P9-DFJ-961

2 —
3/23

JUL 1 2 2011
Palos Verdes Library District

Agewise

Agewise

Fighting the New Ageism in America

Margaret Morganroth Gullette

THE UNIVERSITY OF CHICAGO PRESS
CHICAGO & LONDON

MARGARET MORGANROTH GULLETTE is the author of three previous books, including *Aged by Culture* (2004), also published by the University of Chicago Press. A Nicaragua activist since 1989, she has been a resident scholar in the Women's Studies Research Center at Brandeis University since 1996.

The University of Chicago Press, Chicago 60637
The University of Chicago Press, Ltd., London
© 2011 by Margaret Morganroth Gullette
All rights reserved. Published 2011.
Printed in the United States of America

20 19 18 17 16 15 14 13 12 11   1 2 3 4 5

ISBN-13: 978-0-226-31073-2 (cloth)
ISBN-10: 0-226-31073-6 (cloth)

LIBRARY OF CONGRESS CATALOGING-IN-PUBLICATION DATA

Gullette, Margaret Morganroth.
    Agewise : fighting the new ageism in America / Margaret
Morganroth Gullette.
        p.   cm.
    Includes bibliographical references and index.
    ISBN-13: 978-0-226-31073-2 (hardcover : alk. paper)
    ISBN-10: 0-226-31073-6 (hardcover : alk. paper) 1. Ageism.
2. Aging—Social aspects.   3. Aging—Psychological aspects.
4. Older people—Social conditions.   I. Title.
HQ1061.G8633 2011
305.26—dc22

                                                        2010027054

♾ This paper meets the requirements of ANSI / NISO Z39.48-1992
(Permanence of Paper).

For Vivi (born 2006) and for my mother (born 1914),
for all who believe they will want to commit suicide before they get old,
for all who decide to oppose American decline ideology,
for all who support intergenerational cooperation and an anti-ageist future

CONTENTS

Introduction: The New Regimes of Decline   1
A Historical Tsunami

PART ONE: THE HIDDEN COERCIONS OF AGEISM

[1] The Eskimo on the Ice Floe   21
Is It Aging or Ageism That Causes the Pain?

[2] The Mystery of Carolyn Heilbrun's Suicide   42
Fear of Aging, Ageism, and the "Duty to Die"

[3] The Oldest Have Borne Most   62
Katrina and the Politics of Later Life

PART TWO: IN THE FEMINIST COUNTRY OF LATER LIFE

[4] Hormone Nostalgia   85
Estrogen, Not Menopause, Is the Public Health Menace

[5] Plastic Wrap   103
Turning against Cosmetic Surgery

[6] Improving Sexuality across the Life Course   124
Why Sex for Women Is Likely to Get Better with Age

PART THREE: OUR BEST AND LONGEST-RUNNING STORY

[7] Our Best and Longest-Running Story   147
Why Is Telling Progress Narrative So Necessary, and So Difficult?

[8] The Daughters' Club   167
Does Emma Woodhouse's Father Suffer from "Dementia"?

[9] Overcoming the Terror of Forgetfulness   183
Why America's Escalating Dread of Memory Loss Is Dangerous to
Our Human Relations, Our Mental Health, and Public Policy

[10] Elegies and Romances of Later Life   204
Are There Better Ways to Tell Our Saddest Later-Life Stories?

Afterword: The Next Angels in America   221

Acknowledgments   225
Notes   229
Bibliography   249
Index of Keywords   275

The New Regimes of Decline

A HISTORICAL TSUNAMI

> *I regard the march of history very much as a man*
> *placed astride of a locomotive, without knowledge or*
> *help, would regard the progress of that vehicle.*
> HENRY JAMES TO CHARLES ELIOT NORTON,
> MARCH 31, 1873

Getting Agewise

Suddenly Americans are taking ageism more seriously. Being "too old" is too large a part of the ongoing economic meltdown to ignore. Everyone of a certain age can tell you about somebody who has lost a job, or who is about to lose one, or who has been looking for another and not finding it. Some admit to you that it's themselves they are talking about. In one typical case that went to trial, an employer says to his underlings, "We need young blood"; then employees over forty get fired or don't get promotions.[1] As the film *Up in the Air* showed in actual interviews, even long-term employees get canned swiftly and brutally.[2] Job seekers are cutting years and credentials off their resumes. Personnel directors don't call back. Joblessness lasts longer than for younger people. After age forty-five almost half the unemployed have been out of work long term — more than six months.[3] The official unemployment rate is swollen to almost twice its size with the underemployed, involuntary part-timers, and discouraged workers — people no longer looking. Of the 46 million without health insurance, almost a fifth are of "Baby Boomer" ages between forty-five and sixty-four.[4] Many postpone tests and medical care they need. Between ages fifty-five and sixty-four 10.7 percent die, more than any other uninsured age group.[5]

These economic and health disasters strike people who wear white as well as blue collars.[6] None of this is new. In fact, eliminating midlife workers has become a tacit business practice not only here in the United States but in developed countries worldwide — a disastrous socioeconomic trend extending over decades.[7] Suddenly it is harder to ignore.

An attractive, college-educated white woman who had learned computer skills in her fifties to start a second career writes me:

> Since finishing my grad program I have searched for related jobs and found NONE. I apply and usually get a note back that amounts to "Got your stuff; don't call us, we'll call you." I was interviewed only twice. Friends say my age is a main factor. What 38 year old director of anything wants an assistant who is as old as her own mother?

Carol (not her real name) adds:

> This has been a truly depressing experience. Every application is an act of hope but I have been deflated so often, my pride bruised and my student loan still looms. I had not anticipated this problem. That was naive, I see now. . . .

Underneath every news item about vertiginous drops in 401(k) accounts, corporate and private bankruptcies, chains and franchises closing branches, small businesses vanishing from one day to the next, unpayable mortgages and home foreclosures, are hidden midlife adults, with families, responsibilities, and reasonable self-expectations. In an interview in the *Nation*, Bill Lawhorn, fired for trying to unionize his company, said, "Times really, really got hard. At 52, you shouldn't borrow from your children; you should loan to them. You shouldn't wonder how do you buy your grandchildren a Christmas present."[8] Dan Wasserman, an editorial cartoonist for the *Boston Globe*, has a panel with a kid in a backpack saying, "DAD — STUDENT LOANS HAVE DRIED UP. I MIGHT HAVE TO MOVE BACK HOME." The father, holding behind his back a paper that reads "Credit Crunch," replies, "HOME?"[9] Midlife people are moving in with *their* parents.

It is a shock to discover the disparate impact of the long-term trends on working people who happen to be in their middle years now. Displacement (econospeak for job loss) for workers in their fifties and sixties often results in far lower wages or lasting unemployment.[10] The employment rate of men fifty to fifty-five dropped dramatically over twenty years, from 95 percent to 77 percent. Half of male workers lost

ground economically as they aged into their forties, fifties, and sixties—a figure so big it means the middle class and professionals are affected.[11] In 2000, men between forty-five and fifty-four at the median
(half of men earn less) took in only $41,000. Their median has been
stagnant since.[12] Women at their midlife peak, forty-five to fifty-four,
may earn more than their mothers, but they still earn only 73.6 percent
of what men earn. Bankruptcy filings from people fifty-five and over
rose from 8 percent of all filers in 1991 to 22 percent in 2007.[13] Prematurely drummed out of the workforce or with equity depleted, many
people find their pensions decimated and their other provisions for old
age wrecked or in jeopardy. They keep truckin' even if it's just as greet-
ers at Wal-Mart. "The most notable trend," according to a *New York
Times* article contrasting work in later life from 1986 to 2006, "is that
men and women are both much more likely to keep working than were
their parents in what used to be known as the golden years."[14]

As for the emotional and familial consequences of being fired—uh,
displaced—the lead character in Donald Westlake's thriller *The Ax*
turns on the reader to tell us: "Miss a payday, and you'll feel that flut-
ter of panic. Miss every payday, and see how *that* feels." Burke Devore
is no maniac (although he's killing his rivals to get the one job in his
narrow field). He's meant to be Everyboomer—a pragmatist worried
about his mortgage, his kids losing health insurance, family dysfunction, all the "fringe banes." Sex has gone out of his marriage; his son
almost goes to jail. He refuses to give in completely to despair, although
he realizes that others do: "[S]ome of these people have considered
it and some will do it. (This world we live in began fifteen years ago,
when the air traffic controllers were all given the chop, and suicide ran
briskly through that group, probably because they felt more alone than
we do now.)" Westlake was a screenwriter and popular novelist. Looking back to Reagan's anti-union chop from 1997, he tweaked the classic
populist noir into a Swiftian economic satire. He recognized some of
the long-term villains in "the world we live in" and expressed cold fury
about individual helplessness. One of Devore's high-skilled competitors, working the counter in a diner, sums up the trend: "But this is the
first society ever that takes its most productive people, at their prime,
at the peak of their powers, and throws them away. I call that crazy."[15]

Practices that should be condemned are being institutionalized.
Congress intended to make midlife job discrimination illegal in 1967
by passing the Age Discrimination in Employment Act (ADEA).[16] But
in 2000, in a drastic reduction of civil rights law, the Supreme Court

said in *Kimel et al. v. Florida Board of Regents*, "States may discriminate on the basis of age." Justice Sandra Day O'Connor wrote that "[a State] may rely on age as a proxy for other qualities, abilities, or characteristics that are relevant to the State's legitimate interests."[17] Men typically suffer age discrimination in their mid-fifties, women almost ten years younger. According to Raymond Gregory, the foremost legal expert on midlife job discrimination, underfunding by Congress and a meager 5 percent rate of "for-cause findings" create the impression that "the EEOC [Equal Employment Opportunity Commission] is engaged in discovering where discrimination does not exist rather than where it does." Then in 2009, another Supreme Court ruling (*Gross v. FBL Financial Services*), attacked by four dissenters as "in utter disregard of Congressional intent," gave employers a green light to fire higher-paid workers, especially women and minorities. If you sue in court, many conservative Reagan- and Bush-appointed judges are less sympathetic to the objectives of ADEA. Gregory warns, "Just about every worker . . . has been or will be affected by an employment decision based on age."[18]

The trends suggest that "free-market" capitalism since at least the Reagan years has been eroding job seniority to obtain a cheaper workforce that is demoralized and more flexible. The crazy practices have contributed to reducing American production, elevating working hours for the employed to the highest in the world, keeping wages for most people stagnant, raising personal debt levels to unmanageable heights. People in their middle years have lost faith in the workplace. Under half—roughly 47 percent—are satisfied with their situation, down from 61 percent in 1987.[19]

The degradation of the midlife also changes what it means to age past youth, what it means to be human in our society. Why isn't this unprecedented damage to the life course the biggest story of our time?

THERE'S A SAYING IN SPANISH, "A blow warns, but bleeding teaches." *El golpe avisa, la sangre enseña*. We can't avoid the painful conclusion that age has much to do with these and other savage cuts. Being too old, we are inveigled to believe, is a personal problem, *aging*. Although the word is used with great imprecision, the prevailing idea might be something like this: "Aging means 'old age' and is a universal condition of decline resulting from our biology. There's nothing to do about it until science solves it. There's no story." In the spheres of work and health today, however, this is obviously false. This premature decline is not caused by biology. Now that it is finally and startlingly visible as a collective problem, we can name the global enemy.

Until now, Americans generally didn't pay serious attention to ageism or even notice its precocious spawn, middle-ageism.[20] ("Ageism" alone won't cover the ground, because these victims are only forty-plus.) Some think there never can be a "golden age" for older people, while others think that ours is it. The truth is that aging-into-the-middle-years, or aging-into-old-age, or even aging-past-youth, can be better or worse depending on social context. "Decline" is the name I use for the entire system that worsens the experience of aging-past-youth. It's the opposite of the forces that make living seem a progress worth getting up in the morning for, year after year. Historical forces produce waves of decline. We have been enduring a tidal wave.

I start with the so-called Boomers who are under assault rather than retirees because among the "new old" the huge midlife cohorts were supposed to be home free. The experts said Boomers were in general healthier and (before the recession) better off economically than previous generations and would transform old age to their liking. Yet they too, inadequately prepared, have been shoved headlong into this perilous time.

Whatever happens in the body, and even if nothing happens in the body, aging is a narrative. Each of us tells her own story. But most of us lack an adequate backstory. Not only my own physiology and my personal life experience but societal influences determine my age autobiography.[21] If I can't recognize these influences, my aging narrative can be helplessly naive. In the 1990s and 2000s, I noticed decline vocabulary leaking more and more into my head, tainting my formulations of life's events: "overqualified," "deadwood," "greedy geezer." If wicked cultural stereotypes like racist epithets cannot linger without tending, bizarre age epithets do not emerge in common speech without malice aforethought. Like ethnic hostility, like rape in war, decline culture is insidiously promoted. "Burden" is not a term our grandparents used about themselves. "Elders" used to go with "betters." When my father-in-law said to us youngsters, "I've forgotten more than you'll ever know," it was a boast. The term "senior moment" didn't taint *his* sixties. I use the words they teach me, to paraphrase Samuel Beckett. Or I resist alone, using up tremendous energy.

Even when sideswiped by social change — detrimental developments in biomedicine, media punditry, congressional legislation, and other trends that this book focuses on — I often don't know what hit me. For many reasons, Americans don't get adequate information about the hit-and-run drivers on the life course. Like others, I used to make the mistake of blaming "my aging" for the hits I took.

I am not alone in taking the hits. My granddaughter Vivi is four. When we talk, she confides her important thoughts and the accomplishments she knows I'll admire. I want her to feel all her life long that her sturdy little body has sacred integrity, that living is desirable and precious, that at every age the life course can be blessed. I want her to go on trusting me and thinking I am admirable. But by age six or eight, she may no longer sit as close to an older adult (me!) as to a younger adult.[22] By college, if told she were competing on a test with "old" people, she might confidently predict she'd do well against these "reassuringly inferior" others.[23] By the time her first job has her paying payroll taxes, she might doubt she'll receive Social Security because people she has been taught to call "the aging Boomers" are eating it up. By thirty she may think wrinkles are ugly and be fending off the temptation of cosmetic surgery.

What's age got to do with it? Only this: The older Vivi gets, the greater her exposure to decline ideology. Ageism doesn't damage only people who are old or in their middle years. It's a terrible mistake to think that. While Vivi is still "a little big girl," as she calls herself, ageism may undermine some of the basic lessons she is acquiring from her loving four-generation family. She will overhear condescending and disgusting stereotypes about others and, if she's like other young Americans, believe them. Becca Levy, a Yale psychologist, has a simple explanation for the insidiousness of stereotypes: "There is no psychological need to defend against them when they apply only to others."[24] Meanwhile Vivi may hoard some of the bad stuff inside, to turn against herself later. It may taint her imagination, damage her perceptions, and spoil her expectations of life — the mechanisms known collectively as internalization. Ageism may pollute her mind the way acid rain poisons sweetwater lakes. She too may erroneously blame her own aging.

It's hard work becoming knowledgeable about how we are being aged by culture and history. The least-studied theme in life-course understanding used to be the interplay between historical circumstances and personal experiences. Even now, the practice of demonstrating the interplay is hard, and lags behind the conceptual models.[25] I am a cultural critic interested in age — "age critic" is the term I prefer. I've been intrigued by decline and progress, the two dominant American fables of aging, since my first book, *Safe at Last in the Middle Years*. Progress stories seem so desirable, so homemade, so built-in to American biography and mythology that one has to ask how the counternarratives have gathered strength: What historical circumstances promote or impose decline narratives and ideology? How does decline affect us at different ages? Are there ways to fight the decline system while waiting for Americans to become increasingly agewise?

For me, the breakthrough came when I decided to try out the word "ageism" or "middle ageism" in all the contexts in which we have been instructed to use "aging," plus the contexts in which age critics might use the phrase "being aged by culture." I invented that locution and use it in many contexts. But the material in this book cries out for a term that more forcefully leads us to ask about all the varieties of ageism and the decline systems that expose us to them when we are young and enforce them on us as grow older.

One problem had to be confronted from the start. English has an inadequate vocabulary for discussing either age or decline. Like the term "age" itself, "ageism" has too many referents. It's broad and slippery. Aside from referring to nasty characterizations of older people, it can be used about the serial killer in scrubs who decimates a nursing home. Mortgage vendors who scam older homeowners. The embarrassingly unfunny *Saturday Night Live* skit about "cougars." The twenty-eight-year-old man in a novel who shrieks at the seventy-year-old narrator, "Crawl back into your hole and die . . . old man."[26] The drugstore items purring "anti-aging." The ridiculous tabloid headline, "Look *seven years* younger." Too many disparate things, at disparate moral levels, fall under the rubric. This level of generality makes ageism deniable: nursing-home murders are rare; realtors defraud people of all ages; the humor and the curse and the products are trivial. (Indeed, someone's usually ready to defend any of these instances: "That's not ageism." Or even, "Ageism doesn't exist.")

But decline narratives are ubiquitous. Leaving aside the pathological killer, many such phenomena set the tone of our days but never make it into our uncritical age autobiographies. Our task must be to take them all more seriously for their power to harm. Practice on the local perpetrators: youth-oriented scriptwriters and producers, envious junior colleagues spouting generational claptrap, PR shills, circulation-mad editors. Then move on up. Addie Polk, a ninety-year-old widow who couldn't make her house payments, shot herself when the mortgage servicer sent a deputy to foreclose.[27] It was the local deputy at the door who caused her to pull the trigger, but the other guilty parties include the inventors of securitization, the negligent bank regulators, the legislators who voted to overturn the Glass-Steagall Act, and the mortgage company employees who targeted older women homeowners, luring them to refinance for security during their golden years.[28] Whether people fall into the over forty or over sixty-five or vaguer "old old" categories, many decisions affecting their welfare, ethically considered, should now compel what the Supreme Court calls heightened scrutiny — putting us on guard for possible disparate impacts. Lay people might call this simply extra carefulness.

The local perps link up chain by chain to higher, icier powers. Whether carelessly or intentionally, they create the high-cresting tides in which we struggle to age well and even to survive.

The New Ageism

The word "decline" refers first of all to the major historical forces that have been battering the life course for decades, demonizing and commercializing aging-past-youth. *Agewise* confronts trends and symptomatic events in this new expanded U.S. ageism that have been concealed or misrepresented or underreported even though they do increasing violence to essential aspects of well-being.

We need a little historical revisionism. The biggest and best-educated generations in American history — the Baby Boomers, abused as well as flattered for their supposed might — were in fact unlucky in their timing. The cohorts born between 1946 and 1964 came wailing into the world tagged with an infantile label that I find hard to use without scare quotes. In their years of minority, their numbers had some early effects on culture that were wrongly attributed to their power. Their elders built new schools for them, and expanded the colleges the better-off would need. There were still high-paying blue-collar jobs when they started out. Despite major recessions in the 1970s, 1980s, and 1990s, the economy expanded to encompass them. Helped and pushed by feminism and market demands, women entered the workforce full time. But inequality grew. For many men aging into their middle years, wages declined in comparison to their fathers'.

The idea of generational power as a birthright is an illusion that has

kept many passive as the world turns. Long before the economic debacle of 2008, socioeconomic changes had worsened the experiences
of aging-past-youth. With each passing year, cohort after cohort as
they grew older increasingly ran into constructed job scarcity, weakened unions, downsizing, outsourcing, loss of manufacturing jobs, involuntary early retirement, unemployment, and bankruptcy because
of globalizing and privatizing capitalism. Since at least 1980, the future
of the life course for every cohort has been assaulted by the drive to
weaken labor, seniority, and social welfare. Our nation has been promoting market solutions that pit midlife against younger (or overseas)
workers to drive down wages and benefits and job protections in a race
to the bottom. Boomers have the highest wage inequality of any recent
generation. Younger Boomers — between forty and fifty, ages when they
should be approximating their peak wage — have a 10 percent poverty
rate, the highest level of poverty at that age since the generation born
before World War I.[29]

Ageism lowers wages for people over sixty-five who have to earn
to live. Middle-ageism not only gets rid of midlife workers who
were earning their peak wage but also maligns them as having age-
and cohort-linked defects.[30] In one of the dirty tricks of history,
middle-ageism erupted after millennia when the midlife had continuously been considered the prime of life, and just as the new longevity
was being heralded as a triumph of science. While the oldest Boomers
are turning sixty-five, the youngest are only in their forties. Odd as it
may seem, when such words as "near-elderly," "young old," and "aging"
are thrown around in the mainstream, they often refer to the Boomers.
Some fight back. Age discrimination suits have gone up year after year,
despite the Supreme Court decisions against seniority, and despite having legal recourse too often shamefully denied by the EEOC.

In the annals of middle-ageism, add sedulously advertised youth
culture to rampant individualism and small-government rhetoric. As
each cohort has moved through mid-adulthood, it has smacked harder
into the voracious multi-billion-dollar commerce in aging, increasingly
producing expensive drugs like hormone "replacements" and seeking
to invent what it insists on calling, fallaciously, "anti-aging" products
and surgeries. The prime-timers are told that wanting to look young is
built into their vain and fatuous character.

The psychic and health consequences of midlife job loss can be devastating. This is supposed to be the healthiest midlife group in American history. In some ways they are. But new data suggest many are not

in fact as healthy as their parents. They have more hypertension, heart disease, diabetes, even more difficulties climbing stairs.[31] Many physical conditions are related to work: job strain, insecurity, low and stagnant wages, overwork, lack of sleep, social isolation. Dentists say more midlife patients are losing teeth prematurely, not because of decay, but because they're grinding them in anxiety or fury.[32] Being uninsured is itself a cause of stress and depression.

The Great Recession has only worsened existing trends. However physiological aging occurs, giant economic forces and ideologies are in motion whose convergence has created excess losses as each and every generation grows older.

Since the media started to call them "aging Boomers"—a locution not meant kindly—in the 1980s, when the very youngest were only twenty, the nation has had plenty of warning of their coming retirements. Former administrations should have been saving in order to ameliorate the clearly foreseeable consequences of having giant cohorts start aging into retirement in the era of the new longevity. They knew the date when people born in 1946 would turn sixty-five: 2011. Now the expanding needs of the leading edge of this group are smashing into federal budget cutters in a time of global economic crisis. The victims are likely to be seen not in terms of their second acts—a bitter jibe in the ears of those who won't have them—but in terms of the risk they pose of falling into a state of disease, dependence, and dementia. Despite any current glamour they possess, or control they are supposed to have, they are being depicted as an immense thundering mass, moving along the life course and likely to "live too long." Henry James found the right metaphor for their feelings in this situation.

"Alarmist demography" is the term used by Steven Katz and other historians for this demeaning misreading of the next decades for Americans about to exit from the workforce.[33] As Carol Haber argues, history tells us that in times when "the old" can be represented primarily in terms of disease and dependence, they are most despised, neglected and disadvantaged.[34] To be forced into dependency prematurely (and possibly face uninsured illness) through middle-ageism is no longer unthinkable, even in the middle class. Despite all the boasting about the new longevity, these two dreaded aspects of old age have come nightmarishly closer. Weirdly, old age used to seem further away.

For people on the verge of retiring, "the Golden Years could become 'the tarnished years,'" James H. Schulz and Robert H. Binstock warn in *Aging Nation*. Considering "the public and private institutional arrangements that have provided support in old age for many decades," they conclude that these may be "more fragile than we [Americans] thought."[35]

Our current tsunami of alarmism is vastly different than the concern that brought into being the reforms of the New Deal. People of sixty-five are no longer seen as a worn-out and unprotected population headed for the poorhouse, as they were before the 1930s, when Social Security pulled some of the poor out of abject pauperism, or before the 1960s, when Medicare and Medicaid suddenly gave many people health care they had lacked their whole lives and the Age Discrimination in Employment Act protected some as young as forty from losing jobs to middle-ageism. (Medicare Part D, passed more recently, helps older people pay for prescription drugs only up to a point.)

Since the 1960s, the public has been told, misleadingly, how secure old age has become. One male student in a Harvard class of retirees to whom I lectured came in armed with data about how much it costs the United States to take care of its citizens over sixty-five. As an absolute figure, it sounded pretty big. His aim was to make my warnings about decline ideology seem beside the point, since America has made people over sixty-five so rich. A conservative, writing in a *Washington Post* op-ed, threatens that "workers may get fed up paying so much of their paychecks to support retirees, many of whom (they would notice) were living quite comfortably."[36] Using naked numbers without context, like telling readers they should feel "fed up," is a rhetorical trick. It can construct generational enmity and allow a term like "greedy geezers" to shoot into speech. Such propaganda keeps us drowsily inattentive to those who, slipping unnoticed down through the shredding nets, feel abused and helpless — and keeps us unaware of our own danger.

Long before the 2008 recession, pundits and the media had been treating the big numbers of "old people" as an impending disaster for the nation. They were preparing the ground. Naomi Klein says in *The Shock Doctrine* that capitalists take advantage of disasters to shape society to their ends. With aging-beyond-youth being constructed as a catastrophe, many swarm to take advantage. The forces this book fingers have been ramping up their invective, framing the language of public policy and private desire (or imposing decline without giving notice), over three or four decades.

People retiring now — especially the Boomers — despite having worked hard enough to put surpluses into the Social Security trust fund amounting as I write to $2.5 trillion, are made to seem homogeneous and rich, surfeited and overentitled.[37] The right wing calls its attempts to cut the benefits and make the surpluses available to investment firms "entitlement reform." Social Security doesn't need a rescue on the backs of the elderly, or indeed any rescue. Serious economists — like Nobel Prize winner Paul Krugman — have shown this over and over.[38] But it will be easier to get cuts passed if the group, imagined as enjoying golf, Margaritas, and poetry classes (a mirror image of Ronald Reagan's Cadillac "welfare queens"), doesn't really need its benefits.[39] Both the Bush and Obama administrations' ability to find billions to bail out Wall Street was proof that money can be found for "needs." But one of the greatest human needs — to be well cared in sickness or when dying — may be subordinated to balancing the budget.

In the midst of a weak economy, and after the bailouts, the stimulus packages, and the ensuing enormous deficits, the national conversation on how to pay for 47 million non-old uninsured could have focused on saving money by reforming the bloated for-profit medical system: eliminating insurance companies, curtailing hospital overheads, bargaining for cheaper drugs, training more primary-care doctors, getting doctors on salary. Instead, "reform" homed in on the precious public program, Medicare. After a summit with the health-care industry, the administration promised to cut $450 billion from its safety net. Where will those cuts come from? Medicare is administered thriftily, yet its for-profit providers grow fat. They, however, do not make soft targets. Looking elsewhere, a report from the Congressional Budget Office in 2005 "explored analytical strategies for prospectively identifying which Medicare enrollees are likely to be 'future high-cost beneficiaries.'" These strategies, gerontologist Robert Binstock warns, could be "a preliminary step for identifying those whose care might be rationed."[40] Rationing must be discussed, pundits of all political ideologies say sternly. There are other signs that the soft target is so called end-of-life care, which lacks organized, rich lobbies.

The president himself has given such a sign. Barack Obama was raised by a grandmother he adored, Madelyn Dunham. She was suffering from cancer when she broke her hip. Her doctor recommended a replacement, and she agreed. The family wanted her to live to see if her grandson would win the election. The operation was not overtreatment in the sense of unwanted or unnecessary care. (I know what that means, because an uncle of mine refused all interventions when he was dying and was ignored.) President Obama sweetly declared to the *New York Times* that he would have paid the charges for his grandmother's hip even if Medicare hadn't. It would have been "upsetting" if she had "had to lie there in misery" with a broken hip while dying of cancer. But then he asked, as if cued, "But that's also a huge driver of cost, right?" and raised the "very difficult question" whether "in the aggregate," doing the same for others is "a sustainable model." [41] He passed on bad data. The truth is that of the forty-eight hundred people over sixty-five who die every day, most incur reasonable, low costs.[42] According to the nonprofit Alliance for Aging Research, only about 3 percent incur very high costs.[43] And who assumes the right to say that those 3 percent should be denied care? You and I will be among the forty-eight hundred one of these days. Lacking a rich grandson, we could be victims.

In sidling from talking humanely about loved ones at the most critical time of their lives, to implying that the state might agree to ration health care by age, the president stumbled into ageism. Conservatives, who have been practicing this big shove for decades, have apparently succeeded in making overtreatment seem to many like *the* problem of end-of-life care. But in extremis people want and deserve choices. They are frightened of medical abandonment. Undertreatment is a serious moral issue, but unlike overtreatment, it is absent from many discussions. It should be raised whenever high costs are mentioned. Talk like Obama's drives Americans to think of our future medical needs as unwanted burdens. Obama's interview appeared in April; in September, *Newsweek* produced a feature called "The Case for Killing Granny."[44] I regard such rants as duty-to-die injunctions. There are many.

The British political economist William Jackson explains how in times of general hardship one group is demonized for being dependent (old people) but not another (say, financiers): "Population ageing as a policy problem depends on the level of economic activity. Interest in ageing [peaks] during recessions when public budgets are most stretched."[45] Often resources for caring for people over sixty-five are discussed as if they were intrinsically scarce, rather than the result of policy. So-called reformers save funds for cronyism and making war that might relieve distress. The ageism of the 1960s, when Dr. Robert Butler cannily coined the term, was a weak precursor of the decline ideology of the twenty-first century.[46]

Theories of ageism depend on attitudes toward history. There's some consensus among historians of ageism about the forces operating around 1900 that produced denigration of middle-aged and old people: modernization, urbanization, the cult of youth, technological change, the invention of male midlife sexual decline.[47] Some gerontologists hold, ahistorically, that ageism is an innate and essential psychic wound — gerontophobia — as innate as the Oedipus complex was once thought to be. We cannot know how much truth there is to that before we eliminate many obvious sources of contemporary ageism. Some say that current ageism is an anachronistic relic of a time when most people died young, as if having *more* old people will ipso facto cure hostility to an age class that is currently characterized by some of the most pejorative epithets the culture can devise. Although *Agewise* does not aim to be a full history of the present state of age-related decline, I push hard on the thesis that much of so-called aging, on inspection, reveals the ageist dynamic of decades of socioeconomic and ideological changes.

Capitalism, federal support for free markets, weak enforcement of labor law, the commerce in aging, deficit hawks and small-government advocates, "anti-aging" scientists, and duty-to-die proponents, overt and inadvertent, are among the current masters of decline. Fear them, not aging. With minions puffing decline ideology into the media and its effects sweeping windily through private and public life, decline can be hidden in plain sight, as ubiquitous as global climate change. Like others, I have tried to raise age consciousness. Now I believe the more urgent goal is to raise ageism-consciousness.[48]

How do these hyperborean forces create the pitiless tempests in our backyards? How do they blow into popular culture concepts like "overeducated" and "overtreated," provoking midlife job discrimination and forced retirement while avoiding public outrage? By what process does the erosion of seniority and respect for aging get transformed into geriatric depression and, potentially, elder suicide? When estrogen in hormone treatments turns out to be a carcinogen, how is menopause-deficiency discourse twisted into estrogen nostalgia? How does the manipulation of the cult of youth and fatalism about old age deny and obscure physical beauty and sexual expression in later life? How might ignoring the health needs of frail elderly people make them invisible? How does harping on about demography, forgetfulness, and expensiveness become noxious and even fatal? What are the side effects on younger people of this treatment of later life?

Cultural critics of age are the ones who insist on posing such questions, exposing the deep problems in detail before suggesting tailored solutions. In this book, I try to connect the dots among the concealed or poorly described forces that are undermining our understanding of age. They took my eye as they careened by. They seem urgent. Together they organize the first aspect of my current mission as an age critic: to analyze the threat in its component parts—and to see it whole.

The entire decline system—innocent absorption of cultural signals, youthful age anxiety, middle-ageism, ageism—infiltrating our society from top to bottom, is increasingly a threat to psychological well-being, to healthy brain functioning, public health, midlife job growth, full employment and a growing economy, intergenerational harmony, the pursuit of happiness, the ability to write a progress narrative, and the fullest possible experience of life itself.

Upping the Consequences

I mean this book to be a rational and passionate indictment of the toxins emanating from the new regimes of ageism, a manifesto for fighting back, and a judicious gauge of how well cultural combat is succeeding in some arenas. If the decline system is more controlling and even more lethal than we thought, the fight against it must become correspondingly more pressing. The phrase "the new regimes of decline" could become a shorthand for the mounting evidence that ageism and middle-ageism have become a profound problem for our nation. This new (expanded) ageism is to the twenty-first century what sexism, racism, homophobia, and ableism were earlier in the twentieth— entrenched and implicit systems of discrimination, without adequate movements of resistance to oppose them. At one time, such systems did not seem compelling antagonists to most of those who were not direct victims. The victims, however, felt isolated, anguished, frustrated, and stymied in their activism. Now it is the turn of ageism to be, but not yet seem, urgent.

The Woman Who's Easily Irritated declares, "WHEN I'M IN CHARGE, THERE WILL BE SEVERE CONSEQUENCES IF SOMEONE REFERS TO AN OLDER PERSON AS A CRONE, OLD GEEZER, OLD BIDDY OR THE LIKE." An offstage voice sounds cynical about how much change one ticked-off woman can effect. Our challenge is to make the consequences more severe for all the levels of ageism from the seemingly trivial to the most towering. We must try to change the basic conditions in which we tell our life stories. It cannot be that the American dream of progress in the life course ends for so many so prematurely. Americans need a vision of a more humane and united community,

Figure 1. Nicole Hollander, "Sylvia," *Boston Globe*, October 31, 2006. Doing worse on memory tests that mimic nasty real-life ageism is a response to what is called "stereotype threat." By permission of Nicole Hollander.

multigenerational, willing to expend extra carefulness to sustain all its members from the healthiest possible birth to the best possible death. The elections of 2008 demonstrated that many people once again see our nation ethically, as a whole, dedicated to collective responsibility for its members.

If I am right about how some of the insidious forces work, resistance could focus our dissatisfaction and our critiques—contemptuous, outraged, ironic, humorous, polemical, emotional, persuasive—more justly. We might allocate our positive energies more accurately. Age studies—the field I call my own, also called "cultural studies of age"— could emerge as a guide.[49] Like feminist, critical race and queer studies, and critical/feminist/humanist gerontology, among other watchdogs, age studies monitors the oppressors. It arises out of a commitment to all the ages of life, believing that they are interconnected and that this matters humanly and politically. Age studies analyzes representations and other kinds of pressures, follows trends, investigates the locations where decline thinking intersects other biases. By studying age ideology now and in the past in interdisciplinary ways, it uses the leverage of history—the whisper that "everything can change"—to advance the causes of the vulnerable. As age studies conceives them, those in danger include both Vivi, born in 2006, and my mother, born in 1914.

Anti-ageism needs a self-conscious popular movement behind it, a coalition of the concerned. The focused battle against George Bush's attempted diversion of Social Security trust funds into the bubbling market—the 2005 campaign that fortunately failed all across America—shows that successful resistance is possible. Potential constituencies for a much broader anti-decline movement exist. If all the millions anxious about their jobs joined all the millions being lied to about their midlife bodies and all those furious about being pressured to die prematurely, and they joined teachers and parents who refuse to let kids grow up ageist — a joint war against the regimes of decline could prove heartening. They would be joining the already organized lobbies that stand up for workers and retirees, keeping our adversaries at bay. Our deepest interests unite us. I am hopeful that people will see that. Then the real work begins.

The work laid out for people of goodwill is immense: raising ageism consciousness, cleansing subtle ageist stains from our own hearts and minds, uniting on behalf of a new covenant of extra carefulness. Coalescing into collective anti-ageist activism, we can learn to name the enemies and stand up for better antidiscrimination enforcement and larger resources that should be devoted — logically enough — to the groups that will form a larger fraction of society for the next few decades.

If we can succeed in exposing the effects of decline ideology and creating a sense of urgency, we might be able to assure that the terrible peak of malevolent ageism is behind us, rather than, as now appears, looming ahead. If we can rescue the generation now becoming known as the most expensive by making a progressive revolution in our society's mental imagination of the life course, we can provide a responsible model for the new longevity for the rest of the global twenty-first century.

✳

The United States faces many crises as I write. Some everyone knows — the economy, the Middle East, health care for all, energy dependence and global warming. *This* crisis doesn't yet have a name. The ignorant call it aging, and the enemies make it a scapegoat for others. We must learn to call it ageism, argue that it *is* a crisis, and fight back.

PART ONE

The Hidden Coercions of Ageism

All this interrupts my lessons.
I am studying kindness of heart,
mindfulness.
I have taken a sacred vow
to ban the word "evil" from my mouth.

But words, too, persevere, pry open the jaw.
There it is, caught between my teeth,
where my tongue can't dislodge it.

SUSAN EISENBERG, "FLU VACCINE,"
BLIND SPOT (2006)

CHAPTER I

The Eskimo on the Ice Floe

IS IT AGING OR AGEISM THAT CAUSES THE PAIN?

I've got a lot of art to make . . . instead of ideas drying up and flying
away, I feel like, you know, they're coming, coming, coming . . .
I think about it in that way. God, I want to be here for a long time.

ROBERTA HARRIS, VISUAL ARTIST, WHOSE WORK
APPEARED IN A 2008 EXHIBITION OF WORK OF OLDER
WOMEN ARTISTS AT THE UNIVERSITY OF HOUSTON

Consider "the Eskimo on the ice floe." At first I thought it was nothing but a joke.

In a *New Yorker* cartoon by Lee Lorenz, two figures in parkas are launching a third on a tiny circle of ice: the punch line is "Hold it — we almost forgot his benefits package." This version appeared in 2006, as news about businesses and local governments firing midlife workers was being widely reported. In an earlier cartoon by Sam Gross, also published in the *New Yorker*, an elderly Eskimo floating away calls back to those waving safely from the shore, "Are you sure this ice floe is going to pass by the nursing home?"[1] In the 2008 political season, a quip ran that Republican candidate John McCain, known for his attacks on the provision of government services, boasted: "I'm on Social Security but I'd rather be on an ice floe."

These satirical jokes point beyond their immediate targets to a cultural iceberg that people need to protect themselves from. I want to explain the lethal power of what is four-fifths hidden here. Start with the fact that few versions humorous or otherwise use the word "old," the Eskimo's main characteristic. That doesn't have to be stated. Hidden though it is, everyone already gets it. The ice floe story comes in numerous versions, but is always about younger people sending older people out to die in the cold.

IN SERIOUS CONTEXTS, that "Eskimos" killed their old people is often treated as anthropological fact. In *The Coming of Age* (1970), Simone de Beauvoir mentions several "Eskimo" ways of getting rid of elders, even though she warns that her ethnographic data are of uncertain value.[2] In 2000, the *Journal of the American Medical Association* published an article by a student who had worked in Alaska, recounting how a toothless ninety-seven-year-old Yupik man had come to the point where he said he felt useless, before walking off into the tundra to commit suicide. The problem is, the story wasn't true. The student admitted it wasn't based on an actual person, and the student's tutor, a medical doctor in Nome, said there is no such tradition.[3] *JAMA* apologized. But because the story of native elders forced to die in Arctic cold circulates widely as fact, it has plausibility — enough that *JAMA* accepted the article and that most people are surprised to learn that the myth is just that — a myth.

I admire cultural anthropology because its working attitude is suspicion toward conventional wisdom. My mother, an anti-ageist, then ninety-four years old, objected as soon as I told her the story, "Why would they say this about the Eskimos? Why do they want them to seem so mean?" Geronticide is an old story, but it hasn't always been set near the Arctic Circle. The brilliant feminist contrarian Rebecca West, writing in 1912, mentioned with disdain "the Tierra del Fuego theory that the aged are useless, dangerous, and ought to be abolished, by exposure if possible, by a club if necessary."[4] (People who think that demography rules should note that 1912 came before the so-called new longevity: there weren't even so many of *them*, older people, around then.) It seems there's a history over the past century of the rise and fall and rise of perceptions that senior citizens ought to be abolished.

The point is that the Eskimo geronticide myth is proliferating *now*. As an age critic, the truthiness of this story is important to me and not its truth. The ice floe bearing away a human being is a fantasy of a society in which social murder or coerced suicide or voluntary self-extinction of elderly people as an age class is necessary, or even desirable. Deciding whether such a society is acceptable or a monstrous deviation from human values is one of the struggles I see going on beneath the frozen, glittering surface of our own storytelling.

Why here, why now? Isn't this America, the opposite of the ice floe? We hear about the bounty of the new longevity. Many forces have combined to democratize aging in America. The result is that many more classes of people live longer and for more of that time healthily — a phenomenon known in public health as the compression of morbidity. Some boast about the longevity revolution, as well we should. Longer healthier life could mean relief from overwork and work's frustrations, more outdoor sports, hobbies, "bonus years," sex and remarriage, post-parental friendship with adult offspring, later-life creativity, volunteering, and activism—the progress narratives that some people already live out and that others should have the right to anticipate for themselves. Referring to all the articles beaming out that "sixty is the new forty" or "fifty is the new thirty," Katha Pollitt, a poet and columnist, quips, "Old is the new young!" [5]

We don't see older people much in the mainstream media, but when we do, the images are indeed of robust people with good haircuts and gleaming teeth. Their stories and images abound in certain venues: *AARP, the Magazine*, Sunday newspaper supplements, pop "anti-aging" books, ads for exotic treks and tropic cruises, descriptions of "vibrant" retirement communities. (People say that promoting successful aging improves the image of old age and of older, frailer, more vulnerable people, but many critics doubt that such "success" is transferable. This leisured age class is not considered, by themselves or others, to be really old. "Old" means everything they are not.) If you have picked up whatever you know about later life from such sources, you might think that all older Americans were affluent, fit, happy, and under seventy-five.

Yet if Americans now feel the need to contemplate scenarios of premature death inflicted on the old, it says some extremely important things, not about polar peoples, but about our country's menacing decline ideology today. Ageism is waging undeclared wars against our enjoyment of our longer later life.

Imagining the Future Life Course

Some Americans plan to *be* that Eskimo. In conversations and books, blogs and articles, people mention suicide as a possible out in their own future. They think they can correctly foresee their own decrepit self and will want to act on this image by ending their worthless later life. Baba Copper, a formidable activist for lesbian and anti-ageist causes, was in a group of younger women who, when asked to envision their later lives, said that they would be dead or would commit suicide before getting to be old. In *Over the Hill*, Copper wrote, "I sat there thinking, "Wow! They believe that they would rather commit suicide than be *like me!*"[6] The rock-and-roll song "My Generation" sung by the Who in 1965, notoriously stating the desire to "die before I get old," gets a lot of circulation. For younger people, aging-into-deep-old-age, which is what many people think of as aging, is the future they imagine for themselves. Of course it's imaginary. What else could it be? No one at any age can envision with precision a next self twenty or more years older. But why should the anticipatory image be so decrepit and disabling?

The contemporary shared narrative about later life hammers the inevitable slide into decline, with a better now and a worse later. A much worse later.[7] The younger women did not in fact see Copper herself as their future, which could have been exhilarating. The Boomers, early and often described as aging, are now endlessly told how much they fear it—in gleeful or jeering tones, as if that were a historical anomaly rather than a prudent assessment of later life in the United States. People see ahead of them, in grim shadowy forms, the prospective life-course narrative that the dominant culture provides—an unlivable mind and unrecognizable body, mountainous expense. Some of the evils they anticipate might never occur or could perhaps be prevented—after all, there are countervisions and alternative experiences. But it's as if nobody has a good old age anymore, let alone a good death. Something in American culture blocks out the joyful and the political images, causing people to leap over them to final images of helplessness, decrepitude, pain, abuse, and demeaning death.[8] The Eskimos on the ice floe aren't just old; they are dead men walking. The anticipated image of old age is becoming so one-sided as to be terrifying.

Philosophers explaining why aging might be terrifying usually say because it leads to death, a statement about Thanatos that I used to accept as very likely even though I still don't find aging-into-old-age, in itself, terrifying. But the explanation misses something interesting that is happening in the relationship between these two last things at the present time. Now death—at least imagined way in advance, by healthy younger people, as vaguely, somehow, a choice—can seem preferable to aging-into-old-age. Aging is the new fate worse than death.

ISN'T A DREAD SO fundamental to human nature—the dread of death—immune from history? Apparently not. Here is historical change in a realm where people have not believed history operated. Where does the material come from that fills their heads? We started to see in the introduction how powerful forces, converging, are conferring hideous new meanings on being older and distorting the promises of the new longevity. But who could have expected that one outcome of the new regimes of decline would be a dread contagious to people so young, or that they would feel it intensely?

What do people who believe the story of Eskimo parricide feel about the vulnerable old person exposed on the ice? One woman interviewing a pundit on the Web asked whether the Eskimo family gave the old person vodka; she had a vision of an ordeal that would need anesthetizing. Joni Eareckson, writing a memoir about her relationship to Christianity, describes herself at twelve coming out of a theater with her family after seeing an Anthony Quinn movie called *The Savage Innocents* (1960), in which an Eskimo grandmother is left behind to die. Joni had found the scene heartbreaking: "The image of the old woman had been our long-feared nightmare while growing up," she remembered of her adolescence. Troubled, Joni had asked her father, "Didn't she know she would die on that ice floe?"[9]

The twelve-year-old was doing important imaginative ethical work, breaking down her childlike solipsism and overcoming the inability to imagine being much older than one is. Joni could have been asking about volition, the depth or shallowness of parent-child relations, the degrees of awfulness of ways of dying, and whether it is possible to resist being left to die. But her father missed her anxiety. He answered, in a way meant to sooth, only the part about volition: "She just knew it was her time, honey."[10] The Eskimo's stoic, heroic, self-abnegating willingness to die is crucial to the current myth of the ice floe, one key to its viral proliferation.

A person left to die outdoors by adult children, believing they represent society's will, would feel not only the physical pangs of shivering to death, but also the irrevocable torture of abandonment, the burning sense of injustice and ingratitude, the panic of helplessness — of which we have a close Western model in King Lear on the heath. Wouldn't each of us anticipate our own misery if we were abandoned to die in the cold? Well, not necessarily.

Not Long for This World

Our ability to imagine the feelings of the unwanted matters, because a second set of commentators *won't* be out on the floe. Other people — old people — will be. Ought to be. I remember well the first time I heard this sentiment uttered. A group of us were sharing a friend's summer rental, having cold drinks around the pool. It was a beautiful bright early evening. A sixty-ish New York professional said, as phlegmatically as if he were talking about the price of groceries, "My mother ought to be put on an ice floe. She has a miserable quality of life, she's an enormous expense, we do nothing but care for her." The group listening included his brother and his brother's wife, who actually did care very affectionately for the widowed mother, who herself was paying the expenses.

Do angry filial projections, especially against mothers, explain the widespread references to the Eskimo death fantasy? Not likely. Despite Freud's Oedipal theory, despite the psychoanalytic bugaboo of gerontophobia, despite costly right-wing efforts to create intergenerational hostility in the 1990s, huge majorities of midlife offspring do care. They visit their parents, call them, do their errands, give them presents, enjoy their company. They get advice, child care, gratitude, and gifts in return. If they can, adult offspring protect their parents from scams: bad reverse mortgages, shoddy long-term health-care companies, elder abuse. Millions of people care for their parents if they become frail or sick or suffer from cognitive impairments, even if they did not receive perfect love or find it lacking now. Most are women.[11] As Glory says about her fragile father in Marilynne Robinson's novel, *Home*, "To please him was so potent a motive that it displaced motives of her own."[12] The beautiful culture of caregivers is becomingly increasingly enlightened about the kinds of care that weak and impaired elders respond to best.

It's a mystery of grace how such goodness survives. These normal filial relationships are now heavily laden with popular discourses about parents being burdens and adult offspring being overwhelmed, which misrepresent the situation, dishearten all participants, deny the grave public health issues around unpaid informal care, and bring some old parents to despair. On the other hand, having hundreds of millions of affectionate adult children doesn't stifle the asps writhing out of decline ideology. A senator can love his own darling mommy and still cut Medicare reimbursement.

No, it isn't matricide or patricide with their messy emotional subtexts, but "ageicide" that is in question. Geronticide by ice floe is an imagined social policy in which the victims are not family members like "my parents" or "our grandparents," but "old people" in general. The analogy assumes that those others are unwanted and that society rather than the adult child commits the crime. And it also assumes a society of drastic scarcity so like that of "starving Eskimos" that only their alien solution will work for us.

How can *we* be so like *them*? The paradox is that the United States has both world-historic wealth and rampant inequality on measures like income and health—not to mention world-historic debt. Americans do not understand the complex character of the twentieth century's slow democratization of longevity. They read a lot about a plateau of health that extends the midlife way into what used to be considered old age: this is the new, twenty-first century pattern. But other middle-aged people still live, as it were, in the nineteenth century, without health insurance, access to health information, or up-to-date health care. And whether chronic and degenerative diseases strike at midlife or twenty-five years later, patients encounter a system of research and care still anachronistically set up to deal primarily with acute illness, unequal in quality, extravagantly high in costs, and stingy about desired alleviations like home care, long-term care, and hospice.

The ice floe story hides all this: our two-tier economy and health-care system, the medical model of aging as nothing more than bodily decline and disease, and decades of reactionary hostility to paying for the health and well-being of vulnerable groups, including older citizens on the unlucky side of the new longevity. "Scarcity" will be administered to them, or perhaps they will voluntarily choose it. There's some fuzziness around the details of the myth—specifically, whether Eskimo elders walk out willingly or are left behind. What a choice. This ambiguity curiously matches the frequent fuzziness in the duty-to-die arguments: Will someone in power withdraw costly health services? Will older people refuse them, or will they choose suicide? What is the way for the United States to go when so many people insist on living too long?

Some uses of the myth are obviously about conditions considered problematic in this country rather than about purported ancient Inuit values: "[W]hen the frail elders of the Inuit society *reach a point of senility requiring active nursing care,* or when the food supply becomes perilously low, the demented elders are then *reverently* placed upon an ice floe," writes Stanley Aronson, dean of medicine emeritus at Brown University. Do the Inuit have a special category amid the old of the "demented," as contemporary Americans do? Is it separate from the class of disabled non-old? The objective of Dr. Aronson is to discuss the "merit of care for the neurologically impaired elderly."[13] Would it be possible to abandon anyone, as the Inuit supposedly do, reverently?

Why don't the people advocating this dystopian future ever say to themselves, "That Eskimo might be me"? The odd absence of personal reaction extends even to a ninety-four-year-old man named Burton S. Blumert, musing on his blog about others whom he imagines as needing "scarce" resources.

> I doubt if anybody really believes that the Eskimos abandon their elderly on a chunk of ice. It's a heartless piece of mythology, but at the center of it, is there an underlying integrity?
>
> After all, the folks they deposit on the ice are old, unproductive, sick, and not long for this world. It seems pointless to expend scarce resources on them. Resources that can be better used elsewhere. (Or so it seemed when I was a Randian, and a young one at that.)[14]

But Blumert ends his mini-meditation right there, rather than saying if his feelings and beliefs have changed about the underlying integrity of the concept now that he is of an age to be included with the rest of Ayn Rand's losers.

Erik Erikson talked about the last stage of life presenting two paths, integrity and despair. It seemed to be a choice, albeit a stark one. But now it's a muddle. Are people being persuaded that there is some integrity — the integrity of the social "organism" — in promoting later-life despair and overriding human solidarity? Are we to agree that the United States, although rich, is not rich enough to care for *them* — the old, unproductive, and sick? Hypothermia is supposedly a quick death. That too, is magical thinking.

There's a practical objection, however, to full execution of the fantasy. "We can't put 70 million people on an ice floe," observes Lance Morrow, a journalist who gets the drift (quoted by Mary Ann Hogan in "Welcome to the Rock n' Roll Rest Home").[15] Seventy million, sometimes 76 or 78 million — always a big number — is code for the Baby Boomers, long represented as a powerful and arrogant demographic that controlled the media and had it in for innocent, smart, energetic, tech-savvy, worthy young Generation X.[16] Now, with shocking rapidity — just as the oldest begin to retire — they are being dwindled down into expensive unproductive useless yadda yadda, still dangerous to the young. (It's a feat of popular recharacterization that ought to awe fiction writers.) So how *will* all of them be managed?

Fearing Ageism

They, of course, are *us* — all who are born of woman and may grow old. Some of us realize our collective plight. In the twenty-first century, many people who summon up the image of the abandoned Eskimo do so to criticize the ageism behind a whole range of phenomena. They may feel secure for themselves but worried about others. They see proofs that American society is already too much like the savage Land of Gerontophobia. Aside from death, there's a lot of excess sorrow and early loss to be wrung out of the culture.

The editor of the *Brattleboro Reformer* tells a story about an eighty-year-old widow who was convalescing from heart surgery when the loan company repossessed her car. The bitter point of the article, entitled "No Country for Old Men," is that in this America

> our elderly are better off following the Eskimo tradition of finding an ice floe, getting on, and floating out to sea. . . . Once it has been determined that "old age" has set in and you can no longer contribute to the tribe and your village, you're now just taking up valuable resources for other contributing adults. So in their tradition, you are "pushed" out to sea where you will exit this life without being a burden.[17]

The other keyword secretly buried inside the current use of the legend, aside from "old," is "burden" — a word that carries its small-government politics inside it like a bomb.

A carpenter from a family of modest income tells a friend of mine that her mother gets good individual attention in a boarding house that takes in two or three older people. If her mother were eventually to need more assistance, she shudders at the idea of "putting her in an institution." "Better to put her on an ice floe," she says.

A man who contracted AIDS in the 1980s recounts how he became invisible and untouchable. Then, as understanding replaced ignorance and fear, "he was able to rejoin 'life.'" Now, the author tells us about his interviewee, "he's growing old and it's the same bulls**t all over again. He reminded me of a scene in an old Anthony Quinn movie."[18]

The use of the ice floe story leads us into the horrors of behavioral ageism, especially in medicine. Concerned doctors use it to highlight the fact that in some cases, medical care (like dialysis) is already being rationed by age. For Dr. Erich Loewy of the University of California at Davis, the doubtful fact that Eskimos used to eliminate the elderly should have nothing to do with medical practice. Using age alone is unfair to the patient in front of you. It "denies people equal treatment under the law and . . . is a type of age discrimination. . . . It is irrational to spend hundreds of thousands of dollars, untold amounts of time, energy, and devotion to the 520 gm infant with a gr IV diffuse haemorrhage whose chance of leading a sentient life is close to zero, and to hesitate before using a diagnostic MRI on a patient who is 90 but fully alert and enjoying life."[19]

The ice floe turns out to be a riveting trope. The Eskimo Elder is a figure who has arisen into vigorous cultural life at the intersection of three competing and contradictory attitudes. One group dreads aging-into-old-age. The second dislikes "the aged." The third, cognitively and psychologically dissimilar from the others, is characterized by its fear and criticisms of ageism.

As used by this third group of commentators, the passive recumbent figure illuminates our situation. In their voices we hear Americans groaning and commiserating and fulminating. There's nothing trivial about the assaults to which they are bearing witness. Separately none measures the size or systemic nature of the problem, but together as age critics they are protesting how badly we are being aged by culture, noticing how many ways we are in trouble: "Age prejudice in this country is one of the most socially-condoned and institutionalized forms of prejudice," writes the psychologist Todd D. Nelson (studying ageism rather than aging). "Researchers may tend to overlook it as a phenomenon to be studied."[20] True. Racism, sexism, homophobia, ableism, and anti-Semitism receive far more critical attention and public scorn. In an era like ours, when the mainstream publishes so little against ageism and often blindly manufactures more, the ad hoc pundits I have quoted are performing a patriotic service by getting angry about injustice.

Anger like theirs can be the first step of anti-ageist activism. Put into words rather than left as inchoate rage, wholesome anger can be a blessed warning and a useful tool. Yet these writers doubt that change is possible. A metaphor for the hardness of hearts, the ice floe suggests that many people do not trust their affinity groups, scientific and medical experts, capitalism, or the state to rescue us.

Which groups are more vulnerable than others to ageism? The victim on the ice floe is characterized vaguely. What gender is the Eskimo? Writers and speakers rarely distinguish, but in our country more of the frail and poor old are women than men. The rhetoric of being burdensome is loaded mainly on us. That's a large female enclave out on the ice. "She just knew it was her time, honey," as Joni Eareckson's father said. A woman I know said to me during the 2008 crash, as the stock market was dropping billions, "Social Security's paying out an extra 5.8 percent next year." I was surprised at her mentioning this, as if Social Security made retirees rich. "The average retired woman gets $890 a month," I responded, smiling. Eight hundred and ninety dollars might not cover this woman's Whole Foods bill. In fact, poverty among those older than sixty-five is higher than for those younger, including children. A whopping 18.7 percent of retirees, mostly women, are poor.[21] When in 2010 for the first time in decades retirees were receiving no cost-of-living increase and Obama wanted to give them a one-time benefit of $250, Ellen Goodman, a syndicated columnist, objected, saying children need it more — as if the best way to improve the lives of children were to take a morsel away from elders.[22] Even liberal feminists can fall into such traps.

While this book spotlights many kinds of ageism, they come along mixed up with the interrelated *-isms* associated with class, race, physical ability, sexual preference, and gender. Ageism is rightly a women's issue, worsened by sexism a woman's whole life long. But ageism is also a men's issue — not just because of Viagra ads and impotence and pee jokes, although I think they go deep. If geronticide were to become a more insidiously widespread medical practice, it wouldn't exclude men, even white men of means, because they age into the dangerous age too. They too can be called demented or be judged poor candidates for medical interventions that they would prefer to receive. When divorced, childless, or estranged from their adult offspring, many men lack protectors.[23] The category "the elderly" is a unisex colorless disguise — like "the Eskimo." It keeps the victims undifferentiated, neutered, other.

And what class is the abandoned Eskimo? The joke or myth, set in an allegedly simpler, more homogenous, more primitive society, implies that all the elderly are unprotected; the ice is dotted with fragile figures. Not exactly. "The ruling class that determines the fate of the masses has no fear of sharing that fate," Beauvoir pointed out in *The Coming of Age*.[24] Will Warren Buffett wind up in an understaffed nursing home, without a benefits package, neglected by underpaid aides? Will Leona Helmsley's dogs lack for anything? Below that class, everyone is told to fear aging — meaning, often, outliving your money. An investment brochure reads: "At the ages of 70 and 68, respectively, Charlie and Marie are in good health and view wellness as a top priority.

This, combined with today's longer life expectancies, makes them susceptible *to the risk of longevity*."[25] Perhaps wellness is not such a good idea? The less well off certainly have to fear the risks, given American inequality and the weakness of the safety nets.

But this book is not only about ageist aspects of our culture. Although I need to present evidence about the power of the negative forces, I couldn't bear to write a book limited to them. Even warded off by humor and walled off by analysis, it was too much. "I was overcome by the fumes," as Saul Bellow says in another connection. Age critic though I am, with almost twenty years in the trenches, I have to protect myself from the selfishness, bigotry, hypocrisy and ignorance, greed and exploitation blown toward us from our reeking Chernobyl. I need to armor up for resistance. Now, for relief, I step more or less blithely into a hot shower and make some useful discoveries.

An Epiphany in the Shower

In my youth there was scarcely a part of my body I could look at without criticism. But over time I made peace with some parts I had disliked for decades. My feet, for one. Those broad peasant feet began to look sturdy, smooth-skinned. The toes were charming. After fifty, when menopause discourse led me to expect there would be some kind of bodily "Change," I might have deceived myself but I thought my breasts got heavier. That was an unexpected erotic gain. Like many other women touched by the magic wand of feminism, in midlife I began to overcome the self-hatred that comes of having a young female body in patriarchal, capitalist, consumerist America. Thank the goddess for no longer being so young. Many women, like me, have lived a fair amount of time together in the feminist country of later life.

And then — perhaps as a consequence — in the shower one morning I was twisting to get soap and looked back and down my side. In the shower you can never see your whole self, only parts. Suddenly the curves of my hip, buttock, thigh, calf, and ankle came into view — startlingly elegant, powerful and voluptuous. It was an angle of myself I had never before observed.

I took a longer glance the next time. The view was definitely one a painter might love. Since I was then already into my sixties in a culture increasingly obsessed with youth, this experience was rare. But had I ever seen an image created from the point of view of a woman looking down at her own body from above? Never. Nor could a mirror show it. Certainly no TV or magazine ad had ever captured those satisfying curves. The assumption of our culture is not just ageist but middle-ageist, that bodily decline starts not in old age but ever younger: for women and even some men, as early as thirty. I haven't yet gotten my face to seem astonishingly lovelier, but every time I look down at that arrangement of hip and leg I am rewarded by a jolt of pleasure.

I offer you the same free pleasure. Try it. There is nothing wrong with a little healthy narcissism once in a while, in a steamy bathroom filled with heady aromas of shampoo and olive oil soap. Women who feel they are aging past youth can enjoy such a sight for decades. Suppose that every day, for just two minutes, every single woman in America loved that much of her body. What a different attitude toward ourselves and other women we would carry out of the bathroom and into the world. Men who feel they are aging past youth (which seems to start between thirty and forty for urban middle-class European Americans) also need new forms of solidarity with their bodies that shield them from the angry glare of decline.

These days I don't need to review the fleshly evidence every day. I seem to have absorbed that good sight into my sense of self. Growing older, we can internalize a modest progress view of an "aging" body in the way that others internalize the sense of becoming uglier.

MY DISCOVERY THAT SOME unexpected parts of me looked good naked may be important for others if it clarifies the way one's sense of personal aging is influenced by ageism. The reason that I can admire these parts of the "aging" corpus is precisely because no ad or article has ever focused on them. I hadn't learned to hate them as signs of decline. In the shower I saw them fresh, and there was nothing wrong with them.

As we know, ad campaigns exist only to get us to want their products badly. By giving us views of young, heavily retouched models, they create a critical, ageist, comparative eye. That eye is rapt only by the tall anorexic youthful body. It frowns contemptuously at the average American woman, five foot four inches tall and a hundred and forty pounds, whose median age is in the upper thirties. The commercial and medical purveyors of the Fountain of Youth are the backers of the sour concept "anti-aging." Their nasty age gaze obsessively focuses only on the parts of the body they purport to remedy. "Anti-aging" is a misnomer: no surgery, medication or cosmetic reverses what they call aging. More aptly called the "uglification industry," the commerce in aging targets the body parts it has produced products or services for. The face receives the most minute critique. (It might well be the hardest part of her body for any woman to reclaim.) Fortunately for my graceful lower extremities, no corporate scientist has yet devised a product that could improve that view. Biogerontologists and doctors who appear to know nothing about social construction have also taken charge of telling us what aging is. When the prestigious *New York Review of Books* gets around to the topic, the writers (one a physician) feel free to opine that the body starts "its long preparation for death," a "relentless physical and mental attrition," as early as "the twenties and thirties." Warn the kids. A Harvard pathologist says in the *Boston Globe*, "Disease is a process that prevents you from functioning in an optimal way. *And that's what aging is. I think of aging as a collection of diseases.*"[26] Scientists, bent on getting free advertising for the brave new drugs and devices they dream of, and the associated industries for which any collection of diseases is a financial opportunity converge. As soon as money is to be made, trying to decide whether aging is a disease state or a normal process (that occurs within a narrative and a social system inflicted on us willy-nilly) gets a bend sinister.

Well, I think of ageism as a learned set of beliefs and practices that prevent us from functioning in an optimal way in relation to aging, our own bodies, and people more than ten years older than we are. We have to reeducate the alien mindset, whoever it comes from. Meanwhile, can we focus more often on the body parts we have taught ourselves to find pleasing? Maybe, in time, what we praise could be the whole integrated body-mind, with its spirit, character, charm, and responsiveness. Confession of a new kind would be in order. "Hey, my neck's okay." "My penis is long enough." These wouldn't be boasts about natural endowments, as in the competitive beauty subcultures, but anti-ageist challenges to decline.

Irony on top of insult: Despite all the instances of ageism around and inside our heads, many of us go along naively thinking that aging is just a bodily experience without any history or environmental influences about it. Beauvoir stated the complex truth succinctly in the preface to her book. "Then again man never lives in a state of nature: in his old age, as at every other period of his life, his status is imposed upon him by the society to which he belongs."[27] Women and men alike, we are all imposed upon; we are all aged by culture. If this fact is masked when we are young by the delusory cult of youth, it becomes more salient as we get older or read more age criticism and theory.

What can a hot shower do against the awful chill of the ageist iceberg? Perhaps this book is aimed at levelheaded readers, male and female, who say, "I think I can deal with aging (in *my* meanings of the term). I don't need more confessions of how ghastly it is. Tell me what I need to know, and do, about *ageism*. Help me more with the differences between the two." My first bit of advice? The same I gave myself: When invited to use their term "aging" automatically, try substituting "ageism" instead. We might find thousands of new flashes of insight to share. Let me use the hot shower as a symbol of resistance, which enables us to defend our body-mind from cultural assault as it grows older. Call this armor life-course energy — "The force that through the green fuse drives the flower." Dylan Thomas's metaphor of progressive development could be ours far beyond our first "green age."

Were the steady assault of decline practices more widely recognized as a crisis, many people in later life could certainly be vital enough to confront its commercial/political/economic/medical challenges. Millie Beck, age seventy-four, interviewed by Studs Terkel, says that she became active in her federal housing project when she retired at age sixty-four:

> I wanted an "over-sixty" clinic, because I found that doctors weren't treating their elderly patients right. . . . I got angry. I decided we should have a clinic for elderly people, where, if you're dizzy, they don't just say it's because you're old. We raised $450,000 and we have that clinic.[28]

This is anger in one of its energetic guises, a synonym for "I won't take this anymore."

Along with justified anger, the second emotion we need is hope. Hope comes from discovering weak spots in decline's arsenal, and relying enough on unified action to believe that change is possible. In part 2 of this book, "In the Feminist Country of Later Life," I show how resistance works — or sometimes, given the powers united against it, can't yet prevail — and what can be accomplished when a larger collective develops cannier pushback.

The more clearly we see ageism at work, the less we'll blame aging. The more intelligently we critique the universal biological decline narrative of aging, the better control we might have over our own personal aging narratives. The more empathetic we teach ourselves to become to other victims of decline ideology, the more liberated we'll feel in ourselves, and the more empowered to urge necessary reforms.

Take Another Look!

The question "What's age got to do with it?" could be answered dismissively, "Nothing!" ("Age is nothing but a number," my mother likes to say. I like to hear her say it, because then she goes on, "I am a lucky woman," and lists her good fortunes—her education, her long career as a unionized teacher, the men who loved her, her health, the charming place she lives in, the security she feels, us. That's the way I want her to feel, her whole life long. At the same time she is entirely denying her own body-mind and its place in culture.) Or the question could be answered "Everything!"—without making useful distinctions. I take a different position. If the question really means "What *exactly* does age have to do with it?" then it's an epistemological inquiry about what we can know—given our cultural circumstances, the puzzling nature of some of the evidence, the hidden biases of experts—about the scattered phenomena of enforced decline and the historical chains that bind them.

Ageism can lurk in unexpected places. It can take shrewd sleuthing to detect them. The ice floe jokes are a good introduction partly because the perils they point to come dressed in humor, one of decline's typical disguises. Conan O'Brien says the AARP debate was like all the others, "except the moderator asked the same question over and over." That joke treats AARP—which embraces all of us as soon as we turn fifty, a youngish age these days—as a group marked for senility. Misuse of the growing fear of "dementia" is making progressive forgetfulness seem an inevitable part of later life.[29] I used to think that midlife fear of memory loss was exaggerated but trivial. My mistake.

Ageism is often quiet, factoidal, unheated. Nevertheless, many negative stereotypes and arguments should be considered hate speech. Terms such as "demented" and a new concept like "living too long," when put together, can generate hateful thoughts, promote hateful outcomes. (This book doesn't discuss such matters as whether "feisty" is appropriate only for younger people.) Ageist hate speech may seem harmless even when it concludes that the old have a duty to die, implicitly encouraging practices such as preemptive suicide or medical manslaughter before the elderly cost us — we who are nowhere near old and still on the treadmill — too much. These mortal consequences are beginning to sound rational.

The spokespersons are not called bigots but bioethicists, philosophers, political economists, futurists, biogerontologists, politicians. The distorted genius of contemporary American ageism is that it is managing to expand the hostile class of speakers and actors. They make odd bedfellows. Some no doubt pride themselves on their patriotism for trying to save the country money. Most would be horrified to think of themselves as potential executioners. Ageism's everyday authors are just us, at our various ages: those of us who have not trained ourselves to self-identify as future old people. Watch us in our victimhood squawk like ventriloquist's dummies, repeating embarrassing jokes, "explaining" life to our children as decline, innocently passing on neocon propaganda, praying our parents have saved enough to be independent, passively imagining a dreamy convenient easy exit for our own precious self before we can be led out on the ice. For such reasons, ageism is hard to rebut.

Even I didn't say much at the cocktail party around the swimming pool when the cruel-mouthed son said his mother should be put on an ice floe. Ah, penance. That orphaned son has no doubt washed his harsh anger from the slate of memory. It may not recur to him unless his daughters, like Goneril and Regan, turn him out on the heath. And I have failed on many other occasions of stunned silence, unnecessary politeness to the perp, reluctance to harangue people, or simple idiocy about an appropriate retort. My readers may do better.

Speech is both an act in itself and an index finger pointing beyond itself. Instances of age bias — however lightly spoken — get their persuasiveness from our whole universe of discourse: rejuvenation ads, think-tank reports, scientific "truths." Attitudes get enacted in laws and acted out through relationships. Context is everything. As Nancy C. Cornwell, a feminist theorist, writes, "context is what provides hate speech with its force and its ability to harm." Gordon Allport's scale of prejudice, from which I draw — applicable to racism, sexism, homophobia, and ableism, among others — can also be applied to age.[30] Decline ideology doesn't just stick out its tongue. It leads to shunning behavior, illegal discrimination in hiring, elder abuse, funding cuts (violence by budget), and even death dealing — the dangerous and fatal outcomes some can see around us.

Or don't yet see. Many of the myriad emerging forms of contemporary ageism are puzzling, despite wonderful work by feminists, critical and humanistic gerontologists, and social scientists who function as age critics. Over the course of this book, I want to describe the mechanisms of decline ideology case by case, looking at how the victims are differentially affected, naming our societal losses more clearly. Only within such contexts does it make sense to celebrate heartening sources of resilience. Otherwise celebration is hollow. Middle-ageism prepares younger adults who overhear it for eventually accepting ice floe attitudes toward old people and perhaps themselves in later life. And by describing aging-past-youth mainly as a decline when so many people will in fact be aging longer, American culture is eerily distorting what it means to have a human life course.

The Rescue: To Notice and to Care

My intended audience starts with people of the age to drive, marry, and sign up for the army — old enough to think about life-beyond-youth. Even that young, they have probably already absorbed bias or misinformation, without enough training in age studies to recognize or fight it. I gave a lecture after Hurricane Katrina at which I broke the news few had encountered: that of the people who died right away, a full 64 percent were over sixty-five, and many were between fifty and sixty. I heard some sharp intakes of breath from the spectators. But a young man stood up in the question period, half puzzled, half irritated, to say, "Isn't that what you'd *expect?*"

He assumed that people over fifty are old — and that the business of old people is to die. It's as if it were their profession.[31] In that culture of feeling, there can be no surprise, no outrage. Even Philip Roth, our decline-meister, used to know better. The business of life, he shows in his novel *Everyman*, aside from being kind to others, is usually to live more. That's why the protagonist is about to undergo his *n*th operation in as many years. "Eluding death seemed to have become the central business of his life."[32] A lot more writers are now telling us from their own experience some of the better secrets. One of them is Grace Paley: "It's all life until death."[33] To echo Roberta Harris, the artist whose words stand as the epigraph to this chapter: *God, I want to be here for a long time.*

So the young man who asked the ingrained question got life — the long mysterious life ahead of him — wrong. Like him, like the people who plan to be the Eskimo, most of us have been taught some of the vulgarly comic, politically inspired, greed-motivated, or scientifically scary decline narratives of the life course. They accumulate in us like airborne irritants. Ignorance of later life is a social epidemic, chronic or acute: It can bury our finer feelings, stunt our intelligence, paralyze the body politic. Yet careless ignorance and even bigotry can be remedied — not just by living, which is slow and uncertain, but by reading critically and raising one's consciousness.

That young man needs to question why so many older people died in Katrina and learn why many deaths were avoidable, in order not to ignorantly assume that any death of a person denominated "old" is inevitable. He needs the public health concept of "excess deaths," but tweaked for age. The excess deaths due to ageism sometimes go unsuspected, as they did in Katrina. You have to look for ageism to find it. You have to care, in order to look. An age critic has to have some willingness to bring out these dead, to try to reform the circumstances that shorten their lives. I couldn't have conceived when I started this book needing to argue that old people want to live. But here we are in the new regime.

Ageism, middle-ageism, and decline ideology can spoil a day, steal a job, wound the memory, and kill. Pro-aging literally saves. In another *Sylvia* cartoon by Nicole Hollander, the TV announces, "PEOPLE WHO HAD POSITIVE PERCEPTIONS OF AGING LIVED AN AVERAGE OF 7.5 YEARS LONGER . . . A BIGGER INCREASE THAN THAT ASSOCIATED WITH NON-SMOKING AND EXERCISING." (Sylvia, a midlife mother with a dubious work history but boundless irrational schemes for success, immediately calls for a cigarette and a donut.) The TV fact is true. Becca Levy and her colleagues followed 660 middle-class, mostly white Ohioans who were between fifty and ninety-four, for long enough to discover the advantage. The longer-lived members of the group responded easily to statements like "I am as happy now as I was when I was younger," "As I get older, things are [better than, . . . the same as] I thought they would be."[34] Since decline ideology first strikes Americans not long after birth, and gets worse as we age, the solution is to start teaching anti-ageist conceptions of later life to children. Then society has to provide the conditions in which more people can hold on to these prospective narratives all through the life course.

✳

Children like my granddaughter Vivi need plausible progress narratives, oral or written stories that assure them that getting older is a good thing, and that strengthen them to cope with everything, including ageism. One way or another, our parents are our first guides in constructing life-course stories. My mother is still my informant. Luckily, first she told me a progress narrative about herself, and then, boldly peering forward, arming me for life, she dreamed one for me. I latched on to our best and longest-running story at an early age. And I see my mother now, despite the drastic losses of the last few years, holding on to it gallantly and tenaciously.

Every time one encounters the sad hate words or spots terms like "the new longevity" used as a problem, there's an imaginative benefit to recognizing — as young as possible — that the people referred to are not strangers, not others, but our parents or relatives or mentors or friends. Mark Halliday has a poem in *Keep This Forever* that recognizes the gap of feeling we start with. I think of caregivers primarily as the Daughters' Club, but Halliday is a male member. He cared for his father in his final illness and was there in his last days. The poem begins,

> Everybody's father dies.
> When it happens to someone else, I send a note of sympathy
> or at least an email. It's certainly worth the bother.
> But when my father died, it was *my father*.

The poem ends,

> Everybody's father dies, but
> when my father died, it was my father.[35]

When we are youngsters, our parents are human to us despite the divide of time, innocent as we are of the cult of youth, generation markers, and "lifestyle" divisions. We respect seniority naturally, from its having been founded in the family. The connections may fray at times. But the bonds endure with changes over the decades — perhaps in spite of our parents' aging, perhaps because of their aging, and perhaps by defying the negative meanings of aging. Once we achieve such normal mental, emotional, and philosophical pinnacles, we can practice thinking in the same anti-ageist ways beyond our family — impersonally farther than the people we happen to know. Eventually we may lasso ourselves into the same protective loop, as we too grow older. Our high task, as adults knowledgeable about decline, is to protect everyone's embodied selfhood over time. Like anger and the hope that comes through understanding, activism arises out of love.

SECULAR PEOPLE MAY PRAY for vision and unity. May the generations of our fearful nation grow together in understanding. May our body-minds receive the help they need to age well. May we heighten the resistance to ageism, lessen the irrational fears we have of aging, and learn to know the difference between the two. May our children bless us for redeeming the life course.

CHAPTER 2

The Mystery of
Carolyn Heilbrun's Suicide

FEAR OF AGING, AGEISM, AND THE "DUTY TO DIE"

> *When those who have power to name and to socially construct reality*
> *choose not to see you or hear you . . . there is a moment of psychic*
> *disequilibrium, as if you looked into a mirror and saw nothing.*
> ADRIENNE RICH, "INVISIBILITY IN ACADEME"

In June 2004, a young woman speaking after a National Women's Studies Association plenary meeting started to eulogize the feminist literary
critic, biographer, and mystery writer Carolyn Heilbrun. I was present,
along with a thousand other women. She described how awful Carolyn's suicide had felt to her and how confused she was that Carolyn had
killed herself "to avoid old age." Soon she was sobbing helplessly into
the mic. Carolyn had been a mentor of mine, whose trenchant intelligence I admired and hoped to imitate as I grew older.

When Carolyn ended her life in October 2003, she was a successful
writer of detective fiction who was also celebrated as a feminist literary critic. She was married, with adult children and grandchildren,
fascinating friends who admired and relied on her, financial security,
an apartment on Central Park, a country house in Connecticut, and a
huge following of devoted readers. She was subject to depression but
otherwise healthy, and she was only seventy-seven.

I had heard about the anger expressed at her funeral and thought I
understood it. Her death profoundly disturbed many people, partly because she was loved, but also because she had chosen voluntary death
as she had warned she would: to avoid old age. She called this kind of
suicide rational. Her act, coming in the midst of an apparently envi-
able life, unassailed by illness, and despite her well-known history of

feminist anti-ageism, can, "perhaps inadvertently, feed the prejudices of ageism in others," as Harry Moody, an ethicist and gerontologist, put it in a letter to me.[1] It's the kind of decision that might leave people who hear the story — including quite young people — with the idea that despair is a rational response to normal aging and that feminism can do nothing to alleviate it.

Carolyn and I had not been close enough to have discussed suicide. Her death shocked and amazed me. Later, thinking about the anomalies led me, as an age critic, to interview people who knew her and to read what her friends had published about her states of mind. The more I learned, the more I came to believe that ageism had so diminished her apparently fortunate situation that it exacerbated her long-term depression.

Her story thus raises the general question of the power of ageism in the United States to push older people over the edge into despair. Our thinking about suicide in middle and later life has to factor in, not only childhood, familial, and neurological factors and immediate tensions — the psychological autopsy as defined and practiced by Dr. Edwin S. Shneidman[2] — but also the cultural construction of decline. The pressures brought to bear by the new regimes of ageism can cause even relatively young people to think that perhaps they should make an exit before they become a "burden." So drastic a social change requires a good deal more attention than has been given to it. The key phrase in this connection is neither "right to die" nor "physician-assisted suicide," but "duty to die."

A Psychosocial Autopsy

Carolyn had made celebrated anti-ageist pronouncements about the life courses of women, including a landmark article in the *New York Times Book Review* in 1988: "Women Writers: Coming of Age at 50." Her writings had misled me into thinking that feminism had amply armored her against America's decline ideology. But in 1997 she published a book about life in her sixties that she called *The Last Gift of Time*. We should have paid more attention to the word "last." Although the book begins typically, with Carolyn "savoring a combination of serenity and activity that had hardly been publicly attributed . . . to women in their seventh decade," soon she is explaining why she approves of suicide as an option. She equates the freedom to die with "quit[ting] while you're ahead," thus avoiding becoming "too weak, or powerless, or ill."[3] She is holding that choice in reserve, because her sixties had proved interesting. She assures herself in print that contemplating self-murder is only a strategy for cherishing later life. But that meant treating life in her seventies "as if it were under suspicion," Christine Overall, a feminist philosopher, perceptively commented.[4] It was as if Carolyn were both Scheherazade and the Shah in *The Arabian Nights*. As Scheherazade, the ever-fertile storyteller, she postponed death through prolific imagination, maintaining a day at a time the fragile progress narrative of her life. But she was also the Shah, invincibly suspicious of any female entertainer, who held the power to condemn her.

Carolyn had for a long time held what could be called a suicidal belief system, the collection of feelings suicidologists consider the main prerequisites — necessary but not sufficient — for the act. The surface was her argument that people had the right to choose their death, as women ought to have the right to choose abortions. This appeared to be a feminist argument about control. It was disarming, although feminists presumably would want to distinguish more sharply between ending fetal existence and ending an adult life of achievement and connection.

She could be candid. She told one sympathetic friend what her method would be, and that was the method she chose. (It is the preferred method in Derek Humphry's best-selling *Final Exit*. Kay Redfield Jamison says the percentage of suicides using this method went up 31 percent the year after the book was published.)[5] Some of Carolyn's friends did try to dissuade her. She answered criticisms; she was well armed. And she was formidable. (Although I had never seen her angry, I felt occasionally in our conversations that I was stroking a cat that might turn feral.) Some of her friends shared her conviction about the right to die. In principle, so do I. My father had amyotrophic lateral sclerosis in the 1970s, better known as Lou Gehrig's disease. My mother and I cared for him at home. We promised him that he would die at home and he did. I don't believe he would have chosen suicide, but I wish he had had options about the manner of his dying.

Carolyn talked about voluntary death a great deal, according to a mutual friend who wishes to remain anonymous, but mainly she talked about others: people with degenerative diseases who wished to time their dying to avoid the worst. The surcease, or preemptive, suicide is the main example of a "rational" suicide. Nevertheless, her friend was concerned. She recalled this in an e-mail to me in October 2004: "We were talking about death, dying, as we often did. Why are we talking so much about death? I asked. Because that is what we are confronting, she said. I answered, But not yet." Carolyn led other friends into treating her death talk as if it were a philosophical issue and not a death wish. The summer of 2003 was difficult, I was told. But then she had a better autumn — until she killed herself on October 9. Those who met her that fall, even within days of her act, did not anticipate it.

Many suicides occur with no warning, when stress that "was long coped with in the past" generates "increasing fatigue."[6] The intention may stay latent forever, or suddenly turn impulsive. Jamison says that the average length of premeditation before suicide is five minutes.[7] People who survive their attempts are presumably the source for this estimate. Many people who survive — like James Stewart's character in *It's a Wonderful Life* — never try again.

As far as Carolyn's friends knew, she was nowhere close to being powerless, or ill. If a person has discussed a decision about the timing of her death, this too may lead others to confer the title "rational" on the succeeding act. When suicide occurs at any age, psychiatrists believe it is often related to major depression or other mental illness. Yet neither Carolyn's posthumous power to name her decision rational nor a diagnosis of depression — which her biographer, Susan Kress, seems to accept[8] — precludes investigating her situation, as much as one can, for the ways internalized ageism worsened her psyche-ache.

Retirement can open up vulnerabilities to age bias. There is plenty of evidence in Carolyn's biography. About a decade before her death, she had resigned from Columbia University's English department — famously, because male colleagues were not advancing her protégées. They were denying her the influence that her seniority merited and thwarting her ability to help the feminist movement. Carolyn thus lost a field on which she had been heroically combative. With her credentials — past president of the Modern Language Association, no less — when she left university teaching, she should have been able to join that small coterie of top men who resist ageism through traditional patriarchal means, retaining connections, prestige, and honors. But her retirement proved that her hold on her conferred position as an "honorary man" (a term she had used about other women) was tenuous.

Feeling that she was losing her role as a teacher and mentor — which may not, of course, have been the way her protégées felt about her — left her with writing. But she had stopped writing the Kate Fansler mysteries. Her latest book, *When Men Were the Only Models We Had*, was about three famous male Columbia professors who had not chosen her as their protégée. She had been disappointed in its sales and the paucity of reviews. According to another close friend of hers who also wishes to remain anonymous, a month before her suicide, she suffered a severe publishing disappointment. She had hinted at a similar disappointment to me at dinner five months earlier. Then shortly before her death, her son Robert, a public defender, held a book party to celebrate publishing his own detective mystery—perhaps a sad sign to her that the laurels had passed inexorably to younger heads.[9]

Her voluntary exit from work snowballed into a series of immense identity strippings—as a teacher, as a mentor, as a belletrist and detective-novel writer. Carolyn had solid legacies. She must have lost the good of them, not only through the stoic refusal of nostalgia that she had often praised, but through dejected reinterpretation. It's terrible to think how hard she struggled to revive her sense of self. She tried rereading; she tried intellectual challenge by reading science; she tried writing about this new field. She kept the Shah's fatal menace in play as a goad.

A friend of mine whom I will call Annabelle, who tried to commit suicide in her teens, has written about her own similar strategy: "The plan had been a way of making the interim worthwhile, of keeping pressure on myself to finish the book, of making writing seem important enough to stay up late for, a way of making myself not give up."[10] And then she set a date. Still a writer, Annabelle speaks with the brilliant retrospection that only a survivor can have. The plan deployed to make one's life seem worthwhile actually turned the pressure up wretchedly high.

In her last essays Carolyn listed her losses, evading the appearance of decline by describing them through a rhetoric of later-life flexibility. Her last article in *The Women's Review of Books* is titled "Taking a U-Turn." But the deprivations implied were terrible. She had lost faith in literary criticism, didn't enjoy rereading, had lost her drive for writing when she turned to science, lacked a gripping long-term project, was no longer so motivated by feminist interests, and was losing the attention of critics and her female audience. For a writer and thinker—for Scheherazade—these are signs of depletion.

There are feminist ways to fight stereotype threats and identity stripping, but Carolyn seems to have compared herself to men of her age and status, an impossible ego-ideal. And she certainly knew the wicked generalization that American writers lose creative power as they age. In *Darkness Visible: A Memoir of Madness*, having rejected various other explanations for his suicidal depression, William Styron finally juxtaposes his age — "I turned sixty, that hulking milestone of mortality" — and dissatisfaction with his work.[11] But an alternative explanation — that older writers, however well established, are driven into silence by increasingly ageist attitudes in the increasingly feeble publishing business — is more persuasive in today's youth-oriented climate. One's former enthusiastic editors retire or die or lose interest. Younger editors lose faith in the audience for aging, "second-wave" writers. Midlist writers are written off. Publicity campaigns shrink. Prestige sinks. Fans drift away. One's charisma is evaporating. (In a graduate seminar I took with Robert Lowell, he more than once quoted, "They flee from me who sometime did me seek.")

The victims do not notice that those who have power *choose* to no longer see or hear us, in the metaphors of Adrienne Rich. Writer's block, a condition many writers know young and survive, can be made unsurvivable if unacknowledged ageism turns into dissatisfaction and self-reproach. Instead of recognizing *This is sexist ageism!* did Carolyn's comparative disadvantages as an older woman cause her to regress into that gnawing envy of male privilege so many women writhed under when they were young? Defeatist internalizations — *I no longer have anything to say, this feels worse than when I was young* — weaken self-esteem and affect self-judgment. The career self — the self identified predominantly by its output — may no longer want to go on living if it believes its work plans can no longer be carried to fruition.[12]

My friend Annabelle says that the future had become blank during her darkest days: "Actually, even at the end, I had been able to imagine not doing it, but after imagining the moment of not killing myself there had been a mental blank that I could not fill with anything except more decision-making about killing or not killing myself, and that had been enough to keep me from chickening out."

CAROLYN'S MISTAKE MAY have been to attribute her creative, professional, and emotional losses to aging, considered as an unavoidable process like an incurable illness, rather than to ageism. This is a common error. Because of ageism, "Aging is at least in part a process of coming to terms with where one sits in a social hierarchy," says Katherine Newman, an anthropologist at Princeton.[13] "Aging" often means the shock of finding oneself sitting lower than one had thought.

Carolyn's situation — so full of apparent privilege — suggests a threat aimed at an important historical cohort: women whose work outside the home has been fundamental to their identity. This includes women over forty whose entry into adulthood coincided with the women's movement. Many struggled to change systems that had excluded women; they were among the "firsts." They had talent, energy, a movement — all the good gifts. If they are the biggest group of women ever to work, they will be the biggest to retire. They are ageing into retirement at a historically unprecedented intersection of female gender, privileges that were all-male, an unexpectedly successful midlife, and the new ageism.

What forces might impel women who seem secure to lose solidarity and hope? Whatever else people may gain from retirement — the advantages are all we hear from the mainstream media — in losing institutional backing, many lose income, structure, prestige, community, social life, and identity as a career self. This is true whether you retire from Wal-Mart or Goldman Sachs, at no matter what age. Self-employed people — therapists, private medical practitioners, writers, artists — don't have to retire, but ageism may reduce their clientele. Speaking about the art market's "craze for talent under thirty," MaryRoss Taylor, an independent curator, comments dryly that "women command less attention as they grow older, and becoming invisible is never a good career move."[14]

The sharp difference between an ego ideal maintained throughout the good midlife and what one endures after retirement can turn into sorrow and self-blame. For women, relative disadvantage (realized by comparing oneself to same-age men, to younger women, or to their own former selves) can be felt as fresh humiliation. I too aged into early adulthood in prefeminist decades, first soured and then enraged by being excluded from male privilege. Might I and others like me experience aging-into-retirement as a return of exclusion, in an unappeasable self-hating way? The withdrawal of social capital is defined by capitalist individualism as a personal failure and may be felt as such. Men are supposed to suffer this sense of failure acutely. Now, according to Silvia Sara Canetto, who has surveyed older women's suicides, women seem to be finding the inevitable exit from work more stressful than men do.[15]

Women do not often kill themselves. Over the past decades, the trend has actually been toward much lower rates of women committing suicide at age sixty-five and over. (Women kill themselves at the highest rate before age fifty-four. White men kill themselves far more often than nonwhite. Those who die by suicide come from all levels of education and income.)[16] Over sixty-five, men are four times more vulnerable than women. They account for 81 percent of suicides.[17] Older women apparently have some special later-life strength or wisdom. In recent cohorts, this might suggest the effects of feminist anti-ageism, learned flexibility and psychological resilience, or tolerance for suffering. But no one can take the historical trend for granted. Will the new ageism cause women to start catching up to men in later-life despair, as they have in rates of smoking, drinking, and incarceration?

What Social Forces Construct Age-Related Depression?

There are larger social forces at work that might make everyone, male or female, white or nonwhite, wary of the future. Under American capitalism, with productivity so fetishized, retirement from paid work can move you into the ranks of the "unproductive" who are bleeding society. One vile interpretation of longevity (that more people living longer produces intolerable medical expense) makes the long-lived a national threat, and another (that very long-lived people lack adequate quality of life) is a direct attack on the progress narratives of those who expect to live to a good old age. Self-esteem in later life, the oxygen of selfhood, is likely to be asphyxiated by the spreading hostile rhetoric about the unnecessary and expendable costs of "aging America."

Alarmist demography, as this view has come to be called, has come out of boardrooms and conservative think tanks and flourishes in the public arena. Media discourses warn younger people that old people are becoming too expensive and too numerous, nationally and globally. The *Atlantic Monthly*, usually considered intellectually respectable, published an essay called "The Coming Death Shortage: Why the Longevity Boom Will Make Us Sorry to be Alive," that demonstrates the extravagance of what can get published. The essay, about a transhuman world suspiciously resembling that depicted in Bruce Stirling's sci-fi novel *Holy Fire*, pits "us" — younger people who need careers and families — against "rich oldsters . . . expending their disposable income" on "longevity treatments" like heart bypass operations or implanted defibrillators.[18] Some bioethicists, scientists, lawyers, historians, doctors, and pundits also disdain sick people who are older than they for wanting longer life.

The term "greedy geezers" also began life in a magazine article (in the *New Republic*, 1988), whose author, charging that the budget was "cosseting the old," described as lavish the lifestyles of those featured in *Modern Maturity* (the AARP magazine), argued that sympathy for "the aging" was "understandable if increasingly misdirected" given their power and money, and warned of a "revolt" of the younger against "a massive entitlements system" for the "unproductive." Misrepresenting retirees, some — like the victims of Hurricane Katrina — desperately poor, accompanies calls for reducing safety nets. HMOs limit older patients' appeals of adverse decisions. Hospices were being asked by George W. Bush's Health and Human Services to return money they had already spent because people they cared for lived longer than expected.[19] The day after President Obama's electoral win, the right wing started pushing the ominously named "entitlement reform."

As a hook for her *New York Times* column, "The New Old Age," Jane Gross wrote a sidebar announcing that most people over eighty will spend years dependent on others. "That burden falls to their baby boomer children," whom she described as feeling "overwhelmed."[20] She may have intended to sound empathetic to adult offspring who are caregivers, but such language adds to the effort required to reassure their parents that they are *not* a burden. And concern for midlife offspring, expressed in that form, is like hate speech to the old parents who read it, imagining that the care they may need may come from unwilling adult children.

Summing up the cultural situation, Christine Overall writes, "Long-lived people are perceived as inevitably constituting a debilitating psychological and socioeconomic burden." That perception used to be inflicted on disabled people until the disability movement exerted its muscle. But very old people still lack both empathetic supporters and clout. In *Aging, Death, and Human Longevity*, her carefully argued book, Overall expresses doubt that "any other group in society could be described, with acceptance and impunity, as a 'burden.'"[21]

The diverse pressures on people aging toward old age are in fact coming to a head in a mean-spirited final solution. The injunction to "die sooner" is becoming hauntingly clear. Pundits — starting with former governor Richard Lamm and bioethicist John Hardwig — escalate the argument by insisting that there is a duty to die, which in Hardwig's view includes "a duty [incumbent on older people] to refuse life-prolonging medical treatment and also a duty to complete advance directives refusing life-prolonging treatment." Hardwig piously says he hopes to set a good example. The *New York Times* published an article titled "How to Save Medicare? Die Sooner."[22] Die *cheaper* is the underlying imperative.

Since women live longer than men and are considered to be sicker in old age, the three trends — longevity, alarmist demography, reducing government expense — converge on women. They never die; they just cost more. Women may be more likely than men to be coerced into dying under this new regime. I certainly thought that feminists would have more immunity, but Carolyn's story disabused me of that historical optimism. Many older women, like others of low status, don't get what they want. Does identity stripping make people less assertive, more submissive to authorities, or does it make the authorities more careless? Among people with terminal cancer who expressed a preference for intensive care, white patients were three times more likely than black patients to receive it. Whites were also sure to have their do not resuscitate (DNR) requests heard and honored.[23] There is some evidence that older women are less likely to make requests (for either life-prolonging care or physician-assisted suicide) or to have their requests acted on.[24]

The rhetoric of the duty-to-die proponents already influences medical systems, in a way quite distinct from legislatively defined assisted suicide. According to Stephen Harrison and Michael Moran, the British, although loyal to their system of national health care, already ration dialysis, quietly letting some people die of end-stage renal failure. In the United States, despite systemic incentives to overtreat, some doctors already treat some older patients differently than younger ones, by withholding information, diagnostic services, or treatment, with sometimes negative or even lethal consequences.[25]

When the government announced plans in 2009 to cut about $450 billion from the Medicare safety net, signs appeared that rationing by age — the undertreatment that people fear — might be surreptitiously extended. President Obama, by talking about people who are not his grandmother in terms of "sustainability" in so public a place as the *New York Times*, seemed to assume that denying care to very sick people when they are old is politically feasible. In fact, his comment did not raise a hailstorm of protest. Cost — rather than ethics, need, dignity — has become the mantra. Debates have begun about whether there should be an age limit after which not to provide "heroic" care. The media talk constantly about how expensive dementia is. Many health advocates argue that conversations about advance directives will not only give patients autonomy but save the nation end-of-life expense. Their making a cold-cash argument has enabled the right wing, hypocritically, as the "values party," to call those important conversations "death panels." What we rarely hear is that areas with high health-care spending started with sicker patients but had significantly lower inpatient mortality rates. Joseph J. Doyle Jr., an MIT economist, has found that "[e]xpensive treatment may be found to be effective." Cutting Medicare may jeopardize health.[26]

In deciding how to reduce funding to Medicare if administrative cuts prove insufficient, Congress might rely on bad data and ageist framing. Rationing by age could come about through oblique bureaucratic means. Panels set up by the president or the National Institutes of Health could provide new standards of "care" for classes of patients with chronic conditions, such as cognitive impairment and heart failure, in the presumed last phase of life. Medicare could give teeth to the guidelines, denying certain procedures by cutting reimbursements under the name of efficiencies or regional overuse or through capitation, aka global payments.[27] Whatever you call them, such controversial alternatives to fee-for-service have been criticized for decades for giving incentives for undertreatment.

Who has the power to deny care to those 3 percent who might incur "very high costs"? The onus may pass to doctors. Although a majority of Americans anticipate preferring to die at home, a very sick patient may change her mind despite her advanced directive. She hears of a treatment with some downside, but it might help her live to see a grandchild born. She wants it. In the current climate, an age critic can foresee moments of excruciating doubt and subtle suasion arising. The only relevant criteria — I quote Felicia Nimue Ackerman, an ethicist at Brown University — should be "desire to stay alive, medical need, and a reasonable chance that the procedure will work." But without a law in place that prohibits discrimination by age or by anticipated need for health services, other pressures are already put on doctors, nurses, social workers. Say insurance denies the treatment as inappropriate. How hard will the physician challenge the denial?[28] The patient might become one of the 3 percent! Someone speaks of high-tech dying — with its horrifying implications — or of futile or heroic rather than hopeful interventions. (If the treatment gave a younger person as much time, or relief, would the same judgment be passed? If the patient were Senator Ted Kennedy?) The patient, unsure, fatalistic, trusting the practitioner, is persuaded to forgo treatment. We hear the complaints about overtreatment, but undertreatment is harder to detect. In 2004, I interviewed Dr. Shneidman, the psychiatrist who started the field of "suicidology," about socioeconomic factors in later-life suicide. He warned then, "Don't let the GOP con you into an early death." This con could be bipartisan.

In old people, we may not connect depressive resignation to culture because the label "geriatric depression" implies that there is some distinctive kind of depression incident to old age. Yet in fact older people do not suffer higher rates of major depression than do midlife or younger adults.[29] This is true despite the fact that about a third of stroke victims without previous histories of depression suffer from it afterward.[30] Depression is far from inevitable in later life even under circumstances that younger people anticipate as highly stressful. "Failing strength, isolation, and the fear of death, all of which are associated with aging, though formidable, do not inevitably cause depression," notes Rachel Josefowitz Siegel, in "Ageism in Psychiatric Diagnosis."[31] Even among terminally ill patients, although a majority "discuss their wish to die, to be free of sickness or to have the dying process end," according to John Linder, a social worker with years of experience talking to cancer patients, "many of these references are oblique or symbolic and only a few are overtly suicidal." In a Chicago study of completed suicides, only 13 percent were terminally ill.[32] The surcease suicide to avoid intractable pain or gross indignity is actually rare.

Anxiety and depression may be no more common in later life, but they are less likely to be treated, or even noticed. Many older people who commit suicide had recently seen a doctor or come out of a hospital where their mental anguish had not been noticed or dealt with. In 75 percent of cases, a suicidologist at the University of Pennsylvania found, the victims had told family members or acquaintances of their intention to kill themselves. Depression that is noticed by younger professionals may also go untreated, because of younger people's fatalism about the ills of old age. A report by the Alliance for Ageing Research found that "too many physicians and psychologists believe that late-stage depression and suicidal statements are normal and acceptable" in older patients.[33]

Even if the mediating emotional factor is depression, depression does not always lead to suicide. Ed Shneidman notes, "One can lead a long unhappy life with depression, but acute suicidality is often quickly fatal."[34] The link between depression and suicidality, and perhaps also the refusal of treatment, is the sense that life has become irreversibly intolerable. We have seen many ways ageist coercion might work to make older people more inclined to want to die or to let themselves die by refusing food or treatment. Many psychological burdens are lowered onto frail shoulders under the guise of their being too old to live or the futility of treatment.

Bias—with an empathetic look—also insinuates, for example, that we are right to be deathly afraid of anticipated cognitive impairment. In *The Last Choice: Preemptive Suicide in Advanced Age*, C. G. Prado describes at great fictional length a "reflective aging individual"—a woman—who considers suicide not because of cancer, widowhood, death of friends, or inability to pay for good care. This woman's worry is that she will not recognize her future ratiocinative losses. She anticipates that others will think her judgment diminished, perhaps even before it is. (This is, alas, all too likely.) But she accepts that likelihood as normal aging. Prado describes older people as being treated by others "in a manner too much at odds with their own expectations," so that they come "not to know who they are." He nevertheless writes that "our most recently identified prejudice, ageism, has no adequate basis in fact."[35] Many others familiar with identity stripping (like people of color, disabled people, and women) would be quick to identify such dismissive treatment as ageist.

Feeling compelled to tell a decline narrative about your one and only life is a stressor, a depressant, a psychocultural illness. A list of future circumstances come ready to be applied as too awful to bear: "dementia," Alzheimer's, and, often when old people are concerned, "prolonged high-tech dying." Ageism, middle-ageism, sexism, and ableism can make those aging toward old age or chronically ill likelier to feel unwanted—unloved, sad, outcast, isolated, ashamed, helpless, and depressed, and unable to tolerate such distress.

The Prospective Fantasy of Suicide

The fantasy of the desirable self-inflicted death seems to be proliferating. Donald Sullivan, the protagonist of Richard Russo's semicomic novel on themes of American decline, is a case in point. In *Nobody's Fool*, also a movie starring Paul Newman, Sully often rescues an old woman who has lost her memory and tends to wander; but once as he shepherds her home, just seeing her head lolling brings into his mind a jocular suicide fantasy: "Sully made a mental note to shoot himself before he got like that."[36] It's not just a joke. People say death is a taboo subject, but so-called rational suicide to avoid old age is by no means taboo. At a party, an acquaintance who had just celebrated her fifty-fifth birthday, a working actress, in a tête-à-tête told me that she is preparing to kill herself if need be; she even told me how. There's a sort of folk wisdom out there for people who hate the messy means that are likely to leave you worse off: guns, poison, jumping off bridges. Whatever the means, suicidal ideation is becoming familiar to millions of Americans in a casual, conversational way.

Suicide, I suggest, is a possible cultural outcome of believing that the state, your health-care system, your doctors, and possibly your children find you a burden. Carrying that label is itself a terrible burden. Those of us in our middle years are already being scolded by some media into abandoning our future claims on such treatments. Will the retired in general start believing that they are trapped — too old to live, but too young to die? "Could the idea of a duty to die become one of the proverbial last straws that could precipitate that act?" Overall asks.[37] Exposure to positive stereotypes makes older research subjects likelier to choose life-saving measures, experiments in psychology indicate. In the same way, vicious stereotypes can reduce their will to live.[38] "Concerns about [being] a family burden are a principal reason that patients reject life-sustaining treatments," write Dr. Kenneth Rosenfeld and his colleagues in a study of end-of-life decision making.[39] Felicia Cohn and Joanne Lynn consider how duty-to-die arguments might affect reasoning about the value of life. "Accepting a duty-to-die means that the burden of proof will shift." They suggest that "[i]n American culture, individuals have not been called on to justify their continued existence. . . . It is not clear how anyone could actually make that case."[40] Suicide may come to seem the responsible thing.

As an op-ed writer in the *Washington Post* points out, "Nor, *given the aging of the population*, is the topic of rational suicide likely to disappear."[41] The topic will only burgeon as long as discourses about burdens, population-based medicine, the futility of care, distributive ethics, overtreatment, heroic care, and other rhetorics that lead to age-based medical rationing are framing the discourse. The United States is swallowing a powerful witch's brew of agendas in an era where Congress lacks the political will to cap notorious medical, insurance, and pharmaceutical hyperinflation directly.

Amputees back from Iraq, suffering from posttraumatic stress disorder, still mostly want to live, and the suicides among them are rightly thought shocking. Nobody says they have a duty to die, although every time I hear about their difficulties obtaining benefits from the government it occurs to me that the Veterans Administration is pushing these much younger people onto the ice floe. Since younger people are considered to have a duty to live, suicide may come to sound rational only when elderly people do it. Many Americans, I fear, have come to understand the urge to die preemptively in later life as natural, in far too many, far too vague circumstances.

The prospective fantasy of suicide operates without any hint that sexism, classism, racism, ableism, or ageism might deform it. Many people thought Dr. Kevorkian, who assisted people in suicide, was a hero. As Kevorkian went on, a few feminists pointed out how young some of those dying were, how relatively well many of the patients were — one was said to have played tennis the day before — and how many were women and/or recently disabled.

The suicidal fantasy lacks the practical recognition that for most Americans there is nobody officially able to help us. No states permit physician-assisted suicide except Oregon and Washington; many criminalize euthanasia. I could not have gotten help for my father when he had ALS if he had expressed a wish to die sooner. A kind old doctor told me that many doctors provide lethal prescriptions undercover at their patient's request. But contemporary medicine is not organized to make so private a doctor-patient relationship easy. Anticipating one's own preemptive death in much later life involves a worse failure of the imagination: leaving out of account the will to live even under adverse conditions. I have speculated about finding myself with a body-mind so different that it might threaten selfhood. There are conditions I think now I might not want to endure. But I can imagine deciding to go on living with, say, gradually increasing memory loss if I could be assured of having respectful home care given by people capable of relishing what is left of my selfhood. Many people go through devastating changes (I think of Stephen Hawking) without losing heart, purpose, and self-continuity. Why do people envisioning possible futures underestimate their own defenses?

The very term "rational elder-suicide" ought to be treated suspiciously. It is likely to become far less of a choice than proponents of the right to die think (or than I thought when I began this research). Perhaps it will seem sensible to go through much of the life course fearing the worst of aging and holding the idea of suicide in conscious reserve, as Carolyn did. Might American decline ideology prove so harsh that suicide becomes a rational response to normal aging? At what age should planning for voluntary death begin? At sixty? At forty? Even if age anxiety never turns to suicidal ideation, or suicidal ideation into the isolated, socially unsustained act it now must typically be, it is dreadful to think how much energy is sapped by having to fend off age-linked decline discourse and internalization year by year without the support of a movement. Perhaps this is expectable in a society where people are forced into finding devastating individual solutions for situations that could be dealt with humanely as collective problems.

Keeping Us Out of the Coroner's Office

In our current cultural circumstances, dwelling on prospective declines as if they were entirely natural — physical, personal, ahistorical — is worse than useless. It is baneful. People ought to know better than to deny that aging-as-decline is socially constructed. Age studies warns us to act more urgently. Humanists, responsible gerontological ethicists, suicidologists, and other paladins are ably defending later life. But we need a better-publicized defense, indeed, a new culture war. People need to recognize that the duty-to-die horde is accreting the kind of power I have described. C. G. Prado, quoted earlier as denying ageism, in fact later reconsidered its perniciousness: "[O]ur time's emphasis on personal autonomy regarding elective death is a bit too coincidentally convenient . . . . [given] increasingly grudging social support, more difficult access to health care, and the stigma of appearing to deprive others of scarce resources." In short, "[t]he new social attitudes may unduly influence . . . the decisions [of reflective aging individuals], and thereby render them less than rational."[42]

A few philosophers do feel the need to respond to the duty-to-die forces directly, and they do so by justifying the desire for longevity, as Overall does. Louise Anthony writes, quoting Martha Nussbaum, "'being able to live to the end of a complete human life . . . not dying prematurely' is a level of function that is necessary for a good human life, a life that we would be satisfied to have."[43] Some want us to argue that enfeebled elders have an equal right to life under the Fourteenth Amendment. Felicia Nimue Ackerman believes we should hear much more about the duty to aid, which she opposes to the duty to die.[44]

The right to live ought to be one of the "moral primitives" for which no further justification is needed. Dignity ought to be another, Martha Holstein argues: "Dignity cannot survive alongside humiliation."[45] And yet I fear that even if the corporate media could be pressured into treating the right to live to the end of a complete human life as debatable, current circumstances may not be propitious for winning that debate. The corporate media rarely quote even eloquent social philosophers if they are anti-ageist. A vision of a better life course, kindlier health care, and a respected choice about death may be hard to articulate, given not only public ignorance about ageism, but also fresh helplessness since the 2008 economic collapse about maintaining the health safety nets.

LET'S ASSUME THAT my anxiety proves unfortunately correct, and that more people will want, or say they want, or feel they must want, the right to die in later life. The "right to die" is defined as a patient's power to reject medical, technological, or surgical interventions, overriding a doctor's suggestion. But the term could be expanded to include physician-assisted suicide, as in some European countries where it is legal. Let's say, physician-assisted suicide becomes legal in more states, despite the fact that the "calls for PAS [have arisen] in a social system that [has been] inattentive to the complex physical, emotional, and spiritual needs of patients as they near the end of life."[46] But suppose too that ageism and ableism have come to be widely considered a danger to mental and public health, so people are warier about coerced suicide.

In this scenario, counseling—more than two visits to a doctor—therefore becomes mandatory before one can get medical assistance with suicide, even with an illness diagnosed as terminal. (A friend of mine lived for many years with metastatic breast cancer. People can be living long after they are told they are dying.) Agewise counseling would require that training be developed for practitioners who are already skilled in treating depression, to help all old(er) people (whether they are seriously ill or fear cognitive impairment) through the specific decision-making processes. To date, medical doctors rarely get such training, and many say they feel uncomfortable dealing with depressed or dying people. There is a nationwide shortage of geriatricians and geriatric psychiatrists and little public education about normal old age or living with dying. Ed Shneidman told me categorically in one of our phone conversations, "Our job is to keep that woman [threatening suicide] out of the coroner's office this month." The counselors I hypothesize would like to achieve that goal, but let's say they also believe in the principle of self-chosen death and are willing to take each person's own reasons seriously. People like Carolyn, who rejected therapy or antidepressants, might turn to them.

In this thought experiment, what would the ideal counselor be concerned about? Let's imagine further—the clincher—that age studies has created a new generation of committed anti-ageist doctors and therapists—presumably of all ages, but being older wouldn't hurt. They already know that motives for depression come with cultural contexts. They have received training in ageism awareness: They have analyzed their own fears of dying, chronic illness, dependency, physical failure, cognitive loss. Mirabile dictu, they also know American age ideology well enough to have examined their own relationship to progress and decline. They know how they typically incorporate decline elements into their narrative and can imagine prospectively how they might confront various setbacks. They can identify decline forces in their many disguises.

Psychotherapists who specialize in saving lives know that it is difficult to convince a person bent on ending their pain that they should live. The mutual friend who had often discussed other people's dying with Carolyn reflected on the limits of her role: "I don't know what I would have said to her; it would have been hopeless. Insofar as she was in despair at times, 'This is our lot,' she would have said." Aging, negatively conceived, was to her part of our lot.

Our hypothetical therapists have a more hopeful way to think of depression, as pieced-together, jerry-rigged motives, not as a solid impregnable lot. Imagine a cube of five hundred dice, Ed Shneidman said, made up of all the causes a person has for wanting to die—maybe early childhood neglect, sexual trauma, financial woe, loss of colleagues, some recent distress—all added up, lethally magnifying one another, apparently compact and massy.

Then Schneidman added, "But eliminating one single motive for dying, one die, may be enough."

I responded, "Suppose that ageism is one, even just one, of these five hundred."

With every client over, say, forty, the procedure of our therapists therefore also involves searching out that one die—any of the age-related forces potentially hustling the subject unconsciously toward depression and death. Using the common heading, they would ask, "Do you have some recent fears about aging?" Material might emerge about work (midlife job discrimination, unemployment, "superfluousness"), income (postretirement losses), sexual ageism ("menopausal" women and "andropausal" men), social solitude, disability, and long-term care. "How do your children feel about this? Are you worried about bills?" Finally, "Does the word 'ageism' mean anything to you?"

The training I envision would provide a tilt toward the same kind of search for sustaining resources that therapists make faced with a young adult who has suffered, say, loss of limbs or brain injury. Although able to imagine the despair, the counselor would not withhold therapy because the person in question was *young*. The counselor to an older person would likewise try to find a way to affirm that the client has "lovable traits" and that "things will get better."[47] She or he would help the client look for resilience, conceive of mutual dependency or reciprocity, find heroism in the struggle. A new generation of committed anti-ageists would strengthen selfhood by overtly fighting the deadliest internalized age discrimination, coerced suicide, person by person.

Returning to earth: As citizens we need to face some less hopeful considerations. In the current climate can we improve material conditions sufficiently to make the fantasy of an easy out unnecessary? Will Medicare/Medicaid forbid rationing by age rather than making it inevitable? Hospice doesn't save as much money as advocates believe, but it needs to be expanded. Will Congress keep it only partially funded? Will national health fund the duty to care? Long-term home-based care is cheaper than nursing homes and is what people say they want. You can have a very good quality of life — dignified and independent — while still requiring help, as disabled people with good help know. What does a person — very likely a woman — without means or a compliant family have to look forward to? Who believes that the United States will socialize our caregiving so that the word "burden" never comes up?

✳

In the face of a culture hostile to elders, our instinct ought to be to resist as hard as if the subjects at risk had the same right to the pursuit of happiness as the young do. If Carolyn had comprehended this unequal conflict, the anti-ageist feminist in her, an agent of her kindlier nature, might have revived and warred with the figure I have called the Shah, the hostile sexist ageist she had internalized. If she could have become aware of that ageist piece, she might have extracted it — looking at it critically, not as a piece of selfhood but as some debris of culture. Maybe she would have been outraged at almost losing everything to a dirty die. That might have given her the mission — the energetic distraction — she lacked.

She might have found a different image to live up to: not as an older woman who justified her increasing determination to die as stoic, but as an anti-ageist who would feel guilty about the legacy she might leave by saying age was the cause. Ed Shneidman pointed out in another of our absorbing conversations that living up to one's stated beliefs can have great motive power. Carolyn might have come to believe that her age-linked despair came from powerful forces that could be nobly fought, even if they could not be much changed. The anti-ageist movement could be electrified if potential Carolyns described the near-fatal effects of decline on their psyche and soma.

"[A]ll serious human moral activity, especially action for social change, takes its bearings from the rising power of human anger," said the late John Brentlinger, quoting another philosopher, Beverly Wildung Harrison: "Such anger is a signal that change is called for. . . . Anger is not the opposite of love. It is . . . a feeling signal that all is not well . . . a mode of connection to others, and a vivid form of caring." Fighting back defeats the sadness, bitterness, and isolation that helplessness produces.[48] The intrapsychic is where the germs of revolution begin, but to grow they need to be nurtured with ideas, analysis, vision. Political anger may help heal the rift between the full person accrued over the life course and the wizened, self-depreciating person who absorbs decline. Passionate knowledge can turn the fear of aging into the disdain of ageism. If a larger collective embraces resistance, then the harsher aspects of American decline ideology might not become more cruelly influential.

CHAPTER 3

The Oldest Have Borne Most

KATRINA AND THE POLITICS OF LATER LIFE

The Scandal of the Unasked Questions

Katrina — the hurricane, flood, and diaspora that first hit New Orleans on August 29, 2005 — was a catastrophe first and foremost for older people. Of those who died, 64 percent were over sixty-five, in a city where beforehand a mere 12 percent were over that age. A full 78 percent of the dead were fifty-one or older. Katrina was "one of the worst medical catastrophes for the aged in recent U.S. history," reporter Roma Khanna concluded in the *Houston Chronicle*.[1]

That conclusion may come as no surprise to those who monitored the victims closely. Many searing images of the first week of horror showed old people: a frail emaciated white woman, bent in painful angles, left lying on an empty baggage conveyor. (That sight led me into this story.) An African American woman bundled in an American flag, her brow furrowed in a perplexed frown. White as well as black people died, men died more than women, but age was far and away the most important risk factor.[2]

Yet age has been the underreported story. The nursing-home deaths did receive attention, but they accounted for only 10 percent of the original toll.[3] Even those who knew as early as October 2005 that "most Katrina victims were elderly" (the phrase stood as the title of a *Washing-*

ton Post article) underplayed the loss and disregarded the implications.[4] *Frontline*'s November special "The Storm" reported that the vast majority of the then-counted 1,322 people who had died in New Orleans were old — but *Frontline* gave that fact one sentence in an hour-long show.

By now we know there is no such thing as a *natural* disaster: human decisions and omissions play huge roles before and after nature does its damage. "Excess deaths" is a public health concept that uncovers hidden injustices. Those people didn't die of old age. Many could have been saved.[5]

Suffering excess deaths by age is not peculiar to that event or location. The difference is that in the heat wave of 2003 in Paris, for example, the American press did better: they understood that the deaths had social causes. "Disparate impact of age" in Paris meant, not old people's intrinsic frailty, but family abandonment and lack of communal resources like air-conditioned buildings. In Manhattan after 9/11, Dr. Robert Butler, founding director of the National Institute on Aging, points out that pets were evacuated within twenty-four hours, while older shut-ins and the disabled waited for up to a week without electricity or food.[6]

Why did older adults die disproportionately in Katrina? We need to know. Whatever the next crises might be — heat wave or flood, nuclear meltdown, gas-main or chemical-plant explosion — about 13 million people over fifty have told AARP they would need help evacuating in a disaster. About half of those who would need help said they would need it from someone outside their households.[7] Every adult is one muscle spasm or weakened immune system away from being among them. In an emergency you and I could also be dependent on FEMA, state and local agencies unused to working together, and untrained volunteers. In a society fraught with risk and permeated with ageism, it is time to ask why some die and some do not, and to make sure the future works better.

The bottom line in the Crescent City is that thousands of people over fifty were given painfully fewer choices about everything — being evacuated or drowning; easing back to normal or fighting for every scrap of recovery; getting home fast or spending years in the alien diaspora. Every bad break bespeaks multiple discriminations. In New Orleans the risks of being chronologically older were compounded by poverty, racism, sexism, living alone, mental and physical illness, disability. Theorists call this "intersectionality." Social causes of suffering accrue at these intersections and mount up in people's lives as they grow older. It takes a multilayered analysis to understand this. Since racism and classism were the main if ephemeral focuses of the mainstream media, it's useful to tease out the salience of age, ableism, and ageism. The evidence I found was piecemeal; much is still unknown.[8] But it is possible to pull together facts and hypotheses to explain that startling figure: 78 percent who died were over fifty. The point is to learn from what went wrong and encourage a spirit of collective responsibility for the particular set of perils that can engulf the second half of life.

DROWNING — THE FIRST CAUSE of death — occurred because of one failure: the most vulnerable were not evacuated early. In most cases, prevention is the preferred strategy.[9] In 2002, the Homeland Security director for New Orleans had estimated that in an emergency 100,000 disabled and elderly people would have to be evacuated, but a plan was never operationalized.[10] For those left to deal privately with a last-minute escape, all the risk intersections mattered. Patricia Smith, the extraordinary lyric annalist of Katrina, writes, in "Man on the TV Say":

> *Go.* Uh-huh. Like our bodies got wheels and gas,
> like at the end of that running there's an open door
> with dry and song inside.[11]

Middle-class people, white or black, lived on higher ground or had the wherewithal to go. People of meager resources didn't. African Americans, about 68 percent of New Orleanians, were possibly as high as 80 percent of those trapped inside the city. Many had homes in less desirable low-lying regions, and the highest death counts were in tracts where floodwaters rose rapidly to seven-plus feet. Age deepens lack. Of heads of household over fifty-five, a third did not have access to a vehicle. Women are less likely to have licenses the older they are. Of 484,000 citizens, under a quarter had disabilities, but the figure was 50 percent for people over sixty-five. They couldn't crawl out on roofs, swim through seven feet of water, or set off toward the highways with their backpacks. One young woman I heard fleetingly on NPR said, sobbing, that the family drove away leaving both her mother and their grandmother in the path of what they thought would be merely another hurricane. But people took their children with them, including their ill and disabled children. Only one child under five died.[12]

Lack of social support may turn out to be more deadly for older people. Contacts urge you to leave; they may come by your house to get you out. Older men tend to live alone with fewer contacts. This may explain the fact that although 53 percent of all who died were women, in the population over age sixty-five, men died at higher rates.[13] Maleness was the next risk factor after age.

Some people lacked money to leave because the storm arrived just before they received their Social Security checks. Some stayed behind to care for others. Clementine Eleby, aged seventy-nine, who was bedridden, and her daughter, Barbara Eleby Lee, and other family members stayed because they couldn't find a hospital with a free bed. Long experience told others that hurricanes pass fast but travel out would be hot, slow, and wearing. One black couple over eighty, remembering Hurricane Betsy in 1965, had stayed but bought an ax. The husband had the strength to chop a hole in the roof.[14] Staying would have been a prudent decision if not for the flood that overtopped the levees—the "senseless environmental disaster" that had been years in the making.[15]

People who survived the flood didn't necessarily survive the rescue. The second greatest number of deaths derived from the lack of assistance for those with preexisting health problems.[16] Delay can be fatal. Rescuers—federal troops and the Coast Guard, even the "Cajun Navy" and other volunteers—should have been instructed to search specifically for people who were older, sicker, or more handicapped. On August 30, first responders in a boat offered to take Ms. Eleby's family if they would leave her behind. Her family refused. When a second boat approached, they prudently placed her in it first. After a night spent on a highway, they were taken by truck to the Convention Center, where she soon died. John DeLuca, aged seventy-seven, was helicoptered twice, winding up on an interstate highway. Although buses began to arrive on August 31, he was not evacuated. Ms. Eleby and Mr. DeLuca are two of three elderly residents who, according to a wrongful death suit brought by their families, "were in known peril" and denied "a duty of aid."[17]

Did other young rescuers fail to look for or notice older people—especially if they were black or looked handicapped or "demented"—or did they see them and shrink away from the multiple anticipated difficulties of dealing with these anomalous bodies? "The elderly and critically ill plummeted to the bottom of priority lists as calamity engulfed New Orleans," said a *New York Times* article by David Rohde and others. Ingrid Tischer, a disability-rights activist, makes a case that neglect was broader, and not inadvertent but irresponsible, in fact ableist: "People with disabilities of all ages were shut out of shelters, denied transportation, communications, and left without medication and equipment necessary for survival. We will never know how many people with disabilities who lived in the community lost their lives."[18] But well-coordinated evacuation was possible even amid what has been described as chaos. For predominantly white St. Bernard Parish, it came by ferry, military trucks, and school buses, with relief supplies and Medivac units.[19]

Many older people in New Orleans died of illnesses that can be "easily managed under normal conditions but that become lethal when access to medicine and treatment is cut off."[20] At the Morial Convention Center, for days no agency provided security, water, food, or functioning toilets. (Mayor Ray Nagin said he would not open the Convention Center or the Superdome the next time New Orleanians had to evacuate.) Herbert Freeman managed to get his wheelchair-bound mother, Ethel, on a boat to Morial. Interviewed by Spike Lee for the documentary *When the Levees Broke*, he said he watched her die. Patricia Smith wrote "Ethel's Sestina" in her voice:

> Ain't but one power make me leave my son.
> *I can't wait, Herbert. Lawd knows I can't wait.*
> *Don't cry, boy, I ain't in that chair no more.*[21]

Across the board, older people "had special needs neglected by disaster workers," the *Sacramento Bee* reported.[22] Given the lack of geriatric training in this country, even medical professionals working in shelters may not have been adequately trained. Volunteers may not know that dehydration, for example, comes faster in elderly people and is harder to reverse. Speech that sounds incoherent may be caused by drunkenness, deafness, or a urinary tract infection. Good listening, looking people in the eye, and holding their hands may lower blood pressure and ameliorate panic-related memory loss.

In Houston, some things went the right way. A doctor with geriatric training named Carmel Dyer acted proactively, knowledgeably, and ethically. She not only sought out older people, some of them wandering alone and in confusion through the giant shelter, but also designed a quick questionnaire, SWiFT (Seniors Without Families Triage), so that the neediest could be immediately transported to appropriate facilities.

"Triage" is a term of art in medicine for sorting individuals in chaotic situations of scarcity, to help those with the greatest objective need first. It's doubtful that similar priorities ruled in New Orleans when the city, with almost the entire medical infrastructure destroyed, was officially labeled a medical shortage area. The electric company should restore power first to people who need, say, to refrigerate their diabetes medication. Some agency should be named to locate and provide oxygen for people who run out, and another should be accountable for getting people to facilities for dialysis, asthma treatment, or cardiac problems. (What might make coordination possible is crisis data-pooling, like that provided to humanitarian groups in Haiti by geolocators, texters, and Twitterers after the earthquake.) As it was, in New Orleans many formerly independent people wound up in nursing homes.[23]

The danger in a public operation that doesn't explicitly highlight age and disability is overlooking people who fall into those categories. Decisions about whom to transport, whom to rescue, whom to admit, whom to treat, *first*, are made rapidly, often unconsciously. They are thus likelier — if I extrapolate from work by psychologists like Mahzarin Banaji — to be based on implicit biases.

How do people become invisible or ignorable in plain sight? There are also some reports of African Americans not getting picked up by white "rescuers." The eye of power simply flits by too fast to register the powerless. Retirees, unless white, male, and in suits, are usually absent from councils where emergency plans are being laid and executed. Powerlessness makes oppressed groups invisible. Ageism — as a kind of superiority complex — makes the old appear unworthy of attention when they obtrude.

FOR MANY NEW ORLEANIANS, the years since 2005 have involved layers of trauma, hardship, anger, and grief. Many adult children mourn parents and other older relatives lost in appalling circumstances. Many hundreds of older people were widowed or lost kin and friends. They were forced to witness death and government neglect. Some suffered the displacement of evacuation, not once but many times. Many live in diminished circumstances, whether they have returned to the chaotic city or remain in the exile of the Katrina diaspora, with irreparable losses and ongoing — for some, never-ending — experiences of frustration and uncertainty. Many experience emotional problems they hadn't had before. "'Katrina brain' became a local term describing the fact that we couldn't remember something as simple as a phone number after the hurricane," a psychiatrist named Kenneth Sakauye told me.

(For once, memory loss wasn't age-graded and was connected to anxiety.) People suffered from insomnia, tormented flashbacks, depression, inability to function — signs of posttraumatic stress.[24] Casandra Goins, an evacuee who was a social worker, said, "It's almost like an obstacle course to see what you can endure."[25]

Despite billions in aid, the altruistic support of volunteers and indefatigable nonprofit workers, and for a while the sympathy of the nation, "very few recovery initiatives have specifically addressed the needs of older adults," according to Jennifer Campbell, the director of the Hurricane Fund for the Elderly.[26] For many, life after Katrina has become an unending misery.

Older Exiles in the Inner City

That old woman crumpled on the baggage conveyor: Did she survive? Find an advocate? Get back home to the sludge and garbage? When native New Orleanians dared to return to stinking, debris-filled streets, many found that rents had soared and the city's meager safety net had been shredded. More than 68,000 homes were still vacant, boarded up and moldering. The population of the Lower Ninth Ward, once home to 15,000 — many older African Americans whose families had lived there for generations — went down to 1,400.[27] After the Great Fire, Chicago was rebuilt completely in eighteen months — and that was in the nineteenth century.

With HUD, Habitat for Humanity, and student volunteers on the scene, New Orleans looked for a while like a national goodwill housing project. But dispossession, delays, and aids to gentrification are ruining neighborhoods. Developers and elites hoped to make the Chocolate City considerably whiter, partly by leaving the Lower Ninth and other low bits as "green space." This racist and classist intention was never accepted as a plan, but it has been operationalized, as it were. In 2008, the city council okayed the demolition of virtually all surviving public housing, although there had been no structural damage to the all-brick buildings. Only about half of the city's public-housing residents had moved back by February 2008.[28] Federal housing aid administered under the state Road Home program, cruelly slow in coming, was for owners not renters. People who live with family or friends — which many elderly were doing — were ineligible for housing assistance until they rented another place, but "caught in a FEMA Catch-22," they could not find rentals at decent prices. African Americans whose property had been handed down through generations did not always have clear title.[29]

Subsidies that would help to build three thousand new units of affordable housing for extremely low-income people, a category that includes older and disabled people, single women, and African Americans, have been held up in the House of Representatives. "Most public housing residents, residents of mobile homes, renters, and those lacking insurance are women — often women heading households on their own income alone," writes Elaine Enarson, a professor of Applied Disaster and Emergency Studies, "but rehousing them [was] not a priority." In rebuilding too, the most deprived were likely to get a poke in the eye. Only in 2009 did Obama's HUD give 3,450 families still in trailers or temporary housing priority for rental-subsidy vouchers.[30] With the population halved, homeless numbers have doubled. For the first time, advocates for the homeless say, they are seeing people older than fifty or sixty, people who have worked their entire lives and once owned homes, sleeping rough. Lizzy Ratner, reporting for the *Nation* in 2008, was told about old women suffering severe confusion, an eighty-year-old man, and a middle-aged man with a colostomy bag sleeping every night in Depression-era conditions.[31]

Even if returnees finally restored their houses, it didn't feel like home anymore. Empty houses were marked like crime scenes. Neighbors were gone; no one knew where. For a time, retirees were able to return if they found the title to their land, because then they were allowed to put a trailer on it (renters were generally not permitted to). Younger kin often didn't return, anticipating that they would not find jobs or reopened schools.[32]

New Orleans teaches this: Older people are the cornerstones of families, neighborhoods, local organizing, and church affairs. Networks that grew up around them are dependent on them, perhaps especially on the women — for historical memory, anecdotes and genealogies, the safety of the eye on the street, the sharp tongue of benign authority, raising grandchildren, babysitting to help out working adult children, contributing income from jobs, bringing the family together for crises and holidays. In the dancing at Mardi Gras, the "second line" after the bands included older people, loyal to the West African shuffle step. Describing the musical soul of the city before Katrina, Michael White exults, "Walking canes and crutches that rarely left the ground were suddenly hoisted high. Elderly faces, wrinkled, tired, and helpless from years of struggle — now glowed with youthful joy."[33] All this has been disrupted.

People who finally made their way back found that many of the clinics and medical personnel were still gone, as were the hospitals, pharmacies, and their medical records, which often had no backup. When I went to New Orleans eighteen months after the flood, our guide on the Hurricane Tour was a stocky, white-haired white man who had evacuated, returned, and suffered two heart attacks in the first year. "I didn't know I was so stressed," Chuck said. They took him the first time to a hospital that was still open, but the ER staff told him the wait even for a heart attack would be an hour or more, so he was driven out of town to an overworked suburban hospital. On the tour Chuck pointed out his inundated neighborhood, still lacking a market.

Within a year, most of the medical volunteers from around the country who had bravely taken time from busy practices had left town. Charity Hospital, the last-chance hospital for the uninsured for 150 years, can't reopen. The Louisiana legislature in 2007 refused to use federal block-grant money to rebuild it. According to Kenneth Sakauye, since only the wealthy nursing homes could afford to reopen, few remained.[34] Many were short on staff because their low-wage female employees (like the gravediggers) remain in the diaspora. Louisiana State University cut an entire consortium of geriatric psychiatry services. Many geriatric psychiatrists and physicians, with their institutions closed, found permanent jobs elsewhere. Although the experienced head of AARP warned that recovery funds should not come "at the expense of other older and vulnerable people by chopping Medicare and Medicaid," that was precisely what was happening.[35] The Republican budget cut Medicaid and federal programs for geriatric education even as exhausted elders returned to the Big Easy.[36]

The Older Exiles in the Diaspora

The aftermath of Katrina has also been a catastrophe for older people who evacuated, in terms of the number of people affected, the severity of the dislocations, and their duration. The Gulf area suffered one of the largest migrations of displaced people in U.S. history, according to Jennifer Campbell.[37] They were given "*one-way tickets* out of town!" mayor Ray Nagin said incredulously in *When the Levees Broke*. "No ticket back" — symbolizing a government that was not only inefficient but callous — must be the refrain of rage. An estimated 88,000 people who left the region were over sixty-five; about 45,000 were over seventy-five.[38] They were sent to noisy shelters in thirty-six states, many of them without kin, important papers, medications, eyeglasses, walkers, or clothes other than the ones they were wearing when they locked the front door.[39]

Exile frightens and disorients everyone, but it is perhaps worst for older people who have sunk deep roots in one place. New Orleans was a city full of such people. Over 70 percent of the older exiles had lived in their homes for more than twenty years. Some had built their own houses. Even among renters, over half had lived in their homes for similar lengths of time.[40] They had been surrounded by friends, extended family, pets, and familiar geographies. They lost not just sartorial identity but furniture, photographs, mementos — all the precious supports of selfhood, especially important for those with cognitive impairments.

In one group of exiles between sixty and ninety-seven years of age who wound up in Baton Rouge, two-thirds of them women, three-quarters of them African American, about half had been living alone and had no choice but to escape alone. In the evacuation, these people moved or were removed up to eight times. Over half were still living in a trailer community in 2006.[41] Chuck, our tour guide, lived for a while in a tiny FEMA trailer, gaining weight on Meals Ready to Eat, which are nutritionally dangerous for people with high blood pressure or diabetes. Like other large people and people in wheelchairs, Chuck found he could scarcely sidle into his own bathroom. The trailers leaked formaldehyde. It was rightly called "disaster housing."

Exiles had to deal with crazy-making bureaucracies, including their insurance companies. Many did not receive checks for unemployment, welfare, or Social Security for months. Some were slow to register for help, because "older adults process . . . crisis at a different pace, may be less willing to ask for help . . . may have difficulty getting to or standing in line."[42] FEMA rather than HUD, which has long housing experience and provides rental-subsidy vouchers, was put in charge of housing. Given that college professors puzzle over Medicare Part D, it's hard to see how people in exile, even without "Katrina brain," could get through the labyrinth of regulations produced by multiple government agencies.

Between 10 and 35 percent of the longer term exiles are older people: another small city's worth. In a survey of former residents of public housing, virtually all African American women, more than a third of them over sixty-five or disabled, half said they still wanted to return but didn't know if they could. Affordability and safety of housing were the impediments they mentioned most often. They had plenty else to say. "I need surgery and there's no hospital in New Orleans." "Bus services in New Orleans are nonexistent." "Housing Authority threw all of my belongings out." "$600 Social Security income is the only income I have."[43]

Depletion and Heroism

On the first anniversary of the flood, *Time* magazine asked whether New Orleans was having a "mental health breakdown"[44] Depression and mental illness had risen to staggering heights across the board. Dr. Sakauye, who is a member of the American Association of Geriatric Psychiatrists, told me there was a 61 percent increase in calls to crisis helplines in the months following Katrina, despite the fact that less than half of the population of the city remained. A small survey by the Centers for Disease Control and Prevention in the fall of 2005 showed that more than 40 percent of survivors had signs of posttraumatic stress. Alcohol, drug, and nicotine abuse increased. Most of the local psychiatrists had gone; the number in practice dropped from 196 to 22. The number of beds for patients in psychiatric emergencies dropped 40 percent.[45]

In the midst of the turmoil, some questioned the inner resources of "older people." All evacuees suffer, said an organizer for ACORN, the nation's largest community organization of low- and moderate-income families, but especially seniors, because "they can't bounce back so easily." The chief of geriatrics at Louisiana State University Health Sciences Center varied the metaphor, adding, "A lot of older people are running on fumes."[46] In this decline story, meant to be empathetic, older people lack the resilience that younger people are assumed to have. But many people over fifty, or over sixty-five, are as resourceful and persistent as the silver fox driving a riding mower across the Midwest in David Lynch's film *The Straight Story* (1999) or the women stranded together in the film *Strangers in Good Company* (1990). Indeed, the "rapid recovery and emotional balance" of Pearline Chambers, a widow of eighty-six who spent two days up to her neck in floodwater, suggests that some "healthy elderly people are often able to bounce back from adversity more quickly than younger people."[47] Psychologists believe the best prognosticator of psychological resistance to trauma is experience with travails and the conviction of having survived them—a progress narrative that relates the advantage to age-linked abilities and characteristics.

Interviewing the older New Orleanians who after many moves had washed up in a shelter in Baton Rouge, Karen Roberto and her colleagues indeed found that many were able to reframe their situation positively: "At least I have this." "Compared to my neighbors [I'm okay]." "I'll be able to move on."[48] People who can act to improve their circumstances are likely to feel more resilient. If they were middle-class, older European Americans and African Americans were able to start rebuilding their damaged houses quickly. They had the confidence to deal with bureaucracy and the wherewithal needed to repair their dwellings—$40,000 to $100,000 or more, depending on how high the muddy, toxic water had risen.[49] Poorer whites and blacks are required to be more heroic. After all, it's people without resources who are called "resourceful."

Herbert Gettridge, eighty-two, returned alone from evacuation in Wisconsin in order to fix up his house, even though it had no running water, electricity, or a bed. A fifth-generation New Orleanian, a mason and plasterer since the age of ten, he persevered and became a poster child for the grit required to rebuild, according to June Cross's PBS production about him, "The Old Man and the Storm." He used to have thirty-six grandchildren dropping in. With three hundred relatives mostly in the diaspora, he became intermittently depressed. At one point he goes off camera to cry. Our tour guide Chuck used his bus audience to vent his articulate anger — at Nagin for firing five thousand city workers, at the Army Corps of Engineers for the flooding, at Bush for botching everything. But many survivors couldn't summon enough extra energy for political anger.

Trauma can be soul destroying, brain injuring, and life threatening. Some bereaved adult offspring believe that their parents died of a broken heart. Some were unable to reconstruct a decent life in their wretched abandoned neighborhoods. Others isolated in the diaspora were bewildered by the charmless strange locales they found themselves in. Fifty-nine-year-old Sylvester Major, living in Oklahoma City, officially died of congestive heart failure, but his son says being away from Mardi Gras, the Hornets, and home-cooked food was like "being in a foreign land."[50]

In circumstances of such overdetermined misery, the effects of stress don't necessarily disappear, warns psychiatrist James Barbee IV of Louisiana State University Health Sciences Center.[51] Residents and exiles of all ages were being retraumatized and suffering long-lasting psychic harm. The bitterness against racism in New Orleans was an emotion shared by black people and white sympathizers nationwide. We must admit into our repertory of empathetic feelings the emotions inflicted by ageism: bitterness, the relief of death, anguish, the end of hope. Patricia Smith expressed many of these feelings in her poem "34," in which she writes on behalf of nursing-home residents.

> We are stunned on our scabbed backs.
> There is the sound of whispered splashing
> and then this:
>
> *Leave them.*[52]

Older survivors were likely to learn that death and exile had undone many age peers. Was psychological damage inflicted on people aware that they were considered too old? Do we outsiders also feel in our blind bones that community and nation and some families and rescuers abandoned them on that account? The "No-longers," Philip Roth's Zuckerman calls people his age in his bitter diatribe in *Exit Ghost*[53] — no longer useful, no longer productive, no longer wanted. Us?

People Who "Get Old" Young

A catastrophe like Katrina puts in high relief the economic, social, and health conditions of older people struggling to survive on every corner in this country every day. It should be obvious that seniors are not all rich and secure. But our culture is replete with misinformation about the high status of people called the Boomers and those portrayed as vital seniors. It is therefore worth repeating: Many people are systematically disadvantaged throughout their lives. Their midlife wage-peak is low. Old age — if by that ugly shorthand we mean, as so many do, income declines and physical ailments — for them starts young.

Chapter 2 concerned relatively privileged people. Their well-being turns out not to be secure either, but they are subjected to forms of ageism specific to middle-class accomplishment, suddenly and later in life. In contrast, many of the people this chapter concerns are familiar with lifelong inequities that become exacerbated as they age into their middle years.[54] They are among the 13 million people over fifty who told the AARP they would need help in an emergency.

Low income is highly correlated with poor health. Wages for male midlife workers at the median have been stagnant for decades. Women's jobs not only pay less, they are less likely to provide health insurance or carry pensions. The work may be arduous and stressful. Before retirement—if they can afford to retire—people can be frequently unemployed or underemployed or carry two jobs. The level of debt for people between fifty and sixty-four, earning in the middle of the income scale, more than doubled in the 1990s.[55] Racism worsens all the indicators for people of color.

A lifetime of uninterrupted medical care from childhood on results in better health in later life (and lower Medicare costs). Contrariwise, the consequences of poverty show up in bodily ways at relatively young ages. "Health disparities begin early and can accumulate over the life span of a cohort," writes Angela O'Rand. "In earlier phases of the life course . . . chronic disease and functional limitations emerge unevenly across educational, occupational, ethnic, and gender subgroups," especially among the uninsured. Inequality in a country without national health care, as political scientist Victor Wallis has written, constructs "biologically distinct communities, in which those with the necessary resources will attain formidable physical resistance and longevity, while the excluded sectors . . . will sink to previously unimagined depths of misery."[56]

Many women and men fall to the bottom of this savage distribution as early as their forties, fifties, or sixties, decades younger than in the middle classes. Poverty constructs anxiety, helplessness, ignorance, greater exposure to toxicity, job strain at work, poor diets. As the PBS series *Unnatural Causes* demonstrated, poverty comes with attendant illnesses like asthma, obesity, hypertension, high blood pressure, and heart disease. Life-threatening illnesses may go undiagnosed and untreated because of lack of health insurance, lack of access to medical and psychiatric care, or other ways treatment is rationed by class. Racism and sexism, which worsen poverty, also worsen health outcomes. Physicians make "clinical compromises" that result in "potentially beneficial treatments being withheld from their patients for financial reasons."[57] If people's health-care needs mount when they don't have health insurance and their state, like so many, doles out Medicaid stingily, the most dangerous years come between fifty-five and sixty-four—10.7 percent of the uninsured die in those years, before they can reach Medicare. A quarter of Americans age fifty to sixty-four spend over 10 percent of their income on health care. Most of the early retired, female or male, according to the Congressional Budget Office, are not rich but disabled.[58]

We can begin to comprehend why 14 percent of those who died in New Orleans were as young as fifty-one to sixty, although in the middle class, many people in their sixties, seventies, and even eighties are healthy and are not considered "old." The public health correlatives of economic and social inequality—earlier disability, poorly managed chronic illness, frailty—are inescapable.

As the United States moves toward more complete national health coverage, adequate care earlier could assure that low-income people do not stumble so painfully across the finish line into the arms of Social Security and Medicare. As it is, they get healthier under Medicare but are sicker than they would have been. They possess fewer resources to care for themselves. An updated formula for the poverty rate of Americans over sixty-five, proposed by the National Academy of Sciences, puts it at 18.6 percent, much higher than previously measured.[59] (It should be better known that the federal poverty line is actually set lower for those over sixty-five than those under. To adjust for the current federal underestimation of late-life misery, some sensitive economists combine it with the near-poor rate, 125 percent of the poverty line.) Poor citizens over sixty-five may still require Medicaid, but "the process of applying is so arduous and stigmatizing and the rules of eligibility so restrictive," Madonna Harrington writes, that fewer than one-third of eligible older persons actually receive it. More than 70 percent of older poor people are women.[60]

"Women" was another keyword the media missed, despite the emblematic photos that woke my compassion. In the New Orleans of Katrina, almost 25 percent of the women over sixty-five were poor, according to the Older Women's League.[61] Destitute might be a better word. Were more of the older evacuees women? Certainly African American women are the vast majority of those who remain in the diaspora.[62] Checking early coverage via Internet sources like LexisNexis, I found nobody asking such questions. Ironically, *Off Our Backs*, in an issue that was devoted both to Katrina and to "women and age," barely mentioned older women in its Katrina coverage, focusing on rape, closing of abortion clinics, and difficulties taking care of children. "Women" meant, as it too often does in feminist writing, younger women.

Women tend to wind up alone, as well as sicker or more disabled, and more frequently in nursing homes. The older a woman is, the likelier to be poor. The percentage of black women who fall into the near-poor category rises from 18.3 percent at age fifty-six to 44.9 percent at age eighty.[63] After sixty-five, the women hovering around the poverty line subsist mainly on Social Security. Women get considerably less funding than men. A smaller percentage of black than white women receive any Social Security income. If women sign up early, they'll receive less all their lives. Lesbians, like gay men, cannot get benefits directed to spouses, like widow benefits from Social Security. Never-married women have the highest incidence of poverty, according to Toni Calasanti and Kathleen Slevin in their excellent book, *Gender, Social Inequalities, and Aging.*[64] Carroll Estes, one of the sharpest critical gerontologists, pointed out decades ago that "the old" are divided by government programs into the "deserving" and the "undeserving." Often, given the topsy-turvy American ideal of self-reliance, it is the neediest who are considered most undeserving.[65]

Older women in poor health spend more than half their income on health care, with older women of color spending a higher proportion than white women.[66] These are the ones who eat cat food in order to pay for pharmaceuticals or who take only half their medication to be able to pay other bills. African Americans have the highest rates of disability of any group. African Americans with end-stage renal disease wait twice as long for kidney transplants as white people do. Women are less likely than men of the same age and health status to get put on waiting lists for the transplants. This inequity gets worse as women get older: between ages fifty-six and sixty-five, they are 29 percent less likely to make it to the lists. [67]

Without stereotyping old age or ignoring disabilities at younger ages, one can conclude that people are likely to have special needs as they age into middle and later life. Ageism worsens our country's institutional and individual responses. Those over sixty-five suffer fewer acute illnesses than younger people but more chronic illnesses, which our health-care systems are not nearly as well organized to care for. Even the well-off on Medicare and private insurance suffer from ageism in medicine. Doctors prefer to treat "the worried well rather than the really sick."[68] Even in specialties where professionals will probably treat old people, gerontological or anti-ageist training is not required. People with chronic illnesses may find doctors inattentive or inept. Pain management is not taught properly, so that when it counts older people can be undermedicated as well as overmedicated. Aides to help them age in place can be economically unavailable, deficient, or even abusive. Spouses and relatives who care for older family members are overworked and get inadequate support from public programs.

People with decent incomes sometimes repeat, "We are each responsible for our own health." What can they be thinking?

Not a Good Year for the Life Course

The phenomenon we know as Hurricane Katrina, whatever else it means, should now encompass obliviousness to older people in planning; failure to evacuate them; delay in rescuing them; excess deaths by age; the abandonment of parts of a city where later life enjoyed unusual respect and emotional supports; disregard of the specific needs of older survivors, especially their mental health needs; ignorance, sadly enough, on the part of volunteer medical workers; a painful ongoing diaspora; and, with honorable exceptions, a failure on the part of most media to highlight the category of age. These are staggering consequences for merely growing older.

A democratic society is responsible for acknowledging two complex truths. First, older people have an equal right to life — as much right to survive as younger adults or children. (I find myself needing to say this a second time within two chapters.) Second, a considerable number of older people — say half — have special needs, physical, mental, financial. To give them an equal chance, older people have to be consciously set, along with non-old disabled people, at the top of priority lists.

Katrina was a teachable moment that could have shocked a nation out of its disregard of age. Older people are diverse even if one counts only those from sixty-five to over one hundred. Age is therefore not always a salient category or a good predictor, but it *was* in New Orleans. Such failures of social responsibility need an explanation. "Ageism" was the final keyword missing. A LexisNexis search revealed how many times the word was used in major newspapers and magazines over the six months right after the flood. Zero.

Only that keyword can explain why the old qua old were mostly unseen. Their stories are certainly compelling. Sharpening each major issue, they offer pathos, heroism, morality plays with villains. Yet having discovered (younger) African Americans, reporters in search of other groups went on to investigate prisoners and the "unique" problem of teenage evacuees. Older evacuees and older returnees were interviewed but not to demonstrate their group problems.

Proper coverage would have been a boon not only for the imaginative embrace of the life course but for planning. Prevention prevents disasters from turning into catastrophes. At-risk populations "have needs not fully addressed by traditional emergency preparedness plans," writes Martha S. Wingate in *Public Health Reports*.[69] Peter Fimrite's article about San Francisco's emergency preparedness, "Rights Group Warns Disaster Would Imperil Disabled, Elderly," could still be a model for many local self-exams.[70] In the aftermath of Katrina, age remained the special interest of AARP, social gerontologists, geriatricians, public administrators, aging-services providers, the CDC, rights groups. Their detailed reports, from which I have learned much, should have become the basis of think-tank pieces about, inter alia, training first responders in anti-ageist attitudes and geriatric first aid, urging city and state departments to coordinate with the network of services for old people, or convincing agency buyers to procure adequate amounts of appropriate supplies.

In advance of disasters, mayors should be required to stock special-needs shelters, open specifically for people with disabilities and serious medical conditions. Those scoring highest on the updated SWiFT survey used in Houston should be evacuated early with everything they need: assistive devices, medications, important papers, contact information, and if possible, a companion.[71] Not every city or state has planned for such shelters, nor are they necessarily required to. The CDC is making many changes in emergency eldercare. But a year after Katrina, a major national study that investigated programming for older citizens — including emergency awareness and transportation — found that only 46 percent of towns, counties, and cities had strategies.[72] The best caregivers are those with geriatric medical and mental health education. The United States needs fourteen thousand geriatricians; it has seven thousand. For years Congress has not funded enough geriatric education. Medical schools do not adequately include it in the curriculum.

Indifference to ageism on the part of elites has dangerous consequences. I fear Katrina was a paradigmatic case. Assuming that the next emergency would be coordinated better, that the helicopters would arrive faster, can we trust we'd be picked up or be rushed aid if we were old? Perhaps our names would have to be on a master list that doesn't exist. Some NGOs — like the International Longevity

Center—are trying to find people who aren't on Meals on Wheels and similar lists. Will legislative momentum make agencies responsible for knowing where all the sick or weak elderly and disabled women and men in a community live? Are people inquiring about their own city's or town's disaster plans for older people? Will medical personnel and volunteers be trained to know what help we require to survive? Will ethical reflection change behavior, so that younger people hesitate to leave older relatives behind? Will you and I look around now and pick an older neighbor to help in an emergency, if we are not the oldest neighbors? At many points in our lives—when we are young, hospitalized, injured, convalescent—most of us who consider ourselves independent rely on others. Katrina should teach us that we all live and die by interdependence. The facts marshaled here should not make younger people despair that later in life they too might die disproportionately in an emergency, but scare them into action to avoid it.

Trying to bring together information and stories about the victims of Katrina—and showing the difficulty of doing so—is my attempt to make the travails of the age class more visible and more vivid. In Katrina, of course, the multiple biases I have identified are agglomerated—and sometimes hard to separate out. And coalition politics are necessary both to train us in compassion and to generate political power.

Why argue that the public pay specific attention to "age"? Certainly this is not a claim for superior categorical privilege for people who are old, above, say, people with disabilities—they are often the same people. It is a tactical move to be deployed cautiously. In cases where racism, sexism, classism, and ableism overlap, one way to draw anxious warmhearted attention to the vulnerable can be to foreground their common age. Despite ageism, elders can sometimes draw on devotion that other powerless, stigmatized groups cannot. Dr. Thomas Walsh of the Public Health Service went with a hundred other doctors, nurses, pharmacists, and support staff to care for 250 evacuees after Hurricane Rita. The patients were indigent residents of chronic-care residences, many African American, bedridden, and traumatized. Walsh said that something beside training was necessary to weld his group into a team: They knew they were "caring for the grandmothers and grandfathers of Louisiana children. Many of these patients were the poorest of the poor. . . . There is no greater honor than to care for those who have nothing left."[73] The team's sense of honor can be emulated. (Worded properly. I would prefer to be helped for my intrinsic value as a human being, not because I am someone's grandmother.) If being younger gave that group a sense of superiority, they transformed it into willing service.

Ageism in its many forms blinds people to the literal existence or subjective necessities or intrinsic value of people they consider old. I assume people of goodwill can overcome it. This chapter has developed several caring vocabularies to counter such feelings: the first, a rhetoric of unjust loss, about human beings collectively exposed to special risks. Then, a rhetoric of rescue, about heroic responses. Younger people, identifying with Shakespeare's Cordelia at the end of *King Lear*, mustering her armies to save her father, can be united by pity, honor, and duty. The reproach of injustice, the feeling of chivalry, can rise to activism.

A majority of Americans are willing to pay higher taxes to extend health-care benefits to all. Some might even fight to raise benefits for the old. We could make Social Security bountiful — as proposed by former Bush treasury secretary Paul O'Neill — based on an annuity ample enough to guarantee $50,000 a year.[74] People who care for family members (and lose billions of dollars in wages doing so) might add to their laden days by fighting for universal long-term health care.

Those eighty-five and over are called the "fastest growing segment of the population." "Fastest growing" sounds frightening — an invasion of the living dead — but tells you nothing unless you know the original low baseline. This peculiar fact, repeated even by gerontologists, has the dehumanizing effect of turning the people most likely to need extra help into an empty statistic. The deaths in New Orleans, Paris, and Chicago are warnings to cultivate urgency. *Never again.* "This is a wake-up call," said frantic geriatric social workers in Houston. But to wake up journalists, experts, and government agencies about the profoundly painful effects of ageism, and through them all caring Americans, the alarm bell has to sound a lot louder than the subdued tinkle of 2005.

※

Overall, 2005 was not a good year for the life course in the U.S.A. That summer, just before the August catastrophe, President George Bush spent months traveling around the country trying to weaken Social Security, with an accompanying blare of plutocratic voices announcing that "the old" would bankrupt the nation. Decline ideology in major media became noticeably more shrill. ("The Coming Death Shortage," my nominee for winner of the annual Gross-Out Competition for Blatant Ageism, appeared in May.) In 2005, the Supreme Court promulgated its ambiguous decision in *Smith v. City of Jackson*, saying that seniority in employment was, well, to be honored, but not necessarily acted on.[75] Absent an emergency, many pundits rant about how many old people there are in this country; but when there was a crisis that primarily concerned them, they did not notice or repent.

The ties between culture, public policy, and private behavior are not to be shrugged off. Some courts say a discriminatory atmosphere conduces to discriminatory acts. Any wonder that the voices speaking on behalf of age were absent or muffled? That some didn't notice those white hairs? When a disparate impact by age is as drastic as Katrina, we have no option but to call one of its sources ageism and move forward from there.

The United States badly needs what Katrina could have provided: a vast anti-ageist conversation that will move our hearts, tune up the policy engines, and convince the recalcitrant that later life needs to be spared the excess cruelties that are in the works. Decline ideology is not merely ageist, sexist, racist, and classist. It can be literally fatal — as it was in this disaster and has the potential to be in all the ones to come.

PART TWO

In the Feminist Country of Later Life

CHAPTER 4

Hormone Nostalgia

ESTROGEN, NOT MENOPAUSE,
IS THE PUBLIC HEALTH MENACE

Why Was Menopause Ever Newsworthy?

The biggest news in the history of Western menopause came in 2002, when the WHI (Women's Heath Initiative of the National Institutes of Health) announced that it was taking 16,000 women in a study of estrogen/progestin off the drug early because of the risks it posed of cancers and heart disease. Later studies dramatically confirmed the dangers of taking what had until then been erroneously called "replacement therapy." Taking synthetic (or exogenous) hormones also doubles the risk of developing dementias.[1] In 2008, a follow-up study of the WHI women found they continued to face an increased risk for breast cancer nearly three years after they quit using.[2]

The conclusions were monotonously consistent with earlier randomized controlled studies and the warnings of women's health activists. The medical advice was now straightforward: Far from being a preventive therapy to start early, synthetic hormone was now to be taken warily — only when unavoidable for symptom relief, and then in low doses, for short terms. The precautionary principle "first, do no harm" had, one might assume, finally been applied to midlife women's bodies. Elizabeth Siegel Watkins, a historian of HRT, or rather H"RT," in the twentieth century, says, "The authority of medical science validated feminists' thirty-year battle against the long-term use of estrogen as a treatment."[3] Thirty years of feminist resistance, along with expert analyses of the culture's ageist sexism and studies interviewing women who felt as womanly and healthy "postmenstrual" as they had before, constituted an extraordinary record that has been mostly ignored by pharmaceutical companies, gynecologists, and the commercial media and unknown to many midlife women themselves.[4] The major research discoveries finally had the potential to loosen the grip of a full century of menopause demonization and estrogen hype, two linked phenomena that underpin women's dread of aging and the fantasy of anti-aging medicine.

Whatever its later failures, the mainstream press did cover the estrogen debacle. News outlets of all kinds carried the data and the editorial warnings from the *Journal of the American Medical Association* that accompanied the announcement.[5] This was the study that health activists had told us to wait for. Even the North American Menopause Society, heavily funded by the pharmaceutical industry, called the WHI the "gold standard" of controlled experiments.[6]

At first the revelations seemed to have some effect. In the first year following the report, almost 11 million American women stopped taking hormone treatments — 56 percent of users. Women abroad followed suit. There were legal consequences. In France, some gynecologists still prescribing hormones make patients sign waivers of responsibility. In the United States, a jury awarded $99 million to three women who claimed that H"RT" caused their breast cancer.[7] Five thousand suits are pending. And then in 2006, a study found that the number of women diagnosed with the most common form of breast cancer had fallen dramatically in 2003. Cancer researchers attribute this astonishing drop (breast cancer rates had been rising for decades) in part to the fact that millions of women had stopped taking hormone treatments and fewer had started.[8]

Cancer researchers know what Americans have scarcely been told despite the hormone debacle. Estrogen is a carcinogen. "The link between the female hormone estrogen and cancer is hard to miss," a 1998 article in *Science* began. "It contributes to the development of three of the top five cancers of women — those of the breast, uterus, and ovaries . . . an estimated 240,000 new cancer cases a year in the U.S. alone."[9] Exposure to estrogen — even to a woman's own lifetime production — is an important determinant of the risk of cancer. The more estrogen in birth control pills, the higher the risk of blood clots and strokes. The International Agency for Research on Cancer (IARC), part of the World Health Organization, released a warning in 2005 that moved synthetic estrogen up from the category "possibly carcinogenic to humans" to the highest risk category, "carcinogenic to humans."[10]

The current scientific controversy is over *how* estrogen or its by-products cause cancers. Estrogen both initiates cancer mutations and stimulates the proliferation of existing cancerous cells, according to a review in the *New England Journal of Medicine*.[11] Others are more cautious about its role in initiation. "If any endogenous [normally produced by the body] compound was a strong carcinogen, we'd all be dead," says a researcher quoted in the article in *Science*.[12] From our daily lay reading we can be lured into believing in sci-fi goals based on starving mice, but learn nothing about a scientific inquiry that cautions us about all estrogen-based products.

To a dispassionate observer, it is exogenous hormones, not menopause, that should be the public health issue: their medical risks, commercial manipulation, failed governmental regulation, and the effects of biomedicalization and its accompanying decline ideology on women of all ages.

IT SUDDENLY BECOMES PLAUSIBLE to inquire why menopause was ever considered newsworthy. The end of menstruation is unremarkable, personally, to about 90 percent of the women who go through it — the vast majority who never seek help, according to a study of the typical menopause by Sonja McKinlay, a highly regarded researcher, and her colleagues. Fifteen percent of women barely notice it. Many traditional and poor women — immigrants, African Americans, Latinas, Asian Americans — never hear hormone promises.[13] Some women with the most typical effect — vasomotor flushes — can't afford medical attention. In any case, even if the percentage of complaints were higher, most problems disappear by themselves. For a century, all the attention, worry, definitions of midlife and womanhood, the breaking of women's life course in two, the scientific effort, hype, and lies, have been focused on only about 10 percent of women for only a few years in the middle of their lives. It's a fact that ought to be known but it might as well be a secret.

Menstrual periods end universally, but the experience of menopause is a variable biocultural phenomenon. Younger women learn what to expect from their mothers and from their culture. Although some

Maya women have measurable high skin temperatures, none of them report "hot flashes"; some 80 percent of Belgians do.[14] In a peak year before the debacle, our national rates of estrogen use varied—from a low of 8 percent in Massachusetts to 40 percent in California.[15] In the United States, the only symptoms definitely linked to menopause status are profuse sweating (given a special name because it's midlife female sweat) or lowered secretions (the misogynistically named "vaginal atrophy"). In Japan, the symptoms most associated with *konenki*, the closest approximation, are shoulder stiffness, ringing in the ears, and a heavy head.[16] In trials, some American midlife women received a placebo instead of medication: A full third saw their symptoms disappear—a placebo effect larger than that seen in most medical studies.[17]

The universal menopause is a false decline narrative, like so many prospective cultural scripts. Younger women in some cultural groups are first made to be attentive to the scripts; then they read or hear about the bad things that might happen to their bodies as they grow older. In real life, most women soon forget menopause. Across the world, women in their later years report, in the words of Jane Ussher, "never being happier, never being more at peace" with themselves.[18] If they are not, for about 90 percent menopause has nothing to do with it. The reductionist adjective "postmenopausal"—which, like "premenopausal" and "perimenopausal" serves only to medicalize women and biologize their life course—is irrelevant to them and pathologizes women with symptoms. The adjective "menopausal" can now go into the trash bin of history.

Before 2002, in order to find warnings about estrogen, you had to read feminist anthropologists and women's health activists, who are aware that menopause is sociocultural. Otherwise, in the mainstream, you'd be told about the early biological onset of female decline. Menopause was heavily overreported and misrepresented compared to, say, puberty. In 2002, I was sorry that the 10 percent who felt they needed it didn't have safe treatment, but at the same time I hoped to see the end of the dismal menopause discourse that so distorts the middle years and later life of women. I had a vision of a golden age of feminist change, in which women from their thirties on would no longer be led to expect a raft of monstrous symptoms and women of fifty could get on with their busy lives. Pharmaceutical companies *had* to stop touting synthetic estrogen for benefits they had implied but that were now disproved, since estrogen did nothing to delay Alzheimer's or memory loss, to produce beautiful skin or an air of youthfulness.

It seemed likely that magazine and newspaper articles, having less to sell on this anti-aging front, might find menopause less dire, or even less newsworthy. Since menopause never was a disease like diabetes or hypothyroidism that requires replacement drugs, reporters would have to stop calling estrogen a "replacement" and could then explicitly wither the hormone-deficiency myth that had been taught in medical schools and, in some, still is. Exogenous estrogen could now join thalidomide (effect: birth deformations), testosterone (linked to prostate cancer), and Vioxx (linked to heart attacks) as one of many "therapies" approved by the Food and Drug Administration and promoted and overprescribed without being adequately tested. Journalists might then encourage skepticism about the heady promises of future chemical or genetic medications, including "lifestyle medicines" and anti-aging "enhancements"—which would make not just midlife women but everyone safer. We could then hear more skepticism about the United Soybean Board (soy is a new rival to estrogen) and the nefarious influence of Big PhRMA (the Pharmaceutical Research and Manufacturers of America) on the understaffed and underfunded FDA.

If menopause had come to seem less dangerous, less salient, and less marketable, the "Change" could have weakened as a magic marker of the female life course, the early onset of female decline.[19] The entire commerce in midlife aging—based on creating the need to appear young—could be attacked. The golden-age question, of course, is, "Since 2002, what has been available to read?" Does it fit into a more reliable, informative, and anti-ageist prospective narrative? In a 1993 article in *Ms.* magazine, I said that women had more to fear from menopause discourse than from menopause itself.[20] Is this still true?

Promoting the Hormone Comeback

The hormone debacle, as we'll see, is a case where a major paradigm shift backed by science could have happened but—because of powerful opposing forces—mostly hasn't. Many in the media are in effect promoting the comeback that Big PhRMA wants, starting with a dearth of reporting on major scientific evidence. How many papers reported the 2005 finding of the IARC that estrogen is carcinogenic to humans? According to the Internet search engine, LexisNexis, only the *Herald Sun* of Melbourne, Australia.[21] Not a single British, Canadian, or American paper. The unspoken rule in print seems to be that the words "menopause," "estrogen," and "carcinogen" never appear in the same report. They do on the Web, but you would have to know to put the three words together to find any sites.

Did *anything* change? Yes. Before 2002, with so-called replacement therapy becoming obligatory, a feminist could fear that women who refused it and subsequently acquired osteoporosis or cardiovascular disease might eventually be penalized because they had "neglected their health."[22] That worst-case scenario no longer seems plausible. Globally, smaller percentages are starting on hormones than in the past. In New Zealand, older women with longer use of estrogens are stopping more than younger; in Sweden, younger women are starting in much smaller numbers. In the U.S.A., it's better-informed women who refuse exogenous estrogen.[23] We can hope that this new risk-benefit decision will turn out to be a healthy trend across the globe.

Estrogen ads now come with FDA-prescribed warnings. Some reporting on midlife health has improved. A *Globe Magazine* article, "Health by the Decade" (2005), brought general good sense a bit closer. The page for the fifties highlighted osteoarthritis and sleep deprivation, which strike both genders — and, miracle of miracles, issued a warning to *men* to visit their doctors more regularly. The word "menopause" does not appear. "Hot flashes and night sweats" are mentioned under other causes of reduced sleep, and "stress" is sensibly the first cause. A 330-word *Time* article on hormone prescribing ended, mildly, "Many women find they do just fine without it." The page covering "Treatment" on the Mayo Clinic Web site begins, "Menopause itself requires no medical treatment.[24] Articles occasionally appear showing links between various cancers (including lung) and hormone "therapy."

But this does not constitute a revolution in health care or information. In some medical schools menopause is still being taught as an endocrine-deficiency disease, only now one that doesn't have a single and uncontroversial treatment. Whether the precautionary principle is applied to midlife women's bodies depends entirely on the professionalism of their practitioner. If you have a responsible doctor or gynecologist, says Judith Houck, a historian of menopause, they will no longer routinely promote estrogen treatment to you in your forties.[25] Doctors now have to diagnose the individual who presents with relevant symptoms — in the words of one physician, "by far the difficult bit."[26] Many doctors still rely on their early training, when hormone treatment was considered a magic bullet for the sickly and pathetic state of a female body wrapped around nonfunctioning ovaries. Before

2002, faith in estrogen was so high that women's noncompliance was a major clinical preoccupation. Those doctors remember fondly that they had something to offer. The program director for the National Women's Health Network worries that doctors "find reasons why the [WHI] findings shouldn't apply to their patients."[27]

Since 2002, the makers of exogenous estrogen have not merely counted on inertia in medicine. They have been proactive. They have focused more on men, on testosterone for women and men, and on human growth hormone, according to John Hoberman, a cultural historian. In his 2005 exposé, *Testosterone Dreams: Rejuvenation, Aphrodisia, Doping*, Hoberman shows how the drummed-up disease of menopause has created a model for selling hormones to "andropausal" men. Men who look up the term will find that the female menopause — still assumed to be universally troubling — regularly paves the way toward their equivalent male "problems." And Big PhRMA, still greatly interested in the female midlife market, invests in new products and advertises them in press releases to the media, creating artificial news to keep menopause in the public eye.

My main finding is that since 2002 there are still too many articles about menopause and programs for educating women about it, and the troublesome menopause is still the one we hear about. An Illinois state program using Women's Health Initiative Grants announced in 2008 that it will "teach women *and girls* about the health challenges they may face, such as cancer, heart disease, menopause, and osteoporosis."[28] Osteoporosis, a disease that can often be prevented, is now rightly separated from menopause. But how is sweating or vaginal dryness equivalent to cancer and heart disease? Menopause shouldn't be in such a list at all.

The term "hormone debacle" is rarely seen. General health articles still do not explain how few midlife women have any trouble, or how biocultural a phenomenon menopause is. As I write, the terms "hormone replacement" and "hormone therapy" are still used by the U. S. National Library of Medicine and the NIH. Journalists use the terms as if 2002 had never happened. The category "perimenopause" continues to be used (even in the state-of-the-art manual *Our Bodies Ourselves: Menopause*), backing female sickliness down the life course by construing menstrual problems as early menopause. Christine Overall calls it a "stage only recently created to strike fear and anxiety into the hearts of forty-somethings and even thirty-somethings."[29] We are still being aged by culture younger and younger.

Far from disappearing, "Menopause," a *Washington Post* headline of 2003 told us, "Has Become the New Hot-Button Topic in Women's Health." *USA Today* in 2005 headlined "Change of Life Remains Hard." Women have to "navigate" it, in the tricky-shoals headline of a *Pittsburgh Post-Gazette* article. *Business Week* suggested in 2004 that menopause lasts from the early forties until death.[30] The *Globe* in 2006 published yet another unlikely study tying depression to the "approach to menopause," although the writer noted that two authors have financial ties to antidepressant manufacturers. The nineteenth-century diagnosis of involutional melancholia at midlife casts a distressingly long shadow. The fact is that the least depressed women are those in their middle years.[31]

The *New York Times* published an article on midlife aging in 2006 by a medical doctor who wrote that "[i]n contrast [to men], nature has given women a real challenge." When a woman complained to her husband that he wasn't trying hard enough to find a job, he told her that she was "hormonal" and should "back off." Dr. Friedman explained, "There was little doubt that her annoyance with him was connected to her hot flashes and irritability."[32] After being told this, she reformed. A live instance of using menopause to control a woman: You couldn't make this up. Heather Dillaway, a professor at Wayne State University, likewise found that in familial interactions, women are encouraged to recognize bodily problems and seek treatment.[33]

Rarely do articles report that depression, joint pain, and incontinence have nothing to do with menopause or that libido can rise. Nor do they discuss the benefits of being postmenstrual: no more bleeding, cramps, PMS, pelvic adhesions, fibroids, Tampax, shields, fear of humiliating surprises, and for women who sleep with men, unwanted pregnancy. It means being able to wear white suits anytime. Going off the pill can relieve worry; and going off condoms, if it can be done safely, can make sensations more lively. Surveying lesbians about sex at midlife, Ellen Cole and Esther D. Rothblum found 71 percent listing no changes related to menopause, but life gains included better sexual communication, increased sex, increased orgasms, wonderful sex, positive changes in body fat distribution, having nothing to prove, and feeling more free with adult offspring having left home.[34] (While we're discarding "postmenopausal" for its narrow, negative, biological fixations, we could deploy not only "postmenstrual" but "postmaternal." These positive terms integrate better with other identities.)

If they're responsible, journalists and Web sites repeat "only in low doses for short terms," emphasizing delimited treatment for particular conditions, and put hormone risks before benefits, or they feature the "hormone debacle — the WHI study or the British Million Woman study, which came to similar conclusions. If they're not responsible, writers put benefits foremost and ignore or minimize the dangers. Many sites, including Wikipedia, still use the erroneous term "replacement" and, needless to say, do not refute the belief that menopause is a deficiency disease. The North American Menopause Society, in a 2010 position statement, concludes that the "benefit-risk ratio for menopausal HT is favorable for women who initiate HT close to menopause."[35]

In such ways does pro-estrogen bias persist. You might reasonably conclude from that *Washington Post* article that the millions who stopped treatment all had what the authors called "maddeningly unanswerable" questions.[36] Many articles give midlife women the same implicit character: like addicts going cold turkey, their drugs are being withheld, and they are desperate for new products. I had to find a special study in the *Journal of the American Medical Association* to learn that when women on hormone treatment tapered off, as recommended, only 21.2 percent had a recurrence of "hot flashes."[37]

Two worrying media trends (from which Big PhRMA profits) are at work: to fault or downplay the 2002 WHI study and to introduce untested commercial products. The main thrust — typified by an article in the *Wall Street Journal* — is that the WHI overstated the risks and women are now too frightened of hormone treatments.[38] This is the line that Wyeth, the makers of the hormone treatment on trial, pushed to medical societies and 500,000 health-care providers the day the report broke. According to Sheila and David Rothman in *The Pursuit of Perfection*, the Wyeth commentary convinced 81 percent of gynecologists that women's fears of hormone treatment were overblown. A 2006 article in the *St. Louis Post-Dispatch* quoted one physician who held a chair of obstetrics and gynecology as saying, "The WHI was way overdone . . . the damage has been done."[39] Some journalists now say the WHI data were confusing, denying the original clarity and creating actual confusion. Complicit with the industry, they present its newest products — creams and gels — without warnings, as if they had been successfully tested. Quite a lot of news is about lower-dose versions, which are stabilizing sales, although a Wyeth spokeswoman admits, as reported in a story on Women's eNews, "We do not have data evaluating those particular risks."[40]

Pharmaceutical companies are wistful about their past profits, doctors and gynecologists about their obsolete promises. And many women still link estrogen, irrationally, not to cancer but to a youth-oriented definition of femininity. Wistfulness about the possibility of "rejuvenation" affects the risk-benefit decisions women make. Gina Kolata begins her *New York Times* article "On the Trail of Estrogen and a Mirage of Youth" with an anecdote about a woman who took double her normal dose of hormones to look younger. Where are the articles about women who say, "I was foolish to worry more about youth than health"? Sexual difficulties occur at all ages and probably more among the young—as we will see in chapter 6—but numerous articles on female "dysfunction" overemphasize biology, aging-into-the-midlife, and hormonal "imbalance." Helen Gurley Brown, former editor of *Cosmo*, when promoting estrogen, once said with a shiver that it made her "juicy." Estrogen comes as a powder, but it is still believed to be the liquid that makes younger women *women* and younger women healthier.

The *Globe*'s Judy Foreman wrote a column on whether estrogen, "bathing" women's arteries, might still lower the risk of heart disease (if taken at exactly the right time of menstrual life, which she admits no one can know).[41] The implied readers are still those desperate postmenstrual women. In her *New York Times* article, Kolata faulted the late, indefatigable Barbara Seaman, the author of *The Greatest Experiment Ever Performed on Women*, for holding estrogen critics to a looser standard than promoters, as if even-handedness were still obligatory after 2002.[42] Journalists defending estrogen, and trusting biotech in general, are joined by some scientists. In an article in *Best Practice and Research in Clinical Endocrinology and Metabolism*, the authors conclude that the media caused "panic and confusion" by reporting the WHI results, and argue that the data on extra cancers and heart disease do not mean that "HRT is not safe or efficacious" for symptoms.[43] It certainly isn't safe, and it was not efficacious for most of the symptoms it was prescribed for.

The promotion of untested products, the creation of muddle about WHI's test results, the construction of desperate and deprived "menopausal" women—these rhetorical tricks re-create the illusion the pharmaceutical companies long managed to promote unopposed: that estrogen is still the elixir of rejuvenation. If women could only be freed to get at it! This outcome maintains the estrogen-good hypothesis of the infamous 1968 book *Feminine Forever*. Robert Wilson, paid by Ayerst (now Wyeth), wrote that without drugs, at menopause "no woman can be sure of escaping the horror of this living decay." The estrogen-still-good assumption is mystical.[44] Many gynecologists and researchers still grip the it like fundamentalists the Bible. Women do too, of course. By 2003, studies commissioned by two drug companies found that a quarter of the women who had stopped using hormones after the 2002 announcement had resumed.[45]

The Ugly Culture of "Estrogen Good"

Aside from those extra cancers, hearts attacks, strokes, and dementias, "estrogen good"—a faith manufactured by hormone hype and maintained by hormone nostalgia—produces an ugly culture. It channels age anxieties from numerous sources onto the midlife body, especially for women. For those who accept the theory of menopause as an endocrine deficiency, it functions somewhat as the Freudian concept of female castration used to do, except it comes later in life. The universal menopause represents women as suddenly damaged and desexualized bodies (rather than growing minds, spirits, and agents). Menopause discourse still makes it seem to younger women (and men) as if only women age. But men who accept the belief in midlife decline and deference to the cult of youth can be moved not only to self-consciousness about erections but lured to testosterone, Viagra, and trophy wives (thus constructing midlife women's envy of younger women).[46]

Middle-ageist culture is built on "medicalizing" midlife women — another critical term rarely found in the mainstream. Biomedicalization revved up in the second half of the twentieth century with the widespread diffusion of faith in technoscience and synthetic estrogen. "The very process of aging has been widely reinterpreted as a deviation from the normal, a process against which [to] take major precautions," warns anthropologist Margaret Lock: "living-past-menopause, according to an evolutionary theory that likens women to apes, has by itself been considered 'unnatural.'"[47] The goal of the drug industry, according to Sheila and David Rothman, was that women would take synthetic estrogen from the pill to death.[48] The medical model of the life course — aging as decline — is learned through American dominant culture, and not just in the United States but wherever in the Western world Big PhRMA advertises and influences the media and legislation. The menoboom took off in the 1990s, shortly after a heavily lobbied Congress let pharmaceutical companies advertise directly to consumers. Gail Sheehy's "Let's-all-talk-about-menopause-symptoms-at-dinner-parties" in *Vanity Fair* launched the media frenzy. Estrogen was prescribed for off-label uses overblown in fashion magazines. The cult of youth ("X-er" start-ups, millionaires in sneakers) gave biomedicalization an extra bump. During the menoboom of the nineties, when estrogen was heavily promoted even to healthy women without symptoms, the rate of prescriptions grew — according to one estimate, from 23 percent of women fifty or older to 34 percent.[49]

Women who accept a medical view of menopause have more contact with doctors, more positive expectations of estrogen's benefits, and are more likely to get hormones prescribed, according to numerous studies. Contrary to popular belief, women who use estrogen do not necessarily have more symptoms, but they do believe the drug-makers' claims: for example, that memory loss is common at midlife. Many women *not* taking estrogen believe their memory is still good or excellent; it is users who find this harder to believe.[50] Women who internalize the decline view of womanhood at midlife have to fight harder against depression or to maintain self esteem. Those of us urging better information or caution about treatment are not meanly withholding anything from them; we are fighting for them too.

The troublesome menopause of what might be 10 percent of women has become a centerpiece of the entire commerce in aging. Making it appear universal is fallacious and damaging. When the media repeat it, taking for granted a defective biologized midlife woman (and now, man), they keep the discredited decline narrative alive and hide the cultural work that keeps rejuvenating it. Frankenstein gets a makeover. This multi-billion-dollar commerce includes not just the drug industry, its "longevity" wing, and its advertisers, overselling unnecessary and dangerous drugs, but also the uglification industries (cosmetics companies, plastic surgeons, and their accomplices, the beauty and health magazines and Websites, the movie industry, TV) — all battening on the cult of youth. Sometimes pop culture looks like nothing more than a giant machine for excreting ageism.

To me it is a pleasant wonder that despite all this, so many women are releasing themselves from estrogen culture and enjoying their postmenstrual years — a miracle of common sense and feminist resistance.

Bad Science through "Anti-Aging"

The aftermath of the hormone debacle shows that better science by it-self does not bring the golden age. But why was the science so faulty for so long? One cheerful theory holds that scientists always get it wrong until they get it right. But that doesn't cover the ground in this case. Prescribing and research are both tainted because almost all doctors are directly or indirectly manipulated by the drug companies. As Dr. Marcia Angell, the respected former editor of the *New England Jour-nal of Medicine*, explains, the companies control the results of research, the way medicine is practiced, and even the definition of what con-stitutes a disease.[51] When industry-funded studies are negative, they are frequently suppressed. Getting estrogen past the FDA may have involved lying. Wyeth is known to have paid a medical writing firm to ghostwrite twenty-six articles favorable to its estrogen drug Prempro between 1998 and 2005. The articles, omitting negative trials, were signed by known physicians who had no hand in the writing.[52]

Hormone treatment for women was like the housing bubble: its value rose on faith. In menopause studies, while ignoring the negative studies and warnings from the women's health movement, research-ers made false assumptions: for example, that synthetic estrogen protected hearts because it affected "surrogate" markers like good cholesterol. Estrogen had no beneficial impact on coronary disease.[53] Surrogate markers cannot prove that a treatment reduces cardiovascu-lar risk, Adriane Fugh-Berman and Anthony Scialli write. If estrogen had really been effective against heart disease, men would have been given it. Researchers tried, but the randomized, controlled Coronary Drug Project was stopped early because estrogen increased men's car-diovascular events.[54]

With menopause considered a deficiency state, drugmakers con-structed specific diseases. Osteopenia, for example, is a new bone disease, defined by criteria that would apply to almost any woman over thirty, and its diagnosis is being pushed by Merck, maker of Fosamax.[55] "Osteopenia" means "almost osteoporosis." Like perimeno-pause, osteopenia is an example of disease mongering, inventing disor-ders that expand patient demand and doctors' prescribing behavior. The history of the pill-makers' century-long lucrative claim to the crown of improving midlife women reads like a political allegory, in which a tyrannical cabal refuses to cede their power and wealth no matter how ruinous their sway. Estrogen's fall should serve as a cautionary tale to laypeople and doctors.

Many clinical guidelines prove erroneous. But in this case, the sci-fi fantasy of rejuvenation has a lot to answer for. From the earliest experiments by Eugen Steinach on "middle-aged" mice whose coats were said to get glossier, the makers of hormones always promised the appearance of youth. They constructed the desire in a population that before World War One could not have imagined the prime of life taking such perverse forms. In the 1920s, doctors zapped women's ovaries with X-rays and transplanted monkey glands into men's testicles, all for "youth." Interventions fail but promises never end. In the 1950s, Robert Wilson made the claim as punishingly as it has ever been made. The doctors who prescribed the 1990s' versions of estrogen promoted it for sweating, heart disease, and osteoporosis, dubiously represented as diseases of aging although not every one who ages into their middle years suffers from them. The doctors who prescribed estrogen for off-label uses were even more obviously responding to the fantasies promoted by the pharmaceutical companies' hired guns. So much credulity was made possible by the power of sexism joining middle-ageism within a profit-oriented medical system.

Many of us used to trust science "as the sole exemplar of both genuine knowledge and proper epistemic method," in the words of Barbara Herrnstein Smith, but as she points out, veneration of science is often indiscriminate and minimally informed.[56] The Bush administration disregarded science, cut budgets for the FDA, let the big money interests rule. Officially the FDA mandates follow-up tests from the pharmaceutical companies after drug approval, but according to a 2006 report, 65 percent of 1,231 studies the companies promised to do were still pending years later.[57] After many honest scientists had left the government amid much criticism of FDA practices, the agency tightened its guidelines to exclude from its advisory committees scientists who have considerable stakes in the companies they review or their competitors.[58] It will take further congressional action and time for the FDA to become reliable again. (It will need enough researchers of its own to replace those from pharmaceutical companies providing the data, and independent scientists at its head so that outcomes cannot be politically skewed — as happened in the case of the morning-after pill, long denied approval because some pro-lifers think it tantamount to abortion). Even if research were irreproachable, doctors might still not read it. In one study, the clinicians interviewed rarely relied on research evidence; they got their information from other doctors, patients, and pharmaceutical companies.[59] Since they too ignored feminist anthropologists and women's health activists, any advice they got or gave was likely to rely on studies produced by bias. Gynecologists have been far more likely to recommend synthetic estrogens than GPs or nurses.

As we wait to learn more about estrogen carcinogenesis, should we trust other synthetic hormones? Additional testosterone has been linked to prostate cancer, infertility, and thickening of the blood that might lead to strokes. The "male menopause" or "andropause" uses very similar "facts," tropes, fears, and allures to those of menopause discourse: "drops" in hormonal levels on the one hand, the implication that these levels determine other declines, and promises of increased virility, muscularity, bone density—restored youth, again. Decline ideology and economic disaster are the backdrop for the surge in male midlife anxiety, and in doctor's responses. Testosterone prescriptions more than doubled between 2000 and 2004.[60]

As public reimbursements threaten to fall with health-care reform, people involved in selling anti-aging to the private-pay sector will try endlessly to make it legitimate. "Anti-aging" has taken on the disreputable mantle of "rejuvenation." A Hastings Center report by five highly respected gerontologists in 2003 affirms that "no currently marketed intervention—none—has yet been proved to slow, stop or reverse human aging, and some can be downright dangerous." The entire class of dietary supplements is exempt from regulation by the FDA. New youthening products, usually set to appear only many years hence, if ever, are announced as if they were thrilling news and touted for wishful futuristic properties. Anti-aging flacks, called in the report "clinical entrepreneurs," tend to "exaggerate the state of scientific knowledge" about the specific product they are working on and support the whole scheme of curing humankind of old age. An entity that calls itself the American Academy of Anti-Aging Medicine "hosts an aggressive publicity claim attempting to relegate . . . its critics in biogerontology" to the past.[61]

Implicitly siding with the fantasists, or too lazy to check with the critics, the media scarcely provide equal time to monitor the claims critically. A *Globe* columnist, Alex Beam, refreshingly began an article listing some ridiculous and unproven claims, "I am sick to death of the purported science of longevity."[62] Men as well as women ought to lay the burden of proof on the side of the mystic shills. Responsible doctors warn that in an ill-regulated milieu dominated by commercial greed, being an early adapter of any new drugs (except in desperate situations) is unwarranted. Dr. Angell, describing widespread corruption, sadly but flatly states in the *New York Review of Books*, "It is simply no longer possible to believe much of the clinical research that is being published or to rely on the judgment of trusted physicians or authoritative medical guidelines."[63]

Anti-aging is preposterous as a concept, as well as being phony in practice. Remember the doctor in chapter 1 who said, "Aging is a collection of diseases"? If a disease is what a doctor can charge for, if all the 76 million will eventually be ill, what a huge market that creates. Pill- and device-makers self-servingly presuppose and convince the unwary that aging is something other than a natural life process in which diseases sometimes arise. Which is it? The public must be confused. The five concerned gerontologists wonder how to keep biomedical interventions from "redefining more people as defective, abnormal, or inferior. . . . Pathologizing aging is a seductive way to increase public support for aging research."[64] But pathologizing aging—in particular, as we'll see in chapter 9, the pathologizing of memory loss— also has terrible psychological, aesthetic, sexual, political, and public health effects.

Thus emerge the vague, meaningless names that some biogerontologists and the uglification industries use, and get the media to use, to describe their products and mission. When I see "anti-aging" or "age-management medicine," the word "anti-life" flashes on like a fiery warning light. I wonder, not how they're going to pick my pocket, but what new ashload of ageism they're going to drop into our heads. By all means let honest scientists understand diseases, and if they can, delay their onset or alleviate or cure them, but leave normal aging—and the people who live it—uncontaminated. What could conceivably reverse human aging except the special effects of *Benjamin Button*? The only way to be truly anti-aging is to die younger.

When Commerce and the Media Block Change

When as much money is at stake as it is in the commerce in aging, you don't need to be an age critic to anticipate that even gold-standard discoveries will not cause these high-rolling players to give up. Reforms of medical school pedagogy, research regulations, clinical practice, and institutions, if they come, come slowly. If we care about the midlife, the interpretation of aging, and the value of the life course, we need to resist not just unproven drugs or diets or technologies—every place where decline holds court in the daily lives of women and men—but the commerce in pathological aging and decline ideology as a whole.

Skepticism is a useful weapon on the way to disdain. I started my research on estrogen carcinogenesis and the hormone debacle in 2002 with systematic monitoring of the commercial media, "which gives activists a tool for analyzing broader patterns of media discourse."[65] As with the print media, I found you can't go naively to the unedited Web, full of commercial sites, bias, obsolete material, and current inaccuracy. One careful study of Google's osteoporosis sites found that the best sites do not make it to the top. The Canadian Women's Health Network, "with the most balanced and complete information," was listed at sixty-seven in Google.[66]

When seeking information, especially where later life is at issue, both women and men need to avoid the direct-to-consumer ads and the uglification promoters. Even a few minutes of looking at glossy Photoshopped models makes women feel worse about their bodies. We should read journalism on research findings about menopause as cautiously as if articles too might be ads, knowing how bias can slither in first through Big PhRMA's power and then through fervent fantasies arising from the constructed craving for youth. Relying on the precautionary principle and the history of menopause discourse, we need to put our trust in anthropologically informed, anti-ageist independent media—feminist, progressive, public health oriented—critical scholarly journals, histories of medicine, in short, any writing that keeps the twinings of biology and culture in the forefront.

The clue to going forward in current circumstances of deception, hyperbole, and misinformation is to keep hold of significant concepts, especially if they don't appear in the mainstream. My overarching subject is how women (and men) are aged by culture. If something happens in or on the body, culture is what names it or doesn't name it (think of the Maya women of fifty without vasomotor symptoms). Culture then tells us how we are supposed to feel about what is named. My keywords have included estrogen carcinogenesis, the hormone debacle, pro-estrogen bias, medicalization, the commerce in aging, the corrupt influence of Big PhRMA's spending, medical and media submission to market interests, the biocultural approach. In a world where such terms could be ready at hand, other terms — menopausal, perimeno-pause, anti-aging, replacement — would either disappear or be viewed with the skepticism they deserve. In the aftermath of the hormone debacle, it is still unnecessarily difficult to provide or find and cling to alternative ways of thinking, alternative data, and visions of a better life course. And that is more important than ever.

CHAPTER 5 Plastic Wrap

TURNING AGAINST COSMETIC SURGERY

Given the relentless hype about surgical magic — makeover shows on TV, before-and-after ads, women's magazine features, the once-regular announcements of rises in surgery rates — many feminist commentators, like soft-news journalists and advertisers, have treated cosmetic surgery (CS) as an irresistible desire.[1] Even cosmetic surgeons, who pay for the ads that create the demand, used to express awe at the size of their share of the commerce in aging. Many parties with interests pro and con assume that the "aging" of the midlife cohorts — their sense of being bodies-in-decline rather than the fit, energetic and privileged Babies they are supposed to be — will be the engine of future profits.

The scholarly research on CS has tended to ignore age, but age is relevant in many ways. The primary targets are women between thirty-five and fifty. In 2007 the average age of those receiving surgery was 42.6.[2] To the control of the male gaze and the white gaze has been added the age gaze: "The ideology of beauty work has become increasingly ageist, as evidenced by the use of the term 'anti-aging,'" according to three Canadian researchers.[3] Advertising that promises people they can pass as younger is overt, normalized, unashamed. Targeting ethnic otherness, which makes up 20 percent of the market — Jewish noses, African lips, Asian eyes — is more respectful. Nobody urges, "Defy

Jewishness!" "Look less black!" One sign of the power of American age-ism is that people do not notice the sheer effrontery of ageist puffery.

But the observers of the allegedly irreversible surgical trend are looking in the wrong places. The tide is turning. As women turn fifty, the percentage of those having CS drops in half. The rate of growth in surgeries stalled around 2004–2005. Surgery procedures dropped from a peak in 2005, and the total of all procedures from a peak in 2004. The totals for breast augmentation, which had been central to recon-structed youthful femininity, dropped 11 percent from 2007 to 2008. Liposuction figures went down 9 percent between 2000 and 2006. Eye-lid surgery went down 20 percent in one year, from 2004 to 2005. Half of surgeons reported that their practices were down in 2007, a year before the economic meltdown began. If you think this means a switch to supposedly noninvasive nonsurgical procedures, which had become 82 percent of all procedures, they too dropped — 12 percent — in 2008. The data suggest broad, unreported resistance operating at many levels of culture.[4] "Scary" is emerging as the adjective that best describes the hype, the surgeons, the procedures, and, more frequently, the results of cosmetic surgery.

The Ick Factor

Critiquing cartoonish and botched surgeries and preposterous expec-tations has become a pop preoccupation. A woman with size FFFF breasts, each (we are told) weighing ten pounds, appears on CBS's *Insider* saying she is willing to risk death to enlarge them even more. Another night a woman in a bikini shows her scars from liposuction. Web sites with names like "Plastic Surgery Disasters" and "The 15 Worst Celebrity Plastic Surgery Disasters You Will Ever See" feature before-and-after photo galleries.[5] But such sites are arguments for avoidance. "Before" shows attractive people, men as well as women, of all ages, before their surgery, and "after" shows results that bloggers noisily consider grotesque. One site focuses not on celebrities but on anonymous would-be fashionistas from L.A.'s west side.[6]

Showing off their implants, some women reveal deep, oddly shaped cavities in their Barbie-sized breasts. One displays peculiar criss-cross wrinkles, presumably after liposuction, across her stomach. Many have lips so protuberant they look like sideshows in a Victorian circus. Men are shown with hyperwide eyelifts, eyebrows exaggeratedly high, noses that don't match their faces. One Flickr site invites viewers to "Caption This Disaster."

The blogosphere is one space where the public is free to go negative about cosmetic surgery in a culture that provides little space for anything but raves. Bloggers can be cruel to the victims. The general tone is vindictive, oddly jeering, as if they were saying, "You *wanted* this look? You think this looks *good?*" The mainstream dismisses users through satire. Under the headline "Girls Gone Weird," a writer in the *Boston Globe Magazine* headlined an article about a bridal party that got "peeled, scraped and shot full of sausage poison as a gift."[7] Nicole Hollander lambasted the same "gift" in *Sylvia*. A 2008 cartoon by Barbara Smaller in the *New Yorker* ruefully shows a young couple holding hands and peering into each other's eyes, as she says, "I want someone I can grow old and have plastic surgery with."[8]

"Anti-aging" surgery, supposed to produce youthful looks, is beginning to seem a misnomer. A columnist for *More*, a magazine for midlife women, quotes the designer Isaac Mizrahi as saying, with ageist malice, "If you want to look seventy, get a facelift." Dr. Pauline Chen, the author of *Final Exam*, describes a surgeon as old as her grandfather, "known infamously for his own countless submissions to the . . . knife," as having facial skin "like plastic wrap stretched tightly over a bowl."[9] Other metaphors are also repellently nonhuman: "wax dummy," "clone." In the London *Daily Telegraph*, a celebrity cosmetician from the States summed up the situation as represented on the Web sites and in interviews of nonusers: "Plastic surgery is creating a weird tribe of women who, rather than looking better, just look 'done.' . . . isn't it time for some kind of backlash?"[10] The message of the popular backlash is that cosmetic surgery is uncool.

The pop sites don't have much to say about the cultural forces promoting such desires. One online writer who correctly noted data indicating a higher rate of suicide among plastic surgery patients commented, "It all tracks back to trying to fix the outside when the inside needs the work."[11] The inside/outside binary reflects a misconception that the answer to body dissatisfaction is individual therapy. As feminists have pointed out, these are psychosocial not private problems. Personal dissatisfaction is created or exacerbated by a billion-dollar American commerce in aging that harps on women's — and men's — imperfections and ties them to growing older. Dominant decline culture manages to produce, in great numbers of not-very-old people, what we could call age-related dysmorphia: a belief that some features of one's body, or the whole body, once located within the huge range of normal, has become substandard or even deformed. The business plan of the uglification industries is to make rejuvenation into a hope, shoving people up over the rather high threshold of aversion to going under the knife.

Perceptions of ugliness rise and fall in historical time. The mounting statistics for CS suggest that the worst years of a bad century were from 1990 to about 2005. Deborah Sullivan tells the history in *Cosmetic Surgery*: In postwar America, as the supply of surgeons grew faster than reconstructive demand, doctors decided to create demand for elective procedures. The Federal Trade Commission and then the Supreme Court helpfully made it illegal for the AMA to forbid them from advertising. Lacking oversight, plastic surgeons can operate outside of hospitals and refuse to provide statistics on morbidity and mortality or to police the deficient in their ranks. The availability of financing for procedures on credit brought them within the reach of lower-income women.[12] The cult of youth and youthfulness grew in the 1990s (hi-tech start-ups, ever-younger models). Surgeons, their trade association, the companies that produced devices advertised in the magazines, and the complicit magazines produced articles for women and even teens that paid slight attention to risks. Nevertheless, in the worst time of a bad century, despite the industrial-strength infomercial that millions were happily undergoing elective makeovers, clients and would-be clients together never constituted more than a minority.

A LARGE MAJORITY of women distance themselves. Around the globe, a Nielsen survey found, 80 percent of women say they would never get surgery. Even in data provided by the American Society for Aesthetic Plastic Surgery (ASAPS), 69 percent of American women say it is not an option for them. Among women of color, the percentage of nonusers is even higher. In one study of rural African American college students, aged eighteen to forty-eight, who were asked, "If money was available, would you want any of these surgeries?" 85 percent said no to all.[13]

The data that nonusers far outnumber users have been available to journalists and scholars, but as with data about numbers of women who never took estrogen, the information is never used. Why not? By providing data on absolute and growing numbers of users, ASAPS implied that users are the majority; journalists citing the data made it sound like an endorsement. The few scholars who interview users and nonusers typically choose equal numbers, which implies that the two groups are equally distributed. Nobody says, "Among women it's 70 to 30 against, nationwide. It's 4 to 1 against, globally." In Massachusetts, where I live, a woman might go for decades never seeing a face that's been fixed.

Why are there relatively few users and why have the numbers peaked? This chapter tries to answer the questions. The pro-surgery rebuttal, which wrongly assumes that everyone would do it if they could, is cost. CS is expensive and not included in insurance. (Insurance companies pay for operations only if they fix "deformities" or improve healthy functioning. Insurers may pay to get your breasts made smaller if the weight causes back pain, but not enlarged.) Elective or luxury operations are unlikely to get more accessible even if the United States instituted a single-payer national health plan. It would follow the private market in refusing to pay for procedures that are medically unnecessary.

In my opinion, cost is quite secondary. The public is incredulous about "anti-aging" products and services. Only 4 percent of Americans accept the claims made on television for them, according to a 2002 survey by Harris Interactive. That's a lot of skepticism, a writer for *Aging Today* concludes: "[T]hose considering using the term *antiaging* to describe their products or services, beware."[14] Added to that alienation are powerful positive and personal motives for rejecting surgery. A pro-natural, pro-aging vision has made its way into culture, and strengthens the defense of our underlying bodily integrity.

Feminists have persistently critiqued the culture of body hatred or shame that promotes surgery and eating disorders and have analyzed the mentality it constructs. Many women who became adolescents after 1970 were exposed to such passionate and thoughtful ideas through books and consciousness-raising groups or, if they went to college, through women's studies courses. They learned media critique and could detect the *-isms* and the profit-motives inherent in beauty myths. Like feminists, positive-aging writers also argue (and some cosmetics firms promise) that women can age beyond youth naturally and beautifully. Now many midlife women, not having internalized the hostile age gaze younger, espouse pro-aging too.

Women opposed to surgery have a point of view that rarely gets heard, but they live in a social milieu that is entirely supportive of them. According to interviews collected by Abigail Brooks for her absorbing Boston College dissertation, some nonusers notice the pressure to think of themselves as failed bodies: they are savvy about middle-ageism and ageism in the media. They may notice bodily details they don't like. But they don't act on the pressure. Emphasizing resisters rather than users can help distinguish between the external importunities to think of oneself as declining and women's varied and intriguing reasons for not going along.

In addition to refusing to believe they need a radical change, Brooks's resisters are often dismayed and put off by the way surgery survivors look. Without being angry or dismissive, many refusers think women with fixes don't look normal. ("Normal" is a category that is also important to users: they often say they know surgery won't make them look "beautiful.") An interviewee described a woman with an eyelift as looking as startled as a deer in the headlights. Another said she found it exhausting to interact with a woman whose facelift gave her an intense wind-tunnel look.

Feminists don't like to use the word "normal" because it usually stigmatizes the vulnerable — the cognitively deficient, those born with disabilities, say — as outside the norms. But in the age-related surgery context, "normal" has a different valence because of the temporal dimension. The resisters think "normal" is the way their friends used to look before they succumbed. A woman described a friend who she says lost "the most gorgeous, beautiful eyes, they were her redeeming feature. . . . The bags are gone but the *shape* is different." "Her eye is crooked, definitely," one of Brooks's interviewees reports thinking. Some are disappointed at the lack of expressivity of an acquaintance's face, or upset because a friend "looks sort of ghoulish." This is the real majority speaking, and they are not admiring. Even Nora Ephron, who made so many women feel bad about their necks, points out, "It's a scary thing, when you have friends you actually don't recognize."[15]

Abigail Brooks's resisters feel they are aging naturally and that's what they want for themselves and prefer in their friends. Theorists don't like the term "natural" either, because it implies an essential, precultural, ahistorical embodied self. But context is everything, and aging — if considered a process undergone by the embodied psyche, in culture, over time — provides a different context. In this story, the essentialized body is the former, younger body that some users choose surgery to recover, as they think. It's the resisters, accepting their changing bodies, who use "natural" in a nonessentialized way that admits changes over time and even prefers them to the alternative.

Some mature women actively like their bodies. Grace Paley, in her poem "Here" enjoys her "heavy breasts" and "nicely mapped face": "how did this happen / well that's who I wanted to be."[16] In "Desire Perfected: Sex after Forty," Joan Nestle connects "making aging an honored process" to her "newly acquired erotic territory." Nestle is a lesbian S & M activist. "Gray hair and textured hands are now erotic emblems I seek out. As I curiously explore the lines on my own chest running down to the valley between my breasts, I caress those same lines on the chest of my lover."[17] Martha Holstein, a feminist philosopher, summarizes a good deal of evidence — from Sandra Bartky, Florida Scott-Maxwell, Frida K. Furman — that many midlife and old women live in microcommunities, defying the age gaze and being effusive in their affirmation of one another's appearances. The African American college students from rural Kentucky certainly enjoy that community: 96 percent are happy with their skin color and 55 percent think their hips are "perfect." "God made me this way" was their answer to why they rejected surgery. The harder task is to spread the good news to mainstream culture.[18] It might be easier if people knew that resisters, however unheard through the din of advertising, are the majority.

Miriam Goodman, in her remarkable photograph "The Two Nüts," shows the solid naked body of her friend, the artist Jane Kogan, standing right beside Jane's 1970s life-size painting of the young, slender Egyptian sky goddess (page 110). Nüt, looking like the Queen of Spades and a younger Jane Kogan, needs go-go props: cape and headpiece, kohl-rimmed eyes, lunar attributes, pubic exclamation point.[19]

Nüt, however interesting as a painting, is flat and spiritually one-dimensional, a clownish goddess. Kogan comes out of the encounter looking better. Her later-life flesh self is in the round, statuesque, majestic, with a level gaze — an epitome of the natural. *She's got everything she wants. She's an artist. She don't look back.* She can be naked because she needs no additions. The photograph can be read as Goodman's commentary on Kogan's younger self — scrawnier, more "feminine," more exhibitionist — in contrast to her later-life self, unafraid to be unadorned. The contrast produces an implicit long-term progress narrative. Goodman lit her stately friend beautifully, throwing away thirty-five shots that were badly lit — typical for photographers shooting live models who eschew Photoshop. Goodman's aesthetic process suggests another lesson. There should be a moratorium on making ageism into a visual prophecy by letting only young models be well lit and well posed.[20]

Figure 2. Miriam Goodman, "The Two Nüts." Courtesy of the late photographer and her daughter, Sarah.

The women who like their older faces or hair or bodies are not lying. They live in a state of mind and a collective culture of feeling in which they see their necks, or their chests, or whatever, either less often — having learned to look at the whole — or, as it were, well lit. *That face is mine, a part of my selfhood not a denial of my selfhood.* "Prizing your wrinkles" should not be "a prerequisite for being a feminist," one reader angrily lectured me. I agree, but why not try not to *hate* them. On the spectrum of feminisms, I'm not where Joan Nestle is, but I'm not angry with Nestle because she prizes her wrinkles more than I can mine. I'll see how her sentences work in me and whether they can help me change my eyes more. Anti-ageism is a process in any life course, a train that we can actually drive. Any woman — or for that matter, man — may move into the feminist country of later life any time she or he feels able. No passport, no visa required. Feminists don't patrol the borders like the positive-aging police who want you in the gym or out dying your hair so sixty might look forty. On the contrary, we are looking for new mental citizens moved by whatever waves of resistance they can absorb. And that can happen with a sudden flip of attitude.

Resisters prefer to work on changing their own perceptions of their embodied selves, if necessary, to having their bodies altered from outside. They're not only anti-alteration. They critique the strong pressures on women to conform to narrow, ageist precepts of beauty. Their attitude, like Goodman's, like Nestle's, is a feminist pro-aging position. It's rare but not impossible to find support for this approach in the mainstream press. When the film *Frozen River* opened, a film critic at the *Boston Globe*, Wesley Morris, praised Melissa Leo's face for its "amazing and unlimited capacity for solemnity, grief, despair, and rage. . . . If you've been to a movie lately, you know what an un-nipped, untucked, Botox-free miracle that face is."[21] Pleasing looks and expressivity are good rewards for moving along in the life course. I'd like to see more such miracles at the Academy Awards.

"THERE ARE SO MANY bad examples," reads one response to a post on the Cold Fury blog, "that I'm starting to think there's no plastic surgery that never goes wrong."[22] Even without disaster, disappointment is built into the practice over time because it starts with fantasy. Surgeons not only describe proposed results, they sometimes do glamorous pre-op drawings or computer simulations of features they claim to be able to produce. And some clients imagine that the doctors are sculptors, artists. The metaphor is abused. Fat, flesh, blood, and cartilage are not erasable like pencil. Oil paint doesn't scar. Nor is surgery like lipstick, which women accepted in the early twentieth century in order to look either "American" or upwardly mobile. Lipstick comes off at night. Touch-ups don't require general anesthesia. A woman interviewed by Virginia Blum, an age scholar, was disappointed because her surgeon hadn't given her exactly the nose she had imagined. Blum observes that once you don't like a body part, "the rest of the world looks like an array of perfect examples of just what you lack."[23]

Disappointment is not limited to the so-called polysurgery addicts — the people considered by some psychologists and many surgeons as incapable of being satisfied. Surgeons write articles in their trade journals about how to avoid such people, saying they are obsessive. Unhappy patients often sue. (Some few women seem to be seeking suicide-by-surgeon, a female midlife variant on suicide-by-cop.) Many women decide never again after one experience, or two if they need to correct a bad first job. Despite newspaper stories about people in their sixties and seventies and even a man in his eighties running the risks, after age fifty or fifty-five the percentage of users drops by almost half.[24] The three women I know who have had it won't do it again. One close friend, at about sixty, said briefly, "I'm thinking now about my health." It is still rare to have women bravely come out and say, "I'd never go under the knife again," and warn others. And to be effective such statements would have to appear in women's magazines as well as scholarly articles.

If the surgeons were counting on the female Boomers to help them top up their income, more than half are already past the most vulnerable age. Aging-beyond-wanting-surgery sounds like another blessing of the life course.

Fear, Lies, Pain, Disfigurement, Death

There is a conspiracy to hide the downsides, says David Heilbroner, the codirector of the 2006 HBO documentary *Plastic Disasters*: "Doctors settle lawsuits, which then stay off the books. You really can't find out if your doctor has been sued or not. There's no national center collecting data on botched surgery."[25] The conspiracy of silence — about pain, disfigurement, and death — is in some ways breaking down. Most disinformation about cosmetic surgery is in features pages: the dangers do not get coverage. But some deaths sound alarms — those of a former Miss Argentina after "routine" buttock implants and of hip-hop star Kanye West's mother. It was widely reported that Donda West had been warned by a physician not to go ahead with multiple cosmetic procedures, because of a condition that might cause a heart attack.[26]

Basic facts are what need to be covered. Any licensed medical doctor can perform CS. All kinds of physicians, including dentists, are entering the lucrative anti-aging market. In one Massachusetts death that occurred after anesthesia was delivered for a facelift, no anesthesiologist was present. The American Board of Medical Specialties, which oversees the American Board of Plastic Surgery, does not recognize the American Board of Cosmetic Surgery. Because cosmetic surgery is not paid for by insurance, as former user Alex Kuczynski points out, there is no institution demanding certification of doctors.[27]

Having enough money to pay for a certified surgeon in the best plastic surgery hospitals in the world is no guarantee of perfection, or even survival. Two women died in 2004 at Manhattan Eye Ear and Throat; one was Olivia Goldsmith, author of *The First Wives' Club*, during her eighteenth surgery. These deaths too were well reported. The dreaded MRSA (methicillin-resistant staph infection) is turning up also in some patients who undergo facelifts.[28] *Plastic Disasters* noted that the death rate from liposuction was one in five thousand procedures, ten times higher than the statistic the industry puts out about deaths from cosmetic procedures in general. Dr. Sherwin B. Nuland is the author of *How We Die*, among other well-regarded books. Reviewing *The Pursuit of Perfection* in the *New York Review of Books*, he writes,

> It is ironic that the doctors who choose to perform an operation that is solely cosmetic are willing to accept mortality and complication rates significantly higher than those who restrict their interventions to those required for the treatment of disease. Perhaps this says something about the standards observed by cosmetic surgeons.[29]

Features articles and even some books by feminists typically quote users to the effect that "enhancements" are positive, highly desired beforehand and ego fulfilling after surgery. Women and men with mangled results don't find the experience ego enhancing, as Alex Kuczynski confessed in *Beauty Junkies*. One therapist interviewed by Abigail Brooks, a woman who had been working in a psychiatric emergency room, met a patient who was "beside herself," who looked like "a horror movie," her facial skin "pulling apart [with] all this dark red, about a quarter of an inch, here and here . . . and it was *horrible*."[30] Survivors sometimes find their health destroyed or true repair impossible. *Plastic Disasters* showed three severe cases of bungling. Such cases are not rare. Some 40 percent of breast augmentations will suffer complications within three years.[31] There may be no recourse, as not all cosmetic surgeons carry malpractice insurance.

Even when outcomes are eventually acceptable, the processes can be painful or disturbing. Several respondents interviewed by Brooks did not share with their friends how much pain they had endured. When one woman complained of being lied to, her friend said, "Well, if you told people how painful this would be they'd never do it." A celebrity wife, Sharon Osborne, said in print that at her age—fifty-four—she would never do it again. She is unwilling to take the pain.[32] Women playing down unsuccessful or distasteful procedures have become standard chick-flick patter, according to Laura Capitano in the *Florida Times-Union*. "I'd rather eat a Hardee's Thickburger than sit through . . . any movie that contains . . . the following 'female' film cliches," she says: "Making light of a cosmetic treatment gone awry. Chemical peel burn. Botox paralysis."[33]

Users have rather too naive a faith in "anti-aging" surgeons, perhaps akin to some people's faith in "anti-aging" scientists. It would be rational to avoid radical interventions after reading reports of doctors who have rushed into this lucrative field with little or no training. Unqualified anesthesiologists, working outside of hospitals, are unable to handle complications. Together or apart, these practitioners are disfiguring and even killing women in long elective procedures. The risks rise the more simultaneous procedures a woman has. In Brooks's study, as in Hope Donahue's memoir, *Beautiful Stranger*, some women reported that their plastic surgeon was successful in convincing them to have at least one more procedure than they had originally planned.[34] Looking for bargains? In Australia, qualified surgeons are treating patients for severe complications after they return from "medical tours" to cheap surgery hotspots in Asia.[35]

Cosmetic surgery should be a public health issue. It already is in left and feminist writings that consider surgical talents and other scarce medical resources as wasted on such unnecessary procedures. The conclusion is that a woman can choose to use her discretionary income in better ways.

We'll soon hear a lot more about the dangers of surgery. Not necessarily from the left, the Centers for Disease Control, the numerous university health reports for women, or the mainstream press, but from people who don't give a fig about public health. The well-funded suppliers of botulinum toxin—Botox, Myobloc, Dysportad—are trying to get us to replace one drastic fantasy with another. Such providers have the money to promote their anti-surgery views, which feminists and concerned doctors mostly lack. Reacting to their bad press, surgeons are advertising less extreme makeovers. Friends who know the French fashion magazines tell me they already dictate not getting "done": *Don't cut, just Botox, perfume, cream.* A 2007 article in the *Journal of Aging Studies* concluded that skin-deep procedures "are poised to become the next legitimized and logical intervention that women will be obligated to employ in their socially sanctioned fight against aging."[36] We'll see. The FDA, partway back in the regulatory business, in 2009 required a warning to be handed to patients that botulinum toxin may cause swallowing and breathing problems.[37] When will women journalists, who write the features making CS seem a choice as trivial as hair dye, wise up?

Cultural change happens sometimes when a wide variety of people and groups come together, each for their own motives, each with their own resources: in this case, the multiple anti-surgery forces overlapping with the increasingly vocal pro-aging forces. Snarky bloggers, disapproving fashion dictators, ordinary women who appreciate unretouched aging, competitive Botox providers doing down the competition, concerned doctors and surgeons and journalists upholding professional responsibility, public health progressives, and feminist anti-ageists. It's one of those odd coalitions that might just work to produce intrapsychic and social change.

Why Are There so Many Nonusers?

I believe that CS is becoming more widely regarded with mistrust, aversion, or lack of interest rather than, as its apologists claim, with desire, beauty, or agency. Feminism and positive aging converge in fortifying the resistant instincts of nonusers. Both tap into anger at decline ideology's relentless expropriations. A feminist version of positive aging gives an ordinary woman happier eyes when looking at her natural self. *This is what sixty looks like. Seventy. Eighty. Ninety.* Women in the majority may be choosing happiness. (In Europe they are getting some help, as fashion industries turn against anorexia and, in small ways, the cult of youth. A British ad campaign that raised Dove's share of the market immensely, showed a smiling ninety-year-old woman of color beside two check-off boxes: "wrinkled?" "wonderful?")[38] As resistance grows, choosing to take your healthy body and "causing it harm for the sake of surgically altering appearance," which always required "some explanation," as Rebecca Wepsic Ancheta puts it, will require even more.[39] As the backlash grows, the least extreme thing a woman can do (and the cheapest) as she grows older is to go natural. It's logical that pro-aging would be the default position.

My own theory of why it is in fact the default and always has been, even in the dangerous era of cosmetic surgery normalization, starts with resistant instincts from childhood. Everyone begins with a sense of sacred bodily integrity, and in some people it goes very deep indeed. I had to have a basal cell carcinoma, a mild form of skin cancer, removed from the lobe of my ear. My surgeon came recommended, but I was feeling a little sick to my stomach when I went into her office. She did a delicate Mohs operation (which requires a year of training, she said), and as she did it she discussed with her trainee what she was doing to reconstruct the tiny indentation to make it look when healed like my own original (sixty-plus) ear. Despite my surgeon's skill, I have a palpable scar that feels like a blemish in a way that my laugh-lines do not. Certainly I have no trust in doctors sufficient to let them take my face off and put it back on again, or suck fat out of my body at the risk of fatal dehydration. But apparently I also have a visceral revulsion, amounting almost to nausea, to even the most necessary and invisible of cuts. Bodily integrity, as it is called, is a precious possession. Bodily invasion is a horror. Surgeons undergo long desensitization to undo their innate repulsion.

Freud said, "The ego is first and foremost a bodily ego." And he added that it was not only about skin: "[I]t is not merely a surface entity, but is itself the projection of a surface."[40] Some impressive body theory has developed from the brief remarks Freud made in his 1923 essay. Bodily integrity starts with the parents calming the baby through touch. "The mother's [or father's] body moderates high arousal—anxiety, excitement, distress," writes Roz Carroll, a British body psychotherapist.[41] The infant's sense of bodily integrity depends on good-enough parenting. (This is another, complementary role for parents who teach children good prospective life-course narratives—a role I will return to in chapter 7, "Our Best and Longest-Running Story.")

Bodily integrity builds in childhood. Vivi is developing it, bending forward intently to pedal her tricycle up a little incline or taking long soapy giggly baths. She is simultaneously hearing her first simple progress narratives: instead of denying her something, her parents, Sean and Yto, promise, "You can have that when you're five." Her patience will be rewarded, and patience is a power. In her essay Carroll theorizes links between early skin associations and what she calls the character armor of later life. Adults who can soothe themselves have presumably absorbed adequate amounts of early reassurance that their bodies are a source of pleasure and agency. It's not a stretch to imagine that many adults still have a healthily complacent relationship with their bodies. The bodily ego gets its normal and best reinforcement throughout adulthood through "experiences of skin pleasure through contact" and physical activity that is free of self-consciousness: masturbation and yoga, sex and circle dancing, to name only two of each type that most people even with physical limitations have some access to. Body-centered pleasure helps support a progress narrative. And the narrative itself is another form of character armor.

Before long, however, as I worried in the introduction, the outside world's decline orientation intervenes. "It is broadly accepted in meta-psychology that the ego is that part of the self which has been modified by or adapted to the social environment," Carroll adds. My own self-image has been modified, as I have learned by writing fragments of age autobiography, the history of my ups and downs in relation to decline pressures. I'm a woman, with a female history of a certain class: Vogue-reading in the 1950s sitting beside my well-dressed, upwardly mobile mother; coming of sexual age at a time when even at Radcliffe some girls still came less for the B.A. than for the MRS. At earlier times in middle life, I pulled the skin under my eyes toward my temples to see what it might look like smoother. Not empowering moments.

Carroll warns, "When body image is substituted for body experience (as it is so often in our culture), there is a price to pay." When people look at celebrities, or watch other people's sex (most often younger people's) on TV, for example, they are endangering their sense of integrity. Visually observing other, more-approved bodies raises competitive anxieties, age anxieties. These are heightened in the rituals of social comparison that are so harmful to women — bonding with age peers over hating their necks, scanning fashion photographs, and feeling substandard.

Despite some instants of regret as I let that temple skin go slack, I didn't start looking hungrily at the surgeons' before-and-after ads. What resisted that temptation was complacent bodily ego fortified by my family's habit of deference to its oldest members. My grandfather, who lived to ninety-six, was respected for his solidity, his iron strength, his generosity. I treasure a midlife photo from the 1920s of my grandmother Molly. It is the only photograph of her we have. I never knew her: She died in her fifties when my mother was thirteen. I used to peruse her photo to work out for myself how much I resembled her. She had a strong jaw and two interesting lines that ran from her mouth to her chin. As I get older I see the resemblance more. A number of women who resist surgery say they love the way their mothers or grandmothers looked.

It is a marvel that America still provides backgrounds and subcultures where seniority lifts respect for people as they age and makes pro-aging sentiment possible. I want to include myself in that crowd too. (I'm in both crowds, actually. I still need sudden rescue — in my shorthand from chapter 1: the hot shower effect.) We resisters, then — however close to users in other ways — live a little askew from mainstream culture. The physical changes we are all taught to notice and call aging — wrinkles, whitening hair (I won't list the rest of the body parts made to appear ugly) — simply remain parts of self. Maybe we can live as bodies from the inside out so that, at least some of the time, the *feel* of being me counts more than the *look* I supposedly present to others. This healthy narcissism may help keep our character armor relatively intact and keep solidifying our native horror at bodily invasion. Looking "younger" through cutting would not be an interesting illusion or valid hope to people who experience their own bodies in terms of somatic wholeness and who inherit a legacy of seniority, and who also, as they grow older, practice feminist resistance to ageism, continue admiring their friends' looks, and develop belief in the sanctity of the life course.

Defy Ageism, not Aging

In the developmental theory I am sketching, the ideology of aging-as-decline has to invade people's selfhood harshly enough to overwhelm deeply embedded systems that act as the first robust line of defense. The answer as to why any group of women (and now men) would put themselves at such risk as they get older changes. The forces with a vested financial interest in decline must first *decrease* our quota of ego–bodily satisfaction. The standard concept, that they merely increase our dissatisfaction with our bodies, assumes that aging inevitably carries some level of dissatisfaction. This misses the point that self-liking is to some degree, and starting in infancy, indwelling, and that in nurturing circumstances it strengthens over time. It is self-satisfaction that the forces of decline seek to undo.

Spoiled looks provide the frame that age-surgery users accept. If health were dominant, that motive would support the original motive of bodily integrity and rescue it from internalizing decline. Cultural pressures to make one's body match some temporarily attractive physical ideal vary historically. Ideal noses change their shape. Ideal weights steadily drop. (The latest tiny fad comes from porn-influenced rather than medically necessary alterations of the labia.) Whatever the trendy notions happen to be, they are conveyed by the uglification industries, which on top of the usual suspects now include men's magazines with young buff male models, companies that make implants, and visual media that lack any age spectrum beyond youth.

Age anxiety, often barely conscious, builds on and worsens gender anxiety. Women start out as girls, who already worry at ever-younger ages about their defective selfhood. Some girls cut themselves in private. In some zip codes, parents give their teenage daughters silicone breasts or new noses as a birthday present. Many young adults start reading articles about staying young or looking younger, not good preparation for aging-past-youth. In their twenties, some women are saving up for their first "preventive" cosmetic surgery. Even sites expressing the "ick" response, while they veto surgery, carry the implicit message that many people consider getting older something to try to hide. By acquiring designer body parts, relatively young women and some men try "the normalization of the impossible" as Deborah Asher sagely labels it. Married women, like single women, use surgery, even when their husbands or children say, "No. I don't see why you need it" or "I hate it!" They are instructed in such cases to say they do it for themselves.[42]

Pressures on men as well as women to feel bad about their bodies as they grow older now also come from our economy, from state and local governments as well as private businesses, which are shedding employees or not hiring people because they look too old or cost too much — and because the penalties for discrimination are toothless. Being older equals costing employers more. "Make them redundant" became a kind of murky mantra for managers in the 1990s and 2000s. The age gaze observes physical stigmas in women younger than in men, hurting women in the sexual marketplace. Now stigma follows them into the workplace. Recall that job discrimination suits from women plaintiffs come in on average ten years younger than from men.

But far from sparing men, middle-ageism often raises their unemployment rates higher than women's. For a man now, looking older is not by itself "distinguished." Perhaps it never was, except for the rich. "Be young or else" is a kind of enforcement mechanism. And the uglification industries no longer target women only. The number of men having cosmetic surgery increased 700 percent between 2000 and 2005. In an article in the *New York Times*, the reason men gave for surgery, after looking younger, was to gain "a better appearance in the workplace."[43] If the government ever decided to tax CS, both genders could mentally file costs under "business expense." Midlife job discrimination could still be a generator of plastic desire.

While uglification and economic enforcers are lowering our defenses, the "charlatans fiddle with our hopes," as Adrienne M. Martin writes in an interesting philosophical essay about promises to cure cancer. Sometimes CS promises play on the credulity of self-dissatisfaction blatantly: A supermarket magazine cover recently advertised, "Look seven years younger!" Seven? As if outcomes were an exact science and you could dial up your desire. Seven is a magical number, the way youth is a magical hope. Emotions like hope function as informational filters and modes of interpretation, Martin argues, as well as fists on the scale of weighting schemes. With so much pressure applied from the culture, and some crucial information hidden, a persons' resulting request to pay to be altered cannot be considered a free choice. Surgery users have been given, in Martin's words, "autonomy-impairing hopes."[44] Women with uteruses who still take estrogen for youthfulness, disregarding the warnings, are similarly impaired. Kathryn Pauly Morgan, in a much-cited essay in *Hypatia*, calls the assent to the enticers' lures "coercive voluntarism."[45]

These mechanisms can war inside me, as I have admitted. Ageism can do its worst whenever my psychocultural immune system weakens. In the flash of an angry eye, it strips off my positive age identity and shreds my progress narrative, shoots me up with decline thinking and age anxiety and then tempts me with phony facsimiles of a remade me. This is the battered self I do battle for.

But recognizing this panicky combat has to make a difference. For nonusers, it becomes impossible to stigmatize women and men who lose enough self-satisfaction or enough trust in the fairness of the economic system to decide on surgery. Nor, if users feel regret, should they blame themselves for weakness. In the uglification industries they have an entire regime of decline against them that they formerly took as an ally. Some may refuse to believe any longer that their aging was the culprit. The socially sanctioned fight is really the one against ageism. The larger collective — the one that makes no money from their pain — is on their side when they resist.

✳

How do we help the sorely tempted become less vulnerable? I wish we could deport the surgeons who promise a "younger you" to an island where they have only one another's bodies to critique, instead of the bodies of their patients and wives. Imagine spending your life with a man who sees your wrinkles before you do. The fortune cookie from hell warns, "You will marry a plastic surgeon." It's as much a curse for a woman to *be* a cosmetic surgeon, feeling obliged to argue that the process that begins with such avoidable unhappiness is a celebratory one.

When wide resistance exists but is little known, we cannot improve how we are aged by culture. Discovering this odd emerging anti-surgery coalition, especially its pro-aging wing, has given me the thrill of the longed-for, finally delivered. It's publicity for hidden facts, feelings, and defenses. Potential users might conclude they have less to gain and more to lose than they thought, and more power to resist. Men might return to the idea (once patriarchal, now anti-ageist) that masculine aging doesn't need to be fixed, and assert the same for women.

The motives for rejecting CS turn out to be complex and overlapping: aesthetic, pragmatic, psychological, health related, philosophical, socially conscious. Aging with lowered anxiety about appearance, a form of happiness nonusers have found, might be one strong incentive. Looking younger through surgery is unlikely. With tastes changing, the more you get done, the likelier you are to look done. If users wind up looking less lined and more tautly plastic, that combination doesn't equate with younger in our sharp-eyed culture. Being stared at doesn't elevate a person's sense of competence or confidence. Even if you don't dislike the way you look "after," you may dislike being scrutinized for telltale signs.

If agency is the goal, the means is self-defeating. Even when surgery works, it never works for long. If less is more, eventually doing nothing is best. There's some evidence that people prefer risking live incision to the mere possibility of losing a job or a promotion: Even the idea of age discrimination hurts and diminishes. But the more people there were choosing surgery for this reason, the less likely that the practice would diminish widespread midlife job discrimination or the repudiation of looking old.

Some people may deny that they had to overcome any horror at being cut while unconscious, or that one byproduct of ageist culture was to reduce their innate sense of bodily integrity. (I hope that this sense of loss may diminish as the surgical results soften and the altered part comes to match the rest of the normally aging body.) Others may re-imagine this theory in their own terms. A developmental theory with a preverbal component can be a metaphor. My resistance to uglification's invasive form of ageism feels corporeal, as if it were spread through every cell in my body. The political unconscious of our time also backs up resistance to the commerce in aging, now that all the high risk taking swept up in bubble-headed capitalism feels irrational.

Defying ageism is a transformative goal. Age-related surgery is not merely a personal matter. The public needs to see it as a public health issue in need of regulation, a professional ethical matter — "Do no harm" — a feminist anti-ageist issue, and a civil rights cause. Regula-tors might pick up their responsibilities. Stricter certification could lessen some dangers. Although it must be said that a certification pro-cess does not necessarily produce better practitioners.[46] It depends on who certifies and how often. Certification can provide a false sense of security. But a national registry of deaths, malpractice suits, and de-tails about the second surgeries required to repair previous ones would transform CS into a public health emergency. The risks would ineluc-tably turn up in the mainstream media, perhaps with lively and reassur-ing reports from nonusers and resisters. Chastened surgeons, feeling public censure to "do no harm," might let their age-related procedures dwindle and return to medically necessary practices. Women journal-ists who write features insidiously promoting CS might feel too angry to go on.

Enticements to look younger — like enticements to look whiter, or anorexic, or any other *other* — could finally be rejected as bigotry. En-forcements to look younger must be even more fiercely resisted. Both are the work of heartless, shameless, selfish, ignorant, or indifferent powers. To create a civil rights revolution on behalf of seniority in the middle years, people over forty would have to unionize, sue the bosses who fired them, join OWL and AARP, defeat anti-labor politicians, and agitate to reverse the anti-worker drift of Congress, the NLRB, and the Equal Employment Opportunity Commission.

If you're anti-surgery, sounding defensive is no longer a require-ment. It's opting for surgery that might inspire, not a defense (which tends to repeat the inane language of decline, for example, "to look as young as I feel") but a self-inquiry in relation to culture. "Defying aging" is uglification's marketing tool and hoax. To defy surgery's inherent ageism, just say boldly, "Trust bodily integrity. Rely on instinctive horror. Your normal skin, your normal looks, your normal wrinkles go better with life." Then the truly bad news that everyone sort of knows already, about the psychic and economic deformations caused by our racist-sexist-ableist and ageist culture, in which the fantasies of plastic surgery play a small strategic part, can really sink in.

CHAPTER 6

Improving Sexuality across the Life Course

WHY SEX FOR WOMEN IS LIKELY TO GET BETTER WITH AGE

Time is on my side, yes it is.

JIMMY NORMAN, AUTHOR;
COVERED BY THE ROLLING STONES

"Still Doing It?"

"Still doing it" is becoming the approach du jour to sexuality in positive-aging circles. Women and men in their eighties, seventies, and sixties are being interviewed about their sexual lives. In Deirdre Fishel's award-winning documentary, *Still Doing It*, the women had to be over sixty-five. They included African Americans and whites, lesbians and heteros, swingers and traditional women. One woman in her seventies was having an affair with a twenty-six-year-old; two others were involuntarily celibate. The oldest interviewee, a blind woman, was eighty-six.

Still Doing It is also the name of a book in which the men and women investigated are over sixty. Robert Butler has co-written a sex advice book addressed to people over sixty. Diane Keaton in *Something's Gotta Give*, modestly naked in a long shot—whose character says she is in her fifties—is doing it *again*, with screams and tears of joy. Jane Juska had success in her late sixties with a book provocatively titled *A Round-Heeled Woman*, although the memoir described the underwhelming results of publishing an ad for sexual partners. Late-life and midlife sex are riveting topics. Overcoming modesty, often out of feminist conviction, women who identify as no-longer-young are not just doing it, they're talking about it, invited to do so by pro-sex and positive-aging feminists, psychologists, publishers, and pharmaceutical companies. Implicitly, they say the same thing: they too enjoy sex — like younger women, like themselves as younger women. We're so different we better act (or speak) the same.

In a consumerist hypersexualized environment where bare-midriffed fifteen-year-olds are the pedophilic standard of desirability, becoming older is coded as a set of deficiencies. Youthsex is supposedly "great," the standard. It gets a gloss of rapturous attention, belying the true facts about starter sex. In our culture, the sexual life course is broken in two by age — for women, officially at menopause. Geriatric sex, or more politely, sex in later life, is invisible or treated as jocular. On film it's considered distasteful unless Meryl Streep or Catherine Deneuve is imagined doing it. This hurts the cultural imaginary of ordinary women like me who are labeled older, blearing our self-image, lessening our chances for romance, and reducing the likelihood of our receiving good sexual (medical or psychological) advice.

The still-doing-it approach aims to be a corrective to ageism.[1] An adage current among African American women goes, "There may be snow on the rooftop, but there's still fire in the furnace."[2] This fights the double stereotype that after wild youth they become sexless matriarchs. One of the coupled lesbians in Fishel's *Still Doing It*, Ellen, looking shy and delighted, says, " [Y]ou wouldn't guess what hot numbers we are." For lesbians, "still doing it" fights a psychotherapeutic rumor that lesbian sex gets boring over time and then stops.

But the "still" syndrome doesn't add up to a useful progress narrative. It assumes that if older women *don't* do it, or don't do it the young way, that we've fallen below the standard. My heart sinks at trying to repair a broken-down story of life-course sexuality by plastering a smiley-face emoticon over the second half. I have been married for forty-five years. My husband and I have been reticent, like everyone we know, about our sexuality. The macho sex revolution — the Boys' revolution — spent decades making monogamous sex seem tedious. Will there come a point at which I feel the need to assert that we are "still" doing it? As Darren Langridge and Trevor Butt note, "Proclaiming 'There's nothing wrong with me!' acknowledges the power of an accusation, [and constructs] an internalized dialogue in which steadfast defense is necessary."[3] Even if lots more women were to yell, "*We're* still like the young," it would leave those who don't speak this way under the shadow of failure.

Capitalism demonizes sexual aging not only out of dumb sentimentality for youth but for commercial purposes. Following the money leads to the dysfunction industries — the counterpart of the uglification industries, with some of the same players. To newspaper features and magazines ads for pharmaceutical remedies, add sex therapists targeting the no-longer-young. For the commerce in aging to flourish, victims must be taught that fun and intensity equal "youthsex," that later such pleasures cease, and then sexual difficulties, distastefulness, and dysfunction begin. Some doctors now tell women their problems may begin long before menopause, as young as age thirty-five.[4] The term "perimenopause" survived the hormone debacle of 2002. A "female Viagra" is being sought like the Holy Grail and will be sold to all women, however young, who accept their problem as "low sexual desire."[5] Decline backs down the life course on this ladder too.

With the Viagraboom, aging-past-youth is imagined to bring men too the kind of graduation into ugliness and poor performance that can be slowed down only by expensive, invasive, identity-stripping products. Despite my spam filter, I get e-mails for penis enlargers. As men are added to the clientele of the desperately aging, older men have to signal that they too are doing it. Decline becomes universalized. Middle age is its current site, but "middle age" is a floating signifier, floating youthward.[6] The numbers who are suffering vaguely defined dysfunction grow, as the condition gets biologized even by the American Psychological Association.

Feminist sexologists and health advocates fight this binary by attacking sexist ageism — quite rightly — and by denying through statistics from surveys that deterioration is predictable. If we try to fight capitalist middle-ageism on this ground, which it owns, HBO will eventually produce *Still Doing It at Forty-Five*. College students already expect that aging will lead to a steep decline in sexual activity starting at age thirty.[7] Could age critics fight better, smarter?

No Sexual Paradise for the Young

If the dominant narrative divides the sexual life course between glory and decay, we have to renarrate it resistantly. The first step is to start with younger women, and to treat them as neither opposites nor ideals. Youth for girls and younger women is no sexual paradise. In fact, researchers for the 1994 National Health and Social Life Survey found

that sexual problems were most prevalent in older men—no surprise—and in younger women.[8] From a public health view, teenagers
and emerging-adult women are in a high-risk age. They make a lot of
new decisions, some—like drinking and smoking—likely to turn into
bad habits. Their negative health behaviors increase between the ages
of eighteen to twenty-four. Some have multiple sexual partners. They
have the lowest rates of health insurance of any age from birth to
sixty-four. If heterosexual, they are at risk from young men who rarely
go to doctors and thus rarely get checked for sexually transmitted infections (STIs) or HIV. If women are not in college, they have fewer
safety nets and sources of information.[9]

Sex and sexual orientation may seem at that age the primary badges
of identity, confusingly suppressing other co-identities. The dominant
sexual orthodoxy peddled to the young is that sex is a naturally plea-
surable experience, supposed to be great.[10] But sexuality is not just
sensations, personal or shared. It has a collective side, including contexts, relationships, feelings, (mis)information, and prospective stories, with their influential expectations of what will come. None of the
troubles younger women have is free of social construction. They all
involve "the woman around the vulva," the psyche embodied in culture
over time.

Masculine proponents of the Boys' sexual "revolution" believe that
sex *must* be better now than decades ago, because "Never say no" has
so much more power. For utterly different historical reasons, some
feminists also believe sex is better for younger women. Being a lesbian
can be easier now—being able to come out, assume less rigid gender/
sex roles, openly have partners, raise babies, and in some locales, get
married. In some opposite-sex milieus, there's also less shame or guilt
about being sexually active and more equality in relationships. There
is a rise in masturbation, which is safe and available. (Women are more
likely to experience orgasm through masturbation than through intercourse.)[11] Younger men are supposed to be more capable of having and
interpreting feelings, to know the word "clitoris," to carry a condom.
But many girls and young women are starting toward adulthood with
grief around sexuality (as some of their mothers know, watching them
with concern). Their later histories won't all start, "Those were the best
years of my life," any more than my early sexual autobiography did. And
if you are having a bad time now, being told that it was generally worse
in the 1950s and 1960s is no help.

Feminists locate trouble in some of the familiar zones of cultural combat: body image, ignorance, fear, coercion, violence, and exploitation. Some of the combat zones involve even lower self-esteem, higher risk, and more suffering than in the bad old days.

Body image. If you are female in a patriarchal consumerist culture, disliking your body starts young. Between ages six and thirteen, 35 percent of girls have been on at least one diet.[12] Menstruation is sometimes taught in coed classes where boys overhear and may learn to treat not-bleeding as a superiority. Girl zines — those valuable pseudonymous diaries — report that "if girls show unacceptable emotions, such as anger or depression, it is frequently written off [by boys] as PMS or being 'on the rag.'"[13]

Girls may think their bodies do not conform to the current best-body type, which, for some lesbians, means the boy-dyke; for some heteros, the anorexic. Even one to three minutes of looking at models makes younger white women dissatisfied with their looks. By college age, some believe liposuction is a normal weight-loss strategy.[14] Not just advertising but porn images influence women's self-judgments about their body parts, including the labia. "Will I be normal?" the absurd question that posits a single heteronormative form of sexuality rather than a spectrum, gets established early. Having a female body already promises worse. Even girls, overhearing "menopausal" and other decline discourses, think they know their body's functional fate.

Ignorance. Despite Web sites like Teen Voices (www.teenvoices.com) and other media by and for young women, America is a red-state culture. According to a 2004 report, 30 percent of public middle schools and high schools that taught sex ed taught abstinence (which was the only federally funded program).[15] Sex ed may still mean only a few classes using antiquated textbooks that omit masturbation, homosexuality, transgenderism, premarital relations, contraception, female orgasm, or anti-violence material. Curriculums are littered with falsehoods, portraying boys as experienced, confident, difficult to control, and predatory; girls as without desire.[16]

The number of sexually active emerging women skipping birth control has jumped. Fear of pregnancy — and ignorance about where to get an abortion with so many clinics closed — must be widespread, just as in the past. Some boys are as ignorant as girls are supposed to be kept. Girls sometimes fake their orgasm because neither partner knows how to achieve it. Some boys learn how to have sex (not make love) from the efficiency-driven men's magazines or from porn movies. People can be misled into thinking that sex needs to be kinky or orgasm quick, observes Leonore Tiefer, a brilliant sexologist, in her book *Sex Is Not a Natural Act.*[17]

Fears. Girls have sex at younger ages than girls used to — younger than many of them want to start. Laura Sessions Stepp notes in her book *Unhooked* that few wanted to have sex the first time they did it.[18] Loss of virginity is still a source of fantasies that it will be given and received as a "gift" even though, with boys leading, it is often hasty and awkward. Girls too fear showing ineptitude. Some, especially those who believe they are highly sexual, struggle with fear of being called "sluts."

Coming out as a lesbian — taking one's identity into a public lifestyle and community and losing virginity — can feel triumphant. But it can also be fraught with "shame, anxiety, and denial, exacerbated by stigma and inaccurate knowledge about homosexuals." A National Education Association report evaluating forty-two of the nation's largest school districts on how well they protected gay and lesbian students and teachers from harassment found the average grade was a D.[19]

Given fears of AIDS and STIs, everyone is supposed to forgo privacy in order to share and compel another to share a personal sexual history. Women who insist that potential partners answer questions such as "Have you always used barrier methods?" "Have you ever shared needles?" may then wonder, "Is he or she lying?" Philip Baruth, a communication theorist, has found that any degree of willingness to exchange sexual histories — regardless of the content — often produces enough false confidence to lead to completely unprotected sex.[20]

Coercion. In my adolescence, women were pressured into remaining chaste. Now, despite anxieties about body image and fear of AIDS, younger hetero women are likelier to be teased into exhibiting prominent "sexy" identities. There's early pressure to "hook up." One sixteen-year-old in a 2004 *Seventeen* survey defined the term as "kissing, touching, oral sex — doing anything but going all the way." Thirty-eight percent of the ten thousand younger women who participated in the survey believed you are still a virgin if you've had anal sex.[21] Now, not many years later, hooking up includes casual intercourse. In some milieus, there is little dating, if by that we mean a period of getting to know someone before having sex.

First intercourse is also often nonvoluntary. In one qualitative study, three-quarters of the heterosexual girls recounted "unpleasant" first experiences with boys.[22] The descriptor "hot" implies that the girl in question doesn't require what used to be called foreplay. Girls who go out with boys more than three years older have sex earlier and have more STIs and more pregnancies. If the boy is older or has more class power, they may succumb to pressure, ask fewer questions, be unable to get him to wear a condom.[23] Abuse, haste, carelessness, fear, or lack of privacy spoils many girls' first sexual experience. And a bad first time often leads to lack of sexual interest, genital discomfort, and inability to reach orgasm. Any culture that idolizes "the first time"—as ours does—shows its fundamental puritanism and ignorant youth-centeredness. Cultures truly interested in pleasure don't romanticize inexperience.

In a "culture of promiscuity" or "an unpleasant party scene" (terms used by two hetero Harvard women I interviewed), the question women asked themselves was not "Why?" but rather "Why not?" Being active has become the marker, shorn of desire or pleasure. "There's not *enough* worry about STDs," said the same undergrad who worried about the slut label. About 50 percent of female teens living in U.S. cities acquire at least one of three common sexually transmitted infections—chlamydia, gonorrhea, or trichomoniasis—within two years of becoming sexually active, according to a 2009 study from Indiana University School of Medicine.[24] In one study of 138 African American "experienced" state college students, only 24 percent reported that they always used condoms; 38 percent had had one previous diagnosis of an STI.[25] Girls giving boys head is probably becoming more common—perhaps to avoid penetration, or as a sly contraceptive strategy. Fellatio carries some risk (such as STIs) and is often not reciprocated.

Violence. Violence, mostly by males, is epidemic. In Lynn Phillips's book *Flirting with Danger*, thirty women in a small progressive college with a reputation for being feminist report being hit, pushed, and verbally abused in intimate relationships with domineering boyfriends— yet they still think they are in "good relationships" and resist concepts like male domination. One woman who hoped a same-gender relationship would be gentle and loving was appalled to discover that she herself became sadistic.[26] Half of all rape victims are under the age of eighteen. In a study in which a woman who had been raped was asked whether she felt responsible—a question that should never be asked— one woman said she was, explaining, "Well, I was there." Training in how to protect yourself from sexual assault is inadequate, although African American girls are much more likely than white girls to be given specific information.[27] In some bar scenes, money provides an incentive for some younger women to sleep with strangers, raising the risk of their being abused. Being murdered by a partner is one of the top causes of death for women under forty.

RESISTANCE—NOT TO MENTION empowerment—is harder while you're young. Given the "agency" that even girls are now supposed to possess, if sex isn't great for you, it's your failure. Lacking partners is something a woman can complain about—a poster for a college counseling service says, "My mother gets more dates than I do"[28]—but saying you don't want sex or naming the kinds of sex you do and don't want is more taboo. Young people without experience cannot be sure they know what pleasure is, or whether they are having any. "Is that all it is?" a Stendhal heroine comments after her first time. *Ce n'est que ça?* Still a useful query.

If women want better, how do they get it? Negotiation doesn't seem to be an option. Some walk. In Min Jee Lee's novel *Free Food for Millionaires*, Korean American heroine Casey leaves a hookup with a classy white friend because he phrases his request to be "finished off" in the terms of a racist porn film she knows he's watched. In *H Bomb*, a Harvard literary and arts magazine about sex, H. Bloom writes, "So fuck the sexual revolution. . . . Fuck all the crap about trends . . . which in the long run only confuses me, making me forget that it's about me and what I feel, and not about what popular culture seems to suggest women are experiencing today. And fuck power, because there is no power in sex if you can't control yourself." Soyon Im, in the collection *Colonize This!* declares, "all those dinners, movies, and STD tests have lost their novelty. Yes, Mom, . . . I'm tired of the minirelationships that expire like milk."[29] Some women move early to very committed relationships, perhaps as a way out of hookups, the risks of bar or Internet dating, or solo life.

If sexuality can be considered "an option in life," as Tiefer suggests, then celibacy is another.[30] A brave thirty-three-year old friend told me, quietly, that she was going to "take a celibate year." A. S. Byatt's character Maud, in *Possession*, calls it "the new volupté." But it's not always voluntary. Coupling or marrying at later ages, increasing divorce, slower remarriage, combined with a nasty party or bar scene, probably mean more periods of unwanted celibacy.

Maybe, despite the dismal data and the sad anecdotes, a vast sensible America exists under the radar, in which young people of all kinds are consorting in friendly posses together, learning what they need, and controlling the circumstances of their maturing sexualities. But it can't be denied that sex, not to say romance, has special age-graded risks for younger women. If the culture was simultaneously "punitive and permissive" in the 1950s, as Wini Breines writes, it still is.[31] Confusion reigns. Encouraged to become sexual by the media, peers, and young-adult fiction, girls and emerging adult women are threatened with dangers when they do. Sexual pressure isn't something a girl can just fight off, boy by boy, because the whole cultural gorilla squeezes her brain. She's a "bitch" if she refuses sex and a "ho" if she consents — and not only in rap songs but in real-life college settings. If I were a younger woman, I'd loathe the extremes of American subcultural portrayals, from urban raunch to Bible Belt "Love Can Wait" campaigns and lesbian-baiting.

Feminism's heroic vision — to raise good men and liberate women — has been stymied in many ways. Outspent, outshouted. Feminist visions, nuanced, sororal, egalitarian, theory and research based, have been submerged by gloating *Playboy* and *Cosmo* libertarians, "bimbo feminism" ("worn on the arm like a faux Fendi bag, this feminism goes with everything"),[32] right-wing neo-Victorians, gangsta rap, and the escalating sexual violence of pop culture. The Boys' slogan ("Never say no'") is winning, with many postfeminist women scribbling "my choice" over it like lipstick on a pig. And now, sex trafficking, obscenely built on the cult of youth and the vulnerability of the young, is becoming more rampant.

THESE ARE ALL ASPECTS of younger women's sexualities, and the word "unpleasant" seems to recur. If younger women were asked whether they want more sex, the way older women relentlessly are, and all women were asked if they want less, what percentage would honestly say more? Some young women hope and believe that it will get better. Believing it will get better is a hopeful prospective narrative. Perhaps hope is inevitable: it may be hard for some women to foresee sex getting worse than it was in their teens. Yet hope can be long frustrated. The starter marriage can be a long fight over equality, differences, in-laws, money — you name it — and not everybody likes a fight before bed. Overwork plus child care can lead to the 24/7 no-sex phenomenon.[33] Anxiety about fertility, now constructed earlier in women's lives by the commercial clock-watchers, may inhibit pleasure.

Those who take oral contraceptives with progesterone often experience a marked loss of libido.[34]

Looking at youthful sexuality this way, women my age might be aghast at their own misconceptions. "I thought young women now had it so good!" All this might confirm older women's opinions that they wouldn't want to be young again for anything. "Aging" — they might say, knowing what they mean — cures a lot of problems. This perspective makes the unflinchingly dreary story about later-life sexuality look crazy. Why isn't the sexual life-course story told this way? It's novel, reducible to a sound bite — "youthsex sucks" — and optimistic in providing an unexpected reason for looking forward to aging-past-youth. It just doesn't sell anything.

Same Difference?

Once we have discredited the glory/decay binary by acknowledging early troubles, we can do it another way by marking continuities, good and bad, over the life course. Sexuality is not as age-graded as the surveys assume. Take pleasure. The "pleasant tingling between their legs" that girls or young women usually discover as part of their selfhood — does that ever end?[35] Not automatically. Blake's "lineaments of gratified desire" can be seen on women old enough to have danced the jitterbug.

Gina Ogden, a therapist, psychologist, and sex researcher, told me that after doing fifteen hundred interviews about sexuality she realized how hard it was to distinguish women by age when they were speaking about, for example, the qualities of a good relationship. One of the following speakers is twenty-four, the other sixty-six. Which is which?

> I believe that in some way our souls have connected in a manner that we are at a loss to explain. I know that when we make love, there is a spiritual joining that enhances the sex. I'm not the most beautiful woman ever and he is not the most handsome man in the world. But, I'm his woman and he's my man. Our love is solid and complete and our sex life is like no other.

> I believe sex becomes spiritual when your partner and you share a "psychic" bond. They know what you want, when, where and how. And you know the same for them. Also when the sex goes beyond just sex. It's the complete meaning of "making love." You take your time, and enjoy. No inhibitions, worries, fears. It's a flowing, bending, releasing feeling.[36]

(To discover their ages, go to note 36.)

Whether it's a question of spiritual joining, fear, aversion, or violence, "recurrence" may be more apt for describing sexuality over time than the concept of continuity. Take lack of interest. Women as a group reported it as a top problem in the National Health and Social Life survey.[37] Sex therapists believe that at some points in their lives, most women will experience something they designate as loss of libido or difficulty achieving orgasm. It may not be a problem at all, but if it is, it will usually be a situational and not a medical one. (Being non-orgasmic, Leonore Tiefer says, represents a disability according to the APA, whether or not the individual has any complaints.)[38]

Dating is stressful at any age. Obesity or dislike of one's body, feeling under- or oversexed, can be social and physiological problems at any age. A first-time lover at any age is ignorant about your mind-body: your particular sensitivities, tastes, dislikes, not to mention your deeper apprehensions. College-going people and some out gays are told to request a personal sexual history and taught how to do so by pamphlets and peers. Older people certainly could be educated, but because of the assumption that they are inactive, are not. (HIV/AIDS is growing fast among people over fifty.) Men have potentially even more power over women as they become more scarce, so that in later life a heterosexual woman may feel coerced or deprived of romance in ways that remind her of adolescence. Male violence decreases with age, but it doesn't disappear. Celibacy might not seem so crushing a verdict on your attractiveness if you remember how often in your earlier life you experienced it or that it was sometimes a relief.

The Association of Reproductive Health Professionals found that "sexual satisfaction"—rather an important measure, no?—instead of going down, like desire or frequency, stays level from the fifties through the seventies.[39] If asked whether sex remains good after menopause, most women say it does. Since menopause is a nonevent for about 90 percent of women, this is not surprising. In the 1990 Midlife Women's Health Survey, 60 percent had experienced no change in responsiveness in the prior year. Nine percent enjoyed sex more. The minority who had experienced a negative change responded by wanting to change themselves, to become more passionate, more interested in sex, more romantic. Less often, they wanted their husbands to change, to become more communicative, more affectionate. Twenty-three percent wished they were having sex less often.[40] "Still doing it," we suddenly realize, says nothing about quality. It ignores the 60 percent of women with partners who say their sex life is the same after menopause as before. That could mean either continuously satisfactory or continuously mediocre.

Thirty-two Ways of Discovering Progress

Under what circumstances do women with some experience say sex got *better* for them after young adulthood? Asking anyone, "Do you [still] want sex and how often?" assumes that youthsex was fabulous and treats older sex as a series of metered losses. Questions about frequency over time reveal little but male anxiety, from Kinsey on into recent large-scale surveys, including AARP's. More sensitive questions are, "Has sex gotten better or worse over your life course, when did improvements occur, and why?" It's not just luck. These questions start to get at stories of being aged by culture and experience in a period of American sexual history that was crucial to women (and mostly for other reasons, men) who are now in their middle and later lives.

There are credible explanations for why sex subjectively improved for many women as they aged past youth. Thirty or forty years of enlightenment — contraception, abortion rights, same-sex activism, greater acceptance of divorce and psychotherapy, feminist, disability, and anti-racist empowerment — made possible enormous changes in consciousness and behavior. Women don't find it hard to tell a progress story if they started years ago with brutal or incompatible partners, forced pregnancies, unsafe abortions, ignorance of their own erogenous zones and fantasies, a gender ascription that didn't accord with their sexual selfhood, an ideology of marital duty, religious proscriptions against passion and against various forms of sexual expression including masturbation, exhaustion at work plus child rearing, the tension of the equality wars, or frightening phobias. Linda Gannon recalls that feminist anger at "patriarchal values [was] responsible for some of her most intense disappointments and frustrations."[41] This spilled over onto individual men.

Many women surmounted such problems to discover or heighten their satisfaction with sexuality. They could beneficially ask themselves, How did that happen? Did aging have anything to do with that? If you can define aging without recourse to the medical model, yes.

Some apparently physiological problems or self-esteem issues disappear. You find the right person, maybe a good doctor or a wise feminist therapist. Agency, often scrawny in youth, thrives with knowledge. Technique is not a property of persons, as we believed when I was a teenager. (In high school my friend Nick had a reputation as a great lover; that meant he could "satisfy" anyone. My girlfriends and I were so ignorant, we didn't know that our feelings toward a partner, and our relation to virginity, to mention only two factors, were way more important.) As they age, women acquire experiences that may mature their judgment and lower their risk taking. They often acquire more power, from jobs, money, the raising of children, mentoring. A woman leaves a situation she defines as unpleasant or she learns to negotiate to improve it. Over the same historical period, some male peers also learned more about physiology, individual women, themselves, heteronormativity, and alternative masculinities. Some changed their behaviors to become better partners.

Many women take better care of their health and recount improving their relationship to their body in their middle years. These are foundational moves. Annie Lamott tells one such story about deciding to like her bottom. Annette L. Murrell, an African American woman embarrassed about her big breasts, winds up kissing them. Favored routines may change.[42] A woman with an inept lover may learn how to manage her orgasm anyway. "Being me" sexually could also mean no intercourse, or no sex, or no partner. One story that the film *Still Doing It* omits entirely is that of older women who like celibacy whether they chose it or not. One of the older women in Judith Daniluk's research group finds her long celibacy "incredibly comfortable."[43]

Although a life course is continuous, lived in one single embodied psyche, sexuality may change over the longer term. Christine Jorgensen, speaking about her transsexualism in *A Personal Autobiography*, wrote, "I had left New York an inhibited, introverted half-person and I'd soon be returning to [my parents] as a happy, whole human being." *Lesbian Nuns* tells dozens of short tales of repression followed by liberation, with outcomes ranging from continuing celibacy in orders to leaving orders and breaking the silence, in order to release "powerful sexual and spiritual energy." Jan Clausen's *Apples and Oranges* is the autobiography of a lesbian activist who had been in a twelve-year relationship with a woman when she fell in love with a man. She says, of her identity, "I thought, in fact, that I was what I used to be—I certainly felt like the same person" and she also says "what 'feeling like a woman' means to me has evolved over time."[44]

Given the coercions younger women suffer and accept, women "may reach middle age before accumulating enough experience to discover their own sexual desires."[45] In Deborah Dickson's movie about the relationship of a lesbian activist couple, *Ruthie and Connie: Every Room in the House*, Connie says of her former life in a hetero marriage, "I never had an orgasm for eighteen years." Postmaternal women, with the distraction of children gone, often like sex better. Women, as I noted in chapter 4, may enjoy their bodies more after they can no longer become pregnant. Becoming postmenstrual in a social world that notices its benefits would enable an even higher percentage of women to expect to have good sex in later life.

Gina Ogden has found a basic reason a majority of her older respondents tell progress stories. For them, sexuality means connecting more and more over time with their spirituality—making more eye contact and sharing feelings with a partner, feeling attunement with their God, with the goddess, or with nature.[46] When sex does get better, it's because it has richer meanings than it used to have.

The best phase can come late. Hearing that I was looking for lifetime progress stories, an acquaintance I will call Mary wrote,

> My mother had her best years sexually (and maybe otherwise) in her sixties, after leaving my father and taking up with the family doctor—a bachelor, and good in bed, she let me know. My dad was an alcoholic, and she probably should have left him sooner, but couldn't figure out how. . . . The divorce came at her instigation after all kids had graduated from college. . . . This family doctor had been someone she turned to for advice and sympathy during my dad's depressions.[47]

Alix Kates Shulman found the love of her life at fifty, after two (anorgasmic) marriages. She tells a concise sexual age autobiography in her memoir, *To Love What Is*. After two marriages that ended in death and divorce respectively, my own mother fell in love in her late seventies and had her best loving from a man in his eighties. She would call me weekly to tell me what he said and what she said, and what should she do and what would he think? (The obsessiveness and the adolescent gossip quotient stay the same—another recurrence.) Frances, the eighty-six-year-old in *Still Doing It* who was blind, had a love affair with a sighted man in her nursing home who told her she was beautiful.

A group of women between sixty and eighty-five were asked to compare sex now with the decade of their twenties. A solid minority reported increases in "enhanced sexuality" on one or more measures like interest, strength of urge, pleasure, and satisfaction. The group also reported an increase in masturbation from 10 percent to 26 percent.[48] Another study cited by psychophysiologist Linda Gannon found that 62 percent thought their "sexual interest and comfort" had increased.[49] Decline is taught as a physiological fact in medical settings, textbooks, and feature articles on sex, but when researchers ask new questions of women, decline becomes an artifact of youth bias and assuming that males are the model. *Sooo* twentieth-century.

If feminist age critics like me report such stories of later-life possibilities, it's not to sex up the image of older women in the still-doing-it way. Good stuff happens not because we are still young, but because we are not. (And we want to avoid the adjacent if incoherent stereotype of sex-hungry postmenopausal women.)[50] There's interesting news here for everyone once you mix up the bad and the good of the ages more than current ideology permits and change the language we use. In *Still Doing It*, a couple in their sixties say when they fell in love they had two to three orgasms a night — "Like first love," Harry enthuses. This is a current event, so let him say, "Like real love at sixty!" For everyone's sake, in later life people have to overcome their own ageism in order to consider same-age people and their behaviors sexy (but not "hot") and say so openly. And sometimes Ruth, Harry's partner, says they just laugh in bed. They could plausibly be joking about an episode of impotence, rather than treating it tragically as younger lovers might.

The big change comes through empowerment: women becoming sexual subjects rather than objects.[51] Instead of inquiring, "How must I change," they may say, "I'm fine" or "Finally I am me." You have to learn not what is "normal" — that is unknowable, pragmatically and epistemologically — but what your own range of normal is, and that too may change over time.

The generic arc I have sketched could be criticized for possessing a euphoric pattern — which, Elizabeth Wilson says of feminist confessional fiction, often describes a "journey from victim to heroine."[52] Let's not knock that direction of change. Many girls, emerging young adults, and women have no place to go but up. The arc also shows that sex — believed to be a merely physiological experience — is charged with culture when it's good as well as when it's not. Understanding this holds out the hope — remote I know — that we might improve both culture and experience. But progress is not automatic.

Making Sex Better in Later Life

Obtaining sexual experiences as people age into middle and old age is highly dependent on three things that are often not in one's control: finding a partner, adequate health, and, if a woman is heterosexual, finding a male partner who doesn't believe in midlife sexual decline, his own or hers. My husband's father, George Gullette, used to tell a story about an old college professor who gave a sex-ed class for men only. One day a student shyly asked him what his own sex life was like. The professor hemmed and hawed. Finally, he said, "I would want to tell you . . . only this, sir, that the act of love takes . . . a little longer than it used to. But I do not begrudge the time."

Does anyone begrudge the time? Well, yes. Some men do — in themselves and in their female partners. We can't consider vaginal dryness an inevitable consequence of menopause — indeed, many younger women might report dryness if their lubrication times were measured, and some women who have divorced their husbands describe it as a symptom of a lousy relationship. But given that self-lubrication is supposed to be slower in later life, how much? On average, in one study, it was between one and two minutes slower. Yet twenty-two out of fifty hetero men interviewed in another study felt rejected and even angry because of this.[53] Why don't such men learn some effective techniques and reset their inner watches? In sexual aging, the double standard survives.

Ejaculatio praecox, in youth an embarrassing accident, can become a man's nostalgic ideal. A friend of mine said when her husband took Viagra without telling her, "This is a penis I don't know." She didn't think he needed drugs, and she would have wanted him to discuss it beforehand. Erectile "dysfunction" covers a vast spectrum, and "anti-aging" remedies may be counterindicated. If men are slower to climax than they used to be — to use their own subjective measure — one treatment is to stop regarding this as a decline. In some cases women who felt rushed or got left behind are getting their turn. They may prefer less force or urgency. Retired people need not begrudge the time. As one woman said at a Simmons College sexuality conference, she and her partner can make love on weekday mornings and take their time. (Some of the younger women did an envious double take).

Lacking a partner can happen at any age. But fewer than half of women sixty-five to eighty-four are married, while three-quarters of men that age are.[54] For African American heterosexual women, scarcity begins earlier because of male incarceration, AIDS, and homicide. As potential partners get scarcer, finding a loving partner in later life may feel even more miraculous than at, say, thirty. One problem is that American men die considerably younger than women. Women are genetically stronger even in utero, but much of "excess male mortality" is social, not biological.[55] Japanese men live longer and more healthily than American men.

Some of the chronic diseases that occur earlier for those in lower economic classes or with less access to health care have effects on sex. More than half of African American women aged forty-five to sixty-four have been diagnosed with hypertension, twice the rate for white women.[56] If negative changes in sexuality are "remarkably similar for men and women," as Linda Gannon reports, it may be because women tend to be poorer at midlife and in old age.[57] Health conditions that are not life threatening — like joint pain or asthma — can hamper mobility. So can medications. Sedatives may reduce energy, libido, or flexibility. Americans are an overmedicated people. People often have much younger doctors who, not being geriatricians, understand too little about metabolism to get dosages right and too little about what they see as decline to get advice right. It's said that many older people, women as well as men, would like to have younger sex partners. People sometimes assume that this preference comes from aesthetic disgust at their age peers — ageism as sex snobbery. But seeking the less medicated or the more agile is also plausible.

Sexual longevity is a class-based public health issue that cannot be solved by sex drugs. Men have to live longer. More people, especially minorities and women, have to stay healthy after forty, fifty, or sixty. The only sensible measures are preventive, and prevention is cultural — discursive, social, economic, medical. Health in old age starts in utero, with the health of the mother. We need to lift children out of poverty and boys out of gangs. Sex education needs to teach men while they are young to think about contraception and safety, comfort, reciprocity, meaning, spirit. For themselves and their partners, they should scorn "pleasure" defined by numbers or aroused by violent fantasies.

Men would have higher longevity if the United States had single-payer health insurance, training to avoid male macho behavior, gun control, better anti-alcohol and anti-smoking programs, real education reform. We all need full employment with expanded seniority, creation of good jobs at better wages, structured so that they don't make people hypertense and give them higher risks of heart disease. We need less insecurity in the workforce and the nation: unions and safety laws, a shorter work week like that in effect in France, mandated vacations, and a "slow time" movement that provides leisure for sex not only on the vanishing weekend but during the week. We need doctors and therapists with anti-ageist consciousness, who have broader ideas about sexualities. We need a visual culture that relishes older bodies. This humane socialist-feminist pro-sex, pro-aging vision could actually improve sexuality across the life course.

What Kinds of Sexual Age Autobiographies Do We Need?

Many women do have a better relationship to the sexual part of life — certainly not worse than in youth — as they get older. What would help the culture understand this are a myriad sexual age autobiographies. By definition they would treat sex analytically and historically. To really get the point, we need to know richly detailed trajectories rather than a hyperbolic new arc from bad or so-so to better. Boasting defensively about the present in the value terms of youthsex is not useful. The positive-aging story of the still-doing-it type responds to a chic age-graded message: "You don't stop having sex because you get old, you get old because you stop having sex," in the words of Barbara Marshall and Stephen Katz. "Success" involves exhibiting unending "physical vitality and life enjoyment," says Tiefer.[58] Meryl Streep in a dirndl. Having a partner can come to seem like a health aid, an "anti-aging" practice. Women receive cultural imperatives to act sexy forever, which a Margaret Drabble protagonist says "means nothing [for women] but a sense of unending failure and everlasting exclusion." Like movies focused on frantic youthsex, Tiefer notes, Viagra has raised the bar for what counts as adequate.[59]

And yet there are later-life sexual progress narratives, and they can be distinguished from positive-aging stories. In the former, progress is bumpy. Recurrences are as real as changes. Many losses have no connection to age or aging. Introspective telling would be longitudinal, measured from early adulthood. There is "decline" that isn't loss. Some women prefer no longer being objectified. (Jane Miller, an essayist who doesn't give her age, no longer *wants* sex, no longer feeling the "greedy energy.")[60] In a nuanced progress narrative, the causes would be analyzed, not assumed. Women of seventy or eighty—Mary's mother and my mother and Frances—whose nutshell stories were of finding better love, said so in private afterward because it's nice to talk about happiness when you're looking back. They weren't acting out vitality for show. There's room in the genre for mixed feelings. Bea Freeman in *Women Talk Sex* shares a story of growing out of victimhood, where regrets get mingled with having been "mended with time."[61]

The more intimate and novel the subjective detail, the less phony the arc seems. Tiefer says it is hard to find useful information "about how ordinary sexual routines develop and change" or the role of learning and expectation.[62] We don't know how fantasy gets interpreted, or whether and how it gets turned into behavior, or how impotence brief or permanent is experienced. How does sexual identity—meaning not only orientation but the whole congeries of feelings and behaviors we associate with our way of being sexual—get integrated with other identities? Under what conditions does sex come to the fore or recede? (A woman who has been widowed may learn just how much that greedy energy assails her.) For women, it seems untrue that sex is universally more important in youth and less important in later life. What does its unexpected prominence at different times depend on? Biology doesn't explain much. Having one's sexual life break neatly in two at menopause would probably be rare in full stories: Life, including sexual life, normally contains many other changes and randomness and sudden dips and even tragedies. Such stories could offer young imaginations not just hope but information and matter for curiosity.

Sexual behaviors vary among quite old people who have partners the same way they vary among younger groups.[63] But for some couples, sex expression tends to become less focused on orgasm and more on flirting and cuddling, at whatever age. Cuddling is the most elemental form of love, going back to skin touch and body-mind comforting enjoyed in infancy. Many people learn long before old age that sex is far more than orgasm: it's romance, intimate touch, and visual, olfactory, and oral pleasures, in the context of a relationship. Orgasm may have a delightful but smaller role. There's a youth-centric law about how big a role sex and especially orgasm should have, but it's time to break that law—explicitly. I think I would miss orgasm if it were ever to evanesce, but I wouldn't judge my marriage, my womanhood, his manhood—ah, those nineteenth-century values—or our relationship based on that single factor.

Is it comical to value cuddling? Is it pathetic to feel that having sex only *x* times a month is not a decline or to actually call it a pleasure? Is it disgusting to behave in private the same way young people do on the silver screen? These questions are as biased as similar questions about coming out or going bi. People have to want what they want, not what their subculture or the media say their bodies are supposed to want, or what they wanted in some other phase of life. Physiology is to a malleable extent a verbal story. If something changes, and you are still getting what you want, that is progress. People could say about their slower or less frequent sex that it's "great" or "intense," so the thrilling words don't attach only to hormones and haste. Aging may reveal other unsung benefits.

Later-life sexualities radically spoken have big things to teach. Why not add "interest and comfort" to sex questionnaires for the young? What would happen if girls internalized comfort as a sexual standard? Why not omit that fetish, frequency, from surveys at all ages? Whatever their identities, might younger couples try unpressured, patient, mutually satisfying sex, "devoid of performance imperatives"[64] and accompanied by affection—and say without disdain that it's mature love? Just believing there are thousands of different long-term sexual narratives out there might mean less current suffering, less idiotic information to unlearn, more liberty. Suppose people were to follow their age-uninhibited inclinations at any age? Be celibate at thirty or at sixty? Masturbate guiltlessly at all ages? Refuse to count their conquests with pride at eighteen because that they know it will give them an appalling contrast at eighty? Slow down juvenile experimentation so there is something fun to discover later on to connect with aging? Queering the whole sexual life course we might call it, because it seems a more radical kind of sexual revolution than history has known. Imitate older people in *sex*? By providing relief from compulsion for people at any age and values that serve the whole life course, it would simply be kinder to everyone than our current regime.

Retrospectively discovering age-flavored sexual histories requires writers with enough years on them to get bolder. If need be, write it anonymously, publish it anonymously. Discover what your own landmarks were, with history's guiding hand under your elbow. Aging can clearly lead to a sense of progress, but aside from that what exactly does age have to do with anything? If the answer in many cases is, "Not much" or "Hard to tell," age need no longer be the primary variable in a sex questionnaire, in popular culture, or in women's minds.

Sex needs its mystery. In the world I want, all these multiple tell-ings convince you of one thing: that you know *nothing* about another person's sexual life when you see that she is young, or old, or disabled, or fat, or fit — not her fantasies, behaviors, interests, identifications, capacity for pleasure and love, history, or future. And you would *know* that you knew nothing about that woman's tantalizing private story unless you had the right to ask her and she chose to tell you.

PART THREE

Our Best and Longest-Running Story

CHAPTER 7

Our Best and
Longest-Running Story

*WHY IS TELLING PROGRESS NARRATIVE
SO NECESSARY, AND SO DIFFICULT?*

I can't argue that there is progress in the arts or in global welfare, for "surely to tell these tall tales and others like them would be to speed the myth, the wicked lie" (as Zadie Smith warns in her novel, *White Teeth*) "that the past is always tense and the future, perfect."[1] Then perhaps "progress" has no place in a shorter-term human life story either? But reports from across the life course and from many walks of life show this: Progress in an encompassing form makes its way into people's private dreams and communal dreaming and organizes much life storytelling (oral and written). Moreover, out of the slender urgent goal of progress for self may come "open-ended campaign[s] for improvement" for others. Far beyond merely "assuaging the crying shame of manifest deprivation," self-realization can be transformed into "the metric of justice."[2]

Progress narrative undergirds all these possibilities through affirming the value of aging in time. In good-enough circumstances, that value is inculcated in childhood. Many of us try to keep the story going over our whole life, despite poverty, the deaths of loved ones, and the thousand natural ills the flesh is heir to. And the habit of having long told a prospective progress narrative may help some of us even much later on, in frailty, sickness, or dependency, when the risks of despair can also be high.

Early Socialization

When I was about five, I cut my knee on some metal sticking out of our new used car. The accident left me with two scars. My mother used to say encouragingly, if she saw me fingering the scars, "They'll be gone by the time you're married." The basic notion was about healing. Given enough time, the body (married or not) would get better by itself, without constant scrutiny and tinkering: health was its default. The larger message Betty Morganroth read off her crystal ball was, "Be calm. Don't worry. All in good time." This was a life-course prophecy. Implicit messages about aging are buried in many adults' simple statements about time. My mother's message went bone deep; it has functioned in all my recoveries, lifelong. It gave me an initial bias toward aging, freed of sentimentality.

My two scars in fact never disappeared. But it didn't matter that my mother was wrong. Should she have warned me I'd have ugly scars forever? Her soothsaying—coming from a parent, it was true aging knowledge—strengthened me. She told me jubilantly how her salary as a teacher went up every year. In such powerful sentences and anecdotes, she invented for me a trustful progress story about how the life course would get better. Mine especially.

I've told this story about my mother before without mentioning my father, Martin Morganroth.[3] He too told me a prospective narrative in condensed forms, but his was very different. He didn't spare me tough news about the world we live in. By the time I was in junior high, he owned his own truck and had a beverage route he drove. "Cops are on the take," he said. (This was Brooklyn.) "The bosses don't want people to unionize." "Negroes have been kept down." (This was the 1950s.) Lots of people were poorer than we and might never own a house. He didn't tell only decline stories. Month by month, he said with serious composure, we were paying down our mortgage. Someday we would own our house. But I caught from him the view that progress was dubious and uncertain and unequal and unfair. Nothing to take for granted.

Parents telling stories is one important way for children to learn about the meaning of life-course time, for themselves specifically and by implication for others. The before-and-later stories about aging that each of us internalizes in childhood can be no more than one sentence deep and yet as salient as Pike's Peak. Walter Benjamin says about stories of "the inscrutable world" that "the cardinal point" for listeners is to assure themselves "of the possibility of reproducing the story." He means remembering a precious story accurately.[4] By reproduction, I mean repeating the generic story-shape in one's own life and making it the measure of the lives of others.

In his 2007 novel *Bridge of Sighs*, Richard Russo lets his young narrator hear versions of the very same narratives I learned, only with the genders of the parents reversed. In Lou C. Lynch Jr.'s boyhood, his father, a milkman with faith in others, is the positive thinker. "I was especially comforted by my father's belief that we were living a story whose ending couldn't be anything but happy." As the factories in their region close, his father prophesies, "Another year and everybody'd be back working full-time, even overtime, probably."[5] His mother rubs her temples at her husband's spasms of optimism, gets angry at him, understands other people's motives better. "Not surprisingly, my mother's take on our better life, as well as her estimation of America, was more complex and, to my way of thinking, far less satisfying." She told Lou Senior that his hard work "was no excuse to go around talking nonsense about good things happening to good people, because bad things happened to good people all the time." "I was particularly troubled by my mother's notion of downward mobility.[6]

> I don't know why it troubled me so much that my parents disagreed about how the world operated, but it did, and when I intimated as much to my mother, she replied, "Really, Louie? Which of us should think differently? Your father or me?" I had thought that went without saying. My father's was a more reassuring interpretation of the known facts of our lives and a more elegant, satisfying story to boot.

His mother tells Lou that he will continue to rise farther "if that's what [he] want[s]," but that his parents' progress is finished.[7]

In protected circumstances, children absorb into their age identity some elements of personal progress: an increasing sense of control over material things, authority over themselves, tenderness toward juniors. Somehow these early awarenesses build trust in the future. I see Vivi's chest expand as she grows in any of these domains. Progress narrative projects a moving image of the self through its past and onward to its better future. As I use the term, however, the arc can contain events that are neither elegant nor satisfying. Without losing its grip, "progress" can contain accidents, bleeding, pain, scars, and rage — impediments that might otherwise lead to decline narrative. Lou explains how when his father loses his job (as Lou's mother had foretold) and impulsively buys a failing convenience store, it "brought home to me that . . . the stakes were higher, that the story of our family was being written without any guarantee of the happy ending I'd always taken for granted."[8]

After a certain point, my childish happy story also became confused. When I started going to first grade every weekday, I suffered the first shock of age-related loss. After the exhilarating freedom of playing around in the backyard, building bodily integrity and dirt mounds, I felt my life declining forevermore into discipline. Educational success was supposed to compensate for a stale existence under the clock and the teachers' eyes. Started on my long career of being a good girl, I marched in praise and inhibition toward that insinuated progress. Young as I was, experience had given me a narrative about aging to relate. I felt some satisfaction about possessing a story, even as I told my younger cousins glumly what first grade held in store for them. So the first age autobiography I imparted, at age seven, actually prophesied decline. Along with the feelings inspired by the school regimen, my father's commentaries on injustice and wrongdoing uneasily flowed into the gathering stream of stories next to my mother's, like the blue and brown unmingling rivers at the confluence of the Amazon.

For grownups, the political is personal. The fictional Lynches and the factual Morganroths paid attention to such forces as income, business cycles, deindustrialization, racism. Each of the parents implied progress or decline in their every mention of time. It was always either about historical trends or historical stasis. My mother's salary rising every year. "Another year . . . even overtime, probably." "Negroes have been kept down." "Bad things happened to good people . . . all the time." When judgments are made as to whether lives get improved through social change, who is judging? If the media say the economy is good, that could mean stocks went up because bosses fired long-term employees; but for the workers, income and everything dependent on it went down. If the midlife employees who have been laid off betray their decline story to their children at home, the CEO tells a self-satisfied progress story to the reporters. Progress or decline is always someone's story, based on a judgment about the important underlying direction of change.

Scholars often write about economics, history, or culture without reference to their influences on life-course storytelling. Often people pen auto/biographies and critics write about memoir without reference to the larger contexts that impinge on interpretations of aging. This nonrecognition of the other realm long puzzled me, as an age critic and narratologist. In this chapter, I try to bring the subjective and collective need for progress narrative together with the historical conditions that make it possible, at three different phases of the life course: childhood, adulthood, and old age. This is another way to go deeper into the story too naively called "aging."

Necessary Illusions

"Progress," or its synonym "growth," is the semiofficial prospective life narrative for fortunate children. Progress is a story all children ought to be able to hear first. Was my mother's story good for me? I think so, and I loved her for it, as Louie loved his father for his kindly obtuseness. He didn't love his mother as much. Ultimately, though I didn't discover this for a long time, progress narrative promises children not a charmed life but a resilient self. The story helps produce that self.[9] Who would be so cruel as to deny children the psychic strength and extra hopefulness and energy encouraged by progress narrative? — particularly when we think how often children are exposed to decline stories, gloomy prognostications, and sometimes tragedy, from within the family and without. The bad news filters in even when it doesn't crash through the roof. The self has to be robust, steady, and probably, loved to incorporate bad news and withstand it. The self nourished by progress narrative has an extra boost.

Our next question, then, is what happens or what should happen to progress narrative when children become adults and live and work outside of the protective families and institutions like schools or scouting that provided many of them with secure and progressive age hierarchies? What happens to the sense of rising and growing as those brought up on such expectations age into adult economic life and are exposed to the wider world? Adults continue to build ever more complex age identities, in which disappointments and damages — potentially undoing childhood's sturdy progress narrative — have to be fit into life storytelling. A "predominant feature of the self in European-American contexts is the persistent need for consistency and stability." Yet adults want also to maintain a subjective sense of progress, as cultural anthropology explains. Amos Handel concludes that "[s]tability and progressive aspects of the self-narrative are not inconsistent and may actually coexist."[10] (Jan Clausen's story of feeling the same person after her sexual reorientation is a good example.) Part of progress is not losing ground, which is why stability is important.

Complicating these psychocultural needs is the fact that telling some version of a progress narrative has become almost obligatory in adulthood in the United States, and not just in the middle and upper classes, but down among the aspiring but more precarious adult offspring of the Lynches and the Morganroths and their present-day equivalents. You can tell progress stories about any identity, and people do. (In earlier chapters, I've pointed out modest ones in some women's sexual age autobiographies, in the arc of well-being after menopause, and in pro-aging attitudes toward the body.) But in this country, the favored story in adulthood is of upward mobility from a poor start. Progress is usually envisioned through some version — relevant to your class, race, gender, ableness — of the life-course biography called the American dream. The upward line need not be a steep ascent. For most Americans, it can only be slight. My mother was a unionized teacher who stayed in the profession for twenty-five years. As her upwardly spiraling wage curve taught me, once we are beyond youth, aging well depends a lot on material conditions and the values that ride on them. We need health care to stay on the train all the way to longevity, and second chances and respectful age hierarchies and rising wages, among other things, to do well all along the way.

In the United States, the legend of the American dream — open to all — actually becomes more significant as larger numbers go into economic free fall. The gap between what people might hope for and what they are likely to get grows vast. Margaret Mead describes what is required when social change goes wrong — feels too fast, too intense, too generationally divided, when systems become brittle and individuals less secure. "The idea of progress, which provides a rationale for the unstable situation, makes it bearable."[11] Just before the 2008 election, as the gap grew week by week, nobody said the rhetoric about the American dream was a wicked lie. It was a necessary hope. It made possible an electoral success that few had initially deemed possible. "Change we can believe in" really meant "Progress we can believe in."

The requisites for believing in life-course progress after youth have become more elusive in the United States over the last thirty years, as the country began to produce less, unionization declined, wages stagnated, and income inequality grew. Louis Uchitelle notes in *The Disposable American* that layoffs first appeared as a mass phenomenon, absent a Depression, for the first time over two decades ago. The highest rates of displacement in the 1990s occurred among midlife segments of the workforce.[12] Unemployment is terrible for anyone, but many younger people find jobs quickly when the economy picks up, while many midlife people remain left out of improvements in the business cycle. Even if age is not the cause of a job loss, midlife discrimination can be a problem when looking for the next position. It bears repeating: Displacement among workers in their fifties and sixties often results in lower wages or lasting unemployment.[13] Some are forced out of paid work altogether.

"Financial sin is awfully dull and to appreciate it demands a head for figures. Cruel, mind you, and disastrous for somebody, but undramatic unless there's a suicide at the end," says a character in Robertson Davies's novel *The Cunning Man*.[14] Here are some figures that help estimate the disaster. The typical American household headed by those between forty-seven and sixty-four is not just at risk in an increasingly insecure job market. It is poorer in constant dollars than a similar household was in 1983, despite women working. In 2009, a woman between forty-five and fifty-four, working full time, earning peak pay, at the median took in $37,024.[15] But who knows such facts? Where is the mainstream debate about what kinds of jobs the forgotten midlife workers can find, and what it would take to improve this situation?

Seniority is the reason that any Americans can still acquire life-course benefits like respect as we age into the middle years and past retirement. It is not our own merits per se but the existence of a system of age-graded benefits that enables many of us to climb the ladder of income — up to a point — as we climb the ladder of years. The United States, the richest empire in the history of the world, has been weakening seniority in frightening ways since the 1980s. The Bush administration decimated a well-established system by denying union protections to employees of the Department of Homeland Security, who amounted to one out of twelve government employees. The Supreme Court has weakened the Age Discrimination in Employment Act. The academy is weakening tenure: Between 1975 and 1995, colleges saw a 12 percent drop in professors hired with the possibility of tenure, and a 92 percent jump in positions without possibility of tenure.[16] As business weakens seniority through downsizing, outsourcing, and clawbacks from unions, forces of deprofessionalization are ending it tacitly through losses of authority that affect everyone from judges to doctors.

The "midlife crisis" may have seemed like a hiccup in life-course storytelling when it was first named decades ago, but this innocuous, privatized, misleading term has turned out to disguise a vast national crisis. The degradation of work in America — longer hours, shorter tenure in contract jobs, fewer benefits, high and widespread unemployment levels, eroded or nonexistent pensions — along with the cult of youth, are undermining the security and income support on which self-continuity and progress depend in midlife and beyond. Economic insecurity is the truth offered to more and more Americans, at younger and younger ages, starting earlier for the disadvantaged: "Late capitalism . . . fills [young people] with ambition and aspiration which by definition can only be enjoyed by the fortunate few," Mark Braund writes in *The Possibility of Progress*.[17] Young people may have reasonable, class-based aspirations, but once the majority age past youth, hope for growing material success, more autonomy, efficacy, responsibility, trust — everything good in older Americans' life-course stories — becomes more insecure. The future of their own life course (like their parents') seems less and less in their control. Too often, the only prospective narrative that makes sense is decline.

Life storytelling, I believe, is becoming more edgily poised within the binary of progress versus decline. It's too narrow a choice. There are other humane and justifiable genres — satire, jeremiad, tragedy — that might better serve our turn. The dichotomy has demoralizing political and psychological effects. It suggests that decline is a loser's story — our own fault. Even after mass layoffs and plant closings, most people with pink slips believe they are to blame. Competitive individualism in such circumstances can sap the will to fight. Progress must be pursued but may not be obtainable, and self-continuity may be threatened not by postmodern multiple selves but by radical downward mobility.

To deal internally with the threat of deprivations, to keep our particular narrative going, we try to respond, psychologists say, with a recurrent drive toward identity stabilization or self-continuity. Many Americans manage those drives after a certain age by retorting (perhaps only in public, not in their heart of hearts) with the irrelevant slogans of positive aging: Fifty is the new thirty. We are healthier than our parents. Won't the Baby Boomers automatically get what they need? Aren't women doing so much better than their mothers? — the Lou Lynch Senior form of cloudless forecasting. Lynch is kindly satirized by Russo. In truth, telling progress narratives is not merely a question of temperament, safely under one's own control. "Be happy, be resilient, recover" mocks all the ways in which progress narrative is undermined by cultural contexts — by poverty, insecurity, the hostile *-isms*. My mother knew that.

Adults too need help in maintaining their progress narratives, but it will not come from anti-aging products or blind faith in change. Governments, law, and market forces structure the conditions in which each of us writes our life-course narrative — conditions not entirely of our own making. These help some and deprive or neglect others. *Whose progress is it?*

Second-Chance Plots

My second story about progress narrative and its contexts comes from an outpost of the American empire. Mariposa Duarte (not her real name) is a maid in a hotel in San Juan del Sur, Nicaragua, once a sleepy, provincial, Sandinista port on the Pacific, now a resort experiencing a real-estate bubble, an influx of rich Miamistas and snowbirds, and sex tourism. San Juan also has a more unusual institution, the Free High School for Adults.

The Free High School started its eighth year in 2009 with an enrollment of 568 adult students. More than half come from the rural areas, where there are no high schools. Others come from the poor barrios of the town: many of them couldn't attend the regular public high school because the government used to charge a fee. The private institute charges nothing. The other high schools meet on weekdays, when our students work. The institute meets on Saturdays. Women with babies and people over eighteen are excluded by law from attending public high school. A few of our current students were illiterate in 1997 when they joined our first literacy classes for women. We have had students as old as fifty. The Saturday School, as the students call it, opens its arms to all these rejects. Our students prove to be excellent. Three hundred have graduated. Some go on to higher education. Most get decent jobs. I visit San Juan annually and fundraise for this special place, which is run by my colleague and friend, Dr. Rosa Elena Bello. Years ago we agreed that adults should not be left out of all that education promises. We bring to them as adults a message Jean-Paul Sartre described in *Les Mots*: "All children know that they progress. No one lets them forget it. 'You have progress to make; [you are] in progress, serious and regular progress.'"[18]

Mariposa became one of ours in 2003. She had left school at age

fifteen, over half her lifetime before, because of incapacitating head-
aches, and then she married and became a mother of two. She had
given up the idea of education until the school opened. Her children
were then eleven and five, but she was able to attend because we provide care and a hot midday meal for the children.

When I interviewed her she had been living for eleven years with
an abusive man, the father of the children. She told me a recent story.
He had hit her and one of the children, not for the first time. But now,
she said proudly, armed with her authority as *a woman who goes to high
school*, she and her father had it out with him. He promised to amend
and he stopped taking drugs. Illness still sometimes immobilizes Mariposa. She cried when telling me about not being able to attend school
for pain. That week she had been accidentally hit in the head at the
hostel where she works. "But I want to go forward. I want to," she said
intensely. *Pero quiero salir adelante, lo quiero.* She finished by explaining why the Saturday School matters so much. "It is good for us, the
women. If I had my knowledge earlier, maybe I would have been able
to raise my children without him, alone, on my own. I thank you all,"
she said, smiling as serenely as if, when contemplating her good fortune
in being able to study, she hadn't a care in the world. Not denial, but
hope squares a progress narrative with a harsh, disappointing world.

I am impressed by Mariposa's fortitude. Her husband went back to
some of his bad ways, but she continued to attend the Saturday School.
At thirty-something, she seems to have proof that she has some way of
squeezing out from under economic and social subjections. This optimism is related to narrative agency—being able to say, honestly, "I did
that!" A very little bit of luck, moral support from her teachers, and
mental excitement in her studies have revived all sorts of life energies
that may cohere into a second-chance story. For the time being at least,
this results in her feeling that she and her children actually are going
forward. With a high school degree, she could get a better job—less
taxing, more intellectual, more remunerative. She could send her children to high school. The present is a sight less bad than her past, and it
implies a future in which things might just keep going her way.

There are cultural critics who believe that poor people, especially
poor women, can't tell progress narratives—that this is a bourgeois
form of life-course story, a luxury available only to the powerful and
privileged. The World Bank estimated that globally, in the year of recession 2009, more than 100 million more people would fall into extreme
poverty, dropping to earning under two dollars per day. And political

theorists, looking at billions already at the bottom under globalization, earning only a dollar a day, see hindrances to progress so formidable that chances of improvement over the life course make little sense: traditional, feudal, highly stratified, or totalitarian societies, or situations where progress narrative is largely a male monopoly. Nicaragua is the second poorest country in the hemisphere, after Haiti: inequality has grown in the last decade; machismo is virulent and sometimes lethal. But Mariposa's story and those of 299 other graduates should make us very cautious about denying the possibility of progress narrative to even the most disadvantaged.

In most cultures studied by psychological anthropologists, people seem to need "positive illusions" about themselves. In Japan, for example, a less individualistic society than ours, people exaggerate their share of the abilities most valued there: fitting in with others and behaving interdependently. In Western societies, most of us exaggerate the goodness of our traits, overestimate our personal agency; we also tend to be overoptimistic about our future. Americans lacking these necessary illusions get depressed: failure to maintain "normative esteem-enhancing distortions is the most consistent feature of depressive cognition."[19] For people like Mariposa, life planning involves children and even grandchildren, not the individual life but family time reckoned in generations. Even people who don't know literary forms and whose lives are more subject to random patterns may do this planning and want progress with all their hearts.

Many adult students in San Juan have educational histories as checkered as Mariposa's and determination as fierce as hers. One assignment asked them to describe their dreams—their wishes for their future. Everyone had a dream, even if it was as modest as getting the diploma. I am no longer amazed, but I remain impressed that they struggle to hope in circumstances that strain the credulity of people who lead more privileged lives. Perhaps it doesn't take very much encouragement for progress narrative to flourish. Many plants survive the long dry season.

Nicaragua does have a myth of national progress, with a tense past (the dictatorship of Somoza), a liberation (the Sandinista revolution), and between 1990 and now, the receding likelihood that the free market would produce broad economic gains. In order to maintain their aspirations, Nicaraguans like those in our second-chance school have had to bracket years of neoliberalism, cronyism, corruption. Their own governments have almost abandoned them. The current government, although no longer collecting school fees, doesn't pay a *cordoba* toward the education of the 568 willing, hard-working citizens in the Free High School.

My feelings about Mariposa and our other students include indignation and even outrage. Whoever acts privately on the preferential option for the poor—whether in San Juan, low-income areas of the U.S.A., or anywhere else in the world—is compensating for some basic government neglect or active government harm. Housing, clean water, health care, jobs—most governments in the world don't provide them. They're governing in name. They have a flag and an army. Globalization means that more nation-states can't do it: they are being ground deeper into poverty through debt repayment, exploitation, or resource extraction by multinational corporations and inhumane cuts to health and education via the International Monetary Fund. Even for children, such governments provide only in the barest way. Unless an international outcry focuses on a subcategory of adults—people with AIDS, say, or the famine-stricken—neoliberalism finds a way to justify abandonment, arguing that self-reliance is the highest good (except for the rich), that grown-ups need to pay for what they get, that NGOs helping them ought quickly to become self-financing. (The Saturday School could never be self-financing.) The good work of activists almost always has this other face leering out at it—not a sad or remorseful face, which might be some comfort—but a malicious, blind, or hypocritical face.

Our school aims to make one possible difference. When I meet with my colleagues—the director, Rosa Elena Bello, or her teachers—and we discuss how to continue and improve what we do, I feel that giving adults fresh starts is noble work. I know that Mariposa may not find a better job; better jobs may never come to the backwaters of capitalism. With her knowledge she may now understand why. At least we who work in adult education or job creation or low-interest small-business loans intervene on the side of those who struggle to keep their progress story going in adulthood, trying to change a fate that seemed fixed by class for themselves and their children at birth. Perhaps this attempt is one of *our* necessary illusions.

IT TURNS OUT THAT many of the great political arguments of our time, in the United States and elsewhere, implicitly revolve around this question: Under market capitalism and globalization, which classes, races, ethnicities, sexualities, or genders can continue to tell progress narrative? And the urgent next question, a new question, becomes: For how long in the life course — until what age?

From the story about my scar at age six to Mariposa's story about the difference education made to her at thirty, I have moved from thinking about the development of resilience in children to the maintenance of resilience in adults, from the vulnerability of children to the vulnerability of adults in an unequal world, from the family setting in which my healing was gently narrated by my mother to the harsh global setting in which Mariposa's life chances seemed set. Such complex moves are fundamental to the emerging field of age studies. We start from one age class — childhood — and then turn to others. We follow narrative because we understand the fundamental truth: aging *is* a narrative. We research the contexts of storytelling because we know that storytelling never happens in the vacuum of a solitary mind, however self-affirming that mind may be.

Our Longest-Running Story

My third example of personal progress narrative may seem the most unlikely. Perhaps people can agree that telling a progress story is possible in the face of systemic poverty, partner abuse, and ill health when a person is only thirty or in midlife, despite combined miseries. Hope survives impediments. But what of Jean-Paul Sartre at age sixty-nine, whose health was worsening so rapidly that Simone de Beauvoir feared he might lose his ability to write or speak. Is progress narrative still possible in old age if sickness combines with loss of projects — in the "end-of-life" period that is what people often mean by "aging"? The discussions that Sartre and Beauvoir had at that time, which Beauvoir published as the "Conversations" at the end of *Adieux*, explicitly say yes, it's still possible.

As fresh as paint, the "Conversations" was intended to become "a book about himself . . . concerning [his] literature, philosophy, private life." Initially, the great French playwright, novelist, autobiographer, and philosopher lent himself to the interviews out of ennui: "[S]ince I've not a great deal to do at present, I have to take some notice of myself . . . otherwise I'd have nothing at all." But he could "emerge from abysses," and soon became "completely happy."[20]

In fact, because Beauvoir was an ideal interlocutor, the "Conversations" constitutes an astonishing autobiography-à-deux. The questions she asked Sartre were based on their deep forty-year-long relationship. She had apparently as total recall of his writings as of his affairs. She could and did correct him, jog his poor memory, sum up his positions, and remind him of connections between phases of his life. Sartre said that not only was she at the same level of philosophical knowledge, but "she was the only one at my level of knowledge of myself, of what I wanted to do."[21]

They ran through his life course many times because each new aspect of Sartre's identity (as "action hero," lover, writer) had its own longitudinal story. If one age identity was added, dropped, or changed drastically in his thirties, another changed only at fifty, or in his teens. Telling the narratives of all his identities kept him spellbound. A shah, effecting his own postponements. Beauvoir was curious and even pressing about one particular point: how he felt now about the over-riding arc of his life-course narrative. Sartre had in fact always believed that life had an underlying direction of value, as Beauvoir reminds him in her knowing, assertive way. "There's one idea that has been very important to you—that of progress." That was true. It was a profound element in his formation, as *Les Mots*, his 1964 autobiography, attests in its structure as well its reflections and observations.

Beauvoir might nevertheless have hesitated to repeat this, since Sartre was going blind and finding it very difficult to write. He had certainly despaired at times, and for all she knew he might have given up once and for all on progress. Our view of aging is often reduced to illness, understood, in the words of age critic Kathleen Woodward, "as a demonic force that terrorizes . . . and as hideous bodily confusion."[22] Beauvoir may have been testing on Sartre her own more negative assertions about old age, published just a few years before. In *The Coming of Age* (*La Vieillesse*) she had declared, "But progress at this stage of life is of a disappointing kind."[23] Had Sartre's cherished belief survived his new conditions? He answered unhesitatingly.

> Certainly. I thought my first books would be inferior to those that came
> after. I thought my main work would be completed by the time I was fifty
> and that then I should die. Obviously, this idea of progress came to me
> from the lessons in which progress was taught and from my grandfather
> who believed in it.

Sartre finds continuities in his selfhood, even with a comical younger self who thought he would die at fifty. Beauvoir presses him: "And from your choice of the future too. You think that tomorrow will be better than today."

> BEAUVOIR: [Yours] was a very optimistic outlook, compared with the attitude of all the many people who, like Fitzgerald for example, think that life is a process of disintegration — that the whole of life is a downfall, a defeat.

F. Scott Fitzgerald's *The Crack-Up* serves her, like many others readers, as a locus classicus of the most available antithesis to progress, the view of aging-into-midlife as a decline. She gives Sartre an opening to align himself with those who, whether declining in body or mind, find life a defeat. But Sartre is stubborn:

> SARTRE: I used to think that too. I thought it at various times in my life. Things that had begun and that ought to have been successfully carried out came to a halt. One therefore ended in failure.
>
> BEAUVOIR: The idea of failure is not the same as that of disintegration.
>
> SARTRE: That I never thought. I always thought life was progress up until death — that it must be progress.
>
> BEAUVOIR: What do you think about it now?
>
> SARTRE: The same thing. Progress does stop at some point before death because one is weary, because one is near senility, or because one has private worries. But by rights it should go on for a long time. Fifty's better than thirty-five. . . . As I see it, the moment itself is already progress. It is the present and it flows on toward the future, leaving behind it the poor, disdained, despised, denied past. For this reason I've always readily admitted misdeeds or mistakes, since they were committed by someone else.
>
> BEAUVOIR: You've always been steadfast in your life, both in your work and in your affections; but at the same time you don't possess any deep solidarity with your past.[24]

This exchange is by turns comic, scary, invigorating, and provocative. What is new is certainly not the simple notion of progress that declares, "Fifty's better than thirty-five," which positive aging has made familiar in the English-speaking world, and which treats age simplemindedly as if it were the only variable. Sartre is far more eccentric than the gurus of positive aging. Life must be progress, he says sweepingly, although he had started by talking only about his own writing, not the direction of some putatively universal life course. This is not optimism but a theory about living in time. Or perhaps it is a rule of the good philosophical life.

Some readers may be startled by Sartre's apparent inability to put his sense of the necessary movement of time together with the bodily degeneration Beauvoir has graphically described — incontinence, blindness. Is this what is called denial, as judgmental reviewers of other people's aging narratives often say? Sartre agrees that he thinks occasionally, "I'm seventy: that is, I'm finished."[25] But the tone seems casual, not depressive. Beauvoir was shocked by his bodily "disintegration." It's her metaphor. But Sartre was not shocked. The whole exchange can be read, eerily, as a life review written in a rather impersonal past tense, as if a disembodied talking head had outlived his other selves.

It is quite possible, Sartre notes, for a person's sense of the value of the movement of time to vary from year to year, or even from day to day, depending upon circumstances. And despite Beauvoir and Sartre's implicit pact to defend progress narrative for him, the autobiographies of Sartre's identities told in *Adieux* are not all stories of cure or overcoming or persistence. The "Conversations" opens, at Beauvoir's instigation, with a formidably long list of works he left unfinished, in which the word "failure" comes into play, but not conclusively. He had his dominant narrative: he clung to it from childhood to as close to the end of his life as was recorded.

Beauvoir had shown in *The Coming of Age* how necessary solid socioeconomic support is to a good old age. As Robert Frost admonished, "Provide! Provide!" Sartre had economic resources and friends, admirers, hangers-on. His living room was full of them. But even for the well-provisioned, progress can be a difficult narrative to maintain. Doing so in ill health may take a lot of mental and psychological tricks. This is particularly true in the United States, where ageism makes wholesome denial, sensible distraction, or any good defense against pain and loss much harder. Ageism can shout decline into our ears loud enough to drown out other plausible interpretations of what is happening in our body-mind. Sartre was not just lucky to be male and famous; he was lucky to be French then and not American now. Why did he not say more about his body? Perhaps subjectivity has not much to do with the objective view?

Sartre's devices to hold on are illuminating even to a close student of narrative tenacity. He emphasizes the two-point contrast that Americans usually suppress, that personal progress requires "leaving behind the poor, disdained, despised, denied past." Temperamentally antinostalgic, Sartre tends to evaporate his past selves. "Yesterday is not sharp and clear," he says. He was aided by what we might no longer want to call a weak memory. It was strong in his defense. Beauvoir caps his insouciant rejection of his inferior younger selves by observing, in the lofty language she had used also in *The Coming of Age*, "you don't possess any deep solidarity with your past."[26]

True of many of us. The I has a habit of othering past selves as strangers, while holding tight onto its right to say what they felt and said and did. Is this then a description of autobiography? Perhaps. The danger is to push anti-nostalgia, or Sartre's rule, to the point of minimizing recollections of past happiness, accomplishment, and love, as those in depressive states do — as I think Carolyn Heilbrun did. How does the progress-self deal with continuity when hypostasizing change? I speculate that continuity comes from still feeling like the superior person who others past selves.

People telling their life stories in extremis have the right to lie to the tape recorder, their life partners, even to themselves. But I believe that Sartre's emphasis on progress was sincere, in that the devices were working well enough for him in 1974. Beauvoir was listening to him as intently as ever. He must have been flattered at being so *known*, as any of us would be, in an arena (his own interpretation of his life) in which he of course had the last word.

Beauvoir helps him hold on to progress from different directions. She asserts, "One can never realize one's age oneself — it is not present to us." She reminds him of states of mind to which he has permanent access. A person focused on interior selfhood has great advantages over people who feel bombarded by social gazes and discourses. A man who always thought he was ugly, as Sartre did, has less to lose from the age gaze. A busy political person — whose "consciousness is directed toward the outside world and not toward . . . an image of [the self]" — also is freer. She adds his theory of ego. "You've explained that fifty times. The ego is not in the consciousness, and the consciousness is therefore always perpetually present, fresh, unchanged."[27] This is like the ego I describe in chapter 5, malleable and vulnerable to aging, or as I would say, to ageism. Sartre and Beauvoir put ageless consciousness outside the ego, as if there were a firewall between the two. Would that there were.

Some methods of Sartre's might work for any of us, even though few will have a scribe taking down our age autobiographies. Sartre saw himself as a person suffering a change in physical status who as he speaks does not feel that dying is his future. Having told an ontological progress narrative for so long, he had habit and pride (we might conjecture) to also prevent him from giving it up. Holding on to his theory did him good. It provided him with continuity, even though he had lost many abilities and projects. Beauvoir allowed him to have the last word, and this is what it turned out to be. He convinced her so well that he was living that even much later she hesitated too long, she explains, to ever tell him he was dying.

Sartre's attitude, if I have described it properly, is not easily labeled. Neither "transcendence" nor "denial" fits well. The joint project of the "Conversations" tells the way it feels to an active speaker to be alive *now*, with the whole curious sweep of life to run through at will and a real challenge latent throughout the encounter, to square his story with his life partner's knowledge. No wonder that Sartre was at times happy.

SOME PEOPLE RESIST Sartre's version. Even if they are themselves old, they say that old age is another world, a time of losses, implying that there is only one dominant truth of old age, and progress or continuity cannot be part of it. For them illness and old age are not only intertwined but synonymous. But they might fear the nadir they imagine less, if they listened carefully to true accounts. Failing decline might not be their last act in life. Meanwhile, let them not stop our own ears. Saul Bellow has Augie March explain, "That's the struggle of humanity, to recruit others to your version of what's real." Augie calls the insistent versions of naysayers, "damnation chats." *Ravelstein*, a book about not one but two oldish men, one of whom dies of AIDS while the other survives an acute poisoning, is Bellow's vigorous answer to damnable ageism: "You think we're done! Finito? Wrong." In the words of Bellow's first-person narrator, Chicky, as he and his best friend roar at an old vaudeville joke: "A joyful noise — *immenso giubilo* — an outsize joint agreement picked us up together, and it would get you nowhere to try to formulate it."[28] Like Sartre, Chicky doesn't combat decline narrative frontally. He crowds it out with fresh alternatives.

What brio, what ingenuity, Bellow and Sartre respectively display. Bellow himself had had a near-death experience. Sartre was really ill. They set a high standard for "late style." (This subject has become chic, many years after Kathleen Woodward and Anne Wyatt-Brown developed it as a theme for humanistic age critics.) If people are not in pain, a good deal of liveliness can be left at the "end of life." That's an odd term. What does it mean, anyway? The medical meaning dictated by the cost-conscious — only six months to go to get into hospice — is an accounting requisite, not a fact of life. Experienced doctors say, "We often can't tell in advance when a person will die." Those living with dying don't know.

There's a danger in the increasing attention to later-life eloquence. The bar is rightly set high for fiction or memoir, but that level would be way too high for personal storytelling. Setting expectations too loftily for older people is a kind of bias. We are to be wise, passionate, virtuous, temperate, brave, and stylish, all in a minute. I think sadly of Carolyn Heilbrun's high daily demands on her self. We don't want to ask the impossible from selves — *our* selves — who are increasingly battered by the crosswinds of prejudice as we age.

Readers, let us give one another a break. If you don't require that a thirty-year-old be always in top form, don't ask it of me at eighty. Do not require that I be as scintillatingly sage in sickness as in health. I may be at times sad, mad, bad. Hang on my best words, the way I memorized my parents' unaffected sentences. Mariposa tells her story simply, but her daughters listen in awe. Given how formidable the obstacles put in our way as we move into old age, merely surviving decline day after day has to be seen as a cultural accomplishment. Survival with attitude can itself be saluted as a feat.

Sartre's ability to displace and dispel decline forcefully raises my question again: Who is permitted to tell a progress narrative? Our answer ought to be, Anyone who wants to. One of my subtexts has been that positive aging should not impose progress narrative on people, forcing them to deny their sorrows and the external facts that weigh on them. But neither should dominant culture impose decline narrative as the only possible truth — whether on Mariposa as a disadvantaged woman, on midlife workers threatened with being disposable, on Sartre and other sick people in later life. ("Ageism" is a word I have used rarely in this chapter. When you look at the whole life course, starting young, the name of the enemy that thwarts our desire is "decline.") Once we accept that certain "illusions" are necessary, by what right should they be denied by age, any more than by class, by gender, or by disability?

How fragile progress narrative turns out to be, whether in childhood, as we age past youth, through the long midlife in the workforce, or in old age! If progress is what most people need and want, as my arguments have tended to show, there has to be a collective determination to make it more democratically available, for longer.

Following the wavering but persistent arc of progress through the life course, as I have tried to do here, can lead to a just appreciation of that difficult desire. It can confirm us imaginatively as stakeholders in the politics of the life course, whatever our current age. Perhaps a fuller age consciousness can grow out of this. Looking back on our life opportunities, many of us can discover not only the accidents of chance (which usually loom so large in life stories) but also the contexts that have enabled or disabled our own narratives. We may discover powerful and properly self-interested motives for political resistance.

Decline is real enough. Now progress needs to become more available as a reality. Governments should not be permitted to destroy the socioeconomic and legal bases on which more vulnerable citizens write their progress narratives. Supporting progress from childhood on — through well-regulated national daycare, equal education, fairer systems of social justice, more sacrosanct seniority systems, home care for elders, respect for people with memory loss, wanted and appropriate medical treatment (whatever we find it takes, for all the phases of the life course) seems to me an ethical imperative. But these concerns often treat the issues of childhood or the midlife or old age in isolation, with the specialists focusing even more narrowly through their discipline on the life stage they study. During all the worthwhile discussions that conduce to such ends, it would be wise for us to ask, philosophically, this question: "What are the bases for the whole life course that will let us call it good?"

CHAPTER 8

The Daughters' Club

DOES EMMA WOODHOUSE'S FATHER
SUFFER FROM "DEMENTIA"?

In reading too, age matters. Over a long life our most avid attention swerves. When I first discovered Proust's *Remembrance of Things Past* at seventeen, an age when I craved authoritative information about desire, I read it for its stories of unrequited love. Then for some decades, happily married, upwardly mobile, and Francophone, I read *A la recherche du temps perdu* for the glee of prose style and Faubourg hauteur, skipping the obsessive material about the lost beloved, Albertine. Only with still later readings did I finally notice the key to Proust's underlying values and structure: the figure of the grandmother. The grandmother's selfless devotion to him is young Marcel's model of reciprocated love. Other *amours* and all the social satire aimed at the heartless—which Walter Benjamin called "the physiology of chatter"—are offset by a single person embodying the ability to sense his pain and give comfort. Marcel's dependency on his grandmother's life force explains why he must ignore her worsening illness.

Aging matters as a proxy for our progress in soul making. Experience changes younger people's selfhood, expands their interests, and (Proust implies) opens their hearts to the preciousness of the older people who chose to cherish them young. Aging also matters as a proxy for historical change. My English literature teachers decided their fictional syllabi at a time when ideas of what might claim the attention of traditional-age students were more limited. "The Marriage Plot" was a staple, but its gender baggage was overlooked. As I advanced through my middle years, ambient age culture changed authors, scholars, and readers. In the 1980s I was able to teach the course "Midlife Fictions" because many good writers as they wrote into maturity started publishing novels about complex protagonists almost their age, and sometimes gave them anti-ageist progress narratives.[1] My nontraditional students (midlife women, retirees) were amazed to learn how long it took critics to notice the unromantic supplementary plot—call it "After the Wedding." They devoured novels with non-young protagonists.

Theory occasionally highlighted age, and age critics taught themselves how to read for it. Feminist, anti-racist, left, and queer critics also scrutinized figures of the other tacked into the margins of texts— the so-called minor characters. Scholars began to write on topics that would have been unthinkable or uninteresting before: later-life creativity, grandmothers in children's literature, acting age on stage. Relevant cultural discourses influence what readers can notice at any given age, and whether we can permit ourselves to care.

So in theory I was not surprised on rereading Jane Austen's *Emma* that it was a different novel than the one I had been taught. But, given its fixed place in the canon as a lively courtship novel, it was startling to realize that like Proust, it too, at the deepest level, concerns two generations facing a troubling old age.

Emma and Her Father

In Austen's eponymous novel, Emma Woodhouse's greatest private dread is that she will be left alone, tête-à-tête, with her father. The novel opens at a low point of such anxiety after Emma's former governess, now her one true friend, marries and leaves them. "How was she to bear the change?" is the interior question that leads to a description of Emma's father as "no companion for her . . . a nervous man, easily depressed, [who] made it necessary to be cheerful" even when she feels quite the opposite. On that first sorrowful night alone, she "spared no exertions to maintain [the] happier flow of ideas" that she skillfully guided him into. From this stressful situation the neighborly Mr. Knightley rescues her, by coming to keep them company.[2]

Austen underlines the theme by reiterating Emma's fear toward the end of the book. The same dread now has more warrant, since Emma believes that by her romantic blunders she has also lost Knightley. Her mental soliloquy is full of dismal foreboding. "If all took place that might take place . . . Hartfield must be comparatively deserted; and she left to cheer her father with the spirits only of ruined happiness." Her only hope is that "however inferior in spirit and gaiety might be the following and every future winter of her life to the past, it would yet . . . leave her less to regret when it were gone."[3] The mysterious final "it" cannot refer to her father's death. The antecedent is "every future winter of her life." Her only source of "consolation or composure" is the anticipation of her own death.

This depressive state, and not any common spinster's fate (which Emma doesn't fear), is what Knightley saves her from. In the "profoundly unconventional" ending of the novel, as the American critic Marcia Folsom rightly calls it,[4] he makes the marriage possible by moving into *their* house, so Mr. Woodhouse will not have to change the slightest of his necessary habits. The future husband's remarkable friendship and self-abnegation, and not his willingness to overlook Emma's mild social flaws, is why Knightley is knightly.

In the novel there are scarcely any hints that Austen is describing in Emma's father, Mr. Woodhouse, what many people might now call early cognitive decline or early Alzheimer's or the result of a mini-stroke. Perhaps the most significant marker of his condition can be deduced not as much from his behavior or speech as from hers. Emma's kind and adroit treatment of her father's obsessive preoccupations is an almost unnoticed but immensely important aspect of the novel.[5] Read this way, *Emma* can provide lessons for our Alzheimer's-obsessed era.

Austen never comments on Mr. Woodhouse's behavior as if it were a condition, and Mr. Perry, the apothecary who visits Mr. Woodhouse frequently as a friend, never diagnoses it. In a time before biogerontology and cognitive science and their costly remedies, Mr. Woodhouse is merely a "kind-hearted, polite old man" and a "valetudinarian." Thus his various symptoms — as they would be called nowadays — are simply treated as personal characteristics, like his old-fashioned politeness, fondness for looking at newborns, or adherence to a nursery diet. Yet he is not simply old, like good-natured hard-of-hearing Mrs. Bates. His limited repertory of subjects, his nervousness about being left alone, his craving for the familiar, his ready depressions and fear of having changes made in his routine are among many signs, scattered here and there, of the anxiety and repetitiousness that apparently Austen knew can accompany cognitive impairment. The surface of *Emma* is comedy, but here and there — whenever Mr. Woodhouse comes in — this apparent romance touches very shadowy ground.

Only in retrospect does Austen show how direly his condition might have derailed the romance plot. Emma's former governess, now Mrs. Weston, wonders at the end who else might ever have wanted to marry Emma if the precondition were having to move into her father's house. "And who but Mr. Knightley could know and bear with Mr. Woodhouse . . . ! The difficulty of disposing of poor Mr. Woodhouse had always been felt in her husband's plans and her own [for match-making]."[6] In this light, Emma's often-stated determination to stay single at the then-advanced age of twenty-one seems less like spirited upper-middle-class independence, and more a semiconscious attempt to make a fait accompli appear a decision. To herself, she says concealingly that marriage "would not do for her. It would be incompatible with what she owed to her father, and with what she felt for him."[7] This is close to a lie to herself, but at this late point, when she thinks Knightley will marry someone else, it is also the kind of bravado she needs to carry her through her anticipated ordeal.

And when she accepts Knightley, her joy and relief measure how drearily she had been anticipating the future, not only her father's death but what is sure to precede it, his further mental and physical decline: "Such a companion for herself in the periods of anxiety and cheerlessness before her!"[8] Bharat Tandon, in his book on Austen, rightly noticed that "[e]ven in comparison with its immediate predecessors, *Emma* is unusually tight-lipped about the afterlife of its plot."[9] The explanation is that her father's slow decline and death, and her caregiving, rather than simply marital felicity, is the unusual afterlife of this plot.

Soothing Mr. Woodhouse is a chore that Emma rarely recognizes as such, or, more exactly, that Austen scarcely permits her to recognize. But when Emma finds herself writhing as she recollects her rude and flirtatious behavior at Box Hill, the comparison that comes to her mind is that "[a] whole evening of back-gammon with her father was felicity to it."[10] If Mr. Woodhouse were merely old and somewhat dull, such intense emotion might seem hysterical. But those evening hours she bestows on him are the most "precious" for private occupations, after the daily stress of maintaining his composure and keeping up her own anxious watchfulness. What we sense is her need of relief after strain — a strain that dedicated contemporary caregivers will understand without another word.

One can measure Mr. Woodhouse's potential for agitation by Mrs. Weston's constant efforts, like Emma's, to keep him calm. Emma arranges his thinking to that end, giving him information he needs, reminding him of their joint past — "Do not you remember what Mr. Perry said, so many years ago, when I had the measles . . . ?" — looking on the bright side of every situation.[11] Behind his back, she provides adequate food for his guests. Together, the two women, with presumably much help from servants but no alleviation of responsibility, provide a soothing environment that prevents him from failing worse. They keep him from becoming an object of pity or the butt of jokes.

Mr. Woodhouse can be courteous, but the speech of others must be tailored to his handicaps. He is unable to understand a joke, has few topics of conversation, repeats himself, is persistent in his worries. Without guidance, he fails to follow others' reasoning. In Jane Austen's worlds, where sensitive listening and diverting, empathetic, or appropriate responsiveness are so prized, he is characterized as a defective speaker early on: "He could not meet [his daughter] in conversation, rational or playful."[12] And Jane Austen is usually hard on defective speakers — they are satirized through their own words and by others with superior apprehension and articulateness. Walter Scott complained of the tiresome "prosing" of Miss Bates and Mr. Woodhouse, as if the two characters were equivalent figures.[13] But they are not treated as equivalent. Austen thinks there is no harm in having characters make unflattering observations about Miss Bates in her absence. Mr. Woodhouse encounters no censure, even behind his back.

Austen is kinder, much kinder, to Mr. Woodhouse. Indeed, in her humiliating retrospect on the mean words uttered at Box Hill, Emma reflects that her attitude toward Miss Bates ought to have been modeled on her behavior to her father. (She never thinks that her rudeness to Miss Bates might have been modeled on wished-for but impossible speech toward her father — but we, in a psychoanalytic mood, may.) Why is Emma's father exempt? It is not as if Austen has a habit of sparing alpha men, or fathers, or patriarchs, because of their wealth and status. Witness the amused contempt directed to the arrogant Mr. Elliot in *Persuasion*. Age — or rather, respect for age — has something to do with sparing Mr. Woodhouse, but not everything. The garrulous Miss Bates is younger than Mr. Woodhouse, but she is intelligent enough to understand Emma's sarcasm and be hurt, and also capable of holding her tongue when criticized. (Satire is a reforming emotion: it wants people to improve.) The most plausible reason why Mr. Woodhouse cannot be satirized, that squares with Austen's linguistic and moral values, is because he is cognitively unable to reform.

Emma is grateful to her father for his unstinting love. Her ego is soothed by knowing that she is "always first and always right" in his eyes. Researchers say that midlife offspring caring for elderly parents value the reciprocity, whether it comes as admiration, gratitude, gifts, deference, or advice. But being equally adults together—honest speaking—is impossible between Emma and her father. In controlling her emotions for his sake, she is approved of quite as heartily as Austen approves of Elinor Dashwood's restraint in *Sense and Sensibility*—as heartily but not as openly. *Sense and Sensibility* is structured by contrasts that amount to fulsome praise of Elinor. In *Emma* the theme of daughterly self-control is submerged so deep that some culturally inspired reticence seems to have buried it. Mr. Woodhouse's unnamed condition requires solicitude and manipulation, which are tendered to him without stint—and almost without comment. To Austen this virtue of caregiving, unlike all the others she wants to ratchet up by dint of writing novels in which people talk about how to improve the faulty self, is unsayable.

YET WE MUST ALSO properly appreciate Austen's sweet oblique recognition of the efforts of caregivers. Let me say squarely to generations of literary critics who have missed this, whom I initially read with some astonishment: Emma is a heroine not because her character survives making so many mistakes but because it contains this unnamed and unaccentuated virtue. On these grounds, even her obtuse matchmaking can be better understood—as a distraction that a daughter without work and unlikely to marry, given such a father, must invent for herself. Set in the balance with this degree of filial piety, to any sensitive reader her errors must seem light.

She sets the tone to her crowd in her kind attentiveness to her father. Other characters are measured morally by whether they, like Knightley, can follow Emma's lead or, like Frank Churchill, cannot. Frank has what Emma calls "that greatest fault of all . . . the want of respectful forbearance towards her father." Before the ball, Frank Churchill actually teases Mr. Woodhouse, who is fearful of colds, about people who open the windows at dances. He contradicts the older man's need for deliberation, which requires Emma to interrupt and contradict him.[14] The need to monitor Frank may help her decide that she has no interest in him as a marriage partner. Only one character in the novel notices that what Emma does is work. A newcomer, Mrs. Elton, having learned that Mr. Woodhouse's spirits are "sometimes much depressed," floods her with condescending empathy. "I perfectly understand your situation, however, Miss Woodhouse — (looking towards Mr. Woodhouse) — Your father's state of health must be a great drawback."[15]

I SUSPECT THAT age hierarchy — of the special filial kind I have tried to describe — was imbued in Austen, so sacred to her that she was unable to verbalize it. Austen was careful to construct Mr. Woodhouse's limitations, fretfulness, and anxiety so that they leave other parts of his personality untouched — his generosity, his courtesy, his inability to notice the imperfections of anyone he loves. He is not intelligent, but probably he never had been. Memory loss considerably deeper than his may leave intact other significant and lovable human qualities.

Emma and her sisters in caregiving — the Daughters' Club, joined by a few sons like Knightley — could continue to admire their parents' qualities and treat them, however delicately, as whole persons, in part because they weren't handicapped by a diagnostic label that distinguished them from their neighbors. In Austen's village, they treat Mr. Woodhouse carefully but are able to think it normal to provide him with his habitual social world. "Observations of caregivers in several settings have found that, once the label *Alzheimer's* is applied, even normal behavior is interpreted in terms of disease 'stages' . . . and few opportunities are provided to continue meaningful activity," writes Karen A. Lyman.[16]

The Daughters' Club of that earlier time was not encumbered by the help of prognosis. Nowadays it is hard to avoid being told in advance, "It's early dementia." Early implies late, a grim cascading course of events. The prospective decline narrative is ruthless. Other descriptions — like mild or moderate forgetfulness — are more helpful imaginatively: They leave the sweep of the future open and help us look more attentively for a forgetful person's normal behavior and whole character. At low moments, Emma certainly anticipates her father's growing truly ill and dying. Even so, she may be better off for not knowing his cognitive or physiological future with the exactitude that some experts now seem unable not to impart, although further decline may never materialize, or not in anticipated forms. But fortune-telling with a scientific air continues, increasing everyone's anxiety.

There is something gently persuasive about a social world that did not rush into portmanteau diagnoses like Alzheimer's, given the horror that attends it now. Austen's villagers apparently treated a sufferer — at least a well-to-do courteous patriarch — as an individual, with the seriousness and the clever verbal evasiveness that would give him most comfort. Current caregivers are likely to be the first to admire Austen's most mature novel on these new grounds. A full fifth of Americans, predominantly women, are giving unpaid care to a family member or neighbor or friend.[17] They may be too busy to read: I noted somewhere that the average workday for a live-in caretaker is seventeen hours. But our era may be the first to be able to notice the allusions to Mr. Woodhouse's cognitive state and thus the first to properly appreciate Emma's achievement and, not least, Austen's.

A Mother and a Daughter

Austen's first sentences concerning Emma's stricken state at being left tête-à-tête with her father swept me back with shock to April 2005, when I went to stay with my mother after she fell and broke her sacrum, her second fall in four months. She was ninety-one, and had recently, with hardihood, finished healing from the first. She was initially in terrible pain, and it was hard to find a doctor who would appropriately medicate her. Then she would wake up not knowing exactly who she was. She had lost her ability to play Scrabble. I was tending her alone, with aides. My husband was acting in a play back in Boston, and my son had just moved to another continent to be with his girlfriend.

It is so common now, the midlife daughter taking charge of the parent, the falls, the memory loss, the radical uncertainty, the sudden responsibility of taking on another person's whole life, the daughter's active agitated helplessness, like that of a person who, while watching a whole village burn, darts in and out of the fire rescuing small random accessible objects and dances up and down in anger and grief. So common in America, being in the Club of the Caregivers — daughters, sons, friends, spouses — the common heroism. I learned many things in this hard way, some about my character. I was not a saint like Emma; at times I lost my temper as well as my appetite and my ability to sleep. I could be kind and effective but I lacked Emma's resolute and steady sweetness. When my mother got anxious, though, I behaved like Emma. To ensure that conversation ran smoothly for my mother, I was always alert for "a dangerous opening."

When she recovered, my mother moved nearer to us, into an assisted-living community. *She* wasn't giving up. She recovered. She learned to walk yet again, play good Scrabble, tell jokes, and be the philosophically astute person whom the reader met in the first chapter. I risk a few extrapolations. Even over ninety, people can regain sense and sensibility, not to mention strength. The body can heal. Vivi's bruises heal; my mother's sacrum heals. Every situation of cognitive loss is different, and its outcome is unforeseeable. Subsequently, like other daughters and sons, I fell open to the common task — learning much more about current attitudes to people living with memory loss. The stigma of senility arises from our growing terror of the condition. Facing that down requires a different kind of heroism.

In rereading the novel, I followed Emma's relationship with her father with insatiable curiosity and wondered how I had missed it before. And as I began to be pained by the modern American terror of "dementia," I felt a great envy toward that earlier culture of feeling. How was it lost? What in the world is happening to us?

Before 1900: A More Genial Conceptual Landscape

"The physical and mental deterioration of old age appears to have generated less fear and anxiety" in the late eighteenth and nineteenth centuries than it does today, argues Jesse Ballenger, a historian of Alzheimer's disease.[18] Partly this was a result of age hierarchy. Knightley's great anti-ageist speech after Box Hill is about the continuity of respect due to people "whose notice was an honour" when we were young.[19] Adult offspring, with the habit of deference to more powerful elders, perhaps didn't see deterioration as quickly, and certainly not as one-sidedly, as we do. Compassion and gratitude are more dominant among the emotions Emma and Mrs. Weston feel toward the loved parent of one, the former employer of the other.

Yet filial duty can also be a bitter or tragic emotion. Tolstoy in *War and Peace* portrays the increasingly spiteful senile domination of Prince Andrei's father over Andrei and his sister, Mary. But even as Andrei observes his father decline, nothing in his social class or his reading would have permitted him to derogate from the intergenerational standard established in that family. We can't underestimate the power of norms and the early education of the feelings.

Gerontocracy — rule of the fathers — was defiantly battered down, some say by proto-feminist daughters, some say by angry literary sons (Edmund Gosse, James Joyce, Randolph Byrne). Virginia Woolf in *Three Guineas* comments with awe, "[N]o one word expresses the force which in the nineteenth century opposed itself to the force of the fathers. All we can say about that force was that it was a force of tremendous power." George Orwell noted that after the First World War, "the old-young antagonism took on a quality of real hatred."[20] Historians hold that age hierarchy was weakened also by industrialization, rapidly changing technology, urbanization, and the erosion of patriarchal religion.

We shed no tears for gerontocracy, but ageism has been replacing it stone on stone. "Senescence" was discovered and named by G. Stanley Hall in 1921 and the cult of youth swept through the 1920s. Anti-aging medicine *avant la lettre* (sex hormones) was offered to both genders; the monkey-gland and Voronoff operations were targeted to older men; and cosmetic surgery, developed in the Great War for terrible wounds, was offered to elite midlife women. The belief that aging is a decline has stood on tall biomedical platforms in the United States since the early twentieth century. Before then, one historian of old age believes, illness and old age were intertwined but not synonymous.[21]

Age hierarchy was not entirely crushed. Seniority survived in various less rigid forms, in unions and in families and in nonwork settings as mentorship and earned authority. Benign parenting and conscientious filial caregiving still make aging-into-old-age in a family a more decent and affectionate process than a cultural critic might predict, ticking off the losses to decline since 1900. Emma's caregiving is totally comprehensible to anyone who notices it now.

One of the advantages she had is that mind used to be conceptualized differently. As Austen, Emma, and Mrs. Weston impressionistically saw it, Mr. Woodhouse's mind was an organ with many finely varied faculties. If he was forgetful of the needs of others, as a food faddist, say, he was distinctly generous in other ways. If "he could not meet [his interlocutors] in conversation, rational or playful," his speech was always courteous and gentlemanly. In 1793, in the United States, the distinguished physician Benjamin Rush, who had observed people over the age of eighty for five years, wrote a medical text that summarized his longitudinal observations. Ballenger describes Rush's attitude.

"Rush did not regard memory loss, which he thought inevitable and universal in old age, as particularly alarming, for it was not necessarily an indicator of failing 'understanding' or intellect, and still less an indicator of failing moral and religious faculties."[22]

Perhaps most significant, the differentiated faculties were viewed as independent, so that if one failed it wasn't the end of mentation. More important qualities like judgment and morality were seen to survive memory loss. Not just what can be noticed but what can be valued are cultural constructs. "Senility" was available as a medical label, but it was much harder to apply to a particular old person when many valuable qualities were simultaneously observable.

Mind had not yet been medicalized. It was still the vault for higher functions. Even a century ago, "intellect" or "higher thinking powers" were still separate from, and perhaps superior to, "memory" and "the senses," as Rebecca West put it in a formulation that made sense to both philosophers and laypeople.[23] At about that time the landscape of mind acquired yet more varied features: a conscious and a tripartite unconscious—ego, id, superego. The soul was still a valued possession. In short, memory was only one aspect of mind, and in some realms of value not necessarily the most significant. In contemporary science, a remnant of what might be called the concept of multiple functions of mind remains. "Cognitive health," according to the Centers for Disease Control, means "a combination of mental processes we commonly think of as 'knowing' and includes the ability to learn new things, intuition, judgment, language, and remembering."[24] Around such formulations, a richer scientific and anti-ageist philosophical position could be reconstructed.

Medicalization reduced mind to brain. It turned faculties into physical brain locations with vaguer contents like cerebellum and amygdala. Despite valuable discoveries like neurogenesis—the theory that nerves can regenerate at any age, even developing new neural pathways after stroke—the brain is said to naturally decline. Using their billionaire power, the memory researchers harping on aging-as-forgetfulness reduced brain further to memory. Although other researchers study, for example, vision and hearing, it can be argued that memory gets a lion's share of attention. Memory lights up the brain—if we are to believe scientists, literally.

Memory—normal memory—may have replaced reason as the queen of the mind's functions. In the humanities, the "narrative turn" also sanctifies memory by making it the basis of storytelling and storytelling the basis of selfhood, even though narratologists consider normal memory quite unreliable. (Where in this theorizing is the person who is said to be "losing" memories?) Scientists see different problems than anti-ageists. Steven Weinberg, a Nobel laureate, names the problem that William James had noted over a century before: "how to integrate the conscious *mind* with the physical *brain*—how to reveal a unity beneath this apparent diversity. . . . I do not believe anyone has any good ideas about how to solve it."[25] Will any scheme of integration help brain scientists recognize that their language is causing accidents to older people and their loved ones on the speedway of life?

Since 1980

It is only relatively recently and all too quickly that "dementia" became identified as one of the undeniable characteristics of old age. Since 1980, Alzheimer's specifically has become a focus of mental health, gerontology, biomedicine, public policy, and popular apprehension. It was not the actual prevalence of impairments that drove this convergence. Only one in five people over sixty-five have mild or moderate impairment of memory. The overwhelming majority have none.[26] Even over age ninety, only 37 percent have some form of mental impairment. Sixty-three percent do not. It's less likely than most people think. Of the 3.4 million with some impairment, a full million are estimated *not* to have Alzheimer's.[27]

Biogerontology, neurology, Big PhRMA, the media, and Alzheimer's activists have succeeded in emphasizing the totalizing, degrading, and pathetic aspects of the disease and spreading knowledge of its symptoms and costs. Jesse Ballenger makes the interesting case that in the 1980s a crisis around Alzheimer's was created by well-meaning advocates. Ballenger says that they "legitimated their claims for increased research funding [and assistance for caregivers] by citing the tremendous costs" of caring for people living with the disease.[28] In biogerontology, researchers make seeking a heroic cure seem thrilling: raising funding depends on keeping memory loss as the devil. Pharmaceutical companies have a stake in assuring that millions of damaged memories can be stabilized with expensive "anti-aging" pills, although careful scientists declare there is no good way to measure whether they slow down loss. Ballenger also interestingly suggests an ideological component: that in its troubles late capitalism has created anxiety about the "coherence, stability, and moral agency of the self" and offloaded that anxiety onto a new other, the figure of the senile person. [29] Then former President Reagan revealed he had Alzheimer's.

By 1990 a congeries of different forces had definitively made Alzheimer's a new meme, a term one could scarcely not know, a source of jokes trailing scary connotations. Jaber F. Gubrium very early on observed a public culture with "well-worn expressions" that characterized the "dread disease" and provided a military orientation toward it. [30] We live in what Lawrence Cohen, in his introduction to *Thinking about Dementia: Culture, Loss, and the Anthropology of Senility*, calls the Age of Alzheimer's. [31] Americans over the age of fifty-five fear Alzheimer's more than any other disease, even cancer, according to a survey from MetLife. [32] But laypeople commonly use the words "dementia" and "Alzheimer's" as synonyms; we might as accurately call ours the Age of Dementia. Aging itself since the early twentieth century had off and on been treated as a disease, but anyone could have offered commonsense arguments against that view just by pointing to healthy ninety-year-olds in the general population. Dementia — as a characteristic of old age rather than a characteristic of some old people — has made the case much more difficult to argue. We are turning into a hypercognitive and frightened people. [33]

The tight fearful focus on memory loss has cast into obscurity the victims' coexisting faculties. What is being lost is an alternative view of selfhood — the view that Mr. Woodhouse, whether you admire him or pity him, is one of us. In the United States, memory loss has become the sleep of reason. The gentle old Woodhouses, once presiding at their own tea tables discussing their colds, are morphing into figures from Goyaesque nightmares.

After 1990: What It Takes to Notice and to Care

Over the two centuries since Austen's time, critics could not notice Mr. Woodhouse's cognitive impairment or Emma's devoted caregiving, for reasons similar to hers. They too lived in a culture of feeling when, as Emma says in talking of what she owes her father and what she feels for him, filial responsibility could be unselfconsciously based on the almost automatic moral duty and emotional responsiveness of adult children. In Marilynne Robinson's *Home*, published in 2008, Glory, Reverend Robert Boughton's daughter, is one of them.

The first words of the novel, set in the 1950s, have echoes of *Emma*:

"Home to stay, Glory! Yes!" her father said, and her heart sank. He attempted a twinkle of joy at this thought, but his eyes were damp with commiseration. "To stay for a while this time," he amended. . . . Dear God, she thought, dear God in heaven. So began and ended all her prayers these days, which were really cries of amazement. How could her father be so frail? And how could he be so intent on satisfying his notions of gentlemanliness, hanging his cane on the railing of the stairs so he could, dear God, carry her bag up to her room.

Glory stays on until her father dies, cooking fragrant things "to announce the return of comfort and well-being," coaxing him to eat, hiding from him her brother's wretchedness, providing "moments of near-candor."[34]

We hear just a little of her difficulties: "But oh, the evenings were long!" Boughton, a man capable of commiserating with his daughter, after a stroke speaks once in the presence of his son, Jack, about his disappointment in him, in crazed, sardonic, alienated tones that have *Lear* and the Hebrew Bible behind them but more of Boughton's religion of self-respect and upright conduct. Hiding her own shredded feelings, Glory responds to the outburst, "That was so long ago. Can't we put it aside, Papa?"[35] *Home*, a great American novel, is a precious eulogy to caregivers whether or not they can see themselves in Glory's ready tears, selflessness, and poignant forbearance.

Robinson sees a moral dilemma for midlife offspring in the fact that a parent is deficient in some value they prize. Reverend Boughton, despite the goodness of his heart, is indifferent to the justice of the civil rights movement. This blindness is particularly painful to his son, who is secretly married to an African American woman. Robinson implicitly asks, How ought an adult child behave? Jack tries but cannot find an argument to change his father's mind, except the secret he refuses to reveal. Boughton is unable in this stage of weakness to unlearn prejudice and open his heart. It's too late. Robinson sees this as his ethical failure and also a tragedy: it cuts Boughton off from his son and his country's history. Two hundred years after Austen, another woman writer makes respectful allowances for an old man with unalterable limits.

Many caregivers still live in the world of protective loyalty that is now threatened, ignoring the specter of mental deterioration. They don't seem to fear it for themselves. Dudley Clendinen, a Southerner, wrote a book about the long old age of his mother and her friends.

When his mother first had an incapacitating stroke that left her speechless, he and his sister, Melissa, could not have felt more differently about their mother, he writes. "For Melissa . . . being with the woman in Mother's bed was excruciating because she could see only what was lost. I could see only what was still there."[36] The Dudleys of our time may intuit that calling a mind "failed" or "lost" will weaken their own ability to care for the beloved person or their belief that she merits care. Dutiful and affectionate behavior may depend, for some of us, on sealing ourselves off from heart-freezing public debates about end-of-life care and the personal terror of forgetfulness.

Some readers may deny that Mr. Woodhouse has any form of cognitive impairment, veering back to the simplicities of the "polite old man" characterization by ignoring the tender manipulations of his caregivers that I have tried to put into relief. This is a touching and interesting stance: it might manifest a desire to retake a pre-1990 position. Lose the harsh and trendy meme. Pre-Alzheimer's nostalgia, unlike some other kinds of nostalgia, might fight for better directions for our society.

We might be imaginatively enlarged and politically fortified by a capacity to connect Mr. Woodhouse's condition with our contemporary context. Even though Austen carefully refuses to objectify Emma's father except as one among the elders, we may recognize that he is one of the old people — mostly old women — whom Americans fear most — even, sometimes, when they are our own relatives. It is useful to notice this. As a nation we can't retrieve that kinder time before "Alzheimer's" was a dominant category. But we may get past some of the ignorance, misinformation, unkindness, and terror the blanket diagnosis has inspired. The way backward is forward.

We can go on improving care for the cognitively impaired while understanding Austen's treatment of intergenerational caregiving as an implied criticism of current attitudes. Public long-term-care insurance would be an obvious goal. The need is inexorable, and the alternatives unthinkable. Then even if some individual adult offspring cease to identify with their memory-impaired relatives, the nation as a whole takes on the role of the filial caregivers. We become a nation of sons and daughters teaching a way of being, and thus more likely to be well cared for in our turn.

Our culture has a lost a great deal through our dread of "dementia."

Over the past decades, this has contributed to making American age-ism more panicky and cruel. We are damned by the fake tremors of population aging, and by the erosion of the cautious veneration that was once directed so unconsciously toward vulnerable old persons. We certainly burden our longer lives with earlier fear for ourselves growing older. And we may withhold from the afflicted the thoughtful but difficult consideration that should be their due.

CHAPTER 9

Overcoming the
Terror of Forgetfulness

*WHY AMERICA'S ESCALATING DREAD OF MEMORY
LOSS IS DANGEROUS TO OUR HUMAN RELATIONS,
OUR MENTAL HEALTH, AND PUBLIC POLICY*

> *The largest part of wisdom is kindness.*
> BETTY MORGANROTH

Is That Hate Speech Meant for *Me?*

One evening in the fall of 2009, I was guiding my mother on her walker through the wood-paneled dining room of her residential community to a table with an empty seat. Above the fireplace mantel is an incised panel reading, "The Table Is the Best Center of Friendships." One of the men seated at the table was a dapper Harvard alum, possibly as young as seventy-five, whom I will call Jack. (I have changed all the names.) As we approached the seat beside him, I heard a woman behind us say, with a loud, sneering emphasis, "Jack won't like *that*!" Edith, who suffers from mild Parkinson's, meant that Jack wouldn't like having to pass a dinner hour next to my mother. I heard this chilling remark and wondered with a pang whether my mother had too. Even if she hadn't, it will have wounded others who heard it, by prognosticating their own possible social death.

I continued to seat my mother to Jack's left, sure that he would not be rude. To encourage them to include her, I recounted to the others, who also play Scrabble, that in a recent game my mother had made a full word: REALITY. Going out, I glared at Edith. I was angry. But I didn't say anything. Not out of timidity, or automatic politeness, or shocked silence, or because I am superior to insults.[1] Edith is known to be sharp to people she thinks of as losers; she's also a poor soul who could half foresee her own sad future in those four cutting words. Still, others who overheard were likely to think worse of my mother.

I who am not old have nothing to deny, nothing to prove. But for a person who is viewed as "old" it is different. As soon as she feels the age look fall upon her—a look that is some mixture of fear, disdain, reproach, and brotherly love—she must decide: does she or does she not consent to be that person whose role they make her play? *If an old person has decided that old age does not exist for him, the burden of proof is upon him.*

Edith's sentence was sexist, ableist, and ageist. (Sexist because it deployed one of the few men in the community as if he were an arbiter of group values and tried to wield his prestige against another woman.) Ageist hate speech is unlike other kinds in that it doesn't need to raise its voice. It doesn't yell: "Iron my shirt!" at Hillary Clinton or "Get out of your car slowly with your hands up" at someone driving while black. "We need young blood" is said in a boss's enthusiastic can-do tone. When hate speech is ageist, it may seem harmless because we are less sensitized to its range of effects than to racism or ableism. Edith's remark is like calling a grown man "boy" or a child "moron." Hate speech shatters selfhood. Given social reinforcement, it can be virulent. Given sexism, women as well as men can put women down. Given ageism, someone in your own groups may send you to Coventry.

Context is everything. The harm here comes from the growing dominance of cognitive hierarchies over the entire life span. Cognitive competition starts early in life, as soon as innocent children utter their first words: it can be used to divide even twins. This hierarchy hardens in schools, where grades confer authority on assessments of ability. Then it continues in the kinds of jobs in which mental agility—sometimes measurable only by articulateness—is dominant. Ordinary college students and other non-old people are gobbling up "smart pills." The *New Yorker* published an article about the craze soon after the episode in the dining room.[2]

Ageism and ableism among old people are hard for younger people without experience to understand. They assume that everyone in a retirement community is the same age, aka old, and therefore more or less disabled. Old people are supposed to be not just frail but kind— kind to one another, implying some kind of group solidarity. But Wadsworth, the name I have given my mother's residential community, is full of former knowledge workers—professors, editors, administrators — who not only went through the same lifelong curricula but also now read the memory-obsessed media.

After retirement, hierarchies are based on prior status. But status gets reshuffled. Except for Nobel Prize winners and former presidents, it's a game in which few people get better cards. Retirement communities are a bit like freshman year at colleges: places where individuals start over socially while trying to utilize the status acquired earlier. The difference between the oldest and the youngest at Wadsworth is more than thirty years, and even if everyone there were the same age, in nothing do people differ more than in their aging. Edith might not have dared to attack if my mother were still in ready command of her defenses (including lofty disregard and sarcasm) instead of being mild, visually impaired, and using a walker.

Competition can get fierce, fueled by anxiety about decline in a country going hypercognitive, driven by a "What can you do for me today?" mentality. People fear rudeness à la Michael Kinsley, who reported without any shame in the *New Yorker* that when he met a "tiny old man" who said "I used to be a judge," Kinsley simply looked at him in silence, bungling a social interchange he would have handled with respectful interest had a man of his own age said the same words.[3]

People can be ageist and ableist when they are themselves old, because they have internalized the same negatives we all do, because they don't recognize a positive group affinity, or because they are trying to ward off disability personally, as it were magically, and don't know better how to do this. The most virulent form of ageist superiority is like racism or sexism, assuming that that we, that I, can *never* be them. The younger we are, the more liable to this strain. At older ages or with more common sense, our awareness of the difference age makes functions more like classism or ableism. We admit a remote possibility that we might lose ground, becoming downwardly mobile or afflicted, but quarantine those who have already lost. Edith and Michael Kinsley (who also has Parkinson's) perhaps feel themselves be in the second group, stumbling.

When my mother lived in Florida, her friends there were tender toward one another. They had solidarity. Since she moved to Wadsworth, a community of forty-four residents with one dining area, I have witnessed how hurtful status maintenance can be in a world terrified of forgetfulness. Thus my careful placement of the fact that my mother had made a seven-letter Scrabble word. I wouldn't have boasted about this except at this elite table — maybe not even there if I hadn't been rattled by Edith. Given their adherence to the game of cognitive competition, given my inability to change the rules, given my mother's challenges, I wanted her to maintain her standing as long as possible.

Residents tend to shun those who are not their cognitive peers. Physical disability is often not as high a barrier. A person in a wheelchair who is talkative is welcome at most tables. (Wadsworth doesn't discriminate against people if they can manage by themselves, need only assisted living, or have their own aides.) How do the residents sort their peers cognitively? Superficially, and that's part of the harm. My mother is a good listener although hard of hearing in one ear, charming, appreciative of jokes, a long-term political leftie. On July Fourth, she was wearing blue jeans and a red shirt. An aide, joshing, said, "All you need is white." My mother said wryly, "You don't need white. All you need is a flag and an army."

With her halo of perfectly white hair, delighted smile, and careful grooming, she is more striking than she was as a midlife woman. She was a wonderful first-grade teacher and top teacher-trainer for twenty-five years. She retired without regret, and then, finding south Florida a cultural wasteland, she decided to organize trips to attend theater, opera, and dance events, arranging tickets and buses for hundreds of people. For twenty-odd years, she ran this operation by herself as a nonprofit whose proceeds went to the Brandeis library. Her vocabulary is awesome. Her memory for the twentieth-century songbook, political anthems like the "Internationale," Yiddish idioms, and English Romantic poetry is solid. She is helping one of her foreign-born aides with her Graduate Record Exam, defining words like "accolade" and using them in a sentence for her. And anyone can turn to her for advice if they know to.

My daughter-in-law, Yto, wrote in concern when Vivi, at almost three, said, "I want to cut you." I wrote back, predictably, "She doesn't *mean* it. Tell her you love her." On Thanksgiving 2008, I told my mother the story and asked her advice.

"She learned it at preschool, they should deal with the school."

"Yes, but how should Yto and Sean deal with *her*?"

My mother said, "She doesn't know what it *means*. She knows 'Cut it out,' which is an idiom you can say in an angry voice. She knows, 'Cut the paper.' Give her a scissors and let her cut paper. Say, 'We cut paper, we cut hair.'"

I was instantly convinced that my mother was right. There are crucial differences between my hypothesis, "Vivi doesn't *mean* it," and my mother's, "Vivi doesn't know what it *means*." I repeated the advice to Yto and Sean. "My mother is treating this as a linguistic problem, about teaching Vivi how to use the word 'cut' in all appropriate sentences." One benefit is that treating the problem of violence as a language problem also treats it as an ethical one. What is unsaid is, "We don't cut people." Yto wrote back, "Thanks for the advice; wow, Grandma Betty is amazing as usual." Vivi, handed rubber-tipped scissors, construction paper, and rubber cement, took to collage like a born artist.

As I have in earlier books, I quote my mother in this one. You may already have a sense of her character. Over the past few years, this remarkable woman has lost most of her memory. She has forgotten her first husband, my father; and her second husband, my father's older brother; and the lover she had in her seventies, except for their names. She had a fascinating life story, and she doesn't have it to amuse her anymore. But she has retained so much! She is a remarkable psychologist. Is it that M.A. from Bank Street College of Education? The long years in the classroom with six-year-olds, teaching them how to be human? Raising her own children? It all tells. As the anecdote about scissors shows, she has relational memory, where the mind puts together observations and information learned separately in a new way, not to mention judgment; ethical reasoning, intuition, emotional intelligence, based on long experience. Without being accused of partiality, may I call this wisdom? Is that enough of what the CDC labels cognitive health to align her with the rest of us who are still considered human?

More to the immediate point about being shunned, however, my mother has forgotten the names and stories of her fellow residents. She has difficulty seeing them. Her lovely green eyes are sometimes half closed. Despite her warmth, this makes it hard for new people to want to get closer. Older acquaintances don't have the creativity to figure out how to communicate. (I know this lack firsthand — they were problems I had, adjusting after my mother's traumatic falls.) At Wadsworth, my mother sensed her interlocutors' standoffishness. She often chose to sit with people who had more serious cognitive losses — people who spoke less but welcomed her with smiles. This was hard to watch. Yet no one but Edith turned incomprehension into hate speech.

I have a new view of memory loss from going through this experience of my mother's empathetically and keeping in mind how well my mother reasons despite having much less evidence to weigh. She was a good mother even before she became a specialist in early childhood education. She paid for my college education out of her own savings. We've been close since my early thirties. We held long phone conversations at least once a week.[4] Loyalty is not a prerequisite for better observation, but it can be useful.

Now my mother makes conversation out of her forgetfulness, as she used to do about any important event in her life. "What would I do without your memory?" she asks lovingly when I recall a delicious tidbit about her past. (But sometimes she is bored, the way my son is bored when I tell him about his babyhood. They weren't present.) Or she says, "What I don't remember is an abyss." She says, "I am an absentee" much more calmly than I believe I could. In the fall of 2007, she told me, "I seem to have lost my volition." It was true. She had analyzed what was happening to her as well as a neurologist could have. "I have no frame of reference," she states, factually, about a particular person she remembers once knowing well.

She doesn't stop wondering about memory loss. I say, "The data may still be there, but the synapses aren't hooking it together." I tell her some of the causes. Normal aging is the main one: "You're over ninety, after all." Sometimes she is deeply saddened by thinking that she has "no memory," but other times she says serenely, "My memory is my worst enemy and my best friend." Listening to her, whether she is talking about her great-granddaughter or singing "Avanti Populo," I feel I am hearing from a self that lives, quite vitally and often contentedly, on islands of land around the abyss. My mother is more interesting about memory loss and less frightened of it than younger people who tell me they think they are suffering it. Of course I wonder, "How would it be for me, if I were to have progressive memory loss of this kind?" She is teaching me how to be, as she always has.

The former director of nursing at Wadsworth started to use the word "dementia" in relation to my mother—often a polite code for "Alzheimer's," meaning a slide into total insentience. When we'd meet every six months, the nurse would tell me my mother's ever-lower result on the latest "mini-mental"—a ten-item test of memory (last president, season of year), often abused as a diagnostic tool. *En revanche*, I would smilingly repeat my mother's recent Scrabble score, most original witticism or journal entry—one of the million-odd things still available in her mind. One day, almost in a fury, the nurse said to me, "Your mother is *failing*!" To her, my mother's strengths were irrelevant. My emphasizing them thwarted her need for me to agree with the medical view of reality. Once embarked on the decline story, the reality instructors notice nothing else. She thought I was in denial, rather than delivering an alternative reality with a teeth-baring grin.

Well, as a daughter, I noticed and I grieved. And as a care manager, I lost sleep figuring out how to adjust to the next problem, explain it to my mother, mitigate her shock and my own, and get appropriate help if possible. But as a caregiver, to focus on her losses and my pity would be a waste of the time, emotional energy, and intellectual ingenuity I need to figure out her remaining lifelong abilities and help her relish them.

Sometimes my mother wakes from a nap and says with dismay that her mind is totally blank. She sinks in on herself. I rev her up, as it were, with a joke, a topic on which I know she has an opinion, a song she likes to sing. In a short time she is a participant, animated, laughing.

Much Mind Is Left as Memory Departs

How is it possible, that a mind can be so . . . uneven? My mother has few memories and relatively high intelligence. Having so huge a gap between one mental state and another may not be common, but some disparity between states is one of the things people discover who have a loved one with memory losses. The best answer to the why of uneven-ness doesn't come from neurologists, because all they say is that those white dots on the scan are where some of the brain's lights went out. So how come some lights go on again? Bright new lights appear? At best, tech imaging describes a static snapshot when we need an explanation for a dynamic video. Some researchers understand that the brain is re-silient and grows new synapses throughout life. But the best answer seems to be social support. It has miraculous effects on selfhood.

When my mother feels secure, what she can access alters. She con-nects to her best self—good judgment, appreciation of new informa-tion, smart questions and comments on topics where she has expertise. Data and capabilities are lying in wait for a calmer state of mind to find them. Despite some hearing loss, she listens better than most men their whole lives long. I can't tell you how many times my mother has been given the mini-mental, but never has she been offered a test that measures the millions banked in the megamind. Nor do I observe on the part of most of the nurses, doctors, and social workers I encoun-ter with her any sense that attending to the qualities and powers that remain is their goal. They've seen decline. They know in crude outline how it goes. They think pity is appropriate. I see it in their eyes looking at me. They are wrong. Decline's downward slash has misled them.

My mothers' aides — one of whom worked in an Alzheimer's unit — are notable exceptions. "Your mother is *brilliant*," says Mel, the certified nurse's assistant who has known her the longest and at her worst. "She teaches me so much," says her Bolivian caregiver, formerly a music teacher. They use her as a substitute mother, the encouraging, praise-giving figure every adult child wants. They have discovered her strengths as a by-product of using their time with her to ask her advice. Her affectionate doctor, a geriatrician, says offhandedly, with a touch of condescension, "She's so bright, of course she has a lot more left." The trick for everyone is to be willing to find out what is left — or emerging — rather than what is gone.

That word "failing" — with its old test-based grade-school superciliousness — fails to tell much of the story. My mother in fact has regained her character. She had a period of angry grieving over her forced removal from Florida, resettlement in frigid New England, new dependency on me, and feebleness. And in those years, I couldn't rev her up easily. If it took an hour, I would leave drained for the rest of the day. We visited Florida twice. The second time, when it didn't bring her the joy she had expected, she discarded the fantasy that she could move back. And then she miraculously reclaimed her true temperament, generous and serene. If the gallant effort has been invisible, the uncommon success has been plain.

Given how much we all change over the life course and especially in times of loss or pain, she is remarkably consistent again with her previous best self. Self-recognition is what she wants, and — in line with my past theorizing about multiple sequential selves — is what I want for her. Continuity is more or less a fiction. A happy fiction, it becomes more useful as chunks of memory vanish. "I always have a good appetite," says my mother complacently, having forgotten how she lost twenty-five pounds in her sad years.

Technically speaking, my mother has had TIAs — transient ischemic accidents. Six years ago, we happened to be with her for the first. She fell down in Union Square, not far from her grandson's apartment. Twenty minutes later, having tidied herself up, she was chatting and joking. In a medical biography, her "case" would now fall under the diagnostic umbrella of severe cognitive impairment. Her doctor recently pronounced the word "Alzheimer's." But if *this* is the onset of Alzheimer's, why do daughters begin articles with the melodramatic words,

"She didn't know my name"? Abruptness doesn't square with gerontology or my experience. No loss has come suddenly. The surprises are the gains, like the time recently I first heard my mother sing "Du, du, liegst mir im herzen" like Marlene Dietrich and critically gloss the line, "You don't know how good I am to you."

The mind is capacious. Much mental and emotional ability can survive mere memory loss, as Jane Austen knew. And so do other precious qualities that make us human. What a gracious difference it would make if more people knew this. We could turn cognition-related hate speech into a shameful and infrequent act, make our national conversation about Alzheimer's less searing, improve treatment protocols, reaffirm our collective compact with older people, ease our relationships with people who are cognitively impaired across the whole spectrum at any age, and give hope to prospective life-course narratives. What impedes us?

The Era of Stigmatizing the Victims

Creeping dread of age-related cognitive decline is making us obtuse. This particular prospective decline narrative is now casting its dismal shadows over any progress narratives of middle and later life. Squelch all other demeaning hate speech, level inequality of income, make Americans under sixty-five healthier, restore seniority to the midlife — and still this decline discourse would be left standing. The focus on the horror of Alzheimer's combined with the tendency to confuse it with the other cognitive impairments leads to the false conclusion that we are all liable to get "it."

The denial of the personhood of old people — as I experience it at my mother's side — is a peculiar and maddening cultural phenomenon. But the long-term trends make me anxious also about younger people. Emma Woodhouse did not worry about becoming senile herself. The Emmas of our day do. The humane anti-ageist goal is to bring about a better future, not only for people with memory loss, but for all who anticipate that they are liable-to-become-that.

In our hypercognitive society, outbreaks of memory loss are ratcheting up into an epidemic of dread of age-related forgetfulness. Childhood ADD is memory related. Anxiety causes memory lapses, as teenagers realize when returning from exams. But these we don't remark. We have been coerced into noticing such lapses among people in their middle years, not least by their acquiescence in calling them "senior moments." In our culture, this cliché is not casual: every person who admits a senior moment is another sign of the outbreak. Biomedical discourses cause anxiety, Jesse Ballenger argues, by freighting benign memory loss with images of total dementia: "The elevation of memory loss as the primary symptom of dementia was even more graphic in [media] popularizations."[5]

Even if you have no symptom more serious than a spotty memory—which David Shenk, the author of *The Forgetting*, says is "not really a predictor of the disease"[6]—you may already fear dementia. Although the heritability of Alzheimer's is still a question, many adult offspring of parents with the illness fear it. Some people with minor forgetfulness (like difficulty with word recall) imagine they already have it. Between 12 and 30 percent of people who come to memory clinics do not have any objectively diagnosable problem. Often they are depressed about something like divorce.[7] Memory loss and techno-imbecility can be plausibly attributed to the Boomers, young as they are. "Have you lost your car keys?" once mere absentmindedness, is now becoming a clinical symptom dragging you inexorably toward your doom.

Why is the epidemic of fear spreading now? It is not because memory loss is actually striking more people. Age-related cognitive decline may in fact be decreasing, a study of Americans over seventy found, comparing 2002 and 1993.[8] (If increases were coming at midlife, the cause might be unhealthy work: fatigue from increasingly long hours, multitasking, the dangerous trend of not getting adequate sleep.) The epidemic seems to be a case of hysterical noticing of the symptoms described by Alzheimer's advocates, biomedicine, and the media. The competitive workplace exacerbates the epidemic by drawing intense attention to lapses and drawing hostile extrapolations from them. Job insecurity in the middle classes—where hypercognition might as well be a job qualification—heightens susceptibility to the epidemic. Insecurity is rational, especially for people over forty: it derives from high unemployment rates, deskilling, job turnover, downward mobility, deprofessionalization. People of a certain age fear losing both intellectual capital and the reputation of having it.

"Stereotypes of cognitive functioning in older age are more severe than most actual deficits," say Jennifer Richeson and J. Nicole Shelton. They warn that stereotypes, not unprovable deficits, influence interpretations of ambiguous events.[9] With regard to memory lapses in the non-old, insecurity creates anticipations of humiliation, loss of confidence, fear of speaking, self-silencing. Hesitate during a presentation and who knows what people will think?

We are edging close to accepting a new stereotype that cognitive functioning falls off in midlife. Middle-ageism diminishes the value of the whole age class. Anyone who is potentially viewable as nonproductive is at risk long before old age. Having "Oldtimers' disease" in the current productivity crisis of capitalism is like being physically too old was during industrialization and deindustrialization: a convenient rationale for exploiting the midlife age class as surplus labor or abandoning them. The epidemic also serves Big PhRMA as an opportunity to medicate anxious workers with "steroids for the brain." Cosmetic neurology is likely to be sold like cosmetic surgery, as a source of marvelous anti-aging remedies.[10] If my mother takes Aricept even though its value is doubtful, why shouldn't I? While people can resist plastic surgery as unnatural and unaesthetic, what would be the grounds for refusing to power up your brain?

American culture spreads memory lapse virally, stigmatizes it as memory loss, links it to midlife aging, penalizes it heavy-handedly, and raises it to fear of dementia. The panic is dangerous. It weakens the labor force and demoralizes each succeeding generation. Many midlife people have parents who exhibit all too easily recognizable symptoms. The foreboding of the adult offspring may be a two-edged sword. If you, with occasional absentmindedness, live in growing alarm about forgetfulness, does that make it easier or harder for you to engage people with impairments — to look them in the eye? The new director of nursing says there are residents at Wadsworth who think dementia is contagious.

OUR ERA IS LIKE the 1980s in relation to HIV-AIDS, and not only in terms of scientific ignorance, rumors, bad jokes. It's another era of stigmatizing the victims. People fear dementia for themselves partly because of the anticipated cost of their care. In terms of public policy, the right response to the American terror of forgetfulness is more reasonable collective preparation for the home care or long-term care a percentage of us will need. The right response to house fires was to establish fire departments for everyone rather than letting the houses of poor people burn. The focus in the debate about Medicare has been about cost saving rather than meeting critical needs. Instead of socializing the solutions, the budget-crunchers individualize them, saying, in effect, "Deal with your dementia on your own dime."

In a context where overtreatment gets more indignant attention than abandonment, people may accept the idea of rationing health care even if they love their mothers. Some sick elders may receive the treatment they want or decide against interventions, if hospice funds aren't cut. But quiet ageicide might be the outcome for others. Daniel Callahan's book *Setting Limits* cloaked that unsettling idea in language about bad behavior at the end of life, as if people who want to prolong their lives were greedy children to be punished. Callahan thinks that after our late seventies or eighty, we should all voluntarily refuse expensive medical interventions — or be denied them, including being denied insulin if we have diabetes along with "mild impairment of competence."[11] So far has cognitive ability come as an index of humanity that geronticides are willing to set aside the Fourteenth Amendment's equal protection of the laws.

Sharon Kaufman, who has studied end-of-life situations in empathetic detail, says that "dementia works . . . as a rationale for facilitating death."[12] The argument is that there is no quality of life to consider. (This is *my mother* whom the age gaze refuses to see.) Who would decide what constitutes mild impairment of competence? When "dementia" is in play, cutting off old people in extremis can be practiced quietly. The victims may not protest. People with and without cognitive diagnoses tend to trust medical personnel to give them good advice, and that advice might be to let go. Alert members of the gerontological care–community anticipate that end-of-life care is at risk.

As Tony Kushner said about the AIDS context, "In other countries . . . the agents of what we are calling intolerance are called fascists."[13] As we saw, the so-called duty to die is heavily conferred on those sentient enough to worry in advance about losing their minds. We are supposed to worry about the loss of our life narrative, but that is not very rational: a life does not have to be held together by one single narrative.[14] As Proust showed, selves die, or change over time, and selfhood goes on. Likewise, the self goes on in the memory-impaired in new forms. It is rational, however, to worry about future shunning, rejection by offspring, debt, being a burden. With so many people losing jobs, income, pensions, and houses, not being able to pay for end-of-life care might become a larger factor in projections of later-life misery.

The duty to die could become one of those fringe decline stories that policy and discourse transform into hard facts.

There are many reasons to stop using the term "dementia." It is useless as a differential diagnosis. "The concept of dementia is obsolete," Dr. Vladimir Hachinski writes in the *Journal of the America Medical Association*, "It combines categorical misclassification with etiologic imprecision."[15] Diagnosis depends on which testing criteria are applied, and there are many impairments to differentiate. Aside from four subtypes of possible Alzheimer's, there are the Lewy body type, vascular cognitive impairments, frontotemporal, traumatic brain injury — a range of different types, including those following TIAs like my mother's, and "cognitive impairment without dementia."[16] And there is age-related memory loss, which occurs in a different part of the brain from Alzheimer's, according to neurologist Scott Small of Columbia. Hachinski concludes, "Creating a dichotomy between dementia and nondementia ignores the spectrum. . . . Cognitive impairment should be considered as a continuum."[17] Such critiques leave Alzheimer's a hollow label, but one with malevolent effects. The women or men who are considering preemptive suicide to avoid Alzheimer's — are they really competent to diagnose in themselves a condition that experts are unsure about?

But the clincher for me is that in our world dementia and its synonyms often amount to hate speech. Those harping on population aging incessantly provide us with forecasts about the increase in the number of people over eighty, or over eighty-five, the percentage that will have Alzheimer's, and how expensive "their" care will be. Such forecasts can have hostile effects. It is hateful to have to hear the costs magnified without sympathy for the sufferers. Speakers or writers need to explicitly eschew the duty-to-die argument and make clear that their goal is to remind us of the sanctity of human life and to urge the polity to plan now to fund caregiving. As far as I am concerned, everyone who smiles at the Conan O'Brien joke about the moderator of the AARP debate can stop smiling. Comedy is often calcified bias. Nancy C. Cornwell writes, "The ethic of care recognizes that the harm of hate speech may not be easily quantified, empirically measured, visually observed, or even causally linked to a specific hate speech act."[18] Too true. But with the whole cognitive/cost juggernaut in motion, it could be a quickstep from today's tiresome joke about "Oldtimers' disease" to the decision of some task force — at the Centers for Medicare and Medicaid or Health and Human Services — to link dialysis triage to cognitive diagnoses.

I fear the human, economic, and political consequences of our dread. The memory impaired need to be rescued from the memory obsessed. The memory obsessed need to be rescued from their fears for themselves.

My Mother and I Fall Down

When my mother fell for the first time, at the age of ninety, injuring two vertebrae, I flew to her home in Florida. That was when I first became afraid of her, my darling mother. It happened the instant I arrived. She had refused to go to the hospital; she had weathered the pain for four days. Only when it got really bad did she call me. My trip down had been an agony of apprehension. When the door of her apartment closed on the two of us that first night, she at times shrieking, wailing, "I want to die," with only Tylenol in the medicine chest, I was suddenly responsible for curing the pain immediately, getting her healed, managing her care, her finances, her life — everything. It's hard to talk about that time now; it was so hard to endure. I force myself to write some of it mainly because it enables me to explain as much as I know about the fear, and to talk about how I overcame it. Even though every story is different, that might be useful. Even the anticipation of having to provide care provokes anxiety.[19]

If at first it was her pain I couldn't endure, soon it became her cognitive losses, her disorganization, her loss of selfhood. I had spent my career mostly analyzing the midlife, not studying gerontology or nursing. I was ignorant, unprepared; I let myself be overcome with wearying pity for her and for myself. At the same time, I was forced to be active — get a pain manager, a commode, a wheelchair. Made of iron like her Eisner father, who lived to age ninety-six, and resolute about recovery, she easily learned how to walk again, with a walker and then a cane. She walked through the apartment some mornings looking at the photographs of us, saying, "I don't know who I am when I get up. Lucky I have all these pictures here. They are my joy." The first time she shuffled into the living room with her maid, in her pretty robe, and hobbled from photo to photo, saying sadly, "I don't know who I am," I wanted to fling myself off the balcony on the twenty-second floor to not be a witness.

As she got better, I had to keep reminding her that she was making progress, because she couldn't remember what her old state had been like. Taking the mini-mental, she could subtract sevens backward from one hundred faster than I, but had forgotten how many tiles each player drew for Scrabble. I didn't see how I could ever leave. I remembered Virginia Woolf saying of her father, that if he had lived until ninety, she would never have a life. "His life would have finished mine."

Living in the eternal kingdom of anhedonia, I became stupid from anxiety and insomnia. Even when my husband, David, came armed with computer, disks, and rolodex for me, I couldn't manage anything but what was essential for her. Even when she was asleep and the aide was there, I could find nothing to do to distract myself from the curse laid on us. I wasn't suicidal; I knew I couldn't do that to her, to David, to our son. It just seemed sensible to stare out at the ocean from behind the windows and not from over the railing.

I remembered the four months in 1974 that I spent helping my mother care for my father when he was dying of ALS. But she had been in charge then, a capable woman of sixty, while I had been a mere acolyte of thirty-three. Now I was alone, without her guidance. The responsibility was harrowing. And it was humiliating to think that my mother at sixty had been able to do so calmly and competently what I at the same age but in far less dire conditions did in agitation and wretchedness.

As my mother got better, she was taken off the brain-altering painkillers. I wangled her into making her own breakfast again, persuaded her to exercise. But she refused to take walks even if accompanied. I feared anorexia, muscular atrophy, being housebound, alienation. She couldn't set an hour for a visit from a friend. Was this inability the result of empty memory (the loss of a social habit), vanished initiative, the long-term effects of taking the powerful medications, or depression? And what would I do about any of it if I ever figured it out? I was overwhelmed by a confusion that seemed no more soluble than her own.

It was a miracle, a normal miracle, that her body had healed. But there was still her life, her diminished memory and social life, to deal with. When I left I called every other day, expecting to hear and then hearing how she hated the aides, how the food was cold and bad, how she had no friends. It was, though she never said so, my fault for forcing these strangers and this stifling life on her independent self. And then before I could get my own life back, she fell again, this time breaking her sacrum; and I moved in again and it started all over.

The Enlightened Ones

While the research scientists are trawling the brain molecule by molecule for cures for Alzheimer's with no cure in sight, what do the rest of us do with our growing fear of dementia?[20] People don't yet see that we are in a bad phase of the evolution of social responses to the epidemic of fear. As in the 1980s, they can't imagine an America less terrified. But reducing the dread is possible. Within the scientific community and among writers on cognition, a new consensus is forming about how to respect selfhood that is mingled with forgetfulness and restore the dignity due to everyone who lives to be old. Many experts now favor the spectrum model Dr. Hachinski describes rather than the implicit binary them/us. On a spectrum, everyone can be seen as closer to one another. It isn't as if high I.Q. is an American birthright. High-performing midlifers who complain of new forgetfulness are remembering themselves as more perfect than they were. Mild cognitive impairment (MCI) is what numerous Americans are born with. "Neuroatypicality," another term that is coming into favor, can be applied to people of all ages, including those with autism and Down's syndrome.

"Dementia" might eventually lose ground in mainstream speech as it is slowly doing in neurology, medicine, and gerontology. "The dementias" could come to be preferred because the plural allows for diagnostic differentiations. But many experts and caregivers prefer "cognitive impairments." The term comprehends people of all ages rather than singling out the elderly. Properly used, it might avoid the danger that a disease called MCI could profiteeringly be attributed to everyone as they age into midlife. "Cognitive impairments" has the advantage of leaving room for positive attributes that even the plural "dementias" crowds out. It eschews the pejorative adjective "demented" or the hideous "dementing." The goal is to treat everyone — not only the people we love but also people we don't know — as if each mind were unique. To the best of my knowledge, this is the most advanced age-studies position.

The people who can help us most right now and in the foreseeable future are not the neuroscientists but those who are "imagining a better life for people with memory loss," in the motto of Ann Basting's book and Web site, Forget Memory (http://forgetmemory.org/). In the cartoon strip *Doonesbury*, Garry Trudeau has invented a new character, a young Iraq vet with traumatic brain injury (TBI). He is befriended by the midlife vet, B.D., who lost a leg in Iraq. B.D. now coaches at a football camp and invites the kid to join: "YOU'D FIT RIGHT IN. HALF THE STARTERS HAVE TBI." The kid answers, "HA! NOW YOU COMEDIAN!" and B.D. says, "NO. REALLY. ALMOST NO ONE'S BUILDING MEMORIES."[21] Only a genius could think of making that line a consolation. Trudeau is guessing that Americans may be more open to humanizing a boy with TBI, even in a Goth shirt, than an older person with a TIA. *Doonesbury*, which has become a graphic life-course novel about three generations, is concentrating in this subplot on how to heal our social biases against cognitive ableism.

Artists and writers are going public about their own healing. Alix Kates Shulman has published *To Love What Is* (2008) about living with the love of her life, her husband Scott York, after he suffered a traumatic brain injury. Scott encouraged Alix to publish their story to help others. I discuss *To Love What Is* in chapter 10. Elinor Fuchs's *Making an Exit* (2005) is full of quotations from her conversations with her mother, whose high gibberish was fluent, funny, Beckettian, and marked at times by total lucidity. Elinor reacted to some of it with equivalently playful speech. She participated in conversations with her mother's fellow nursing home residents not with irritation or haste but by companionably following their lead.

One of the art therapists with new ideas, Elizabeth Lokon, has made a video about helping people with Alzheimer's produce beautiful abstract art. Watching, we first see two vivid paintings side by side. "One was done by my husband [an artist]," she says, "the other by a man with Alzheimer's. Which is which?" In the audience we couldn't tell. Her big idea for volunteer teachers and activities directors is that their model can't be art for preschoolers, with coloring books that have to be filled in or the idea that a task has to be done correctly. These projects set people up to fail, and failing feels bad. It is cruel to believe that people with cognitive loss don't know when they fail, so that it doesn't matter if you set them up to do so.

In Elizabeth's video, a heavyset older man carefully dipping his brush into gold paint and then gilding his paper, working in utter absorption, illustrates "being in the flow." Lokon asks the participants in her workshop to sign their art if they can, shows them their art the next week (some recognize it), and praises it again. Lokon studied with

Anne Basting, the pioneer whose work with Alzheimer's patients produced poems that Basting worked into a fine play, *TimeSlips*.

The coalition of the like-minded includes not only a cartoonist, memoirists, and art and poetry teachers but, importantly, caregivers, who are personally interacting with people with memory loss, and scholars from all fields who are theorizing and historicizing and personalizing cognitive disability — feminists, phenomenological psychologists, humanistic gerontologists, ethicists, medical anthropologists — in short, people from all walks of life who have not fled the experiences but come closer to them in spirit. The guru of the movement is an Englishman named Tom Kitwood, a psychiatrist who taught himself a whole new paradigm he describes in *Dementia Reconsidered: The Person Comes First* (1997). His book is like a calm hand on a fevered brow.

This anti-ageist coalition revitalizes the concept that memory is only one aspect of mind — not necessarily the most important aspect of selfhood. We have to believe it sincerely. Some writers are attending to "the *gifts* of persons with memory loss and mental confusion," in the graceful words of Susan McFadden, a psychologist, and her colleagues.[22] Many theorists are, like me, emphasizing such other values as intelligence, logic, creativity, warmth, humor, empathy, imagination, moral judgment, which survive for a long time in people living along the whole spectrum of impairments. This recognition enables caregivers to change too, becoming more empathic toward people who may feel "terrifyingly incompetent" or "outclassed," as Tom Kitwood puts it, by reaching into our own similar experiences of feeling powerless and abandoned. We may also slow ourselves down through physiological empathy, enjoying — as I sometimes find I do with my mother — a relaxation response. Caregivers get back something wonderful from the people they soothe, he says knowledgeably. "The quality of interaction is warmer, more rich in feeling, than that of . . . everyday life."[23]

Science, it seems fair to say, will not eliminate the category of old people living with memory loss, either through prevention or cures. But we can learn how to relate better to our loved ones, strangers, and our possible future selves. All of these enlightened people teach us. Perhaps it is too much to call this loose coalition a movement, but it is the primary current hope for reducing the agonies of the terror of forgetfulness. And all my contacts with it, although they came late in the process, helped me, and my mother, get back up.

My Mother and I Get Up; or, What I Learned

In time — a lot of time — I overcame pity and terror. I overcame terror as everyone does, by getting closer to the feared object, in this case my dear mother. I did it by being attentive to her selfhood, by trying out ways of talking to her that helped her through her anger and anxiety and me through mine. I had somehow forgotten in the travail how loving she was, how unusual our relationship had been, how she edited my work, bought me clothes, praised my successes. I had relied on her as a guide, friend, and parent, a model for caregiving with her father and my father. I always told my son how remarkable she was, suggested he turn to her for advice. I had set her up as an example to my friends (in my enthusiasm forgetting that other people did not always have good mothers). I had written about her in book after book. Her belief in progress had been a guide through my life, emotionally and cognitively.

I got my writing life back once she healed after the second fall and moved here. I stopped feeling her mental state might be contagious. That must have happened unconsciously as I discovered that I didn't have to match every negative emotion she experienced. I didn't have to follow her lead into sorrow, or berate her out of feeling bad. Berating her produced an angry cycle that, as a good mother, she would break with an apology, or a calming, "Let's change the subject, dear." But when she could no longer be benevolently maternal, I was the one who had to become pacific. For a while in Florida I had treated her as badly as some people treat their seventeen-year-olds: not smart enough, not outgoing enough, not living up to her potential. She had long before internalized the same standards. After I stopped, she would still say, "I'm doing my best." I say, lovingly, squeezing her hand, "Your best is very good indeed." She accepts that truth.

I continually reinvent a conversational style that suits her and that I can maintain. It has fewer low notes about politics or culture and omits sad revelations about the family. I have to practice concealments. But it has virtues. It has a lot of singing and joking and teasing. Since she is free of pain, I always ask with apparent concern, "How do you feel, Mum?" so she can answer, "Perfectly well, baby." When her eyes became too bad for Scrabble, I invented a kind of anagram game with Scrabble letters.

But how did I escape grief? That is the burning question for loving caregivers, I assume, how not to be disabled. Would that Austen had addressed that issue! In me terror and pity and anger were so intertwined at the beginning that I was overcome. Even though I knew I would perform better if I could control them, I couldn't do it without help.

Kitwood might say that eventually I dealt with the psychospiritual crisis that often afflicts family members: "our own issues of love, and grief around the failures of love."[24] I had to grieve over what my love would fail at, to be sure, but take solace in how it could succeed at giving companionship, comfort, security, recognition, occupations, interests. At the same time, I fought the temptation to drop into prospective decline narrative. I refused to read *The 36 Hour Day*, which Alix Shulman and others recommend. It sits dusty on the bookshelf beside my bed. If my mother were not going to take the expectable path — if no one takes the exact same path — I would have to figure out what path she was taking and follow her where she went. There were really no shortcuts for that.

As a literary critic, I long ago felt dismay at decline narrative and mild aversion to some of its fictional expressions. As a progressive cultural critic, I came to detest the ugly carelessness of the powers foisting decline on the midlife masses below, who found henchmen to distract them with "Boomer power" and to deride radical social change. All the prospective decline stories — about sexuality, the body, cognition — were at bottom complicit: hope-denying and deluded about the power of resilience. Lately I see how blind decline ideology is to the interests of people like my mother — pressing on my temples to reduce her to a banal character in a preordained plot. If my antagonism to decline goes deeper than before, that's the reason.

Now, I don't repeat her saddest lines to myself; I don't write them here. If I call the situation "progressive forgetfulness," it's because I have noticed what has really happened over the past four or five years, not because I imagine how it will get worse. I refuse crystal balls. If this is naiveté, leave me to hoard my tiny hot spark of hope.

I always come in with good news. I can still share with my mother the kind of problems that enable her to use her optimism to encourage me, as she always did. Sometimes it's the same good news or problems I used earlier in the week or even the day before. Elinor Fuchs's high example originally discouraged me: I can't be an actress like her, I convinced myself. But I came to like conversational routines, even rather silly routines. I enjoy making them up or reminding my mother of her own, knowing they'll give her a pleasant conversational opportunity. I enjoy performing them. My mother has a marvelous laugh. She likes to laugh.

I had to stop thinking, "This is a tragedy," although the situation could be said to have the ingredients Aristotle taught us to look for. For a long time I dreaded the moment when *she* would decide that her life had become tragic. Even when things went smoothly, I would ask myself, "How will I live with a woman, my darling mother, who has spent her whole life believing in progress narrative and making it real, and watch as she realizes that now it is ending?"

What helps most is the fact that she stays with her progress narrative. If I wanted to experience her old age as a decline, I would have to dwell on it when she merely mentions it, or remind her of it when she forgets. Otherwise I would be doing decline pretty much alone. Her story has changed a little. It is about how lucky she has been, what a lovely life she had, how dear her aides are to her. "Why is everyone so kind? How do I deserve it?" How she manages her charming generous equanimity is a temperamental secret of her own. (I fear that I did not inherit enough of it to make me, if I live to old age, the adorable and adored person she is.) I marvel at this ability. I admire her.

CHAPTER 10

Elegies and Romances of Later Life

ARE THERE BETTER WAYS TO TELL
OUR SADDEST LATER-LIFE STORIES?

*When someone remarked in his hearing that he had lost
an eye in the war to free the slaves, the abolitionist preacher
said, "I prefer to remember that I have kept one."*
MARILYNNE ROBINSON, *GILEAD*

Not everyone tries to avoid decline narrative. Some readers and writers even prefer it, the more apocalyptic the better. Cormac McCarthy's *The Road*, in which a man and his young son roam an infernal world where food no longer grows and cannibals stalk the highways—the two are doomed as soon as we discover the donnée—has won critical praise and been made into a movie. Anyone picking up Annie Proulx, another much-admired American writer, knows that her hardscrabble characters are going to be relentlessly mowed down by war, work, accident, poverty, the oppressions of gender or sexual identity.

The grim atmosphere of decline—its scarring details, its steady lunges toward the disaster foretold, the reader's rush of adrenaline and accelerating heart rate as the risks rise for the protagonists—carries a subtextual message. Decline implies that losing, viewed realistically or allegorically, is the way the world goes. It's our doom.[1] Analysts of decline's fictional conventions might say that readers can be judged by how much of its purported realism they can endure.

Aging-as-loss can't sustain me as a writer forever.
DOROTHY BARRESI, POET

The narrative of decline-through-aging has its aficionados too, for similar reasons. I think they like the shudder. The unkindness of the story arc is a punishment they accept. They defend its truth-value: Aging-as-decline is a fact of science, declaimed from those high biomedical platforms with unshakeable faith. The body-mind is a time bomb attached to fuses of unknown length (sometimes called telomeres, but the name changes). Although many old people happily seem not to act or speak as if their fuses were lit, decline fiction confirms aging-as-loss through its chosen protagonists or narrative voices. Time — lifetime — is the enemy. Anxiety and dread are the appropriate responses. We are all inevitably victims. In Philip Roth's *Everyman*, a not-very-old body relentlessly deteriorates, watched by a sour mind. "Old age," as a character says, "isn't a battle; old age is a massacre."[2] The biogerontologists promise that they alone, like Foreign Legionnaires coming over the dunes to the rescue, can make it a "battle."

In narratives where aging is intrinsically a decline, there are psychological versions in which character becomes as fixed a fate as biology. The protagonist needn't be old physically; many decline writers choose midlife as the time of life by which determinism already rules. Nabokov's Humbert-Humbert in *Lolita* (1955) is in his middle years, but no possible change in the world or the self can ameliorate his condition. Pedophilia is almost too perfect an allegory of decline's relationship to growing older. The perpetrator, as if no other identity but being an aging being mattered, cannot control his drive to try to recapture the remote, wondrously remembered sensations of his youth.[3] His obsessive behavior — say, in marrying Lolo's unattractive mother to get at the nymphet herself — might seem peculiar to readers with a different relationship to their own puberty, time, or midlife women. What makes sense out of Humbert-Humbert's feelings is decline's cult of youth. An oblique adoration of one's past, a one-sided fixation on losing over time — many people identified with this in the 1950s and still do. Men may romanticize their adolescence more than women do, which would lay them open to midlife angst even if they don't lose their jobs, their hair, their erections, or other identities that decline strips from them or reminds them of every other day.

Decline narrative even sans pedophilia can insinuate to its non-old readers — always presumed to be healthy and beautiful — a very American inflection of hostility to eventual "losers." Its ageism is often success oriented, "looksist," and ableist. No disability movement, no positive-aging vitality, has so far subdued decline's disgust with the non-young body and the thrill of the vocabulary that conveys it. Squeamishness drags riveting details of organic processes and helplessness into fancy language in creative writing classes and little magazines.

It takes both high art and plausible philosophy to make determinism palatable. To me, *The Road* is repulsive as an imaginative vision, even if its goal is to warn against nuclear winter. Its suspense is phony, since a dreadful death is inevitable for father and son as well as for the cannibals. The only suspense is *how*. The future horrors I am forced to keep in mind — and my thwarted hopes that the hardened, obstinate father might protect his vulnerable son — jointly overwhelm me. It's not good for me to smash my precious instinct of empathy against the dense steel of such plots. That's not what I need to learn about dealing with inevitabilities.

If critics object to the genre, we can be taunted: "Can't face the facts?" It's a judgment on the reader, not the writer if, anticipating decline's rigid patterns, I refuse the narrative experience — to be vicariously defeated — and close the unfinished book for good. Dorothy Barresi, who now says decline can't sustain her writing, once wrote that as we round forty our children kill us:

> The young are God's gun.
> Our DNA, re-
> mastered in a cool gel matrix
> wearing a little slip of a sundress . . . [4]

It would be useful if writers who formerly used decline for its literary and emotional turn-ons were not only to turn against it but explain why and what now sustains them.

Beauty, love, endurance, for starters. Proulx's novella *Brokeback Mountain* has enough of all three to make its arc bearable. The beauty of style confers vividness on the landscape, on unexpected youthful passion, and most of all on an enduring same-sex love that does harm to wives but survives the death of one of the partners and the aging of the survivor. *Brokeback Mountain* admires a lover who can weather violence and time. It's not a decline story, finally, but a toughminded elegy.

Refusing Decline through Elegy

Marilynne Robinson's *Gilead* (2004) — from which I have drawn the epigraph that opens this chapter — is a tender elegy. *Gilead*, in my view an even greater novel than Robinson's *Home*, is told by John Ames, who is only seventy-six but suffers from angina. He tells his young son in the first sentence of his first letter to him that his father "might be gone sometime." Telling the truth, but through euphemism letting him down easy.[5] John Ames's late marriage and fatherhood have finally enabled him to feel "very much at home in the world." He has a lot to lose, but he's going through the anticipatory period calmly and deliberately. *Gilead* dispels Ames's doom and the conventions of decline through the triumphant creation of a plain, kind, funny, homely, respectful, narrative voice, a voice that refuses self-dramatizing rhetoric, self-pity, and the bitter side of irony. It's rather amazing that elegy, a genre traditionally used for eulogizing another, can be achieved through autobiography, by definition a self-centered genre. A modest man can shed sweetness over our precious world through his praise-filled observations. Only later do we discern that Robinson has also written an elegy for Ames through his own voice. *Gilead* refuses attrition also by giving the narrator a plot, in Ames's case, an ethical plot about repelling his own jealousy. Plots are fictional signals that *wanting* is going on: Wanting, for most of us, is a synonym for living. Wanting to become a more perfect being in relation to others is one of the ageless goals anyone can aim for.

We defy our animal dooms, of which we are humanly conscious, through love, friendship, grace, rage, humor, through prayer, forgiveness, and hope. We do so also from a need to protect normalcy, an ability to expand our definition of the normal. Level-headedness may grow out of self-reflection and self-acceptance. You may know a number of common abilities this list leaves out. My point is, Defy the harsh depressiveness of doom first.

There's far less need to deny loss once we have carefully named what has also been retained or newly achieved. It's actually my father's example, rather than my mother's, that first helped me live my way into understanding this difference when losing is truly dreadful. I came to help my mother care for him as the amyotrophic lateral sclerosis was taking away his speech and swallowing ability. In the popular mind, ALS is perhaps the most doom-laden of diseases, a synonym for decline. In the 1970s it was also exceedingly rare. Its progression (as doctors horribly call it) is always uncertain. I knew his future — our future — in only a mercifully vague way. I saw my father then and I see him now as a heroic figure. This hardheaded man, so powerful in his hatred of injustice, was never angry at those who were caring for him, never openly angry at the unfairness of dying at sixty-nine, so comparatively young and strong. Only in my thirties then, I started off terrified, my brain screaming that he was dying. I was wrong. I saw him die. But the "end of life" was all life.

Conscious and stoical, letting us help him without complaint or embarrassment as he came to need more help, he read his newspaper. He continued to work in the garden for as long as he could. After he couldn't speak, he laboriously wrote out a poem he had memorized in his youth — Emerson's "The Rhodora." He didn't want pity. It was all life, those active determined months when he yielded no unnecessary inch in the fight to be in control of his body. His living went on until that last early morning in August when his final soft breath sighed forth clearer than birdsong. I wrote a book about all this, never published, called *Determinations*.[6] The title meant both what the disease decided, unbeknownst to us, and how he, and my mother and I, resistantly responded. Did my father get any important part of what he wanted? He got us. He got to die at home. That's what he had said he wanted. Did it count? It's because I didn't know his answer that the memoir was meant as an elegy — to my father, to my mother, to their mismatched but eventually united marriage.

Elegy is one exit from decline's dangerous highway. Tragedy is another. An elegy is a tragedy written ten years later, or whenever the bitterest shock starts wearing off. On the last page of an elegy, there may seem to be next to nothing left for the empathetically weary reader, but the completed story affirms that something of value, now lost, is being appropriately mourned. We do lose, over and over, but as Elizabeth Bishop says in her incantatory poem, there can be an art to it.

PERHAPS THE QUESTION should be, What counters despair's taste of iron? There are other generic ways of dispelling aging-as-decline. These ways do not harp on older people's status as losers or on the subtractions of time. Nor do they merely encourage us to remember that even the physically challenged survive every minute — "except," as John Updike says somewhere, "the last." The most successful narratives about aging-into-frailty or aging-toward-death go beyond that remedial task. They fortify us for the work of coping with terrible challenges in our own lives or the lives of others close to us. I have called — dared to call — some resistant fictions "progress narrative." Doesn't that get less plausible as the situation gets more stark? We'll see to what extent any definition of progress fits the two groundbreaking memoirs I describe below.

Leaving aside Beckettian black humor, what most often helps readers endure vicarious loss are the protagonists' subjective qualities and close human relations, surviving the vicissitudes. If we stick with such novels, it's because the characters we grow old or sick with are more interesting than the clichés. Defiance, equanimity, rejection — we welcome the punch of complexity when the alternative is the monotonous pornography of decline: at regular intervals, another collapse ascribed to aging. Resilience sometimes even seems to grow through mounting hardship. In Doris Lessing's innovative novel *Diary of a Good Neighbor*, Maudie Fowler, a ninety-two-year-old woman who is one of the "infinitely deprived"—weak, poor, ill-housed, and sick with cancer, proud, angry, charmed by life, and befriended by a midlife fashion editor — is imagined as saying "Dreadful, dreadful" and is actually heard to say, "This is the best time of my life."[7] Both are credible. Lessing is wise to include the second. Anti-ageist literature challenges the grueling negativity and automaticity of decline but not by facing away from loss.

To Love What Is

Alix Kates Shulman's memoir, *To Love What Is*, is a thrillingly balanced meditation about confronting losses by naming the survivals and gains just as carefully. The book starts when Alix's beloved husband, Scott York, then seventy, falls out of their loft in the middle of a dark night, dreadfully injured and far from medical help. The suspense that opens this artfully structured book doesn't let up in the events that follow Scott's fall. Suspense deprived of hope creates dread, but true suspense leaves outcomes open. Suspense here means that to the author as well as to a character some goal really matters — rescuing a person, discovering truth, finding romance. Suspense can be a sign of caring and a way of getting the reader to care.

In *To Love What Is*, two people are made to matter: Scott, the victim, and more indirectly, Alix, the narrator and caregiver. The first suspense is Alix's about Scott: Can he be rescued? Will he live? What brain functioning will he have after a second accident in the hospital? As he starts to recover, will he learn to make art again? What will happen to their relationship when it is no longer equal? Scott's condition more or less stabilizes — in the sense that a dubious war is going on between the healing that can follow traumatic brain injury and the deterioration expected from his Alzheimer's. "Once again, irony rules. If time is the one thing in Scott's favor when it comes to TBI, it's also working against him when it comes to the dementia. The former, time alone may help, while the latter, time can only worsen. Entering the final stretch, better and worse again run neck and neck, racing each other against time."[8]

"Dementia" is a word Alix uses sparely. Scott's behavior alters, but not entirely. From time to time he shouts even at Alix, and once he strikes her — she calls the police but he is himself again when they arrive — he can curse at his caregivers and drive them away. But the memoir shows how much of his character is left intact despite his cognitive and emotional impairments. Scott comments on each section of the book as Alix reads it to him. An artist, he is entranced by beauty and remembers Christo's Gates in Central Park. His social skills are unflawed, charming. He loves her; he is grateful to her.

AS WE ACCEPT HIS unexpected human status, midway between the extremes of progress and decline but poised toward further loss, Alix's story, more latent, comes more to the fore. The suspense about Alix also starts early, but it is internal and psychological. Can she cope with finding her husband crumpled on the floor, naked, unconscious? (She finds her cell phone in the dark and calls 911.) Can she face understanding how the accident happened? (She doggedly lists five mistakes she made that led to it.) Can she bear her fourteen-hour-a-day hospital stakeout to keep him safe? "Now I'm a lioness stalking prey," she says of her attempts. Can she give a year of her life to his recovery? "There was no one else to do it and nothing else remotely worth doing. It became my mission, my passion, my obsession, displacing every other."[9]

The suspenseful issues are proxy experiences for readers to estimate their own limits and powers when so many kinds of worsening decline threaten. Alix's mistaken belief that Scott will recover within a year gives her fortitude: Can that survive into the second year? Can she bear to live with a man so different from the man she married, with a new implied contract? — "And now our solitude and freedom have been reduced to mere abstractions, as all privacy is wiped out and his disability renders him utterly dependent, making prisoners of us both." She is necessary—"I alone can detect subtle changes in his condition and anticipate his needs"—but is that sufficient?[10] The middle of the book is actually harder to bear than the end—bringing him back so changed to their beloved home, getting him to accept strange "Scott-Watchers," patient companions who can bear his outbursts and relish his personhood as she can do.

What is not in suspense is that this is a love story, about two people and "the enchantment of life" (crucial words crucially located on page 2). The memoir starts from the marriage vows they made in midlife, almost two decades before; and right after the 911 operator sends help, the narrative jumps back to the moment she first fell in love with Scott—"blond, blue-eyed, and fabulous"—in a college classroom, fifty-five years earlier. The past continues to break through the present, in alternating sections. The past is not forgotten, it's not even past, in Alix's mind. She remembers every meeting distinctly: first date, first sex (Scott even now remembers the motel room number). After a brief affair, they married other people, divorced, and met and fell in love again later. She wanted him, and she finally got him.

Do they still have sex? (Yes, and a brief sexual autobiography follows, about how she discovered orgasm in later life with Scott.) At night they often cuddle in bed with frozen yoghurt watching movies. "If it doesn't bother him that he doesn't know what's going on and forgets the movie the minute it's over, it doesn't bother me that my wry commentaries go over his head. . . . When he kisses my hand and says for the hundredth time, 'I can't believe how lucky we are,' I know it's not the brain injury talking, because in that moment I feel the same." She clears away decline conclusions first. "[T]hose who assume we're in mourning for our former life are wrong." "He is mine, and I am his," she writes, more ambiguously.[11]

Alix changed herself in ways most of us probably can't imagine accepting. She started the process when Scott had an earlier heart attack: "[T]he self-protective resistance I'd cultivated all my life melted away as I embraced instead devotion."[12] Feminism had abetted her native independence: she had watered it with intellectual fearlessness, love of solitude on her island, self-sufficiency, political activism, and literary success. She was one of the fiery second-wave few who fought sexism almost alone. She became famous as a writer: *Memoirs of an Ex-Prom Queen* has sold a million copies.

Now, in her seventies, with this new emergency, she undoes some of what embattled feminism enabled. She had begun to think about giving up the future-oriented career self, based on "work accomplished, knowledge accumulated, habit inculcated, skills expanded." But she is under no illusions: "Still addicted to hope, which always faces forward, and with no diminishment in energy despite my age, I knew it might take considerable effort to pull off such a change."[13]

Even a partial change of selfhood takes mastery. In desperate hours of Internet speed-cramming, Alix finds the best research on cognitive impairments and shares it. She learns from texts how to deal with changes in mood and cognition, and then must make the advice habitual: "I know I must *prevent a crisis before it starts*, but I can't be better than I am or do more than I can do." She learns from Scott, who has not only a traumatic brain injury and Alzheimer's but his own continuing selfhood, how to care for his unique self. No two impairments are the same, she teaches us, as the how-to books cannot. What she successfully learns to do — although she doesn't name it herself — is phenomenological psychology.[14]

She doesn't say much about the toll of this enforced learning and doing, except by describing a brief depressive breakdown. She describes how she finds it in herself to master sorrow and many other disabling emotions I feel I might have succumbed to.[15] She details the final practical compromise. She gives up her day to Scott, who lives in the present tense, except for five or six hours for writing, and several for reading after he goes to bed, with her first project being this memoir, an account of this harrowing punctum in time. The editor of *Aging Today*, the percipient Paul Kleyman, soberly puns, "It's a love story for the ages."[16]

Endnotes

Endnotes, a memoir by Ruth Ray, is another. As a romance, it is even more extraordinary. In her forties, a writing teacher training to become a gerontologist, Ruth goes to a nursing home (here called Bedford) to conduct writing exercises with the residents. She falls in love with a man of eighty-two. Superficially, it's preposterous. There's no fifty-year relationship behind it, from the days when he was twenty and gorgeous. No mental superimposition of an image of past virility. His Parkinson's is the first thing she and we learn about him. When she meets him, she sees "he didn't take up much space. He was a very small, quiet man." Once he stops walking. "Move, dammit!" he said to his feet. "I have to remind myself to walk," he apologized. "It's Parkinson's." She finds him asleep one day, with his pants unfastened, unshaven, looking more frail. She makes no adverse comment; she isn't put off.[17]

The suspense here comes from wondering how far this odd couple will go in this anaphrodisiac setting. Ruth is drawn first to Paul's writing, admiring his vivid eye for sensory detail and character, his good nature, his humor. Coming late to class, he apologizes. "'Someone volunteered to cut my throat, and it took a while.' He had a piece of toilet paper stuck to his neck."[18]

The dialogue has to be good to create both characters at the same time and to make the rapid love story plausible, and it is. Paul treats her sweetly. He's open, appealing. He lets her know he thinks she's "a beautiful girl"; he complains about living in a cage. As narrator, Ruth is a bit reticent: one of the charms of the book is having to read between the lines of her very private character. She overcame something to tell this story. She had been married and divorced; she wasn't looking; the affair took her by surprise. She soon responds to him as a man. Only professional ethics while doing research keeps her from undertaking an oral history with him every day. The day she is saying goodbye, he reaches over to put his hand on top of hers.

> I found myself leaning down and rubbing my cheek gently over the top of his hand.
> "I love you," Paul said. He looked straight into my eyes.
> "I love you too," I said, looking right back at him.
> The other man didn't seem to be paying attention. . . .
> His fingers, cupped together, had landed in the middle of my spine, like a small bird come to rest for a moment on a branch. "I guess I should be going," I said, clearing my throat.

When she leaves, he kisses her lightly on the lips.

> Without a second's thought, I returned the kiss.
> As I walked across the parking lot in the shimmering heat, my brain took over. What on *earth* was I doing? But I couldn't stop smiling.[19]

RUTH IS A NAÏF, in American cultural terms. She doesn't evade decline in the common way by avoiding the other residents or brushing Paul off. It doesn't occur to her. There's no learning curve emotionally—which should teach us something, contrasted to our own steep learning curve as we read. Her friendliness to old people with impairments seems like the most ordinary thing in the world. It would be ridiculous to wonder how Ruth overcame common aversion when we see her so quickly captivated by Paul. She doesn't explain; she just shows it. On New Year's Eve, she breaks a date with another man to spend it with him at Bedford. In fiction this would scarcely be credible; on film Paul would have to be tall with a full head of hair and no perceptible shaking. Within four or five months, they are talking on the phone or seeing each other every day. Ruth tells him she doesn't want to write a scholarly book; she wants to write a love story.

First date, first sex. The overtures to intercourse are familiar—and perhaps shocking to those readers who are thinking about his age, and her age, all the time. They discuss sex, contraception. Inviting him to her house, she buys pink satin sheets because she's read in a book called *Caring for the Parkinson's Patient* that satin sheets help a person slide out of bed. His physical problems become naturalized through the love story. He sleeps over, waking often, needing to pee. Only when it's relevant do we learn that he has had prostate cancer. The frankness of all this—and its pedagogical shock value—remind me of Jane Fonda and Jon Voight, he playing a paraplegic vet, in the film *Coming Home*. Perhaps geriatric disabled sexual romance is now in the position young disabled sexual romance was a generation ago—ready for prime time if treated not as a clinical procedure, but as the outcome of desire.[20] When Ruth told me the story, years ago, she said his was "the best loving" she'd ever had.

Their affectionate joking chats and cheap dates alternate with descriptions of his condition and clinical details about the coming stages. They both defuse anxieties. "When you're tired, you're just tired. It doesn't mean you're going to die," he explains. They have a difficult morning getting to church, and he says weakly, "You didn't bargain for this." Ruth offers, "Let's look on the bright side. . . . You're teaching me to accept the things I can't control." His dying is mentioned several times. Paul says,

> "Going doesn't bother me so much, but I don't like the idea of leaving you to the wolves. I don't like it one bit."
>
> "I think you worry too much about those wolves," I replied. "I don't see any wolves circling."

She gives him an assignment, to watch over her, "from wherever you are." Paul sighs contentedly, "That was a true lover's speech."[21]

But when Paul unilaterally tells his son, the first time she meets Dan, that he wants to move in with her, she panics about being overwhelmed. "I wanted *me* to be at the center of my life." After hearing him out, she tells Paul privately that living together won't work for her, as forthrightly as she would have told a same-age, healthier man. "You are a passionate man, and I am a careful, deliberate woman," she explains. He, remarkably, understands.

> "Part of me wants you all to myself," Paul continued. "But another part says, 'Go, learn, work earn!' The world is yours, my darling! . . . Oh, honey, I love what we have now."

They decide to live apart together. She doesn't have to bend over backward to treat him specially. Neither love nor anti-ageism could lead her to go against her selfhood. They cruise the nursing-home grounds on his scooter. He knows her book, and says, "I'm proud to be a part of it."[22] It's a normal affair, if a reader accepts it as such. Even though Ruth critiques bureaucracy and depersonalization in nursing homes, the fact that much of their love affair takes place in one, in which people are abuzz about the spectacle, humanizes the nursing home for people who know about them only from books and films in which they are treated as the waiting rooms for death.

Then Paul dies suddenly. Why isn't this book an elegy, then? For one thing, it's about gerontology, and Ruth moves on to tell us how to read through that lens. The reader's experience is partly dependent on tone, and Paul's wit makes this a very funny book. Neither Ruth nor Paul lost their equanimity. She is a cool customer, and how she mourns she doesn't say. But the real reason is that *Endnotes* doesn't have the feel of pastness, of experience or romance recollected in tranquility. It seems to have been *lived* in tranquility, a different matter.

TWO LOVE STORIES for the ages in one year. Both published in 2008, they seem landmarks within the literature of old age and the struggle against ageism or ableism. (Disclosure: I know both Alix and Ruth, Alix since 1990. Ruth told me her story when we first met in 1997. My husband and I were about to visit Alix and Scott on their island when he fell. But none of this interferes with my objectivity, I believe, about the two achievements.)

These two beautiful memoirs abet the long bumpy development process that makes us more human the more deeply we learn about the life course and identify with its entire trajectory, including its contingent accidents and illnesses. The long multiple endnotes of life still seem like foreign and frightening territory to younger people, because North American culture keeps younger people — here I include myself too, as I once was — mostly ignorant and distant. But even if we knew Paul and Scott socially, we wouldn't get to know them the way Ruth and Alix represent them.

The writers' skills mean that every one of the four major characters becomes lovable, and especially the two men who are impaired. These books thus directly allay our fears of disability. They may also allay fears of what we call old age. (Jane Somers, Lessing's narrator in *Diary of a Good Neighbor*, says more accurately, "I no longer fear the old."[23] Jane is listening to and caring for women in their nineties, most of whom are frail or ill but long remain independent.) The category "older," so automatically conflated with "disabled" or "diseased," can be kept conceptually distinct. Neither Scott nor Paul is aging normally — if I may rebelliously use the word "normal" to describe old age. Alix can be said to be aging normally. The men are the victims of accident and illness. But this distinction can go mainstream only when we demedicalize old age and undo the terrifying and inaccurate equation of old age and dementia.

Even the most passionate nonfiction books about aging-into-old age cannot dispel these fears or teach us to avoid shunning as well as these memoirs do. These two women propel even the age critics among us farther across the abyss of ageism, the way a thirteen-year-old can leap a wider gap than an eight-year-old. The simplest point might be that love can be stronger than ageism and ableism because love is so enthralled by the particular. We have to absorb the consequences of this fully. As a result of making a brain-damaged man and a man with Parkinson's lovable, these memoirists show where value lies inside later life; they create value in unsuspected places. Lovingly, they show us how to write feelingly about — and quote — people with disabilities who also happen to be (for many readers) old. Respect is nothing to this. More generally, they teach us how to live carefully and equally in a world that contains more and more people who are old, many of whom will be not merely old, but also disabled or living with dying. Our imaginations leap over aversion into a better set of relationships.

But these memoirs go farther. Many of us have already decided how unendurable later life will be on the basis of the vague ignorant fears that prospective decline narrative concocts for the young. Could I myself live with brain damage? With Parkinson's? We can't know our personal future: I might have a mild, healthy old age and be all alone — a likely and relatively lucky fate for a woman, if she also has financial resources. (I might then be a good candidate for a plucky positive-aging story.) But having empathetically read these experiences, now I can imagine not only being Ruth or Alix, but being Paul or Scott, and even thinking, as Scott says, "How lucky I am."

The memoirs show that one can write without embittering nostalgia about a life course that held a better time before. (Ruth Ray has also written a book called *Beyond Nostalgia*.) Alix believes that nostalgia saved her — not the sentimental kind that pretends to draw value from faded experiences, but the inescapable feelings and images that continue to be vivid. She loves Scott because she has always loved him. Ruth didn't have a past with Paul to wax nostalgic over.

Neither Alix nor Ruth, I daresay, set out consciously to write her way out of decline narrative. People live their lives forward in their own natures, after all — then that's what they remember. After the fall, Alix fought Scott's physical and mental decline because she was desperate for him to heal. As the situation grew more grave, her dedication grew, the optimistic and resistant sides of her temperament kicked in. For both their sakes, she had to save herself from anger at him, depression, and despair. Ruth had not the slightest intention of falling in love with one of her writing students in the nursing home, not to mention holding his hands and rubbing his back as his condition worsened.

But perhaps each woman did undergo pressures to shape her unexpected adventures in later life keeping in mind the genre debate about progress versus decline. Alix perhaps felt some pressure in a business where trade editors push for upbeat positive-aging stories — people who climb the Himalayas and win the Purpose Prize. Ruth, who has academic interests in narrative, is knowledgeable about the debate, and was publishing *Endnotes* in Columbia University Press's End-of-Life series, must have felt an interior pressure to write responsibly as what she calls a "social-change agent . . . providing alternative images and conceptions of aging and old age."[24] For these very different reasons, both writers might have felt some need to keep their works from becoming too dark. No one writes memoir in a cultural vacuum.

On the other hand, these are women for whom honesty is a kind of instinct. Ruth might have felt that Paul's adorable nature would shield her odd love story and give her adequate freedom about how to tell it. And Alix wound up pulling no punches about Scott's condition: "If all else fails we'll use our tragedy for making art."[25] Certainly neither of these books evades the facts of physical decline. The writers took risks. They crammed in as many as they imagined the reader of the contemporary progress narrative of old age can take.

The two memoirs are obviously not about progress in any common definition. Do I want to apply the term merely because the writers saved themselves from succumbing to decline's momentum? I hesitated, but then fortunately I was able to decide: Let *them* speak. Alix says she and Scott "manufacture optimism" by "our stubborn resistance to viewing our lives as other than blessed."[26] Whether anyone else but Alix would be capable of taking that valiant stance may occur to a reader only after some reflection. Alix refuses to use words like heroic with regard to herself, perhaps to encourage us all to think ourselves capable of loving care, managing what is sometimes called the thirty-six-hour day. Alix mentions a nursing home as an option, but within the pages she remains the watchful, loving, hands-on caregiver. She is still in part the future-oriented solitary creative and independent self that she always was; as the demands of her situation increase, she proves equal to them. Even if tragedy were her last word, tragedy too is an exit from decline, ennobling the lost beloved and the lovers who lose what they prize.

Paul said about being with Ruth, "It was a long time coming. I waited my whole life for it. But I couldn't have recognized it until now." Ruth, quoting my book *Safe at Last in the Middle Years* on how aging can be a psychic cure for youth's prospective terrors of the life course, writes, "I think of *Endnotes* as a progress narrative in which a midlife woman (who is also a gerontologist) releases some of her youthful fears and, with the help of a good friend, comes to a better understanding of aging, decline, and death."[27]

Recall Sartre's holding on to the idea that "life was progress until death — that it must be progress." Instead of adoring the past, allegorized as youth, Sartre had been glad to chuck it behind, "the poor, disdained, despised, denied past." The person he was who had formerly lived in that body-mind was someone else, more liable to error.[28] We are lucky to have Sartre's forceful position to chew on: it's an odd hors d'oeuvre of philosophy. Making use of it depends on believing in multiple sequential identities, rudely dismissing younger selves and solidly lodging in one's current body-mind.

Positive-aging books and speakers also praise resilience, but they make it look too easy—by minimizing the dreadful, the deprivations, by creating luckier characters. How to describe radical later-life progress narrative as it has been evolving away from positive aging to include more sorrow, more realism, and more heroism? I have tried to define the term for two decades, and each time I have to include other yet more unlikely examples of loyalty to progress thinking in the service of selfhood. The ones I cherish come not from mere observers of the infinitely deprived, who have their own reasons for needing to call what they witness progress, but from first-person survivors like the fiery Civil War veteran in *Gilead* who had learned at some point after his wounding to say of his lost eye, "I prefer to remember that I have kept one." Or, since he and Maudie Fowler are fictional, think of reporters like Sartre, pushing progress ahead of him like a toboggan he's holding onto. Scott York saying, "I am lucky." And my mother at ninety-six, charming, smiling, going blind, less and less mobile, her intelligence grasping and wielding whatever is left of her past and her command of language, asking, "What could be worse than to lose all your memory?" and yet declaring, "I have a wonderful life." And however absorbing and deprived their situations, nothing precludes their being in loving and appreciated relations with others. Companionship and advocacy shield them. They are not alone.

If we ask again what exactly age has to do with it, it's not aging but disability or illness and their social deprivations that assault them. The body-mind challenges may rise high for any of us, like Katrina's waves overtopping the levees. Some spectators feel they would drown in like circumstances. (None of these writers deals with pain that if not adequately treated takes over the whole universe, or the kind of chronic illness that starts in a person's twenties or forties and requires attention and expense and may involve repeated medical failures lifelong. Other writers do that.)

In the midst of what may seem obvious, inescapable, and pitiable loss, those we call sufferers often prove to be moral and emotional survivors. All of them say, at a minimum, "I haven't lost as much as, at the worst, I anticipated." It's tricky and perhaps untenable to argue against what trustworthy people say they've lost or kept or won. It may be for them a precarious balance, not a fixed position but not a vertiginous seesaw either. They have all my respect. If you started this book calling the whole later-life package — including not only midlife job loss and ill health but normal old age — decline-through-aging, do you still want to call it that?

The Next Angels in America

The exemplary figures in these memoirs — Scott, Paul, Jean-Paul — catch one break that helps us peer a little way ahead of contemporary culture. By good luck it is mainly illness they suffer from. Illness they can bear, with the companionship of Alix, Ruth, and Simone. We know the facts and the breaks because illness now has its poets and memoirists, as Virginia Woolf wished when she wrote her important essay "On Being Ill." But Woolf was talking only about bouts of critical illness, where "All day, all night the body intervenes."[1] Even more critical to our understanding, these new narratives are accounts of chronic illness, where normal distractions — romance, humor, beauty — may make their bodies' clamoring solitude intermittent. Telling chronic illness is important news for all, since this is the spreading fate in the developed world, not only for the old but for those who often get ignored in policy and cost discussions focused on longevity: the sick and disabled under sixty-five.[2] For our six protagonists, discouragement comes if it comes in bouts. All day and night, *life* intervenes. Late life happiness is no oxymoron.

   Ah, but with minor exceptions, none of our protagonists is fighting ageism — or middle-ageism — or decline ideology. Decline is the great Nihil in charge of the runaway train of history. Decline is the source of much long-term despair, as the haunting image of the lonely figure left on the ice floe indicates. A part of the American political unconscious speaks through this image. Nothing defeats the soul more than the sense of being forsaken or about to be forsaken on the basis of an ascribed category (age, race, sexuality, gender, ableness) that I cannot—that no one can—control. It doesn't help to know that indifference or abandonment are likely to become my lot through the ignorance or apathy of others, when knowledge and sensitivity are increasingly available.

And it wounds painfully when these harms come from individuals, institutions, or national leaders who appear to know better by the very lip service they pay to age. How can it be that my need at midlife or in late life will be in some sense known but ignored? Or that neglect of my age class will be publicly warranted at the highest levels because the money to alleviate my suffering is supposedly needed for something else? Age critics wonder, Can materialism be operationalized yet more viciously against the life course than we have yet witnessed? Human malice may cut as deep as untreated pain. Indeed, untreated pain in later life—which doctors sometimes refuse to alleviate, if they even notice it, on such grounds as "We don't want to get her addicted"—is precisely a cruel form of ageism. Such doctors inflict that extra violence onto the helpless body-mind. Would the double sufferers be able to say whether the physical torture or the callousness causes them the greater harm? Not while in pain. But later, free of physiological pain, let them testify. Wrongdoing on the part of those with power to prevent distress may be a greater harm, because it is morally and intellectually inexcusable.

The potential victims of decline include not only those in middle and later life but all the rest—like the younger women who said in Baba Cooper's hearing that they didn't want to get old or the people who tell me over drinks that they plan to commit suicide. *What shall we say to them?* I keep wondering. I ask myself, I ask others. We must take this question seriously.

The brisk retort is, "You *won't.* You *won't* want to commit suicide."[3] The life force will speak for itself. Would that we could rely on it. But no good societal answer can come out of putting so much weight on any single person's élan vital. Each of us alone is too fragile a creature of culture, borne along on the locomotive. If decline ideology is not successfully slowed or halted, its spreading powers will more and more perceptibly destroy old age and the midlife and generational solidarity and all early anticipations of the later life course, not just in the United States but country by country across the globe.

Because it is a product of human invention, and because we all potentially have skin in this effort, decline ideology can be opposed. It can be fought even if its unswerving interests and economic might make it too strong to be eliminated. It can be more effectively decried. It can be fought argumentatively, by convincing scientists and pundits that biogerontology needs humility: medicalization does not have the last word on aging and scarcely knows the first word on the human natures that are passing through the cultural fire. Decline can be fought legally and politically, on such grounds as economic rights for workers, antidiscrimination, the value of seniority, and patient rights. It can be combated ethically, on the grounds of respect for our parents, equal rights for elders, and civic responsibility for the whole life course. And it can be fought imaginatively, through the illuminations of our best and longest-lasting stories.

But where are the writers, including poets and journalists, who regularly monitor lethal ageism and inveterate decline thinking and reflectively fight back? At stake is a willingness to attack the high and mighty rather than only correcting the people we happen to know. Do those who fight racism and sexism and classism lack the courage in this case? Or is this world of later life a corner of vulnerability that has been made to seem so alien, repulsive, or boring—as ghettoes were made to seem by Nazi propagandists in the 1930s—that only dedicated age critics can wish to bring out of the shadows the metaphorical death-march offstage? Let writers make the bitterness and perplexity and humiliations of decline real, but not only by describing bodily aging. Some will be the laureates of our broader illuminations. Anti-ageism needs its own Angels in America, those who empower us for the fights.

We are only beginning to even want to understand how contemporary people are making sense, emotionally and theoretically, of all the baggage that aging-into-later-life in America now heaps on most of those exposed to mainstream culture as they grow beyond youth. But demography is not destiny. We in the lead within the longevity societies may bring about two remarkable phenomena through resistance: a wiser literature of progress narrative and the collective will to defeat decline politically and save the life course. Insofar as we survive ageism and ableism on our own behalf, watching ourselves do so and wondering how in the world we are managing the trick, *that* will be something to celebrate and to describe.

✳

It should be a boast that the United States provides conditions in which the so-called new old can turn away from despair, strive for progress in the life course, and teach younger people to look forward. We all have a role to play in making this possible. Like the Buddha in the Sukhavati Ceremony, may we help our country "manifest the victorious vision of kindness."

ACKNOWLEDGMENTS

The growing crowds in age studies provided the nutrient medium for this book. My age studies posse, once few enough to be listed on a dedication page, is now spread over Europe, the United Kingdom, Canada, and the United States. For encouragement and wise critique, in person and through e-mail, I thank these scholars and theorists at the cutting edge, from whom I learn so much. I particularly thank my hosts, Heike Hartung (Germany), Aagje Swinnen (Holland), and Roberta Maierhofer and Heidi Moertl (Austria).

The Women's Studies Research Center (WSRC) at Brandeis University, under the directorship of Shulamit Reinharz, has given me a collegial home since 1996, a lecture space for trying out my chapters to crossover audiences, grants from the Tavris Fund that made it possible for me to present my work in distant venues, and participation in two relevant writing groups—on the memoir and on social issues—whose members gave me valuable critiques.

I have had the best editors in and out of the business. David Gullette, First Editor, with a red-pencil background in both *Ploughshares* and *New Political Science*, read the whole, checking for everything from logic to word usage to metaphors. He handled the joke meter. In the charrette of finishing, he ran beside my cart offering cold drinks and calm comfort. Sean Gullette, with years of professional experience editing his own cultural magazine, pared three unruly chapters into closer-to-topiary elegance. Andrea Petersen gently applied her sharp tools as a lawyer, editor, and cultural critic to a number of chapters. Frinde Maher, a co-editor of *Radical Teacher*, made smart pithy comments about both style and substance. Paula Caplan cheered me on with generous praise and learned commentaries.

Tom Cole and Ruth Ray urged me to write about aging and social trends for an edited collection. Accepting that task changed this book in a powerful way, reorienting it more toward what might be called the current history of decline. Bob Binstock, Rick Moody, and Bob Ross answered some urgent last-minute questions with knowledge and patience. Dr. Michelle Holmes gave authoritative information about some hard-to-answer questions.

Deborah Haynes, a sculptor, gave me the text of the Sukhavati Ceremony, which provides the closing words of my argument. Dorothy Austin, Sedgwick Associate Chaplain in the Memorial Church at Harvard, has invited me on several occasions to give the 8:45 A.M. sermon at Appleton Chapel, once on a topic in age studies. These experiences, building on John Brentlinger's moving and politically powerful example, taught me the value of the secular sermon.

The book came together in a startling way when I realized that the themes of my talks, sermons, essays, and even blogs were inextricably and multiply linked, as if an unacknowledged core obsession had been working its way free. Many sections of the book were delivered at conferences. I had to read aloud so people from other disciplines or outside the academy could understand. I was able to gauge which arguments and structures had force. Writing for live audiences helped make my American English that much more like speech.

Some chapters started as short articles or essays, which grew from exposure to editors and my own critical rereadings. The epiphany in the shower in chapter 1 is based on a twelve-hundred-word piece I wrote for Women's eNews (http://www.womensenews.org/, August 3, 2005); it subsequently appeared in a shorter form in the Boston Women's Health Book Collective, *The Our Bodies Our Selves' Guide to Menopause* (2006). A friend said that doing the exercise in the shower was transformative for her, so that helped me decide to include it pivotally.

Thanks to Nan Bauer-Maglin and Donna Perry for help with editing an earlier unpublished version of chapter 2 on Heilbrun and the "duty to die." Part of chapter 3, in a brief different version, was also published by Women's eNews (December 14, 2005). Another section appeared as "Tragic Toll of Age Bias," *Boston Globe*, August 27, 2006. A third was given as a talk, "Preparing for the Next Catastrophe," to the American Association of Geriatric Psychiatrists, New Orleans, on March 2, 2007. M. Christian Green invited me to lead a discussion on ageism during Katrina in her ethics course at Harvard Divinity School, which was attended by Harvey Cox. The chapter was published in an earlier form in

There Is No Such Thing as a Natural Disaster, edited by Chester Hartman and Gregory D. Squires (New York: Routledge, 2006). At a late stage, when they could be most helpful, my colleagues in the social issues writing group at the WSRC tackled my handling of the difficult issues of the intersectionality of age with other social categorizations. Susan Eisenberg gave me lucid notes, each one of which sharpened the argument. At every venue, attendees involved helped me improve the text.

Early short versions of chapter 4, "Hormone Nostalgia," were delivered to a large public, including colleagues at the WSRC on December 12, 2006, and sociology graduate students and faculty at Suffolk University in the fall of 2008, under the auspices of Professor Amy Agigian. A section appeared in the *American Prospect*, under the title "Pause for Concern" (http://www.prospect.org/, January 23, 2007). A version also appeared as "Hormone Nostalgia: Menopause Discourse after the Debacle," in *Women, Wellness, and the Media*, edited by Margaret Wiley (2008).

A brief section of chapter 5, "Plastic Wrap," was published by Women's eNews as "Plastic Surgery (Thankfully) Goes under the Knife" (November 26, 2008). Another small section, "Look Again," appeared on my own blog on the Women in Media and News site (http://www.wimnonline.org/WIMNsVoicesBlog/author/mgullette/, April 16, 2007).

A section of chapter 6, "Improving Sexuality across the Life Course," appeared in a different version under the title "Then and Now: What Have the Sexual "Revolutions" Wrought?" in the *Women's Review of Books* 25, no. 1 (January/February 2008): 22–23.

An earlier version of chapter 7, "Our Best and Longest-Running Story," appeared in *Narratives of Life: Mediating Age*, edited by Heike Hartung and Roberta Maierhofer (Munich: LIT Verlag, 2009). A version of the section on Ruth Ray's *Endnotes* appeared in *Journal of Aging, the Humanities, and the Arts* (2009), a Taylor and Francis publication.

A shorter version of chapter 8, "The Daughters' Club," appeared as "Annals of Care-Giving: Is Emma Woodhouse's Father 'Demented'?" *Michigan Quarterly Review*, winter 2009, and was reprinted in the *Journal of Aging, Humanities, and the Arts* (2009). The editor of the *MQR*, Laurence Goldstein, by asking for a one-paragraph introduction, gave me an opportunity to meditate on how reading changes over a lifetime.

Many member of the Daughters' Club were at my side for chapter 9, "Overcoming the Terror of Forgetfulness," with their own great stakes in the subject, enabling me to revise what I once thought I would never be able to write. The members of my social issues group at the WSRC helped me improve an earlier version.

The WSRC Scholar-Partners Program has provided me for many years with resourceful undergraduates who have helped with research, and sometimes with editing, these chapters. My warmest thanks to Nora Berenstain for the research she did on sources on menopause and sexuality, especially for her bibliographies and her ability to chase down documents online. Dawn Schwartz avidly followed up details on Katrina and cosmetic surgery. Stephanie Spiro tracked down important materials, especially on surgery, took great initiative in pursuing interviewees and material about Katrina, and helped improve the index. Sarah Kinsler helped me update the media responses to the hormone debacle. Jake Weisberg was helpful checking data for the references.

Many thanks to my team at the University of Chicago Press, headed by my long-term editor David Brent, who kept faith in my book through the depths of the Great Recession. As she had with *Aged by Culture*, Carlisle Rex-Waller provided clear, sensitive guidance during the editing process.

Dozens of other people, uncredited, helped me build this book. Some requested anonymity. Others whose names I don't recall said or wrote a single sentence that (often long after, when I was finally ready) made me see a subject in a fresh light. It takes a village.

INTRODUCTION

1. Counsel for Amicus Curiae AARP, *Brief Amicus Curiae*.
2. Mendenhall et al., "Job Loss at Mid-life," esp. 195, 197, 201. Most of those affected are male middle-class professionals and managers.
3. U.S. Bureau of Labor Statistics, *Current Population Survey*, table 31.
4. U.S. Department of Health and Human Services, "Overview of the Uninsured," fig. 3.
5. Wilper et al., "Health Insurance and Mortality," table 1.
6. Ehrenreich, *Bait and Switch*, 1–13; Mendenhall et al., "Job Loss at Mid-life."
7. I discussed this in "The High Costs of Middle Ageism," *Aged by Culture*. See Estes, Philippson, and Biggs, *Social Theory, Social Policy, and Ageing*.
8. Kaplan, "Can Labor Revive the American Dream?" 13.
9. Wasserman, "Credit Crunch," *Boston Globe*, September 11, 2008.
10. Chan and Stevens, "Job Loss and Employment Patterns of Older Workers," 17.
11. Madrick, "Enron, the Media, and the New Economy," 18. For a fuller version of these midlife developments, see Gullette, "Ageism and Social Change."
12. My thanks to Robert Ross of Clark University for help with the data, mainly from the U.S. Bureau of Labor Statistics from 2000 to 2009, using the consumer price index. The male midlife median in 2009 was $50,284 ($41,000 in year 2000 dollars = $51,045 in 2009 inflation-adjusted dollars — so the midlife median was actually higher in 2000).
13. Sedensky, "Number of Older Americans Filing for Bankruptcy Soars," A5.
14. Norris, "She Works, Her Grandson Doesn't," 12.
15. Westlake, *The Ax*, 13, 220, 47, 104.
16. For a brief summary of evidence of differential treatment of midlife workers prior to the ADEA, see Neumark, "Age Discrimination Legislation in the United States," 304–5.
17. *Kimel et al. v. Florida Board of Regents 528 U.S. 98–791* (2000), p. 19; *Kimel v. Florida Board of Regents*, 120 S. Ct. 631 (2000).

18. Gregory, *Age Discrimination*, 116, 185; Lazarus and Munoz, "Supreme Court Undermines Protections"; Gregory, 14.

19. Conference Board, "U.S. Job Satisfaction at Lowest Level."

20. I introduced the concept of middle-ageism in *Declining to Decline* (1997) and was the first to use it as a defining term. Most economists employ the term "older worker," which misleads the public about the age at which people are losing jobs or any hope of work. I call them "midlife workers."

21. See the chapters on age autobiography and aging as a narrative, in Gullette, *Aged by Culture*.

22. Isaacs and Bearison, "The Development of Children's Prejudice," 175–93.

23. In Becca Levy's experiment, young people, on the other hand, became *less* confident if told that the old people were wise. Levy, "Improving Memory in Old Age," 1105.

24. Levy, "Mind Matters," P203.

25. On the "lag," see James, "This American Life," 24.

26. Roth, *Exit Ghost*, 104. The curse is uttered by a young man "savage with health and armed to the teeth with time" against the respected seventy-year-old writer Nathan Zuckerman.

27. Boyer, "Eviction," 48–53.

28. Ginty, "Women's Key," refers to a study of former lenders conducted for a class-action suit.

29. Hughes and O'Rand, "The Lives and Times of the Baby Boomers."

30. Gullette, "'The Boomers' vs. 'the Xers': A Contrived War," in *Aged by Culture*.

31. Stein, "Aging Boomers Facing Increased Health Problems."

32. Rattigan, "Tight Jaws in Tough Times," N01, N07.

33. Katz, "Alarmist Demography."

34. Haber, "Anti-Aging: A Historical Framework," 12.

35. Schulz and Binstock, *Aging Nation*, 3, 7.

36. Samuelson, "Economic Death Spiral," A19.

37. Data on surpluses from Ohlemacher, "Seniors' Job Losses," A8.

38. See, for example, Krugman, "America's Senior Moment," 6–11; Kuttner, *Obama's Challenges*, 77–84. My late cousin Robert Eisner, former president of the American Economics Association, wrote several books about fraudulent attempts to make Social Security seem at risk.

39. On right-wing attempts to cut social insurance, see Kuttner, *Obama's Challenges*, 76–87.

40. Binstock, "Our Aging Societies," 8, quoting the 2005 Congressional Budget Office report "High-Cost Care Beneficiaries."

41. Leonhardt, "After the Great Recession."

42. From Colello et al., "End-of-Life Care," table 1, p. 2. The alarming figure Obama then used—80 percent of the total health care bill—is wrong. Sixty percent of the costs for health care overall come from chronic illnesses occurring in the non-old (Butler, *Longevity Revolution*, 22).

43. Schulz and Binstock, *Aging Nation*, 190.

44. On fear of medical abandonment, Colello et al., "End-of-Life Care," 3, citing a report from the Institute of Medicine; Thomas, "The Case for Killing Granny." For a rebuttal, see Gullette, "In Medicare Blame Game."

45. Jackson, *Political Economy*, 202.

46. Butler, "Age-ism," 243–46.

47. "Male midlife sexual decline" is my own addition: see Gullette, "Male Midlife Sexuality," 58–89, and "Midlife Discourses," 3–44.

48. I found the term "ageist-consciousness" in Reinharz, "Friends or Foes," 507.

49. I invented the term "age studies" in 1993 ("Creativity, Aging, Gender," 45–46). See the chapter, "What Is Age Studies?" in *Aged By Culture*.

CHAPTER I

Epigraph: Harris was interviewed by Tracy Hughes Karner, for a videotape shown at the conference "Gender, Creativity, and the New Longevity," sponsored by the Women's Studies Department, University of Houston, November 13–15, 2008. Karner kindly sent me the excerpt.

1. The Lorenz and Gross cartoons appeared, respectively, in the *New Yorker* issues of September 11, 2006, and November 22, 1999.

2. Beauvoir, *The Coming of Age*, 51; her doubts about the ethnological record are on 44. Many recent gerontologists cite these pages of Beauvoir, some critically, but without including her caution. It's worth asking why anyone uses the myth without question or analysis.

3. Josefson, "JAMA Falls Foul." Older Inuit now receive medical care and pensions. Formerly, they boasted a communal infrastructure for taking care of sick people or frail elders. Rare "altruistic suicides" occurred only "in dire circumstances," according to Savishinsky, quoted in Shield and Aronson, *Aging in Today's World*, 203.

4. West, *The Young Rebecca*, 375.

5. "Old Is the New Young" was the title of Pollitt's plenary address at the conference "Gender, Creativity, and the New Longevity," University of Houston, November 13–15, 2008.

6. Marshall quotes Copper in "Teaching Ripening."

7. On aging as a narrative, see my *Aged by Culture*, chapters 1, 7, and 8.

8. Some gerontologists divide the "third age" from the "fourth." Bill Bytheway notes, quoting Young and Schuller, that "elevating the third [age] by comparison is only done by treading down the fourth . . . even older and more defenseless people" ("Ageism and Age Categorization," 369). Treading down the fourth has a terrible effect on younger people's own life-course imaginary. (But it was not the gerontologists naming a fourth age who had the power to force people to leap imaginatively over the third.)

9. Tada, *The God I Love*, 243. (In chapter 1 of *Aged by Culture* I discuss research on the difficulties children have imagining very far along in the future life course.)

10. Tada, *The God I Love*, 243.

11. If we include spouses in "eldercare," 80 percent of the caregiving is provided by

women. See Brewer, "Gender Socialization," 218, citing Hooyman and a large social science literature.

12. Robinson, *Home*, 101.
13. Aronson, "Commentary — Dignity of the Old with Dementia," C5 (my emphases).
14. Blumert, "An Answer to Old Age."
15. Hogan, "Welcome to the Rock n' Roll Rest Home."
16. See Gullette, "'The Boomers' vs. 'The Xers.'"
17. "No Country for Old Men," July 30, 2008.
18. Rothstein, "Gay Elders," April 3, 2007. Asterisks in original.
19. Loewy, "Age Discrimination," abstract; see also Rothenberg, "Withholding."
20. Nelson, "Ageism," 207.
21. Associated Press, "New Formula," A2.
22. Goodman, "The $250 Donation to Elders," A15.
23. Schulz and Binstock, *Aging Nation*, 179.
24. Beauvoir, *The Coming of Age*, 6.
25. Fidelity Investments brochure, *Planning for Retirement Income* (my emphasis).
26. Johnson and Murray, "The Patient Talks Back," 24–27; David Sinclair of Harvard Medical School, quoted in "Rethinking the Definition of Aging," 74 (my emphasis), was connected to Sirtris Pharmaceuticals, developing resveratrol and other substances as drugs to "slow" or "treat" aging.
27. Beauvoir, *The Coming of Age*, 9.
28. Terkel, *Coming of Age*, 452.
29. Quoted in Schwartzmann, "50 Years of seniority," A4. "Progressive forgetfulness" is used by Susan McFadden, personal communication, November 6, 2008.
30. Cornwell, "Rethinking Free Expression," 113. Susan Koppelman, inviting me to speak on a panel about hate speech, gave me Allport's Scale of Prejudice from *The Nature of Prejudice*.
31. Ed Hill, an artist, says, "I have to be honest: as a child, I believe my vision of older people was that what they did was age. It's like it was their profession" (in Barber, Goeser, and Taylor, *Thrive*, 53).
32. Roth, *Everyman*, 71.
33. Shulman, *To Love What Is*, epigraph.
34. Hollander, "Sylvia," *Boston Globe*, November 5, 2008; Levy et al., "Longevity Increased," 261–70. Levy believes attitude was the primary difference, more important than money or good health.
35. Halliday, "Chicken Salad," in *Keep This Forever*, 12–13.

CHAPTER 2

Epigraph: Adrienne Rich's "Invisibility in Academe" is quoted in Kress, *Carolyn G. Heilbrun*, 177.

1. Moody, personal communication, April 16, 2008.
2. Shneidman's deeply moving book, *Autopsy of a Suicidal Mind*, also influenced my decision to research Carolyn's last years.
3. Heilbrun, *Last Gift of Time*, 7, 9.

4. Overall, "Feminist Ended Her Life Journey."

5. Jamison, *Night Falls Fast*, 189. The total number of suicides did not increase. The method, with a plastic bag, suffocates. The phrase "air hunger" hints at the agony. Some people planning suicide select a way they suspect will be painful as a deterrent.

6. Motto, quoted in Shneidman's *Autopsy of a Suicidal Mind*, 55.

7. Jamison, *Night Falls Fast*, 189.

8. Kress, *Carolyn G. Heilbrun* (216–21) lists many plausible sources of Carolyn's distress, including the fact that her unloving mother had died at age seventy-seven. Kress doesn't consider ageism.

9. Holt, "Holt Uncensored," no. 385 (May 27, 2004).

10. Annabelle, who wishes to remain anonymous, has given me permission to quote.

11. Styron, *Darkness Visible*, 76.

12. Overall, *Aging*, 186.

13. Newman, *A Different Shade of Gray*, 4.

14. Blue-collar retirees may be exhilarated but later feel a sense of exclusion and invalidation (Bauer-Maglin and Radosh, *Women Confronting Retirement*, 7); Taylor, "Essays," in Barber, Goeser, Taylor, *Thrive*, 5.

15. Canetto, "Elderly Women and Suicidal Behavior."

16. Clark, "The Puzzle of Suicide in Later Life," 146.

17. Centers for Disease Control, "Suicide Data Sheet."

18. Mann, "The Coming Death Shortage," 94.

19. Fairlie, "Greedy Geezers," 19, 20, 19; Prado and Taylor, *Assisted Suicide*, 138, citing Robert Pear; Sack, "In Hospice Care," A1.

20. Gross, "The Beginning of Something New," July 2, 2008.

21. Overall, *Aging*, 57.

22. Hardwig, "Is There a Duty to Die?"; Altman, "How to Save Medicare? Die Sooner."

23. Loggers et al., "Racial Differences," 5. Their data have not yet been examined by gender.

24. Parks, "Why Gender Matters," esp. 35.

25. Harrison and Moran, "Resources and Rationing"; Calasanti and Slevin, introduction to *Age Matters*, 6, citing Robb, Chen, and Haley in *Journal of Clinical Geropsychology* (2002).

26. Doyle, "Risky Business."

27. This scenario is described — approvingly — by Gillick, "Is Death Optional?"

28. Ackerman, private communication, August 2009. This question about challenging denials comes from Wolf, "Health Care Reform," 28.

29. Clark, "The Puzzle of Suicide in Later Life," 149.

30. Robinson et al., "Can We Prevent Poststroke Depression?"

31. Siegel, "Ageism in Psychiatric Diagnosis."

32. Linder, "Oncology," 704; on the Chicago study, see Clark, "The Puzzle of Suicide in Later Life," 147. Sixty-three percent of the Chicago suicides had relatively good health for people their age.

33. Reported in Brody, "A Common Casualty," D7; Quoted in Dembner, "Ageism Said to Erode Care."

34. Shneidman, *Comprehending Suicide*.
35. Prado, *The Last Choice*, 25, 21.
36. Russo, *Nobody's Fool*, 39.
37. Overall, "Concepts of Life Span and Life Stages."
38. Levy, Ashman, and Dror, "To Be or Not to Be."
39. Rosenfeld et al., "End-of-Life Decision Making."
40. Cohn and Lynn, "A Duty to Care Revisited," 104.
41. Lerner, "A Calculated Departure," F1 (my emphasis).
42. Prado, *The Last Choice*, 36.
43. Anthony, "Natures and Norms," 137.
44. Ackerman, "Patient and Family Decisions," especially 60–61.
45. Holstein, "A Normative Defense," 28, 29.
46. Cohn, "Physician-Assisted Suicide: Con."
47. Jamison, *Night Falls Fast*, 260.
48. Brentlinger, "Thanksgiving," quotes Harrison's *Making the Connections*. Woodward, "Against Wisdom," uses Cynthia Rich as a wise example of using anger for activism.

CHAPTER 3

The title of the chapter is derived from *King Lear* 5.3.
1. Khanna, "Katrina's Aftermath." The accounting of 64 percent over age sixty-five is based on a study of 850 dead, by the Louisiana State University Health Sciences Center (Pope, "Katrina's Toll on Elderly"). The 78 percent over aged fifty-one comes from earlier data from the Louisiana Department of Health and Hospitals in November 2005. The numbers of dead were 88 aged fifty-one to sixty, 150 aged sixty-one to seventy-five, 268 from the over-seventy-five group. The percentage of people over sixty-five prior to Katrina — 12 percent — comes from Sharkey, "Survival and Death in New Orleans," table 1, 488.
2. The photograph of the woman on the conveyor belt appeared in the *Boston Globe*. The woman in the flag appears in Burford, "The Tale of a Photograph,"142. Men died at a higher rate than women, African Americans more than white. The death rate for men over sixty-five was 81 per 10,000 versus 60 per 10,000 for same-age women. The death rate for African Americans over sixty-five was 74 per 10,000 compared to 52 per 10,000 for Euro-Americans (Sharkey, "Survival and Death in New Orleans," 489).
3. O'Neil, "Evacuee Finds Comfort," A1.
4. Christofferson, "Study."
5. Amartya Sen, now a Nobel Prize winner in economics, wanting to explain the higher rate of female deaths in India and China, found that unnecessary deaths were caused by such socially constructed means as sex-selective abortion, female infanticide, neglect of birthing women at childbirth, abandonment of widows. Sexism was the origin of the inequalities. Klinenberg says that the heat-wave deaths in Chicago in 1995 were also mainly of old people — 73 percent over age sixty-five — and that the media did not recognize this (*Heat Wave*, 18, and chapter 1).

I would be pleased if my chapter provoked a book-length "social autopsy" of the deaths in New Orleans of the high quality of Klinenberg's.

6. Butler, *Longevity Revolution*, 41.

7. The AARP study is widely cited.

8. The best summary of risks is probably Benson and Aldrich, "CDC's Disaster Planning Goal."

9. Off, "A Look at the Victims." Off's data, from the Centers for Disease Control (CDC), are based only on eight hundred "hurricane-related" deaths, when the largest number of victims over age sixty-five drowned.

10. Miron and Ward, "Drowning the Crescent City," 155.

11. Smith, *Blood Dazzler*, 7.

12. Seager, "Natural Disasters Expose Gender Divide," on the racial divides; Sharkey, "Survival and Death in New Orleans," 494, on the highest death counts; Jenkins, Laska, and Williamson, "Connecting Future Evacuation to Current Recovery," 50, on the lack of a vehicle specifically in households headed by someone aged fifty-five or older; Golant, "The Gender Inequalities of Eldercare," 3, on licenses. The first figure on disability from Tischer comes from the National Council on Disability, (www.Jfanow.org/jfanow/index.php?mode=A&id=2497). The second figure comes from Fussell, "Leaving New Orleans," based on 2000 census data. The comparison of child deaths comes from the Louisiana Department of Health and Hospitals, "Vital Statistics."

13. The data on the over-sixty-five male/female toll comes from Sharkey, "Survival and Death in New Orleans," table 2, 489.

14. Malveaux, " An Interview," 77.

15. "Senseless Environmental Disaster" is the telling subtitle of Johnson's article "Environmental Justice and Katrina."

16. Off, "A Look at the Victims."

17. See *Herbert Freeman, Jr, et al. v. United States of America*, no. 08 — on petition for a writ of certiorari to the United States Court of Appeals for the Fifth Circuit, 4–5, 6. On DeLuca see also Filosa, "Appeals Court Takes Up Case of Elderly Deaths."

18. Tischer, private communication.

19. Lance Hill, executive director of the Southern Institute for Education and Research, private communication, June 15, 2009.

20. Fussell, "Leaving New Orleans."

21. Smith, *Blood Dazzler*, 46.

22. Teichert, "Katrina's Lasting Storm."

23. Campbell, "Belonging and Belongings." Other details come from dozens of articles.

24. Minerd, "USPsych."

25. Quoted in Krupa and Warner, "Across South, Displaced Chime In," 1.

26. Campbell, "Belonging and Belongings," 7.

27. Fausset, "New Orleans Economy Dodges Effects," A15; Williams, "Movin' On Down," 9.

28. Williams, "Movin' On Down," 9; Whelan et al., "Housing Authority of New Orleans," 1.
29. Crowley, "Where is Home?" 136–37; Hartman and Squires, "The Social Construction of Disaster," 281.
30. "Katrina Victims Can Stay in Their Trailers," A2.
31. Reckdahl, "New Orleans Has More Homeless People," cites Martha Kegel, director of Unity for the Homeless; Ratner, "Homeless in New Orleans," 18.
32. Lance Hill, private communication by e-mail, May 12, 2008.
33. White, "New Orleans's African American Musical Traditions," 92.
34. Deslatte, "Plans for New Charity Hospital Stall"; Dr. Sakauye, telephone interview.
35. Novelli, "Katrina's Legacy," 35.
36. Levkoff, "Assault on the Elderly," A19.
37. Campbell, "Belonging and Belongings."
38. Gabe et al., "Hurricane Katrina," CRS-17.
39. Markley and Garza, "Katrina's Aftermath."
40. Gabe et al., "Hurricane Katrina," CRS-17.
41. Roberto, Henderson, and Kano, "Surviving Hurricane Katrina."
42. Wade, "Meeting Needs of Older Americans."
43. Whelan et al., "Housing Authority of New Orleans," 25, 23–24.
44. McCulley, "Is New Orleans Having a Mental Health Breakdown?"
45. Allen, "Harvard to study Katrina's long-term psychological toll," A4; Pope, "N.O. Is Short on Doctors, Dentists," 1; *New Orleans Times-Picayune*, editorial, "A Hurdle to Mental Health"; also see Weisler, Barbee, and Townsend, "Mental Health and Recovery," 4–5.
46. Duncan, "Combating Katrina."
47. Harden, "With Age Comes Resilience": A24.
48. Roberto, Henderson, and Kano, "Surviving Hurricane Katrina."
49. Hartman estimates the bills in "Report from New Orleans," 4.
50. Roberts, "Families Say Stress of Katrina Hastened Deaths of Loved Ones," A12.
51. Quoted in McCulley, "Is New Orleans Having a Mental Health Breakdown?"
52. Smith, *Blood Dazzler*, 53.
53. Roth, *Exit Ghost*, 256.
54. Calasanti and Slevin, *Gender, Social Inequalities, and Aging*, 23.
55. On midlife debt, see Gist and Figueiredo, "Deeper in Debt."
56. O'Rand, "When Old Age Begins," 112; Wallis, "Species Questions," 505.
57. Simms, "Opening the Black Box of Rationing," 715, quoting Marshall P. Kapp.
58. Wilper, "Health Insurance and Mortality," table 1; Lazar, "Prickly Policies," G5; for data on people aged fifty to sixty-one not in the labor force, see Congressional Budget Office, "Disability and Retirement."
59. Associated Press, "New Formula," A12.
60. Hooyman, "Is Aging More Problematic for Women?" 126.
61. Older Women's League, *Newsletter*, 2005.
62. Whelan et al., "Housing Authority of New Orleans."

63. U.S. Bureau of the Census, 2005. For white women the rate rises from 9.8 percent at age fifty-six to 21.6 percent at age eighty.

64. Calasanti and Slevin, *Gender, Social Inequalities, and Aging*, 101.

65. Estes, "The Politics of Ageing in America," 18–20.

66. Calasanti and Slevin, *Gender, Social Inequalities, and Aging*, 114.

67. Frances Kissling, private communications, March 29, 2009, following up on her Salon.com essay, "Whaddaya Have to Do to Get a Kidney around Here?"

68. Weil, *Healthy Aging*, 56.

69. Wingate et al., "Identifying and Addressing Vulnerable Populations," 422.

70. Christofferson, "Study"; Fimrite, "Rights Group Warns," B5.

71. Faffer, "In the Eye of the Storm."

72. Krisberg, "Emergency Preparedness"; Benson and Aldrich, "CDC's Disaster Planning Goal," 3–4; Powell, "Communities Called Unready," A6. The national study was cosponsored by the National Association of Area Agencies on Aging, or N4A.

73. Walsh, Orsega, and Banks, "Lessons from Hurricane Rita."

74. Alperowitz and Williamson, "A 'Top Ten' List of Bold Ideas," 16.

75. *Smith v. City of Jackson*, no. 03-1160 (2005); *Smith v. City of Jackson*, 544 U.S. 228 (2005). In legal language: "Although the Court's recognition of a disparate impact claim under the ADEA is well-grounded, the restrictions that it placed on disparate impact claims under the ADEA rendered the theory of liability all but useless to employees" (Sturgeon, "Smith v. City of Jackson").

CHAPTER 4

1. The dementia risk appeared in a report in the *Journal of the American Medical Association* in May 2003; see Fugh-Berman and Scialli, "Gynecologists and Estrogen," on the absence of health benefits; also on revelations of risk (120).

2. "Breast Cancer," March 21, 2008.

3. Watkins, *Estrogen Elixir*, 274.

4. Dillaway lists many such feminist researchers, "Menopause is the 'Good Old,'" 398–401.

5. Reports of declining use of "replacement therapy" appeared in such journals as *Obstetrics and Gynecology*, *Annals of Internal Medicine*, *British Medical Journal*, and the *Journal of the American Medical Association*. See Ekström, p. 3 and notes 10–14.

6. The description appears in a fat brochure, *Menopause Guidelines*, that was given out by my HMO in 2005.

7. "Jury Awards $99m to 3." On American drop-off in usage, see Ginty, "After Health Scare." Sales dropped only 38 percent. Data differ on what percentage of women dropped hormone treatments. On French waivers, see Demey, "Peut-On Reprendre des Hormones?" 14.

8. Kowalczyk, "Breast Cancer Diagnoses," citing M. Ravdin et al., "The Decrease in Breast Cancer Incidence in 2003 in the United States," *NEJM*, 356, no. 6 (2007). See also Marchione, "New Study Strongly Connects Hormone Use to Breast Cancer," A18.

9. Service, "New Role for Estrogen in Cancer?"
10. Yager and Davidson, "Mechanisms of Disease," 271, 270; on the estrogen-stroke connection, Harris and Berenson, "Legal Strategy Boosts Drug Makers"; International Agency for Research on Cancer, "IARC Monographs Programme."
11. Yager and Davidson, "Mechanisms of Disease," 270–82.
12. Joachim Liehr, quoted in Service, "New Role for Estrogen in Cancer?"
13. Woods and Mitchell, "Symptoms during the Perimenopause," 14, cite a 1992 study by McKinlay, Brambilla, and Posner on the typical menopause before the 1990s' menoboom. See also Gullette, "What to Do When Being Aged by Culture."
14. Ussher, *Managing the Monstrous Feminine*, 131.
15. McNagny, Wenger, and Frank, "Personal Use," 1997.
16. Lock and Kaufert, "Menopause, Local Biologies, and Cultures of Aging," 499.
17. Bonetta, "Coping with the Change."
18. Ussher, *Managing the Monstrous Feminine*, 173.
19. To my knowledge, I was the first to use the term "magic marker" in this context. See Gullette, "Menopause as Magic Marker." The North American Menopause Society (NAMS) used to say that 5,700 women every day "mark the end of" their reproductive period, according to Dr. Marcie Richardson in a talk I attended.
20. Gullette, "What, Menopause *Again*?"
21. Houlihan, "HRT Cancer Link Found." The National Toxicology Program first listed "estrogen, steroidal" in its *Tenth Report on Carcinogens* (2002).
22. Bettina Leysen is quoted to this effect in Hoberman, *Testosterone Dreams*, 7–8.
23. Ekström, "Trends in Middle-Aged Women's Reports," 11, 12.
24. Gorman, "Menopause: A Healthy View"; Mayo Clinic, http://mayoclinic.com/ (accessed March 2010).
25. Houck, *Hot and Bothered*, last chapter.
26. Genuis and Genuis, "Exploring the Continuum," 6, quoting Porta.
27. Berger, "Two Years After."
28. [Illinois] State News Service, "Governor Blagojevich Announces" (my emphasis).
29. Overall, "Concepts of Life Span and Life Stages," 313.
30. "Change of Life"; Carpenter, "Choosing Different Paths," F1; Freundlich, "Menopause."
31. Johnson, "Studies Tie Depression Risk to Approach of Menopause," A6; Solomon, *Noonday Demon*, 174.
32. Friedman, "The Waist May Expand," G10.
33. Dillaway et al., "Why Can't You Control This?'"
34. Cole and Rothblum, "Lesbian Sex at Menopause," 186, 190.
35. North American Menopause Society, "Position Statement," 242.
36. Mundy, "Better Living through Chemistry," 2003.
37. Ockene et al., "Symptom Experience," 192. The *JAMA* study followed 8,400 women who had stopped taking estrogen eight months before.
38. Parker-Pope, "The Fear Factor."
39. Rothman and Rothman, *Pursuit of Perfection*, 100; Jackson, "Trouble Connecting?"

40. Amy Allina, quoted in Berger, "Two Years After."
41. Foreman, "Hormones."
42. Kolata, "On the Trail of Estrogen."
43. Quoted in Ussher, *Managing the Monstrous Feminine*, 133.
44. Wilson quoted in Hoberman, *Testosterone Dreams*, 135. Woodman points out in "The Women's Enron," 6, that Wyeth paid Wilson to extol its new drug. On the persistence of Wilson's arguments, see Redmond, *Sex, Drugs, and Middle Age*.
45. Ginty, "After Health Scare," 3.
46. On the convergence, see Gullette, "All Together Now?" in *Declining to Decline*.
47. On the use of the term "technoscience" to "invoke the inseparability of . . . culture and science," see Joyce and Mamo, "Graying the Cyborg," 99–121 and 116 nn. 1 and 2; Lock, "Accounting for Disease and Distress," 269.
48. Rothman and Rothman, *Pursuit of Perfection*, 74.
49. Collins et al., *Commonwealth Fund 1998 Survey*.
50. Ekström, "Trends in Middle-Aged Women's Reports," 12; Melby, Lock, and Kaufert, "Culture and Symptom Reporting at Menopause," 499.
51. Angell, "Drug Companies and Doctors."
52. Singer, "Drug Company Paid Ghostwriters," A7.
53. Genuis and Genuis, "Exploring the Continuum," 7.
54. Fugh-Berman and Scialli, "Gynecologists and Estrogen," 118, 117.
55. Public Citizen Health Research Group, "New 'Diseases' often Invented" 1–2.
56. Herrnstein Smith, "Figuring and Reconfiguring ," 22.
57. Bridges, "FDA Says Firms Still Lagging," A7.
58. Office of Management and Budget, "FDA Issues New Conflict of Interest Guidelines."
59. Study cited in Genuis and Genuis, "Exploring the Continuum."
60. Information on testosterone from the Mayo Clinic Web site, http://www.mayo clinic.com/ (accessed fall 2006).
61. Juengst et al., "Biogerontology: 'Anti-aging' Medicine," 23.
62. Beam, "Want a Long Life?" G23.
63. Angell, "Drug Companies and Doctors," 12.
64. Juengst et al., "Biogerontology: 'Anti-aging' Medicine," 26.
65. Hoynes, "Consider the Source," 13.
66. Wallace et al., "Evaluation," 936.

CHAPTER 5

1. Virginia Blum argues, "Little by little we are all becoming movie stars — internally framed by a camera eye" (*Flesh Wounds*, 288). But surgery wouldn't necessarily follow.
2. On the scholarly neglect of age, see Clarke, Repta, and Griffin, "Non-Surgical Cosmetic Procedures," 70. Exceptions are Kathryn Bayer, "The Shifting Gaze," and Abigail Brooks, "Growing Older," two dissertations focused entirely on surgery and age. Data from March 2008 on the average age come from the American Academy of Cosmetic Surgery, posted on Medical News Today (http://www

.medicalnewstoday.com). Data vary on the ages of users. According to the American Society for Aesthetic Plastic Surgery's posted statistics (http://www.cosmetic plasticsurgerystatistics.com/statistics.html; hereafter ASAPS) in 2007 people age thirty-five to fifty had the most procedures, and were 46 percent of the total.

3. Clarke, Repta, and Griffin, "Non-Surgical Cosmetic Procedures," 71.

4. Foreman, "Is Liposuction Safe?" C2; Teitell, "Yes I'm Cutting Back," D7. According to the posted statistics for ASAPS at the height of the CS boom, nonsurgical procedures rose 431 percent from 1997 to 2003. Surgical procedures rose only 87 percent.

5. CBS TV, "Insider," October 29 and 30, 2008. "Plastic Surgery Disasters" is found on the Web portal Frances Farmer's Revenge (http://www.francesfarmersrevenge .com/stuff/archive/plasticsurgery/); "The 15 Worst Celebrity Plastic Surgery Disasters You Will Ever See," on the Web site Topsocialite (http://www.topsocialite .com/the-15-worst-celebrity-plastic-surgery-disasters-you-will-ever-see/). See also the Web site Awful Plastic Surgery (http://www.awfulplasticsurgery.com/) and the cosmetic surgery portal Surgery Sagas, which attracts readers who have searched phrases like "liposuction gone wrong" (http://www.surgerysagas.com/2007/07/lipo suction_gone_wrong.html).

6. "Cosmetic Surgery World," images posted on Flickr (http://www.flickr.com/ photos/malingering/sets/1802082/).

7. Pierce, "Girls Gone Weird," 9.

8. The cartoon appeared in the issue of November 3, 2008.

9. Chen, *Final Exam*, 203. Mizrahi is quoted in Jackson, "Looking Old?"

10. The British cosmetician is quoted in Thomas, "Why do Women Want to Look Plastic?" 23.

11. "Bbb," posting on the Royal Forums portal about "royals having plastic surgery" (http://www.theroyalforums.com/forums/f161/). On the suicide studies and the questions they raise, see Nowak, "When Looks Can Kill," 18–21.

12. Sullivan summarizes these changes in *Cosmetic Surgery*, 189.

13. McDaniel and Malone, "Bootylicious." See also the 2007 news release posted for ASAPS.

14. Milner, "'Active' v. 'Anti' Aging," 9. The Harris Survey came out in its *Health Care News* 2, no. 23 (2002).

15. Brooks, "Growing Older"; Ephron is quoted in Kachka, "Sticking Her Neck Out."

16. Paley, "Here." Dorothy Barresi quoted this poem at the conference "Gender, Creativity, and the New Longevity," sponsored by the Women's Studies Department, University of Houston, November 13–15, 2008.

17. Nestle, "Desire Perfected," 181, 182.

18. McDaniel and Malone, "Bootylicious"; Holstein, "On Being an Aging Woman," 322–331.

19. My oldest friend, the artist Marsha Weiss Leinberger, made the point about Nüt looking like the Queen of Spades.

20. I interviewed both Miriam Goodman and Jane Kogan after I first saw Goodman's

photograph at a Cambridge Arts Society show, where it had won a prize. Bob Dylan's lyrics capture their intention.

21. Morris, "It's All About Face," N10.
22. Cold Fury blog, http://coldfury.com/ (accessed March 2008).
23. Blum, "Becoming the Other Woman," 104.
24. People between fifty-one and sixty-four had only 25 percent of procedures, compared to 46 percent for the fifty and under group (posted statistics for ASAPS). Eskenazi, in *More Than Skin Deep*, says the majority are between forty-five and fifty-five. Several hundred thousand operations performed on patients eighteen or younger bring down the average age.
25. Heilbroner, "Plastic Disasters."
26. Details on the death of Donda West are widely available on the Internet. For the essential facts, see the entry "Kanye West" on Wikipedia, under the heading "Mother's Death."
27. Pitts-Taylor, *Surgery Junkies*, 3, cites Deborah Sullivan's book, *Cosmetic Surgery*; Saltzman, "Suit Ties Death of Woman to Face Lift," 1; David Heilbroner is quoted on the American Board of Medical Specialties in "Plastic Disasters," the HBO interview on his documentary of the same title; Kuczynski, *Beauty Junkies*, 98.
28. See Landman, "Struck Twice," on Goldsmith's death. "Superbug Warning for Face-Lift Patients," appeared as a news item as part of the "Daily Briefing" on the Web site Boston.com, March 18, 2008 (http://www.boston.com/news/nation/articles/2008/03/18/three_more_bodies_pulled_from_rubble/).
29. Nuland, "Getting in Nature's Way," 34.
30. Brooks, "Growing Older," 35, 43.
31. Kuczynski, *Beauty Junkies*, 289, citing FDA data.
32. Osborne's comments were recorded on a Carefare Web site posting May 23, 2007 (http://www.carefair.com/html/Sharon_Osbourne_too_Old_for_Pain_of_Cosmetic_Surgery_2232.html; accessed November 2007).
33. Capitano, "This Woman Doesn't Get Chick Flicks."
34. Brooks, "Growing Older," 35.
35. McArthur, "Asian Cosmetic Surgery Disaster."
36. Clarke and Griffin, "The Body Natural," 199.
37. Public Citizen Health Research Group, "FDA Grants Public Citizen Petition," 14.
38. Dove's share rose from 1 percent to 6 percent. See "Spectacles of Moral Decline."
39. Quoted in Pitts-Taylor, *Surgery Junkies*, 91.
40. Freud, *The Ego and the Id*, 16.
41. I quote throughout this section from Carroll's "The New Anatomy."
42. Asher, "Strange Fruit," 25; Sullivan, *Cosmetic Surgery*, 177, also 180.
43. CBS Evening News, "Nips and Tucks"; Brown, "Maturity Is in Demand," C5, citing a survey from *Prevention*.
44. Martin, "Hope and Exploitation," 51, 52.
45. Morgan, "Women and the Knife," 2.
46. I am indebted to Paula Caplan for making this point to me (private communication).

CHAPTER 6

1. See also Jones, "That's Very Rude," describing counternarratives.
2. Quoted by Brenda Allen, "Hair Matters at Midlife," 77.
3. Langridge and Butt, "A Hermeneutic Phenomenological Investigation," 49.
4. Hales, "Embrace 'the Change,'" 4.
5. In December 2004, the FDA decided not to approve a testosterone patch from Procter and Gamble. "It remains to be seen whether higher testosterone levels contribute to increased sexuality or vice versa" (McNeill, "Blood, Sex and Hormones," 62).
6. On decline backing down the life course toward younger ages, see Gullette, *Aged by Culture* and *Declining to Decline*. On the way men are being constructed as also aging, consult the section "All Together Now?" in *Declining to Decline*.
7. Calasanti and Slevin, *Gender, Social Inequalities, and Aging*, 78, citing a study by Zeiss.
8. Loe, *The Rise of Viagra*, 18.
9. Rutstein-Riley, "I am More than My Medical Record!" (citing M. J. Park and others). Rutstein-Riley prefers the term "emerging-adult women" for those between the ages of eighteen and twenty-four.
10. Brekhus, "Social Marking," 504. Tyler, "Managing between the Sheets," discusses the "managerial ethos" constructed by "lifestyle" magazines. The binary is "great sex" or "bad sex" (95) with no spectrum.
11. McNeil, "Blood, Sex, and Hormones," 70.
12. Gibbons, "Teen Magazines."
13. Schilt, "I'll Resist," 89.
14. Hamilton, Mintz, and Kashubeck-West, "Predictors of Media Effects on Body Dissatisfaction," 397–402; Students of Rutstein-Riley in a survey at Lesley University (Cambridge, Mass.) uncovered a 67 percent willingness to use cosmetic surgery.
15. NPR, "Profile," February 7, 2004.
16. Ashcraft, "Adolescent Ambiguities," 43.
17. On neglect of birth control, see Kaplan, "Just Say No to AIDS," data from the National Center for Health Statistics; Tiefer, *Sex Is Not a Natural Act*, xiii.
18. Stepp, *Unhooked*, 8.
19. Talburt, "Constructions of LGBT Youth," 1.
20. Baruth, "Consensual Autobiography, " 118.
21. Gold, "The Hook-Up Report," 98, 99.
22. Carpenter, "Gender," 352–53. Some men regret losing their virginity with casual partners.
23. Schilt, "I'll Resist," 85.
24. Tu et al., "Time from First Intercourse," report based on 381 teens, aged fourteen to seventeen.
25. Lewis et al., "Factors Influencing Condom Use."
26. Phillips, *Flirting with Danger*, 4, 7–8, 21, 46; Maguire, *Men, Women, Passion and Power*, 196.
27. Tolman, *Dilemmas of Desire*, 11; Holland et al., *Pressured Pleasure*, 17; Wyatt, *Stolen Women*, 245.

28. Seen November 2004 posted on a wall leading into the Harvard campus.

29. Bloom, "Sexually Liberated Urban Twenty-Something," 22; Im, "Love Clinic," 140.

30. Tiefer, *Sex Is Not a Natural Act*, 145.

31. Breines, *Young, White, and Miserable*, 88.

32. Johnson, "Fuck You," 23.

33. Loe cites a *Newsweek* story about "a handful" of couples (*The Rise of Viagra*, 174).

34. McNeil, "Blood, Sex, and Hormones," 62–63, citing Bancroft and Sartorius.

35. Douglas, *Where the Girls Are*, 69.

36. The first speaker is sixty-six years old; the second is twenty-four.

37. Loe, *The Rise of Viagra*, 18.

38. Ginty, "Sex Drugs for Women Flood the Market"; Tiefer, *Sex Is Not a Natural Act*, 52.

39. Lacy, "Mature Sexuality," 7.

40. Mansfield et al., "Qualities Midlife Women Desire," 289.

41. Gannon, "Sexuality and Menopause," 114.

42. Lamott, *Traveling Mercies*; Murrell, "Autobiography as a War Machine"; Adams and Turner, "Reported Change in Sexuality," 127.

43. Daniluk, *Women's Sexuality across the Life Span*, 344. The age of the woman is not given.

44. Jorgensen, *A Personal Autobiography*, 137; Curb and Manahan, *Lesbian Nuns*, xxxi; Clausen, *Apples and Oranges*, 227, xx.

45. Adams and Turner, "Reported Change in Sexuality," 129, citing Lillian Rubin.

46. Ogden, "Sexuality and Spirituality," esp. 13–14.

47. Private communication, November 2004.

48. Adams and Turner, "Reported Change in Sexuality," 129, 134. Women in Winterich's group discussed husbands' complaints about dryness ("Sex, Menopause, and Culture," 633, 635).

49. Gannon, "Sexuality and Menopause," 103, citing Leiblum and Schwartzman.

50. Gannon warns against creating a new stereotype (ibid., 106).

51. Travis and White, *Sexuality, Society, and Feminism*, 199–200.

52. "Euphoric" is Nancy K. Miller's disparaging term for a roseate genre in Wilson, "Tell It Like It Is," 22. The authors Wilson discusses were young and writing fiction, not life-course analyses.

53. Gannon, "Sexuality and Menopause," 105–6, citing Philip Sarrel.

54. Statistics from a U.S. Census press release on older married couples, May 20, 2003 (http://www.census.gov/Press-Release/www/releases/archives/aging_population/001122.html).

55. For a summary of gender differences, see Desjardins, "Why Is Life Expectancy Longer for Women?"

56. Statistics from Kaiser Family Foundation, "Racial and Ethnic Disparities," 1.

57. Gannon, "Sexuality and Menopause," 107.

58. Marshall and Katz, "Forever Functional," 62; Tiefer, *Sex Is Not a Natural Act*, 8.

59. Drabble, *Seven Sisters*, 278; Tiefer, *Sex Is Not a Natural Act*, x.

60. Miller doesn't say whether she has a partner or explain why her libido is gone ("Not Wanting Things," 150–57).

61. Freeman, "Going through Changes for the Better," 28.
62. Tiefer, *Sex Is Not a Natural Act*, xiii.
63. Walker, *Sexuality and the Elderly*, 113.
64. Tyler, "Managing between the Sheets," 98.

CHAPTER 7

1. Smith, *White Teeth*, 448; the locus classicus of the argument in regard to the arts is William Hazlitt's "Why the Arts Are Not Progressive." Immanuel Wallerstein gives a succinct overview of why progress as a theory of history was shared by the left, center, and part of the right for most of two centuries, in "A Left Politics . . . ?" (143–45). The failure of international aid organizations (IMF and World Bank) and donor nations to develop the Global South has silenced even the right-wing ideologues of the theory of progress.
2. I am borrowing Samuel Moyn's view of these relationships from "This Seeming Brow of Justice," 40.
3. In order to expand my arguments here, I draw on a few sections of *Aged by Culture*.
4. Benjamin, *Illuminations*, 97.
5. Russo, *Bridge of Sighs*, 53, 98.
6. Ibid., 53, 54, 55.
7. Ibid., 55.
8. Ibid., 111.
9. *Aged by Culture*, chapter 1, takes up the subject of the anguish of children — like First Nations Canadians — who are denied all possibility of progress narrative.
10. Markus, Mullally, and Kitayama, "Selfways," 24; Handel, "Perceived Change of Self among Adults," 327.
11. Mead, *Culture and Commitment*, 46.
12. Uchitelle, *Disposable American*; Hipple, "Worker Displacement in the Mid-1990s," 15–32.
13. Chan and Stevens, "Job Loss," 17.
14. Davies, *The Cunning Man*, 197.
15. Porter and Walsh, "Retirement Becomes a Rest Stop"; based on Robert Ross's analysis of data from U.S. Bureau of Labor Statistics, "Usual Weekly Earnings of Wage and Salary Workers," News Release for Third Quarter 2009, http://www .bls.gov/news.release/archives/wkyeng_10162009.htm.
16. Russell, "Northeastern Allots $75 Million to Recruit 100 Professors," A16. The 2002 study was commissioned by the Association of American Colleges and Universities.
17. Braund, *The Possibility of Progress*, 170.
18. Sartre, *Les Mots*, 195–96 (my translation).
19. Koenig, "Depression and the Cultural Context," 65.
20. Beauvoir, *Adieux*, 71, 176, 73–74.
21. Quoted in Rowley, *Tête-à-Tête*, 335.

22. Woodward, "Telling Time," 6. I quote an unpublished version of Woodward's essay.
23. Beauvoir, *The Coming of Age*, 409.
24. Beauvoir, *Adieux*, 414–15.
25. Ibid., 35, 418.
26. Ibid., 421, 415. In *The Coming of Age*, 362, Beauvoir creates a binary between the mass of old people who cling to a more youthful past self nostalgically, versus the superman whose project is "to advance" beyond "the self he is no longer."
27. Beauvoir, *Adieux*, 417, 420.
28. Bellow, *The Adventures of Augie March*, 402, 128, and *Ravelstein*, 118.

CHAPTER 8

1. My first book, *Safe at Last in the Middle Years*, treated midlife themes in four novelists of the late twentieth-century.
2. Austen, *Emma*, chap. 1: 5, 6, 7. I use Frances Ferguson's edition here.
3. Ibid., chap. 49: 314, 315.
4. Folsom, "The Challenges of Teaching *Emma*," xliii (paraphrasing Claudia Jonson).
5. As Folsom notes, "the novel rarely emphasizes Emma's steadfast kindness to Mr. Woodhouse" (ibid., xxii).
6. Austen, *Emma*, chap. 53: 348.
7. Ibid., chap. 48: 310.
8. Ibid., chap. 52: 335.
9. Tandon, *Jane Austen*, 172
10. Austen, *Emma*, chap. 44: 281.
11. Ibid., chap. 29: 188.
12. Ibid., chap. 1: 5.
13. Scott is quoted in Southam, *Jane Austen*, 1:68.
14. Austen, *Emma*, chap. 11: 73, 188.
15. Ibid., chap. 32: 204.
16. Lyman, "Bringing the Social Back In," 342.
17. Centers for Disease Control, *Assuring Healthy Caregivers*.
18. Ballenger, *Self, Senility, and Alzheimer's*, 4.
19. Austen, *Emma*, chap. 43: 280.
20. Woolf, *Three Guineas*, 138; Orwell, *A Collection*, 230.
21. Haber, "Anti-Aging," 10. In the early twentieth century, most authorities subscribed to the view that aging was a disease destroying both body and mind.
22. Ballenger, *Self, Senility*, 6.
23. West, *The Young Rebecca*, 341.
24. Centers for Disease Control, *The State of Aging*, 5.
25. Weinberg, quoting Colin McGinn, "Without God," 74 (emphasis added).
26. Moody, *Aging*, 276.
27. Plassman et al., "Prevalence of Dementia in the United States: The Aging, Demographics, and Memory Study," is quoted in Lokon's talk, "Opening Minds through Art." Lokon says that "other sources tend to have higher estimates but the Plass-

man study is the most solid, with a nationally representative sample" (personal communication, November 2008).

28. Ballenger, *Self, Senility*, 119.
29. Ibid., 9.
30. Gubrium, *Oldtimers and Alzheimer's*, 118–19, 121.
31. Cohen, "Thinking about Dementia," 7.
32. Cited in Greenberg, "Just Remember This," 10.
33. "Hypercognitive society" is used in Shabahangi et al., "Some Observations," 11, citing S. Post.
34. Robinson, *Home*, 3, 252, 254.
35. Ibid., 19, 295.
36. Clendinen, *A Place Called Canterbury*, 203.

CHAPTER 9

1. This list of possible motives is used by Susan Koppelman in order to raise the complex question of why people are often silent in the face of hate speech, including ageist speech.
2. Talbot, "Brain Gain."
3. Kinsley, "Mine Is Longer," 38.
4. For more about my mother, see "My Mother at Midlife," and "The Other End of the Fashion Cycle," in *Declining to Decline*.
5. Ballenger, *Self, Senility*, 98
6. David Shenk, quoted in the *Washington Post*, June 7, 2004.
7. Smith, "Negotiating the Moral Status of Trouble," 64, citing work by others.
8. Dembner, "Mental Acuity in Seniors," A1.
9. Richeson and Shelton, "A Social Psychological Perspective," 177, 178.
10. Talbot, "Brain Gain," 35.
11. Quoted in Destro, "Target — the Elderly," 48.
12. Kaufman, "Dementia-Near-Death," 23.
13. Kushner, *Thinking about the Longstanding Problems*, 43.
14. Elliott, *A Philosophical Disease*, 137.
15. Hachinski, "Shifts in Thinking about Dementia."
16. Graham, "Diagnosing Dementia," 86, 87.
17. Small cited in Greenberg, "Just Remember This," 12; Hachinski, "Shifts in Thinking about Dementia."
18. Cornwell, "Rethinking Free Expression," 113.
19. Laditka and Pappas-Rogich, "Anticipatory Caregiving Anxiety."
20. I borrow the phrase "molecule by molecule" from Greenberg, "Just Remember This," 14.
21. The cartoon can be found in the Doonesbury archive on the *Washington Post* Web site (http://wpcomics.washingtonpost.com/client/wpc/db; June 7, 2004). It reran in the *Boston Globe*, March 17, 2009.
22. McFadden, Frank, and Dysert, " "Creativity in the 'Now' of Advanced Dementia," 146.

23. Kitwood, *Dementia Reconsidered*, 128, 89.
24. Kitwood here quotes Frena Gray Davidson, ibid., 81.

CHAPTER 10

1. In the hands of astute observers like Proulx, however, some critique of the social world is implied. If that world were otherwise, despite the limitations or faults of the characters, things might not go quite as badly for them.
2. Roth, *Everyman*, 156. That tough pronouncement conveys the automatism of decline narrative, passes for smarts about "aging." But it's not Roth's last word, at least in this novel, which is also about friendship and resilience and persistence. Pulling off the word "massacre" about universal mortality and vanishing like the Cheshire Cat, Roth gets to make a sophisticated metaphysical joke about the unfairness of dying.
3. Humbert-Humbert's attempt is more grandiose and romantic than that of any average man who feels he is exiled in adulthood, partly because it is obsessively limited to one lost beloved.
4. Barresi, "Ephebephobia."
5. Anna Deveare Smith gave her 2008 performance piece the title *Let Me Down Easy*.
6. A chapter, "Going Home," was published in the *Massachusetts Review* (autumn 1981) 425–45.
7. Lessing, *Diary of a Good Neighbor*, 114, 127, 126.
8. Shulman, *To Love What Is*, 126.
9. Ibid., 47, 42.
10. Ibid., 63, 64.
11. Ibid., 67, 64.
12. Ibid., 92.
13. Ibid., 74, 75.
14. Ibid., 143; for a description of "phenomenological psychology," see McFadden et al., "Creativity in the 'Now' of Advanced Dementia," 138–40.
15. Shulman, *To Love What Is*, 83.
16. Kleyman, personal communication, 2008.
17. Ray, *Endnotes*, 19, 38.
18. Ibid., 22.
19. Ibid., 22, 26, 29, 30.
20. Their approaches to sex seem to me very different from some rather clinical stories published early in the disability movement.
21. Ibid., 70, 100–101, 129.
22. Ibid., 136–37, 170.
23. Lessing, *Diary of a Good Neighbor*, 166.
24. Ray, *Endnotes*, xi.
25. Shulman, *To Love What Is*, 81.
26. Ibid.
27. Ray, *Endnotes*, 171, 173.
28. Quoted from Beauvoir, *Adieux*, 414–15.

AFTERWORD

1. Woolf, *The Moment*, 10.
2. O'Rand, "When Old Age Begins," 111–12: "The chief limitation of many of the excellent studies [about the disability-free years of later life, is that they] thereby ignore earlier phases of the life course (especially midlife) when chronic disease and functional limitations emerge unevenly."
3. I told this story at a plenary at a conference in Maastricht, and asked the question, "What shall we say to them?" A young American, a gay activist from New York City who knows many people with AIDS, came up afterward to offer this answer. But he surely meant that the growing AIDS movement provides much-needed social and emotional support, so that even those who are living with dying may feel included and comforted.

Ackerman, Felicia Nimue. "Patient and Family Decisions about Life-Extension and Death." In *The Blackwell Guide to Medical Ethics*, ed. Rosamund Rhodes, Leslie Francis, and Anita Silvers, 52–68. Malden, MA: Blackwell, 2007.

Adams, Catherine G., and Barbara F. Turner. "Reported Change in Sexuality from Young Adulthood to Old Age." *Journal of Sex Research* 21, no. 2 (1985): 126–41.

Allen, Brenda J. "Hair Matters at Midlife." In *Age Ain't Nothing but a Number: Black Women Explore Midlife*," ed. Carleen Brice, 72–77. Boston: Beacon, 2003.

Allen, Scott. "Harvard to Study Katrina's Long-term Psychological Toll." *Boston Globe*, January 6, 2006, A4.

Alperowitz, Gar, and Thad Williamson. "A 'Top Ten' List of Bold Ideas." *Nation* January 23, 2006, 16–18.

Altman, Daniel. "How to Save Medicare? Die Sooner." *New York Times*, February 27, 2005, sec. 3, 1.

American Society for Aesthetic Plastic Surgery (ASAPS). "Cosmetic Plastic Surgery Research," Plastic Surgery Research Info, http://www.cosmeticplastic surgerystatistics.com/statistics.html.

Angell, Marcia. "Drug Companies and Doctors: A Story of Corruption." *New York Review of Books* 56, no. 1 (January 15, 2009).

Anthony, Louise M. "Natures and Norms." In *Feminist Theory: A Philosophical Anthology*, ed. Ann E. Cudd and Robin O. Andreasen, 127–44. Malden, MA: Blackwell, 2005.

Aronson, Stanley M. "Commentary—dignity of the Old with Dementia," *Providence Journal*, January 28, 2008, C5.

Ashcraft, Catherine. "Adolescent Ambiguities in *American Pie*: Popular Culture as a Resource for Sex Education." *Youth and Society* 35, no. 1 (September 2003): 37–70.

Asher, Deborah. "Strange Fruit." *Old Trout* (Winter 2006): 25.

Associated Press, "New Formula Shows More Live in Poverty." *Boston Globe*, October 21, 2009, A2.

Austen, Jane. *Emma*. Ed. Frances Ferguson. New York: Pearson Longman, 2006.

Ballenger, Jesse F. *Self, Senility, and Alzheimer's Disease in Modern America: A History*. Baltimore: Johns Hopkins University Press, 2006.

Barber, Diane, Caroline Goeser, MaryRoss Taylor, eds. *Thrive*. University of Houston, Women's Studies Program, 2009.

Barresi, Dorothy. "Ephebephobia." Reproduced in a feature on the poet in *Poetry Magazine*, spring 2005, http://www.poetrymagazine.com/archives/2005/Spr005/Features/barresi.htm.

Baruth, Philip E. "Consensual Autobiography: Narrating 'Personal Sexual History' from Boswell's *London Journal* to AIDS Pamphlet Literature." In *Getting a Life: Everyday Uses of Autobiography*, ed. Sidonie Smith and Julia Watson, 177–97. Minneapolis: University of Minnesota Press, 1996.

Basting, Anne Davis. "Creative Storytelling and Self-Expression among People with Dementia." In *Thinking about Dementia: Culture, Loss, and the Anthropology of Senility*, ed. Annette Leibing and Lawrence Cohen, 180–94. New Brunswick, NJ: Rutgers University Press, 2006.

Battin, Margaret. "Age Rationing and the Just Distribution of Health Care: Is There a Duty to Die?" *Ethics* 97, no. 2 (January 1987): 317–40.

Bauer-Maglin, Nan, and Alice Radosh, eds. *Women Confronting Retirement: A Nontraditional Guide*. New Brunswick, NJ: Rutgers University Press, 2003.

Bayer, Kathryn Jeanne. "The Shifting Gaze: Medical Aesthetics and the Technologies of the Aging Self." M.A. thesis, Georgetown University, 2004.

Beam, Alex. "Want a Long Life? No Worries." *Boston Globe*, February 23, 2010, G23.

Benjamin, Walter. *Illuminations: Essay and Reflections*. Ed. Hannah Arendt. Trans. Harry Zohn. New York: Shocken Books, 1955.

Beauvoir, Simone de. *Adieux: A Farewell to Sartre*. Trans. Patrick O'Brian. New York: Pantheon, 1984. (Originally published as *La Cérémonie des adieux*, 1981.)

———. *The Coming of Age*. 2nd ed. Trans. Patrick O'Brian. New York: W. W. Norton, 1996. (First edition published 1972; originally published as *La Vieillesse*, 1970.)

Bellow, Saul. *The Adventures of Augie March*. New York: Viking, 1953.

———. *Ravelstein*. New York: Penguin, 2000.

Benson, William F., and Nancy Aldrich. *CDC's Disaster Planning Goal: Protect Vulnerable Older Citizens*. Centers for Disease Control and Prevention Healthy Aging Program, March 2007, http://www.cdc.gov/aging/pdf/disaster_planning_goal.pdf

Berger, Leslie. "Two Years After: On Hormone Therapy, the Dust Is Still Settling." *New York Times*, June 6, 2005.

Binstock, Robert H. "Our Aging Societies: Ethical, Moral, and Policy Challenges." *Journal of Alzheimer's Disease* 12 (2007): 3–9.

Bird, Caroline. *Lives of Our Own: Secrets of Salty Old Women*. Boston: Houghton Mifflin, 1995.

Bloom, H. "Sexually Liberated Urban Twenty-something." *H Bomb* (Spring 2004): 20–22.

Blum, Virginia. "Becoming the Other Woman: The Psychic Drama of Cosmetic Surgery," *Frontiers* 26, no. 2 (2005): 104–31.

———. *Flesh Wounds: The Culture of Cosmetic Surgery*. Berkeley and Los Angeles: University of California Press, 2003.

Blumert, Burton S. "An Answer to Old Age." Lew Rockwell Web page, http://www.lewrockwell.com/blumert/blumert103.html (accessed October 2008).

Bonetta, Laura. "Coping with the Change." *Sage News and Views*, May 2, 2005.

Boston Women's Health Book Collective. *Our Bodies Ourselves: Menopause*. New York: Touchstone Books, 2006.

Bowman, Lee. "Katrina Response May Require Greater Mental-Health Resources." *Scripps-Howard News Service*, May 15, 2006.

Boyer, Peter J. "Eviction: Anatomy of a Foreclosure." *New Yorker*, November 24, 2008, 48–53.

Braund, Mark. *The Possibility of Progress*. London: Shepheard-Walwyn, 2005.

"Breast Cancer." *Drug Week*, March 21, 2008, on NewsRx, http://www.newsrx.com/newsletters/Drug-Week.html (accessed September 2008).

Breines, Wini. *Young, White, and Miserable: Growing Up Female in the Fifties*. Chicago: University of Chicago Press, 1992.

Brekhus, Wayne. "Social Marking and the Mental Coloring of Identity: Sexual Identity Construction and Maintenance in the United States." *Sociological Forum* 11, no. 3 (1996): 497–522.

Bretlinger, John. "Thanksgiving." Unpublished manuscript.

Brewer, Loretta. "Gender Socialization and the Cultural Construction of Elder Caregivers." *Journal of Aging Studies* 15, no. 3 (September 2001): 217–35.

Bridges, Andrew. "FDA Says Firms Still Lagging on Follow-up Drug Studies." *Boston Globe*, March 4, 2006, A7.

Brody, Jane E. "A Common Casualty of Old Age: The Will to Live." *New York Times*, November 27, 2007, D7.

Brogden, Mike. *Geronticide: Killing the Elderly*. London: Jessica Kingsley Publishers, 2001.

Brooks, Abigail. "Growing Older in a 'Surgical Age': An Analysis of Women's Lived Experiences and Interpretations in an Era of Cosmetic Surgery." Ph.D. diss., Boston College, 2007.

Brown, Paul B. "Maturity Is in Demand." *New York Times*, July 15, 2006, C5.

Burford, Michelle. "The Tale of a Photograph." *Essence*, http://www1.essence.com/news_entertainment/news/articles/thetaleofaphotograph (posted October 31, 2007).

Butler, Robert. *The Longevity Revolution: The Benefits and Challenges of Living a Long Life*. New York: Public Affairs, 2008.

———. "Age-ism," *The Gerontologist* 9 (1969): 243–46.

Byatt, A. S. *Possession: A Romance*. New York: Random House, 1991.

Bytheway, Bill. "Ageism and Age Categorization." *Journal of Social Issues* 61, no. 2 (June 2005): 361–74.

Calasanti, Toni M., and Kathleen F. Slevin. *Gender, Social Inequalities, and Aging*. Walnut Creek, CA: Altamira Press, 2001.

———. Introduction to *Age Matters: Realigning Feminist Thinking*, ed. Toni M. Calasanti and Kathleen F. Slevin. New York: Routledge, 2006.

Campbell, Jennifer. "Belonging and Belongings: Lessons from Katrina." *Aging Today*, July/August 2006, 7.

Canetto, Silvia Sara. "Elderly Women and Suicidal Behavior." In *Women and Suicidal Behavior*, ed. Silvia Sara Canetto and David Lester, 215–33. New York: Springer, 1995.

Capitano, Laura. "This Woman Doesn't Get Chick Flicks." *Florida Times-Union*, September 16, 2008.

Carpenter, Laura. "Gender and the Meaning and Experience of Virginity Loss in the Contemporary United States." *Gender and Society* 16, no. 3 (June 2002): 345–65.

Carpenter, Mackenzie. "Choosing Different Paths: Three Years Out from Blockbuster HRT Findings, Women are Navigating Menopause in Increasingly Personal Ways." *Pittsburgh Post-Gazette*, December 21, 2005, F1.

Carroll, Roz. "The New Anatomy: Is the Ego More than Skin Deep?" A talk given at Springfield Hospital, September 18, 2001, posted on Thinking Through the Body, http://www.thinkbody.co.uk/papers/is-the-ego-more.htm (accessed November 2008).

CBS Evening News. "Nips and Tucks for Senior Men: More Men Deciding You're Never too Old to Look Younger." News report, July 20, 2005. *CBS Evening News*, http://www.cbsnews.com/stories/2005/07/20/eveningnews/main710504.shtml.

Centers for Disease Control (CDC). "Suicide Data Sheet," 1999. Posted on the CDC page for Injury Prevention and Control: Violence Prevention, http://www.cdc.gov/ViolencePrevention/pdf/Suicide-DataSheet-a.pdf .

Centers for Disease Control and Prevention and the Kimberly-Clark Corporation. *Assuring Healthy Caregivers: A Public Health Approach to Translating Research into Practice. The RE-AIM Framework*. Neenah, WI: Kimberly-Clark Corporation, 2008.

Centers for Disease Control and Prevention and Merck Company Foundation. *The State of Aging and Health in America 2007*. Whitehouse Station, NJ: Merck Company Foundation, 2007.

Chan, Sewin, and Ann Huff Stevens. "Job Loss and Employment Patterns of Older Workers." *Journal of Labor Economics* 19, no. 2 (2001): 484–521.

"Change of Life Remains Hard." *USA Today*, September 26, 2005.

Chen, Pauline W. *Final Exam: A Surgeon's Reflections on Mortality*. New York: Vintage, 2007.

Choi, Precilla Y. L., and Paula Nicolson. *Female Sexuality: Psychology, Biology and Social Context*. New York: Harvester Wheatsheaf, 1994

Christofferson, John. "Study: Most Katrina Victims were Elderly." *Washington Post*, October 24, 2005.

Clark, David C. "The Puzzle of Suicide in Later Life." In *Before Their Time: Adult*

Children's Experiences of Parental Suicide, ed. Mary Stimming and Maureen Stimming. Philadelphia: Temple University Press, 1999.

Clarke, Laura Hurd, and Meredith Griffin. "The Body Natural and the Body Unnatural: Beauty Work and Aging." *Journal of Aging Studies* 21 (2007): 187–201.

Clarke, Laura Hurd, Robin Repta, and Meredith Griffin. "Non-Surgical Cosmetic Procedures: Older Women's Perceptions and Experiences." *Journal of Women and Aging* 19, no. 3/4 (2007): 69–87.

Clausen, Jan. *Apples and Oranges: My Journey through Sexual Identity*. New York: Houghton Mifflin, 1999.

Clendinen, Dudley. *A Place Called Canterbury: Tales of the New Old Age in America*. New York: Viking, 2008.

Cohen, Lawrence. "Thinking about Dementia." Introduction to *Thinking about Dementia: Culture, Loss, and the Anthropology of Senility*, ed. Annette Leibing and Lawrence Cohen, 1–19. New Brunswick, NJ: Rutgers University Press, 2006.

Cohn, Felicia. "Physician-Assisted Suicide. Con: A Better Prescription." http://biomednet.com/hmsbeagle/1997/07/people/op_ed.htm (posted May 2, 1997).

Cohn, Felicia, and Joanne Lynn. "A Duty to Care Revisited." In *Ethics in Practice*, 3rd ed., ed. Hugh LaFollette, 103–13. Oxford: Blackwell, 2007.

Colello, Kirsten J., et al. "End-of-Life Care: Services, Costs, Ethics, and Quality of Care." Congressional Research Service, February 23, 2009, http://opencrs.com/document/R40235/.

Collins, Karen Scott, et al. "Health Concerns across a Woman's Lifespan: The Commonwealth Fund 1998 Survey of Women's Health." *Commonwealth Fund*, May 5, 1999.

The Conference Board. "U.S. Job Satisfaction at Lowest Level in Two Decades." Press release, January 5, 2010, http://www.conference-board.org/utilities/press Detail.cfm?press_ID=3820.

Congressional Budget Office (CBO). "Disability and Retirement: The Early Exit of Baby Boomers from the Labor Force." CBO paper, November 2004, http://www.cbo.gov/ftpdocs/60xx/doc6018/11-22-LaborForce.pdf.

———. "High-Cost Care Beneficiaries." CBO paper, May 2005, http://cbo.gov/ftpdocs/63xx/doc6332/05-03-MediSpending.pdf.

Cornwell, Nancy C. "Rethinking Free Expression in the Feminist Classroom: The Problem of Hate Speech." *Feminist Teacher* 12, no. 3 (1998): 107–18.Counsel for Amicus Curiae AARP. *Brief Amicus Curiae of AARP in Support of Respondent*. American Bar Association Supreme Court Preview, February 2008, http://www.abanet.org/publiced/preview/briefs/feb08.shtml (accessed May 2009).

Cross, June. "The Old Man and the Storm." PBS TV documentary, aired January 6, 2008.

Crowley, Sheila. "Where Is Home?" In *There Is No Such Thing as a Natural Disaster: Race, Class, and Hurricane Katrina*, ed. Chester Hartman and Gregory D. Squires: 121–66. New York: Routledge, 2006.

Curb, Rosemary, and Nancy Manahan, ed. *Lesbian Nuns: Breaking Silence*. Tallahassee, FL: Naiad Press, 1985.

Daly, Gay. "Hundreds of Man-Made Chemicals Are Interfering with Our Hormones and Threatening Our Children's Future." *On Earth* 27, no. 4 (winter 2006): 20–27.

Daniluk, Judith C. *Women's Sexuality across the Life Span: Challenging Myths, Creating Meanings.* New York: Guilford Press, 1998.

Davies, Robertson. *The Cunning Man.* New York: Viking, 1994.

Dembner, Alice. "Ageism Said to Erode Care Given to Elders." *Boston Globe,* March 7, 2005.

———. "Mental Acuity in Seniors Improving, Study Suggests," *Boston Globe,* February 21, 2008, A1.

Demey, Juliette. "Peut-On Reprendre des Hormones?" *Elle* 29 (May 2006): 147–48.

Desjardins, Bertrand. "Why Is Life Expectancy Longer for Women than It Is for Men?" *Scientific American,* September 18, 2004, http://www.scientificamerican.com/.

Deslatte, Melinda. "Plans for New Charity Hospital Stall due to Lack of Support." WWLTV (Louisiana), February 16, 2007, http://www.wwltv.com/.

Destro, Robert A. "Target—the Elderly." In *Set No Limits: A Rebuttal to Daniel Callahan's Proposal to Limit Health Care for the Elderly,* ed. Robert L. Barry and Gerald V. Bradley. Urbana: University of Illinois Press, 1991.

Dickson, Debra, director. *Ruthie and Connie: Every Room in the House.* Documentary film, 2003.

Dillaway, Heather. "Menopause is the 'Good Old': Women's Thoughts about Reproductive Aging." *Gender and Society* 19, no. 3 (June 2005): 398–417.

Dillaway, Heather, et al. "'Why Can't You Control This?' How Women's Interactions with Intimate Partners Define Menopause and Family." *Journal of Women and Aging* 20, no. 1/2 (2008): 47–64.

Donahue, Hope. *Beautiful Stranger: A Memoir of an Obsession with Perfection.* New York: Gotham Books, 2004.

Douglas, Susan J. *Where the Girls Are: Growing Up Female with the Mass Media.* New York: Times Books, 1994.

Doyle, Joseph J. Jr. "Risky Business: Cutting Health Care Costs." *Boston Globe,* October 11, 2009, K9.

Drabble, Margaret. *Seven Sisters.* New York: Harcourt, 2002.

Duncan, Jeff. "Combating Katrina: Elderly Veterans Are Hard Hit by the Hurricane." *New Orleans Times-Picayune,* June 7, 2006, 1.

Ehrenreich, Barbara. *Bait and Switch: The (Futile) Pursuit of the American Dream.* New York: Henry Holt, 2005.

Ekström, Helene. "Trends in Middle-Aged Women's Reports of Symptoms, Use of Hormone Therapy, and Attitudes Towards It." *Maturitas* 52, no. 2 (October 16, 2005), doi: 10.1016.maturitas.2005.01.010.

Elliott, Carl. *A Philosophical Disease: Bioethics, Culture, and Identity.* New York: Routledge, 1999.

Enarson, Elaine. "Women and Girls Last? Averting the Second Post-Katrina Disaster." *Understanding Katrina: Perspectives from the Social Sciences*, June 11, 2006. http://understandingkatrina.ssrc.org/Enarson/.

Eskenazi, Loren. *More Than Skin Deep*. New York: HarperCollins, 2007.

Estes, Carroll L. "The Aging Enterprise Revisited." In *Critical Gerontology: Perspectives from Political and Moral Economy*, ed. Meredith Minkler and Carroll L. Estes, 135–46. Amityville, NY: Baywood Publishing, 1999.

———. "The Politics of Ageing in America." In *Dependency and Interdependency in Old Age: Theoretical Perspectives and Policy Alternatives*, ed. Chris Phillipson, Miriam Bernard, and Patricia Strang, 15–29. London: Croom Helm, 1986.

Estes, Carroll L., and Karen W. Linkins. "Critical Perspectives on Health and Aging." In *Handbook of Social Studies in Health and Medicine*, ed. Gary L. Albrecht, Ray Fitzpatrick, and Susan C. Scrimshaw. London: Sage, 2000.

Estes, Carroll L., Chris Philippson, and Simon Biggs. *Social Theory, Social Policy, and Ageing: A Critical Introduction*. Maidenhead, UK: Open University Press, 2003.

Faffer, Jaclynn I. "In the Eye of the Storm: Responding to Senior Needs Before, During, and After." *Journal of Jewish Communal Services* 83, no. 1 (fall 2007): 70–74.

Fairlie, Henry. "Greedy Geezers." *New Republic*, March 28, 1988.

Fausset, Richard. "New Orleans Economy Dodges Effects of the Global Recession." *Boston Globe*, April 5, 2009, A15.

"FDA Issues New Conflict of Interest Guidelines." Report on OMB Watch, April 3, 2007, http://www.ombwatch.org/node/3241.

Filosa, Gwen. "Appeals Court Takes Up Case of Elderly Deaths after Katrina." *New Orleans Times-Picayune*, August 6, 2008.

Fimrite, Peter. "Rights Group Warns Disaster Would Imperil Disabled, Elderly." *San Francisco Chronicle*, October 7, 2005, B5.

Folsom, Marcia McClintock. "The Challenges of Teaching *Emma*." In introduction to *Approaches to Teaching Jane Austen's "Emma,"* ed. Marcia McClintock Folsom, xvii–xliii. New York: Modern Language Association of America, 2004.

Foreman, Judy. "Hormones: Does Timing Make a Difference?" *Boston Globe*, February 20, 2006.

———. "Hormones Given through the Skin Are Worth a Look." *Boston Globe*, December 12, 2005, C1.

———. "Is Liposuction Safe?" *Boston Globe*, November 13, 2006, C2.

Freeman, Bea. "Going through Changes for the Better." In *Women Talk Sex: Autobiographical Writings on Sex, Sexuality, and Sexual Identity*, ed. Pearlie McNeil et al., 15–28. London: Scarlet Press, 1993.

Freud, Sigmund. *The Ego and the Id*. Rev. and ed. James Strachey. Trans. Joan Riviere. New York: Norton, 1962.

Freundlich, Naomi. "Menopause." *Business Week*, August 30, 2004.

Friedman, Richard A.. "The Waist May Expand, but the Libido Stays Fit." *New York Times*, October 24, 2006, G10.

Fugh-Berman, Adriane, and Anthony R. Scialli. "Gynecologists and Estrogen: An

Affair of the Heart." *Perspectives in Biology and Medicine* 49, no. 1 (winter 2006): 115–30.

Fussell, Elizabeth. "Leaving New Orleans: Social Stratification, Networks, and Hurricane Evacuation." *Understanding Katrina: Perspectives from the Social Sciences*, June 11, 2006.http://understandingkatrina.ssrc.org/Fussell/.

Gabe, Thomas, et al. "Hurricane Katrina: Social Demographic Characteristics of Impacted Areas." Congressional Research Service of the Library of Congress, November 4, 2005.

Gammel, Irene. "Parading Sexuality: Modernist Life Writing and Popular Confession." In *Confessional Politics: Women's Sexual Self-Representations in Lifewriting and Popular Media*, ed. Irene Gammel, 47–61. Carbondale: Southern Illinois University Press, 1999.

Gannon, Linda. "Sexuality and Menopause." In *Female Sexuality: Psychology, Biology and Social Context*, ed. Precilla Y. L Choi and Paula Nicolson, 100–124. New York: Harvester Wheatsheaf, 1994.

Genuis, Shelagh K., and Stephen J. Genuis. "Exploring the Continuum: Medical Information to Effective Clinical Practice." *Journal of Evaluation in Clinical Practice* 12, no. 1 (February 2006), doi: 0.1111/j.1365-2753.2005.00609.x.

Gibbons, Sheila. "Teen Magazines Send Girls All the Wrong Messages." Women's eNews, October 29, 2003, http://www.womensenews.org/.

Gilleard, Christopher, and Paul Higgs. *Cultures of Ageing: Self, Citizen and the Body*. Essex, UK: Pearson, 2000.

Gillick, Muriel. "Is Death Optional?" *The Hastings Center Health Care Cost Monitor*, May 27, 2009, 1–2.

Ginty, Molly M. "After Health Scare, Menopause Treatment Matures." Women's eNews, July 10, 2005, http://www.womensenews.org/.

———. "Sex Drugs for Women Flood the Market." Women's eNews, November 29, 2004, http://www.womensenews.org/.

———. "Women's Key to Home Ownership Opened Debt Trap." Women's eNews, January 15, 2010, http://www.womensenews.org/.

Gist, John, and Carlos Figueiredo. "Deeper in Debt: Trends among Midlife and Older Americans." *AARP Public Policy Institute Data Digest*, April 2002.

Goodman, Ellen. "The $250 Donation to Elders." *Boston Globe*, October 23, 2009, A15.

Golant, Stephen M. "The Gender Inequalities of Eldercare." *Aging Today*, March/April 2009, 3.

Gold, Sunny Sea. "The Hook-Up Report." *Seventeen Magazine*, December 2004, 98–99.

Goldman, Norma. "What Do Menopausal Women Want?" *Menopause Exchange Newsletter*, autumn 2002; *Practice Nurse* 25, no. 7 (April 11, 2003).

Gorman, C. "Menopause: A Healthy View." *Time*, May 8, 2005, 57.

Graham, Janice E. "Diagnosing Dementia: Epidemiological and Clinical Data as Cultural Text." In *Thinking about Dementia: Culture, Loss, and the Anthropology of*

Senility, ed. Annette Leibing and Lawrence Cohen, 80–105. New Brunswick, NJ: Rutgers University Press, 2006.

Greenberg, Michael. "Just Remember This." *New York Review of Books* December 4, 2008, 10–14.

Gregory, Raymond F. *Age Discrimination in the American Workplace: Old at a Young Age*. New Brunswick, NJ: Rutgers University Press, 2001.

Gross, Jane. "The Beginning of Something New." The New Old Age, *New York Times*, July 2, 2008.

Gubrium, Jaber F. *Oldtimers and Alzheimer's: The Descriptive Organization of Senility*. Greenwich, CT: JAI Press, 1986.

Gullette, Margaret Morganroth. *Aged by Culture*. Chicago: University of Chicago Press, 2004.

———. "Ageism and Social Change: The New Regimes of Decline." In *A Guide to Humanistic Studies in Aging*, ed. Thomas R. Cole, Ruth E. Ray, and Robert Kastenbaum. Baltimore: Johns Hopkins University Press, 2010.

———. "Beauvoir, Sartre, and 'The Conversations': From Life Storytelling to Age Autobiography." In *Writing Old Age*, ed. Julia Johnson, 64–79. Buckingham, UK: Open University and Centre for Policy on Ageing (Ageing and Biographical Studies), January 2004.

———. "Creativity, Aging, Gender: A Study of Their Intersections, 1910–1935." In *Aging and Gender in Literature: Studies in Creativity*, ed. Anne M. Wyatt-Brown and Janice Rossen. Charlottesville: University Press of Virginia, 1993.

———. "The Exile of Adulthood: Pedophilia and the Decline Novel." *Novel* 17, no. 3 (spring 1984): 215–32.

———. "In Medicare Blame Game, Seniors Aren't at Fault." *Boston Globe*, January 4, 2010.

———. "Male Midlife Sexuality in a Gerontocratic Economy: The Privileged Stage of the Long Midlife in Nineteenth-Century Age Ideology." *Journal of the History of Sexuality* 5, no. 1 (July 1994): 58–89.

———. "Menopause as Magic Marker." In *Reinterpreting Menopause: Cultural and Philosophical Issues*, ed. Paul A. Komesaroff, Philipa Rothfield, and Jeanne Daley. New York: Routledge, 1997.

———. "Midlife Discourses in the Twentieth-Century United States: An Essay on the Sexuality, Ideology, and Politics of 'Middle Ageism.'" In *Welcome to Middle Age! (And Other Cultural Fictions)*, ed. Richard A. Shweder, 3–44. Chicago: University of Chicago Press, 1998.

———. *Safe at Last in the Middle Years*. Berkeley and Los Angeles: University of California Press, 1988. Available on iUniverse, http://www.iuniverse.com/.

———. "What to Do When Being Aged by Culture: Brief Annals of the Twentieth-Century Hormone Wars." *Tikkun*, July/August 2003, 63–65.

———. "What to Do When Being Aged by Culture: Hidden Narratives from the Twentieth-Century Hormone Debacle." In *Listening to Older People's Stories*, ed. Anne M. Wyatt-Brown. Special issue of *Generations* 27, no. 3 (fall 2003): 71–76.

———. What, Menopause *Again?*" *Ms.* (Summer 1993).

Haber, Carole. "Anti-Aging: A Historical Framework for Understanding the Contemporary Enthusiasm." *Generations* 25, no. 4 (Winter 2001/2002): 9–14.

Hachinski, Vladimir. "Shifts in Thinking about Dementia." *JAMA* 300, no. 18 (November 12, 2008): 2172–73.

Hales, Diane. "Embrace 'The Change.'" *Parade*, October 10, 2004, 4–6.

Halliday, Mark. *Keep This Forever*. Dorset, VT: Tupelo Press, 2008.

Hamilton, Emily A., Laurie Mintz, and Susan Kashubeck-West. "Predictors of Media Effects on Body Dissatisfaction in European-American Women." *Sex Roles: A Journal of Research* 56 (2007): 397–402.

Handel, Amos. "Perceived Change of Self among Adults: A Conspectus." In *Self and Identity: Perspectives across the Lifespan*, ed. Terry Honess and Krysia Yardley-Matwiejczuk, 320–37. London: Routledge, 1987.

Harden, Blaine. "With Age Comes Resilience, Storm's Aftermath Proves." *Washington Post*, September 14, 2005.

Hardwig, John. "Is There a Duty to Die?" *Hastings Center Report* 27, no. 2 (March/April 1997): 34–42.

Hareven, Tamara. *Family Time and Industrial Time*. Lanham, MD: University Press of America, 1993.

Harris, Gardiner, and Alex Berenson. "Legal Strategy Boosts Drug Makers." *Boston Globe*, April 6, 2008.

Harrison, Stephen, and Michael Moran. "Resources and Rationing: Managing Supply and Demand in Health Care." In *Handbook of Social Studies in Health and Medicine*, ed. Gary L. Albrecht et al., 493–508. London: Sage, 2000.

Hartman, Chester. "Report from New Orleans." *Poverty and Race* 14, no. 6 (November/December 2005): 3–5.

Hartman, Chester, and Gregory D. Squires. "The Social Construction of Disaster: New Orleans as the Paradigmatic American City." In *Seeking Higher Ground: The Hurricane Katrina Crisis, Race, and Public Policy Reader*, ed. Manning Marable and Kristen Clarke, 271–94. New York: Palgrave Macmillan, 2008.

Hazlitt, William. "Why the Arts are Not Progressive: A Fragment (Jan. 1814)." In *William Hazlett: Selected Writings*, ed. Jon Cook. Oxford: Oxford University Press, 1991.

Healy, Patrick. "Kerry Revives <apos>92 Election Theme to Attack Bush." *Boston Globe*, May 19, 2004, A3.

Heilbroner, David. "Plastic Disasters: These Scars are Forever." HBO interview with Kate Davis and David Heilbroner, http://www.hbo.com/docs/programs/plasticdisasters/interview/html (accessed March 2008).

Heilbrun, Carolyn G. "From Rereading to Reading." Guest column, *PMLA* 119, no. 2 (March 2004): 211–17.

———. *The Last Gift of Time: Life beyond Sixty*. New York: Dial Press, 1997.

———. "Taking a U-Turn: The Aging Woman as Explorer of New Territory." In "Women Aging," special issue of *Women's Review of Books*, July 2003, http://www.wellesley.edu/womensreview/archive/2003/07/special.html.

——. "Women Writers: Coming of Age at 50." *New York Times Book Review*, September 4, 1988, 1.

Herrnstein Smith, Barbara. "Figuring and Reconfiguring the Humanities and the Sciences." *Profession*, 2005, 18–27; doi: 10.1632/074069505X79035.

Hipple, Steven. "Worker Displacement in the Mid-1990s." *Monthly Labor Review*, July 1999, 15–32.

Hoberman, John. *Testosterone Dreams: Rejuvenation, Aphrodisia, Doping*. Berkeley and Los Angeles: University of California Press, 2005.

Hogan, Mary Ann. "Welcome to the Rock n' Roll Rest Home." Special report to the (*South Florida*) *Sun-Sentinel*, posted on Wholestory, http://www.wholestory.com/stories/welcome_to_the_rock_n_roll_rest_home/ (accessed September 12, 2008).

Holland, Janet, et al. *Pressured Pleasure: Young Women and the Negotiation of Sexual Boundaries*. London: Tufnell Press, 1991.

Holstein, Martha. "On Being an Aging Woman." In *Age Matters: Realigning Feminist Thinking*, ed. Toni M. Calasanti and Kathleen F. Slevin, 322–31. New York: Routledge, 2006.

Holt, Pat. "Holt Uncensored," no. 385 (May 27, 2004), http://www.holtuncensored.com/members/column385.html.

Hooyman, Nancy R. "Is Aging More Problematic for Women than Men?" In *Controversial Issues in Aging*, ed. Andrew Scharlach and Leonard W. Kaye, 125–35. Boston: Allyn and Bacon, 1997.

Houck, Judith A. *Hot and Bothered: Women, Medicine, and Menopause in Modern America*. Cambridge, MA: Harvard University Press, 2006

Houlihan, Liam. "HRT Cancer Link Found." *Herald Sun* (Australia), August 1, 2005, 8.

Hoynes, William. "Consider the Source." *Extra!* 19, no. 1 (January/February 2006): 13.

Hughes, Mary Elizabeth, and Angela O'Rand. "The Lives and Times of the Baby Boomers." Report for the Russell Sage Foundation and Population Reference Bureau, October 2004, http://www.prb.org/Articles/2004/TheLivesandTimesoftheBabyBoomers.aspx.

"A Hurdle to Mental Health." Editorial, *New Orleans Times-Picayune*, September 20, 2006, 6.

Hurricane Katrina Community Advisory Group. "Overview of Baseline Survey Results." Report for the Harvard Medical School, Department of Health Care Policy, August 29, 2006, http://www.hurricanekatrina.med.harvard.edu/pdf/baseline_report%208-25-06.pdf.

[Illinois] State News Service. "Governor Blagojevich Announces More than $1.2 Million to Help Keep Women in Illinois Healthy." Press release, September 9, 2008, http://www.idph.state.il.us/public/press08/9.9.08OWH_InitGrants.htm.

Im, Soyon. "Love Clinic." In *Colonize This!* ed. Daisy Hernandez and Bushra Rehman, 133–41. New York: Seal Press, 2002.

International Agency for Research on Cancer. "IARC Monographs Programme

Finds Combined Estrogen-Progestogen Contraceptives and Menopausal Therapy are Carcinogenic to Humans." IARC Press Release no. 168, July 29, 2005.

Isaacs, Leora W., and David J. Bearison. "The Development of Children's Prejudice against the Aged." *International Journal of Aging and Human Development* 23 (1986): 175–93.

Jackson, Harry, Jr. "Trouble Connecting?" *St. Louis Post-Dispatch*, September 4, 2006, H1.

Jackson, Kate M. "Looking Old? Do Something about It." *Boston Globe*, January 3, 2008.

Jackson, William A. *The Political Economy of Population Ageing*. Cheltenham, UK: Edward Elgar, 1998.

James, Jacquelyn B. "This American Life: A Discussion of the Role of History in Developmental Outcomes." In *Historical Influences on Lives and Aging*, ed. K. Warner Schaie and Glen Elder, 21–34. New York: Springer, 2005.

Jamison, Kay Redfield. *Night Falls Fast: Understanding Suicide*. New York: Knopf, 1999.

Jenkins, Pamela, Shirley Laska, and Gretchen Williamson. "Connecting Future Evacuation to Current Recovery: Saving the Lives of Older People in the Next Catastrophe." *Generations* (Winter 2007/2008): 49–52.

Johnson, Carla K. "Studies Tie Depression Risk to Approach of Menopause." *Boston Globe*, April 4, 2006, A6.

Johnson, Diane, and John F. Murray. "The Patient Talks Back." *New York Review of Books*, October 23, 2008, 24–27.

Johnson, Glenn S. "Environmental Justice and Katrina: A Senseless Environmental Disaster." *Western Journal of Black Studies* 32, no. 1 (2008): 42–52.

Johnson, Merri Lisa. "Fuck You and Your Untouchable Face: Third Wave Feminism and the Problem of Romance." In *Jane Sexes It Up: True Confessions of Feminist Desire*, ed. Merri Lisa Johnson, 13–21. New York: Four Walls Eight Windows, 2002.

Jones, Rebecca L. "'That's Very Rude: I Shouldn't be Telling You That': Older Women Talking about Sex." *Narrative Inquiry* 12, no. 1: 121–43.

Jorgensen, Christine. *A Personal Autobiography*. New York: Paul S. Eriksson, 1967.

Josefson, Deborah. " JAMA Falls Foul of Fabricated Suicide Story," *BMJ* 323 (1 September 2001): 472, doi:10.1136/bmj.323.7311.472, http://www.bmj.com/cgi/content/full/323/7311/472/a (accessed September 10, 2008).

Joyce, Kelly, and Laura Mamo, "Graying the Cyborg: New Directions in Feminists' Analyses of Aging, Science, and Technology." In *Age Matters: Realigning Feminist Thinking*, ed. Toni M. Calasanti and Kathleen F. Slevin, 99–121. New York: Routledge, 2006.

Juengst, Eric T., et al. "Biogerontology, 'Anti-aging' Medicine, and the Challenges of Human Enhancement." *Hastings Center Report* 33, no. 4 (2003): 21–30.

"Jury Awards $99m to 3 Nev. Women from Wyeth." *Boston Globe*, October 15, 2007.

Kachka, Boris. "Sticking Her Neck Out." Interview with writer Nora Ephron, August 6, 2006. *New York Magazine*, http://nymag.com/arts/books/profiles/18854/.

Kaiser Family Foundation. "Racial and Ethnic Disparities in Women's Health

Coverage and Access to Care: Findings from the 2001 Kaiser Women's Health Survey." Issue brief, March 2004, http://www.kff.org/womenshealth/upload/Racial-and-Ethnic-Disparities-in-Women-s-Health-Coverage-and-Access-to-Care.pdf.

Kaplan, Esther. "Can Labor Revive the American Dream?" *Nation*, January 26, 2009, 11–16.

——. "Just Say No to AIDS." *Nation*, January 31, 2005.

"Katrina Victims Can Stay in Their Trailers." *Boston Globe*, June 4, 2009.

Katz, Steven. "Alarmist Demography: Power, Knowledge and the Elderly Population." *Journal of Aging Studies* 6, no. 3 (1992): 203–25.

Kaufman, Sharon R. "Dementia-Near-Death and 'Life Itself.'" In *Thinking about Dementia: Culture, Loss, and the Anthropology of Senility*, ed. Annette Leibing and Lawrence Cohen, 23–42. New Brunswick, NJ: Rutgers University Press, 2006.

Kessler, Ronald, et al., for the Hurricane Katrina Community Advisory Group. "Mental Illness and Suicidality after Hurricane Katrina," *Bulletin of the World Health Organization* 84, no. 11 (November 2006): 1–21.

Khanna, Roma. "Katrina's Aftermath." *Houston Chronicle*, November 27, 2005.

Kinsley, Michael. "Mine Is Longer Than Yours." *New Yorker*, April 7, 2008, 38–43.

Kitwood, Tom. *Dementia Reconsidered: The Person Comes First*. Buckingham, UK: Open University Press, 1997.

Klinenberg, Eric. *Heat Wave: A Social Autopsy of Disaster in Chicago*. Chicago: University of Chicago Press, 2002.

Koenig, Linda J. "Depression and the Cultural Context of the Self-Serving Bias." In *The Conceptual Self in Context: Culture, Experience, Self-Understanding*, ed. Ulric Neisser and David A. Jopling, 62–74. Cambridge: Cambridge University Press, 1997.

Kolata, Gina. "On the Trail of Estrogen and a Mirage of Youth." *New York Times*, July 5, 2003.

Kowalczyk, Liz. "Breast Cancer Diagnoses Took Sudden Drop in '03." *Boston Globe*, December 15, 2006, A1.

Kress, Susan. *Carolyn G. Heilbrun: Feminist in a Tenured Position*, Charlottesville: University Press of Virginia, 1997.

——. "The Mysterious Life of Kate Fansler." *Tulsa Studies in Women's Literature* 24, no. 2 (2006): 257–64.

Krisberg, Kim. "Emergency Preparedness a Challenge for Older Americans." *The Nation's Health* (American Public Health Association), April 2007, 14–15.

Krugman, Paul. "America's Senior Moment." *New York Review of Books*, March 10, 2005, 6–11.

Krupa, Michelle, and Coleman Warner. "Across South, Displaced Chime in with Own Ideas for Rebuilding N.O." *New Orleans Times-Picayune*, December 3, 2006, 1.

Kuczynski, Alex. *Beauty Junkies: Inside Our $15 Billion Obsession with Cosmetic Surgery*. New York: Doubleday, 2006.

Kushner, Tony. *Thinking about the Longstanding Problems of Virtue and Happiness*. New York: Theatre Communications Group, 1995.

Kuttner, Robert. *Obama's Challenges*. White River Junction, VT: Chelsea Green Publishing, 2008.

Lacy, Katherine K. "Mature Sexuality: Patient Realities and Provider Challenges." *SIECUS Report*, December 1, 2001.

Laditka, Sarah B., and Maria Pappas-Rogich. "Anticipatory Caregiving Anxiety among Older Women and Men." *Journal of Women and Aging* 13 (2001): 3–18.

Lamott, Annie. *Traveling Mercies: Some Thoughts on Faith*. New York: Pantheon, 1999.

Landman, Beth. "Struck Twice." *New York Magazine*, March 8, 2004, http://nymag .com/nymetro/news/trends/columns/cityside/n_9981/.

Langridge, Darren, and Trevor Butt. "A Hermeneutic Phenomenological Investigation of the Construction of Sadomasochistic Identities." *Sexualities* 7, no. 1 (February 2004): 31–53.

Lazar, Kay. "Prickly Policies." *Boston Globe*, April 26, 2009, G1.

Lazarus, Simon, and Sergio Eduardo Munoz, "Supreme Court Undermines Protections for Older Workers." Commentary on New America Media, January 11, 2010, http://news.newamericamedia.org/news/view_article.html?article_id=91 a4d44663fc59e865ed063af50a6bd0.

Lee, Min Jin. *Free Food for Millionaires*. New York: Warner, 2007.

Leonhardt, David. "After the Great Recession," *New York Times Magazine*, April 28, 2009, http://www.nytimes.com/pages/magazine/ (accessed May 2009).

Lerner, Barron H. "A Calculated Departure: For Someone in Good Health, Can Suicide Ever Be a Rational Choice?" *Washington Post*, March 2, 2004: F1.

Lessing, Doris. *The Diary of a Good Neighbor*. (Part 1 of *The Diaries of Jane Somers*.) New York: Vintage Books, 1984.

Levkoff, Sue. "Assault on the Elderly." *Boston Globe*, January 13, 2006, A19.

Levy, Becca R. "Improving Memory in Old Age through Implicit Self-Stereotyping." *Journal of Personality and Social Psychology* 71, no. 6 (1996): 1092–1107.

———. "Mind Matters: Cognitive and Physical Effects of Aging Self-Stereotypes." *Journal of Gerontology: Psychological Sciences* 58B, no. 4 (2003): P203–11.

Levy, Becca R., Ori Ashman, and Itiel Dror. "To Be or Not to Be: The Effects of Aging Stereotypes on the Will to Live." *Omega* 40, no. 3 (1999/2000): 409–20.

Levy, Becca R., et al. "Longevity Increased by Positive Self-Perceptions of Aging." *Journal of Personality and Social Psychology* 83, no. 2 (2002): 261–70.

Lewis, Lisa M., et al. "Factors Influencing Condom Use and STD Acquisitions among African-American College Women." *Journal of American College Health* 49, no. 1 (July 1, 2000): 19–23; PubMed index, http://www.ncbi.nlm.nih.gov/ pubmed/10967880.

Linder, John. "Oncology." *Living with Dying: A Handbook for End-of-Life Healthcare Practitioners*, ed. Joan Berzoff and Phyllis R. Silverman, 697–722. New York: Columbia University Press, 2004.

Lock, Margaret. "Accounting for Disease and Distress: Morals of the Normal and

Abnormal." In *Handbook of Social Studies in Health and Medicine*, ed. Gary L. Albrecht et al., 259–77. London: Sage, 2000.

Lock, Margaret, and Patricia Kaufert, "Menopause, Local Biologies, and Cultures of Aging." *American Journal of Human Biology* 13 (2001): 494–504.

Loe, Meika. *The Rise of Viagra: How the Little Blue Pill Changed Sex in America*. New York: New York University Press, 2004.

Loewy, Erich H. "Age Discrimination at Its Best: Should Chronological Age Be a Prime Factor in Medical Decision Making?" *Health Care Analysis* 13, no. 2 (June 2005): 101–17.

Loggers, Elizabeth Trice, et al. "Racial Differences in Predictors of Intensive End-of-Life Care in Advanced Cancer Patients." *Journal of Clinical Oncology* 27 (2009): 5559–64.

Lokon, Elizabeth. "Opening Minds through Art (OMA): Creativity and Dementia." Paper delivered at the conference "Gender, Creativity, and the New Longevity," Women's Studies, University of Houston, November 14, 2008.

Louisiana Department of Health and Hospitals. "Post-Katrina Death/Suicide Rate Study." Summary released by the State of Louisiana, http://www.dhh.louisiana .gov/offices/publications/pubs-87/Orleans%20Death%20Study.pdf.

———. "Vital Statistics of All Bodies at St. Gabriel Morgue." Death statistics released by the State of Louisiana, November 14, 2005, http://www.dhh.louisiana .gov/offices/publications/pubs-145/DECEASED%20Victims%20released _11-14-2005_publication.pdf.

Lyman, Karen A. "Bringing the Social Back In: A Critique of the Biomedicalization of Dementia." In *Aging and Everyday Life*, ed. Jaber F. Gubrium and James A. Holstein, 340–56. Malden, MA: Wiley-Blackwell, 2000.

Madrick, Jeff. "Enron, the Media, and the New Economy." *Nation*, April 1, 2002, 17–20.

Maguire, Marie. *Men, Women, Passion and Power: Gender Issues in Psychotherapy*. Hove, UK: Brunner-Routledge, 2004.

Malveaux, Suzanne. "An Interview with Judge Ivan L. R. Lemelle." In *Seeking Higher Ground: The Hurricane Katrina Crisis, Race, and Public Policy Reader*, ed. Manning Marable and Kristen Clarke, 75–83. New York: Palgrave Macmillan, 2008.

Mann, Charles C. "The Coming Death Shortage: Why the Longevity Boom Will Make Us Sorry to be Alive." *Atlantic Monthly*, May 2005, 92–104.

Mansfield, Phyllis Kernoff, Patricia Bathalow Koch, and Ann M. Voda. "Qualities Midlife Women Desire in Their Sexual Relationships and Their Changing Sexual Response." *Psychology of Women Quarterly* 22, no. 2 (June 1998): 285–303.

Maranan, Julia Tolliver. "50 to 59." The Wellness Issue, *Boston Globe Magazine*, December 4, 2005, 39.

Marchione, Marilynn. "New Study Strongly Connects Hormone Use to Breast Cancer." *Boston Globe*, December 16, 2008, A18.

Markley, Melanie, and Cynthia Leonor Garza. "Katrina's Aftermath: Reaching out to Aid the Elderly, Frail." *Houston Chronicle*, September 10, 2005.

Markus, Hazel Rose, Patricia R. Mullally, and Shinobu Kitayama. "Selfways:

Diversity in Modes of Cultural Participation." In *The Conceptual Self in Context: Culture, Experience, Self-Understanding*, ed. Ulric Neisser and David A. Jopling, 13–61. Cambridge: Cambridge University Press, 1997.

Marshall, Barbara, and Stephen Katz. "Forever Functional: Sexual Fitness and the Ageing Male Body." *Body and Society* 8, no. 4 (December 2002): 43–70.

Marshall, Leni. "Teaching Ripening: Incorporating Lessons on Age Identity, Aging, and Ageism into the Humanities Classroom." *Transformations: The Journal of Inclusive Scholarship and Pedagogy* 19, no. 2 (fall 2008/winter 2009): 55–80.

Martin, Adrienne M. "Hope and Exploitation. " *Hastings Center Report* 38, no. 5 (September/October 2008): 49–55.

Martin, Norah. "Physician-Assisted Suicide: Weighing Feminist Concerns." In *Recognition, Responsibility and Rights: Feminist Ethics and Social Theory*, ed. Robin N. Fiore and Hilde Lindemann Nelson, 131–42. Lanham, MD: Rowman and Littlefield, 2003.

McArthur, Grant. "Asian Cosmetic Surgery Disaster," *Herald Sun* (Australia), August 31, 2007.

McCulley, Russell. "Is New Orleans Having a Mental Health Breakdown?" *Time*, August 1, 2006.

McDaniel, Karen Cotton, and Angela W. Malone. "Bootylicious Body or Barbie." Talk at the National Women's Studies Association Annual Conference, Atlanta, November 2009.

McFadden, Susan H., Vanessa Frank, and Alyssa Dysert. "Creativity in the 'Now' of Advanced Dementia: Glimpses of the Lifeworld through Storytelling and Painting." *Journal of Aging, Humanities, and the Arts* 2, no. 2 (April/June 2008): 135–49.

McNagny, Sally E., Nanette Kass Wenger, and Erica Frank. "Personal Use of Postmenopausal Hormone Replacement Therapy by Women Physicians in the United States." *Annals of Internal Medicine* 127, no. 12 (December 15, 1997): 1093–96.

McNeill, Erin. "Blood, Sex, and Hormones: A Theoretical Review of Women's Sexuality over the Menstrual Cycle." In *Female Sexuality: Psychology, Biology and Social Context*, ed. Precilla Y. L. Choi and Paula Nicolson, 56–82. New York: Harvester Wheatsheaf, 1994.

Mead, Margaret. *Culture and Commitment: A Study of the Generation Gap*. Garden City, NY: Natural History Press / Doubleday, 1970.

Melby, M. K., Margaret Lock, and Patricia Kaufert. "Culture and Symptom Reporting at Menopause." *Human Reproduction Update* 11, no. 5 (May 2005): 495–512.

Mendenhall, Ruby, et al. "Job Loss at Mid-Life: Managers and Executives Face the "New Risk Economy." *Social Forces* 87, no. 1 (September 2009): 185–207.

Meyer, Madonna Harrington. "Family Status and Poverty among Older Women: The Gendered Distribution of Retirement Income in the United States." In *Social Problems across the Life Course*, ed. Helena Z. Lopata and Judith A. Levy, 243–58. Lanham, MD: Rowman and Littlefield, 2003.

Miller, Jane. "Not Wanting Things." *Raritan* 29, no. 1 (Summer 2009): 144–57.

Milner, Colin. "'Active' v. 'Anti' Aging." *Aging Today* (March/April 2008): 7.

Minerd, Jeff. "USPsych: 'Katrina Brain' Pervasive after Hurricane." Paper delivered at the U.S. Psychiatric and Mental Health Congress, New Orleans, November 16–19, 2006. Posted on MedpageToday, November 22, 2006, http://www.medpagetoday.com/MeetingCoverage/USPsychiatricMentalHealthCongress/4582 (accessed December 2006).

Miron, Luis, and Robert Ward. "Drowning the Crescent City: Told Stories of Katrina." *Cultural Studies / Critical Methodologies* 7, no. 2 (2007): 154–68.

Moody, Harry. *Aging: Concepts and Controversies*. Thousand Oaks, CA.: Pine Forge Press, 1994.

Morgan, Kathryn Pauly. "Women and the Knife: Cosmetic Surgery and the Colonization of Women's Bodies." *Hypatia* 6, no. 3 (1991): 25–53.

Morris, Wesley. "It's All about Face." *Boston Globe Magazine*, August 24, 2008, N10.

Moyn, Samuel. "This Seeming Brow of Justice." *Nation*, December 7, 2009, 35–41.

Mundy, Liza. "Better Living through Chemistry: How Menopause Has Become the New Hot-Button Topic in Women's Health." *Washington Post*, October 5, 2003.

Munt, Sally, et al. "Virtually Belonging: Risk, Connectivity, and Coming Out On-Line." *International Journal of Sexuality and Gender Studies* 7, no. 2/3 (July 2002): 125–37.

Murrell, Annette L. "Autobiography as a War Machine (or, Wild Titties I Have Known)," *Auto/biography Studies (a/b)* 16, no. 1 (Summer 2002): 141–55.

National Cancer Institute (NIH). "Decrease in Breast Cancer Rates Related to Reduction in Use of Hormone Replacement Therapy." NIH Press Release, April 18, 2007, http://www.cancer.gov/newscenter/pressreleases/BreastIncidence Drop (accessed June 2008).

Nelson, Todd D. "Ageism: Prejudice against Our Feared Future Self." *Journal of Social Issues* 61, no. 2 (June 2005): 207–21.

Nestle, Joan. "Desire Perfected: Sex after Forty" In *Lesbians at Midlife: The Creative Transition*, ed. Barbara Sang, Joyce Warshow, Adrienne J. Smith, 180–83. San Francisco: Spinster Books, 1991.

Neumark, David. "Age Discrimination Legislation in the United States." National Bureau of Economic Research, NBER Working Paper no. 8152 (March 2001).

Newman, Katherine S. *A Different Shade of Gray*. New York: New Press, 2003.

"No Country for Old Men," *Brattleboro Reformer*, July 30, 2008 (accessed Lexis-Nexis, October 2008).

Norris, Floyd. "She Works, Her Grandson Doesn't." *New York Times*, September 3, 2006.

Norris, Michelle. "Written Testimony of American Association of Homes and Services for the Aging." Report to the House Financial Services Committee, Subcommittee on Housing and Community Development, September 15, 2005, www.aahsa.org/WorkArea/DownloadAsset.aspx?id=958.

North American Menopause Society (NAMS). *Menopause Guidebook*. Cleveland: NAMS, 2003.

——. "Position Statement." *Menopause: The Journal of the North American Menopause Society* 17, no. 2 (2010): 242–55.

Novelli, William D. "Katrina's Legacy." *AARP Bulletin*, November 2005, 35.

Nowak, Rachel. "When Looks Can Kill." *New Scientist* 192, no. 2574 (October 26, 2006): 18–21.

NPR. "Profile: History of Sex Education in American Public Schools," *Weekend Edition* with Scott Simon, reported by Wade Goodwyn, February 7, 2004.

Nuland, Sherwin B. "Getting in Nature's Way." *New York Review of Books*, February 12, 2004, 32–35.

Ockene, Judith K., et al. "Symptom Experience after Discontinuing Use of Estrogen Plus Progestin." *JAMA* 294, no. 2 (July 13, 2005): 183–92.

Off, Gavin. "A Look at the Victims of Hurricane Katrina." *Scripps News*, February 20, 2008.

Ogden, Gina. "Sexuality and Spirituality in Women's Relationships: Preliminary Results of an Exploratory Survey." Paper published by the Wellesley Centers for Women, 2002, http://www.wcwonline.org/.

Ohlemacher, Stephen. "Immigrant Number Hits Record 37.5m." *Boston Globe*, September 12, 2007, A4.

——. "Seniors' Job Losses, Early Retirements Hurt Social Security." *Boston Globe*, September 28, 2009, A8.

Older Women's League. *Newsletter*. November 16, 2005.

O'Neil, Tim. "Evacuee Finds Comfort in Arms of Family." *St. Louis Post-Dispatch*, December 22, 2005, A1.

O'Rand, Angela. "When Old Age Begins: Implications for Health, Work, and Retirement." In *Contemporary Challenges to Age-Based Public Policy: The New Politics of Old Age Policy*, ed. Robert B. Hudson. Baltimore: Johns Hopkins University Press, 2005.

Orwell, George. *A Collection of Essays*. Garden City: Doubleday Anchor, 1954.

Overall, Christine. *Aging, Death, and Human Longevity*. Berkeley and Los Angeles: University of California Press, 2003.

——. "Concepts of Life Span and Life Stages: Implications for Ethics." In *Feminist Moral Philosophy*, ed. Samantha Brennan, 299–318. Calgary: University of Calgary Press, 2003.

——. "Feminist Ended Her Life Journey—but Was It Really Finished?" *Kingston Whig-Standard* (Ontario), October 27, 2003.

Paley, Grace. *Begin Again: Collected Poems*. New York: Farrar, Straus and Giroux, 2001.

Parker-Pope, Tara. "The Fear Factor: Women Continue to Shy Away from Hormone Therapy." *Wall Street Journal*, October 11, 2005, D1.

Parks, Jennifer A. "Why Gender Matters to the Euthanasia Debate: On Decisional Capacity and the Rejection of Women's Death Requests." *Hastings Center Report* 30, no. 1 (2000): 30–36.

Phillips, Lynn. *Flirting with Danger: Young Women's Reflections on Sexuality and Domination*. New York: New York University Press, 1999.

Pierce, Charles. "Girls Gone Weird: Remember, Bridesmaids, It's OK Sometimes to Just Say No." *Globe Magazine*, August 24, 2008, 9.

Pitts-Taylor, Victoria. *Surgery Junkies: Wellness and Pathology in Cosmetic Culture*. New Brunswick, NJ: Rutgers University Press, 2007.

Plassman, B. L., et al. "Prevalence of Dementia in the United States: The Aging, Demographics, and Memory Study." *Neuroepidemiology* 29 (2007): 125–32.

Pollitt, Katha. "Old Is the New Young." Keynote address, "Gender, Creativity, and the New Longevity," Women's Studies Department, University of Houston, November 13, 2008.

Pope, John. "Katrina's Toll on Elderly Shows More Evacuation Help Needed." Newhouse News Service, August 21, 2007.

———. "N.O. Is Short on Doctors, Dentists." *New Orleans Times-Picayune*, April 26, 2006, 1.

Porter, Eduardo, and Mary Williams Walsh, "Retirement Becomes a Rest Stop as Pensions and Benefits Shrink." *New York Times*, February 9, 2005, A1.

Powell, Eileen Alt. "Communities Called Unready for Seniors." *Boston Globe*, September 28, 2006, A6.

Prado, C. G. *The Last Choice: Preemptive Suicide in Advanced Age*. 2nd ed. New York / Westport: Praeger Press / Greenwood Press, 1998.

Prado, C. G., and S. J. Taylor. *Assisted Suicide: Theory and Practice in Elective Death*. Amherst, NY: Humanity Books, 1999.

Proulx, Annie. "Brokeback Mountain." In *Close Range: Wyoming Stories*. New York: Scribner, 1999.

Public Citizen Health Research Group. "FDA Grants Public Citizen Petition for Botox Warning." Statement by deputy director Peter Lurie, *Public Citizen News*, May/June 2009, 14.

———. "New 'Diseases' Often Invented by Drug Industry Marketing Departments to Sell You Drugs." *Public Citizen Health Letter* 21, no. 9 (September 2005): 1–2.

Ratner, Lizzy. "Homeless in New Orleans." *Nation*, February 25, 2008, 13–18.

Rattigan, David. "Tight Jaws in Tough Times Lead to Pain." *Boston Globe North*, May 7, 2009, NO1.

Ray, Ruth. *Endnotes: An Intimate Look at the End of Life*. End of Life Care series. New York: Columbia University Press, 2008.

Reckdahl, Katy. "New Orleans Has More Homeless People and Fewer Services for Them." Newhouse News Service, August 7, 2007.

Redmond, Ann-Marie. *Sex, Drugs, and Middle Age*. Documentary film, 2005.

Reinharz, Shulamit. "Friends or Foes: Gerontological and Feminist Theory." *Women's Studies International Forum* 9, no. 5 (1986): 503–14.

Richeson, Jennifer A., and J. Nicole Shelton. "A Social Psychological Perspective on the Stigmatization of Older Adults." In *When I'm 64*, ed. Laura L. Carstensen and Christine R. Hartel, 174–208. Washington, DC: National Academies Press, 2006.

Roberto, Karen A., Tammy L. Henderson, and Yoshinori Kamo. "Resilience and

Resources of Aging Families." Poster at the Meeting of the Gerontological Society of America, Dallas, November 2006.

Robinson, Barrie. "Ageism Teaching Module." Berkeley: School of Social Welfare, University of California, 1994.

Robinson, Marilynne. *Gilead*. New York: Farrar, Straus and Giroux, 2004.

———. *Home*. New York: Farrar, Straus and Giroux, 2008.

Robinson, R. G., et al. "Can We Prevent Poststroke Depression? *JAMA* 299 (May 28, 2008): 2391.

Rohde, David, et al. "Vulnerable and Doomed in the Storm." *New York Times*, September 19, 2005.

Rosenfeld, Kenneth E., et al. "End-of-Life Decision Making." *Journal of General Internal Medicine* 15 (2000): 620–25.

Roth, Philip. *Everyman*. Boston: Houghton Mifflin, 2006.

———. *Exit Ghost*. Boston: Houghton Mifflin, 2007.

Rothenberg, Leslie S. "Withholding and Withdrawing Dialysis from Elderly ESRD Patients." Part 2, "Ethical and Policy Issues." *Geriatric Nephrology and Urology* 3, no. 1 (February 1993): 23–41.

Rothman, Sheila, and David Rothman. *The Pursuit of Perfection: Promise and Perils of Medical Enhancement*. New York: Pantheon, 2003.

Rothstein, Richard. "Gay Elders: The Second Gay Health Crisis." Queer Sighted, April 3, 2007, http://www.queersighted.com/2007/04/03/gay-elders-aids-the-second-wave/.

Rowley, Hazel. *Tête-à-Tête: Simone de Beauvoir and Jean-Paul Sartre*. New York: HarperCollins, 2005.

Russell, Jenna. "Northeastern Allots $75 Million to Recruit 100 Professors." *Boston Globe*, Feb. 11, 2004, A1.

Russo, Richard. *Bridge of Sighs*. New York: Knopf, 2007.

———. *Nobody's Fool*. New York: Vintage, 1994.

Rutstein-Riley, Amy. "'I am More Than my Medical Record': A Relationship-Centered Approach to Emerging Adult Women's Health." Lecture, Women's Studies Research Center, Brandeis University, November 15, 2007.

Sack, Kevin. "In Hospice Care, Longer Lives Mean Money Lost." *New York Times*, November 27, 2007, A1.

Saltzman, Jonathan. "Suit Ties Death of Woman to Face Lift." *Boston Globe*, March 4, 2010, 1.

Samuelson, Robert J. "Economic Death Spiral." *Washington Post*, 2005, A19.

Sartre, Jean-Paul. *Les Mots*. Paris: Gallimard, 1964.

Schilt, Kristen. "I'll Resist with Every Inch and Every Breath: Girls and Zine Making as a Form of Resistance." *Youth and Society* 35, no. 1 (September 2003): 71–97.

Shneidman, Edwin S., ed. *Autopsy of a Suicidal Mind*. Oxford: Oxford University Press, 2004.

———. *Comprehending Suicide: Landmarks in Twentieth-Century Suicidology*. New York: American Psychological Association, 2001.

Schulz, James H., and Robert H. Binstock. *Aging Nation: The Economics and Politics of Growing Older in America*. Westport, CT: Praeger, 2006.

Schwartzmann, Paul. "50 Years of Seniority Gives AARP the Benefit of Strength in Numbers." *Boston Globe*, September 6, 2008, A4.

Seager, Joni. "Natural Disasters Expose Gender Divide." *Chicago Tribune*, September 14, 2005.

Seaman, Barbara. *The Greatest Experiment Performed on Women*. New York: Hyperion, 2003.

Sedensky, Matt. "Number of Older Americans Filing for Bankruptcy Soars." *Boston Globe*, August 28, 2008, A5.

Service, Robert. "New Role for Estrogen in Cancer?" *Science*, n.s. 279, no. 5357 (March 13, 1998): 1631.

Shabahangi, Nader, et al. "Some Observations on the Social Consequences of Forgetfulness and Alzheimer's Disease: A Call for Attitudinal Expansion." *Journal of Aging, Humanities, and the Arts* 3 (2009): 38–52.

Shapiro, Judith. "Transsexualism: Reflections of the Persistence of Gender and the Mutability of Sex." In *Same-Sex Cultures and Sexualities: An Anthropological Reader*, ed. Jennifer Robertson, 138–61. Oxford: Blackwell, 2005.

Sharkey, Patrick. "Survival and Death in New Orleans: An Empirical Look at the Human Impact of Katrina." *Journal of Black Studies* 37, no. 4 (March 2007): 482–501.

Shield, Renee Rose, and Stanley M. Aronson, eds. *Aging in Today's World: Conversations between an Anthropologist and a Physician*. New York: Berghahn Books, 2003.

Shulman, Alix Kates. *To Love What Is: A Marriage Transformed*. New York: Farrar, Straus and Giroux, 2008.

Siegel, Rachel Josefowitz. "Ageism in Psychiatric Diagnosis." In *Bias in Psychiatric Diagnosis*, ed. P. J. Caplan and L. Cosgrove. New York: Jason Aronson, 2004.

Simms, Mary. "Opening the Black Box of Rationing Care in Later Life: The Case of 'Community Care' in Britain." *Journal of Aging and Health* 15, no. 4 (November 2003): 713–37.

Sinclair, David. "Rethinking the Definition of Aging." Interview in the *Boston Sunday Globe*, July 7, 2008, 74.

Singer, Natasha. "Drug Company Paid Ghostwriters to Back Hormones." *New York Times*, August 5, 2009, A7.

Smith, André P. "Negotiating the Moral Status of Trouble: The Experiences of Forgetful Individuals Diagnosed with No Dementia." In *Thinking about Dementia: Culture, Loss, and the Anthropology of Senility*, ed. Annette Leibing and Lawrence Cohen, 64–79. New Brunswick, NJ: Rutgers University Press, 2006.

Smith, Martin. "The Storm." *Frontline*, November 22, 2005.

Smith, Patricia. *Blood Dazzler: Poems*. Minneapolis: Coffee House Press, 2008.

Smith, Richard. "Curbing the Influence of the Drug Industry: A British View." *Public Citizen Health Letter* 21, no. 11 (November 2005): 1–3.

Smith, Stephen. "Risk Found by '02 Hormone Study Challenged." *Boston Globe*, April 4, 2007.

Smith, Zadie. *White Teeth*. New York: Random House, 2000.

Solomon, Andrew. *The Noonday Demon: An Atlas of Depression*. New York: Scribner, 2001.

Southam, Brian C., ed. *Jane Austen*. Volume 1, *1811–1870: The Critical Heritage*. 1979. Reprint, London and New York: Routledge, 1995.

"Spectacles of Moral Decline: Representation of Ageing Femininity in Celebrity Culture." Unpublished manuscript.

Stein, Rob. "Aging Boomers Facing Increased Health Problems." *Boston Globe*, April 22, 2007.

Stepp, Laura Sessions. *Unhooked*. New York: Riverhead, 2007.

Strickland, Bonnie. "Beauty and the Butch." *Journal of Lesbian Studies* 3, no. 4 (1999): 107–15.

Sturgeon, Jessica. "*Smith v. City of Jackson*: Setting an Unreasonable Standard." *Duke Law Journal* 56 (2007): 1377, http://www.law.duke.edu/shell/cite.pl?56+ Duke+L.+J.+1377 (accessed May 2009).

Styron, William. *Darkness Visible: A Memoir of Madness*. New York: Random House, 1990.

Sullivan, Deborah A. *Cosmetic Surgery: The Cutting Edge of Commercial Medicine in America*. New Brunswick, NJ: Rutgers University Press, 2001.

Tada, Joni Eareckson. *The God I Love: A Lifetime of Walking with Jesus*. Grand Rapids, MI: Zondervan, 2003.

Talbot, Margaret. "Brain Gain: The Underground World of 'Neuroenhancing' Drugs." *New Yorker*, April 27, 2009, 32–43.

Talburt, Susan. "Constructions of LGBT Youth: Opening Up Subject Positions." *Theory into Practice* 43, no. 2 (spring 2004): 116–21.

Tandon, Bharat. *Jane Austen and the Morality of Conversation*. London: Anthem, 2003.

Taylor, MaryRoss. "Essays." In *Thrive*, ed. Diane Barber, Caroline Goeser, and MaryRoss Taylor. Houston: University of Houston, Women's Studies Program, 2009.

Teichert, Nancy Weaver. "Katrina's Lasting Storm: Disaster Plans for Seniors Reviewed." *Sacramento Bee*, September 13, 2005.

Teitell, Beth. "Yes I'm Cutting Back on My Spending BUT . . ." *Boston Globe*, October 9, 2008, D1.

Terkel, Studs. *Coming of Age: The Story of Our Century by Those Who've Lived It*. New York: New Press, 1995.

Thomas, Evan. "The Case for Killing Granny." *Newsweek*, September 12, 2009, http://www.newsweek.com/id/215291.

Thomas, Lesley. "Why Do Women Want to Look Plastic?" *Daily Telegraph* (London), July 5, 2006, 23.

Tiefer, Leonore. *Sex Is Not a Natural Act and Other Essays*. 2nd ed. Boulder, CO: Westview, 2004.

Tolman, Deborah. *Dilemmas of Desire: Teenage Girls Talk about Sexuality*. Cambridge, MA: Harvard University Press, 2002.

Toth, Emily. "Dishing with the Girls . . . Oops, the Women." *Women's Review of Books* 24, no. 2 (March/April 2007): 16–18.

Travis, Cheryl Brown, and Jacquelyn White. *Sexuality, Society, and Feminism*. Washington, DC: American Psychological Association, 2000.

Tyler, Melissa. "Managing between the Sheets: Lifestyle Magazines and the Management of Sexuality in Everyday Life." *Sexualities* 7, no. 1 (February 2004): 81–106.

Tu, Wanzhu, et al. "Time from First Intercourse to First Sexually Transmitted Infection Diagnosis among Adolescent Women." *Archives of Pediatric and Adolescent Medicine* 163, no. 12 (December 2009): 1106–11.

Uchitelle, Louis. *The Disposable American: Layoffs and Their Consequences*. New York: Knopf, 2006.

U. S. Bureau of the Census. *Current Population Survey*. Washington, DC, 2005.

U.S. Bureau of Labor Statistics. *Current Population Survey* (September 2009), table 31, Total Both Sexes. (Unpublished tabulations.)

———. "Usual Weekly Earnings of Wage and Salary Workers." News Release for Third Quarter 2009, http://www.bls.gov/news.release/archives/wkyeng_10162009.htm.

U.S. Department of Health and Human Services, Office of the Assistant Secretary for Planning and Evaluation. "Overview of the Uninsured in the United States: An Analysis of the 2005 Current Population Survey." ASPE Issue Brief, http://aspe.hhs.gov/health/Reports/05/uninsured-cps/index.htm (accessed June 2009).

Ussher, Jane M. *Managing the Monstrous Feminine: Regulating the Reproductive Body*. London: Routledge, 2005.

Wade, Leigh. "Preparing Early, Acting Quickly: Meeting the Needs of Older Americans during Disasters." Report for the Senate Special Committee on Aging, October 5, 2005. Washington, DC: GPO, 2006; http://www.access.gpo.gov/congress/senate/pdf/109hrg/26545.pdf.

Walker, Bonnie L. *Sexuality and the Elderly: A Research Guide*. Westport, CT: Greenwood, 1997.

Wallace, Lorraine S., et al. "Evaluation of Web-Based Osteoporosis Educational Materials." *Journal of Women's Health* 14, no. 10 (2005): 936–45.

Wallerstein, Immanuel. "A Left Politics for the 21st Century? or, Theory and Praxis Once Again." *New Political Science* 22, no. 2 (November 2, 2000): 143–59.

Wallis, Victor. "Species Questions (*Gattungsfragen*): Humanity and Nature from Marx to Shiva." *Organization and Environment* 14, no. 1 (spring/summer 2000): 500–507.

Walsh, Thomas J., Susan Orsega, and David Banks. "Lessons from Hurricane Rita: Organizing to Provide Medical Care during a Natural Disaster." *Annals of Internal Medicine*, August 14, 2006.

Watkins, Elizabeth Siegel. *Estrogen Elixir: A History of Hormone Replacement Therapy in America*. Baltimore: John Hopkins University Press, 2007.

Weil, Andrew. *Healthy Aging: A Lifelong Guide to Your Physical and Spiritual Well-Being*. New York: Knopf, 2005.

Weinberg, Steven. "Without God." *New York Review of Books*, September 25, 2008, 73–76.

Weisler, Richard H., James G. Barbee IV, and Mark H. Townsend. "Mental Health and Recovery in the Gulf Coast after Hurricanes Katrina and Rita." *JAMA* 296 (2006): 585–88.

Weitz, Rose. *The Politics of Women's Bodies: Sexuality, Appearance, and Behavior*. New York: Oxford University Press, 1998.

Wenger, G. Clare. "What Do Dependency Measures Measure? Challenging Assumptions." In *Dependency and Interdependency in Old Age: Theoretical Perspectives and Policy Alternatives*, ed. Chris Phillipson, Miriam Bernard, and Patrician Strang, 69–84. London: Croom Helm, 1986.

West, Rebecca. *The Young Rebecca: Writings of Rebecca West, 1911–1917*. Ed. Jane Marcus. New York: Viking, 1982.

Whelan, Bob, et al. "Housing Authority of New Orleans Pre-Katrina Resident Survey." New Orleans: Housing Authority of New Orleans, 2008.

White, Michael. "New Orleans's African American Musical Traditions: The Spirit and Soul of a City." In *Seeking Higher Ground: The Hurricane Katrina Crisis, Race, and Public Policy Reader*, ed. Manning Marable and Kristen Clarke, 88–106. New York: Palgrave Macmillan, 2008.

Williams, Patricia. "Movin' On Down." *Nation*, July 14, 2008, 9.

Wilper, Andrew P., et al. "Health Insurance and Mortality in US Adults." *American Journal of Public Health* 99, no. 12 (December 2009), table 1.

Wilson, Elizabeth. "Tell It Like It Is: Women and Confessional Writing." In *Sweet Dreams: Sexuality, Gender and Popular Culture*, 21–45. London: Lawrence and Wishart, 1988.

Wingate, Martha S., et al. "Identifying and Addressing Vulnerable Populations in Public Health Emergencies: Addressing Gaps in Education and Training." *Public Health Reports* 122 (May/June 2007): 422–26.

Winterich, Julie A. "Sex, Menopause, and Culture: Sexual Orientation and the Meaning of Menopause for Women's Sex Lives." *Gender and Society* 17, no. 4 (August 2003): 627–42.

Wolf, Richard. "New Orleans Symbolizes U.S. War on Poverty." *USA Today*, December 22, 2006, 13A.

Wolf, Susan M. "Health Care Reform and the Future of Physician Ethics." *Hastings Center Report* 24, no. 2 (1994): 28–41.

Woodman, Sue. "The Women's Enron." *Nation*, September 2/9, 2002, 6.

Woods, Nancy Fugate, and Ellen Mitchell. "Symptoms during the Perimenopause: Prevalence, Severity, Trajectory, and Significance in Women's Lives." *American Journal of Medicine*, December 18, 2005, 118; suppl. 12B, 14–24.

Woodward, Kathleen. "Against Wisdom: The Social Politics of Anger and Aging." *Cultural Critique* 51 (spring 2002): 186–218.

———. "Telling Time: Aging and Autobiography." Unpublished manuscript. Another version appeared in *Generations* 27, no. 3 (fall 2003): 65–70.

Woolf, Virginia. *The Moment and Other Essays*. New York: Harcourt Brace Jovano-
vich, 1948.

———. *Three Guineas*. San Diego: Harvest/HBJ, 1938.

Wyatt, Gail Elizabeth. *Stolen Women: Reclaiming Our Sexuality, Taking Back our Lives*.
New York: John Wiley, 1997.

Yager, James D., and Nancy E. Davidson. "Mechanisms of Disease: Estrogen Carcinogenesis in Breast Cancer." *New England Journal of Medicine* 354 (2006): 270–82.

ableism, 15, 30, 54, 56, 64, 65, 66, 80, 184, 185, 215
   cognitive, 199
   fighting ageism and, 58, 216, 223
   See also disability; ageism-consciousness: intersectionality
activism, 135, 211. *See also* anti-ageist activism
adolescence, 25, 129, 134, 205. *See also* women, emerging-adult
adult offspring, relationships with parents, 2, 26, 29, 50, 64, 73, 137, 176, 194
   author and her mother, 117, 174–75, 183–91, 194, 196–98, 201–3
   as caregivers: Daughters' Club, 40, 173; grief at failure of love, 201–2; learning about old age/disability, 26; portrayed as overwhelmed, 26, 50
   daughters learning from mothers, 87, 118
   foreboding about memory loss, 193
   grief at deaths, 67
   portrayed in novels, 168–74, 175–76, 179–81, 191
   rescuing their parents, 26, 65, 66
   son(s), 26, 37, 40, 66
   See also parents of adult offspring
African Americans, 62, 64, 65, 67–69, 71–73, 76, 77, 78, 80, 234n2

   midlife and old/er women, 71–72, 76–77, 140
   women, 62, 87, 106, 109, 124, 125, 130, 136, 234n2
age, 30, 62–63, 185
   ascribed category, 222
   as cultural construction, 6, 16, 143, 168, 215: made to appear natural, biological given, 4, 57, 75, 100; as marker of difference between young/er and old/er people, 2; neglect of category by media, 78; reason to foreground in anti-ageism, 80
   See also other age *entries*; aging *entries*; generations
age anxiety, 12, 41, 119, 120, 185
   channeled to midlife body, 95
   onset at young ages, 15, 23–24, 57
   See also ageism *entries*; age-related emotions; decline *entries*; memory loss in midlife and beyond: terror of
age auto/biography, 7, 150
   critical, 5, 117, 141–42
   sexual, 127, 137, 142–43, 152
age class, 14, 22, 23, 80, 159, 193, 222
age classes, named. *See* adolescence; childhood; midlife *entries*; old age; women, emerging-adult
age-class transitions, unnamed. *See* aging-into-old-age; aging-past-youth

age critic(s), 7, 14, 38, 160, 164
    author as, 15, 22, 32, 43, 100, 138, 150
    emphasis on whole life course, 166
    on late style, 164
    reading for age, 168
    resisting decline, 30; 52, 222
    revising sexual age narratives, 126,
        138
    writers as, 216, 223. *See also* age stud-
        ies; gerontologists
aged by culture (theory of social con-
    struction of age), 7, 30, 34–35
    aims to improve life course, 121
    being "aged" starts ever younger, 91
    inquires how we are so aged, 6, 101,
        121
    notes confusion of "aging" and "age-
        ism," 7, 14, 17, 33–35, 47
    terms like "middle-ageism" or "age-
        ism" useful to, 7–8 passim
    See also ageism-consciousness; age
        studies
age discrimination
    every worker likely to be affected
        by, 4
    gendered, 4, 119–20, 121
    in medical care for old/er people, 30,
        51, 52
    in midlife employment, 1–4, 9, 14, 15,
        37, 119, 153
    multiple discriminations, 63
    See also middle-ageism, as a historical
        phenomenon: economic construc-
        tion; midlife job loss; stereotypes
        of later life
Age Discrimination in Employment Act
    (ADEA), 3–4, 11; weakened by
    Supreme Court, 4, 153
age gaze, 33, 103, 119, 163, 184, 194
    visual progress narratives, 109, 115
    women who defy it, 107, 109–10
age hierarchy, 152, 173, 175
    consideration for elders, 181–82
    versus gerontocracy, 175–76
    See also seniority
ageicide, 21–28, 194. *See also* "Eskimo . . ."

age identity(ies) across time, 149, 160
    continuity in relation to changes, 56,
        136, 142, 160, 162–64, 190, 194
    full selfhood accrues over life course, 6
    identity-stripping in later life, 46, 51,
        54, 126, 205
    psychocultural immune system, 120
age ideology of United States, 16, 27–28,
    59, 60. *See also* decline *entries*
ageism, 5, 58, 71, 176, 223
    against women, 8, 30–32, 45, 51
    among old/er people, 134, 184
    aspect of "decline," 165
    class-based, 31, 74
    confused with "aging," 6, 14, 17, 33–35,
        47, 100, 163
    hard for young/er people to under-
        stand, 58, 184
    invisibility of old/er people, 42, 47,
        48, 65, 67
    learned by children, 6, 15
    "the new," 8–15, 17
    too many referents for, 7
    worse than other biases, 30, 50, 103–4
    youth as cultural superiority, 6, 68,
        81, 85
    See also other ageism *entries*;
        anti-ageism; decline *entries*;
        middle-ageism *entries*
ageism, analyzed, 13, 34, 36–37, 63–64
ageism, as a historical phenomenon, 6–7,
    9, 14, 22–24, 57, 175–76
    crisis created around Alzheimer's,
        178–79
    fantasies of committing suicide to
        avoid aging/old age, 23–25, 54–56,
        60, 222
    memory loss being pathologized as
        "dementia," 100, 191–93
    right-wing policy of cutting social
        safety nets, 12–14, 29, 31, 50, 70, 81
    sources of "the new regime" of de-
        cline, 14–15, 33, 39, 87, 96, 120
    worsening in our era, 11, 13–15, 50,
        103, 182
    See also decline *entries*; "duty to die";

memory loss in midlife and beyond: terror of; middle-ageism, as
a historical phenomenon
ageism-consciousness, 14
  ageism compared to other "isms,"
    15, 30
  interplay of history and personal life
    course, 6
  intersectionality, of ageism and other
    biases, 16, 31, 54, 56: ageism and
    ableism, 58, 216, 223; in Katrina,
    63–65, 67, 75, 80
  raising of, 17, 39, 59: cartoons, 16, 39,
    199; education for children and
    younger people, 39, 167–68; en-
    lightened caregivers, 198–200; love,
    216; novels and memoirs about late-
    life love, 164, 204, 206, 207–20
  See also anti-ageism; feminism;
    middle-ageism, resistance to
ageism in behavior, 140
  cognitive competition, 184–86,
    199–200
  cuts in Medicare, 52, 70
  health-care system, 12, 26, 27, 55, 99
  lethal ageism: age-related deaths
    in Katrina, 38, 62–66, 74, 234n2,
    235n12; medical homicide, 29–30,
    51, 194
  lower wages, 9
  in medical practice, 35, 51, 77–78, 230
  neglect of old/er people in
    public-health emergencies, 65–
    68, 78
  neglect of women's end-of-life
    wishes, 51
  no COLA in Social Security, 31
  shunning, 37, 183–86, 194, 216
  See also ageicide; pharmaceutical
    companies
ageism in language and images, 118,
    195–96
  "anti-aging" sales pitches, 7, 9, 33–34,
    86, 96, 99, 100, 103, 176, 178
  concept of "population aging" as bad,
    190

denial of personhood to old people,
    81, 191
  fiction of decline through aging, 206
  hate speech, 50, 183–84, 187, 191, 195,
    232n30: "burden," 5, 13, 26, 50, 55,
    60, 194; "demented," 36; jokes, 31,
    36, 37, 179, 193; "geezer," 5, 11, 15,
    50; language of "sustainability"
    about costs of health care, 11–14,
    51–52, 193–94; proposing a "duty
    to die," 27, 37–39, 51, 55–56, 195;
    stereotypes, 6, 10, 16, 55, 192;
    threats of killing old sick people,
    21–31, 51
  See also "anti-aging" products,
    services, ideology; cult of youth;
    "duty to die"; "Eskimo . . ."; media,
    mainstream: and ageism
ageism, psychological risks of, for old/er
    people, 43, 55, 57, 74
  identity-stripping, 46, 47, 54
  internalization of losses of value, 6,
    43, 138, 162
  possible suicidal ideation, 51, 54–57
  sex snobbery, 138, 140
ageism, resistance to. *See* anti-ageism;
    decline (through aging), as system:
    opposition to
ageless consciousness, 163
age narratives, aka life-course narratives,
    35, 156, 160, 199
  ability to repeat generic story-shape
    of, 149
  conditioned by culture and econom-
    ics, 150, 154–45
  decline through aging, 7, 54, 61, 72,
    88, 96, 164, 165, 173, 191, 204, 205,
    217, 247n2: dominant in American
    culture, 24; nonfiction, fiction,
    and poetry about, 161, 175, 205–6;
    personal age autobiography, 59,
    150; with preordained plot, 189–
    90; prospective (about sexuality,
    body, cognition, beauty, ability),
    24, 57, 125, 154, 173, 202; taught to
    children, 6, 148–50, 151

age narratives (*continued*)
  decline versus progress, 35, 59, 148–50,
    160–61, 164, 218–19: the two
    dominant fables of aging, 7; posed
    as a binary, 154
  literary alternatives to decline (ro-
    mance, tragedy, elegy), 154, 164,
    206, 207–18, 221
  positive aging, 219: different from
    progress narratives, 141, 165, 219
    (*see also* positive aging)
  progress, 7, 15, 23, 168, 244n9: affirms
    value of aging, 147–49; of author's
    mother, 40, 44, 148, 201, 203;
    becoming obligatory in USA, 152;
    bodily, material, social conditions
    that support telling a, 117, 152, 155,
    156–57, 159, 165; class elements of,
    148–51, 154–59, 165–66; continu-
    ation despite sickness, disability,
    old age, 159–65, 209, 218–19;
    decline elements possible in, 147,
    149; denial and other defenses
    against loss, 162; evolving from
    positive aging, 219, 223; produces a
    more resilient self, 151; as resistant
    fictions, sexual, 109, 141; taught to
    children, 39–40, 116, 147–49, 151,
    162, 165; undermined by poverty,
    insecurity, bias, 155
  prospective, 39, 59: change possible
    in, 89; of cognitive decline, 173,
    191; fantasy of need for suicide,
    54–55; frequently about false
    decline, 24, 56–57, 88, 202; told by
    parents, 116, 148–55.
  See also age auto/biography; memoirs;
    novels; writers and artists
age-related emotions, 222
  cautious veneration, 182
  dysmorphia, 105–6
  hopes, 35, 120, 132
  political anger, 30, 35, 61, 73
  terror of memory loss, in hypercogni-
    tive society, 24, 54, 175, 181, 188–89,
    191–93

  See also age anxiety; ageism, psycholog-
    ical risks of; fears of aging/old age
age studies, 38, 57, 59, 198, 225
  importance of studying whole life
    course, 166
  monitors the oppressors, 16
  studies intersectionality of ageism
    with other biases, 16, 31, 54, 56, 63,
    64, 65, 66, 67, 75
  teaches age consciousness, 168
  treats aging as a narrative, 159
  See also ageism-consciousness
"aging," 59, 118
  attributed prematurely to Baby
    Boomers, 20, 24, 103
  confusion about difference between
    ageism and, 6, 7, 14, 17, 33–35, 47,
    100
  a costly "aging" America, 11, 49
  described: as choice of narratives
    about time, 5, 150, 159; as loss of
    status, 45–48; as normal process,
    34, 43, 108, 179; as outliving your
    money, 31
  imagined as deep-old-age, 24
  involves being aged by culture, 7, 30,
    34–35, 91, 101, 121, 135
  means "old age," 4
  through medical model as disease
    state, 27, 34, 176
  proxy for historical change, 167
  in recessions, 13
  viewed positively, 14, 73, 167
  See also age *entries*; *other* aging *entries*;
    body
aging-into-old age
  abilities linked to, 73
  decline interpretations of: biological
    universal deterioration, 4, 27, 34,
    35, 176–77; "new fate worse than
    death," 24, 30, 205 (*see also* ageism
    entries; decline *entries*)
  in families, 176
  fiction about, 164, 205
  not synonymous with illness, 219
  as positive experience, 167

as progress (*see* age narratives: progress)

aging narratives. *See* age narratives

aging-past-youth, 4, 5, 11, 161
 constructed as a decline in era of longevity, 9, 38, 119, 125, 126
 constructed optimistically, 33, 133, 218
 medicalized, 95, 96
 men also targeted by decline young, 33, 126
 nonfiction and poetry about, 161, 206
 See also decline *entries*; progress

AIDS, 29, 129, 134, 140, 164, 193, 248n3

"alarmist demography." *See under* longevity (the new)

Alzheimer's, 88, 169, 175, 188
 crisis created around, 178–79
 improving attitudes towards people with, 179, 190–91, 200
 as label that impedes caregiving, 173–74
 as part of ruthless decline narrative, 54, 173–74, 190–91
 rising terror of, 54, 169, 174, 178–79, 191
 See also cognitive impairments; "dementia"; "dementias"; *memory loss* entries

Alzheimer's, people with
 art and poetry by, 199–200
 gifts of, 200

American dream of progress in the life course, 15; becoming more insecure, 152–54

anti-ageism, 6, 8, 15, 34–35, 37, 40–41, 61, 81
 deinternalizing decline, 17, 34, 60–61
 and feminism, 43, 44, 46
 helps tell progress narrative, 40
 imaginative embrace of whole life course, 74, 79, 116
 obstacles to, 37, 57
 political anger, 30, 35, 61, 73

anti-ageist activism, 15–17, 30, 58
 "duty to aid," 57, 65
 duty to care, 6, 60, 80–81

equal right to life for enfeebled elders, 24, 57

improved caregiving for people with cognitive impairments, 26, 190, 199–200, 202

improves conditions of life storytelling, 15, 39

as a movement, 16–17

prayer for, 41

role of government, 10, 16–17, 31, 79–81

social changes needed, 15–17, 39, 61, 122

suicide counseling, 58–60

visual progress narratives, 109–10, 115

See also middle-ageism, resistance to; pro-aging; progress

"anti-aging" products, services, ideology
 ageist sales pitches: 7, 9, 33–34, 86, 96, 99, 120, 122, 176, 178; addressed to men, 91, 99, 119; for cosmetic surgeries, 103 passim, 120; for "curing" old age, 99; for "lifestyle medicines," 89; promises of rejuvenation through estrogen, 7, 120–21; by uglification industries, 34, 96, 100–101, 106, 119–20, 122
 arguments against, 34, 89, 96–97, 98–101
 See also commerce in aging; rejuvenation

Asian-American women, 87

author, 42, 116, 127, 142
 as age critic, 15, 22, 32, 43, 138, 150
 learning pro-aging and anti-ageism, 117, 148, 151–52, 159
 relation to decline, 202–3
 relationship to mother, 174–75, 183–91, 194, 196–98, 201–3
 revelation in the shower, 32–33
 telling first decline story in childhood, 150

author's father (Marty Morganroth), 44, 148, 207–8

author's father-in-law (George Gullette), 5, 139

author's granddaughter (Vega Violet, aka Vivi), 6, 16, 40, 116, 149, 175, 186–87

author's mother (Betty Morganroth), 16, 22, 36, 137, 142, 175, 183, 186–87, 208
  lifelong progress narrative of, 40, 44, 148, 201, 203
  memory loss versus what remains, 187–91
  physical recoveries of, in nineties, 196, 197, 201

"Baby Boomers" (born 1946–64), 23
  as "aging," 20, 24, 103
  alleged to have "Boomer power," 28, 202
  considered the most expensive generation, 17
  debt of, doubled in 1990s, 75
  duty to die of, 28
  health of, versus parents' generation, 10
  historical bad luck of, 3, 5, 8–10, 17
  inequality among, 9
  lack of national planning for old age of, 10
  misrepresentations of, 6, 9, 10, 23, 28, 50, 74
  wage inequality among, 9
  women as, 103, 112
  See also midlife *entries*; middle-ageism *entries*

beauty in later life
  age-related dysmorphia, 105
  feminist and pro-aging views of, 107–11, 115, 117–18
  and ethnicity, 103–4, 109
  fantasies of youth, manipulated by commerce in aging, 114
  rituals of social comparison, 14, 117
  socially constructed as declining with age, 6, 33–34, 105–6, 125
  versus visual cult of youth, 32–33, 109, 115

beauty industries. *See* cosmetic surgery; rejuvenation; uglification industries

bioethicist(s), 37, 49, 50

biogerontology. *See* gerontology

body, "the," 5, 221
  anticipated as declining young, 23, 24, 33, 34, 118
  biocultural approach to, 101
  decline decreases satisfaction in, 118
  discourse of "dysfunction" of, past youth, 94, 126, 139
  disgust with the non-young body, 140, 206
  "essentialized," 108
  female, 32–34, 85, 92, 101, 128–29
  images substituted for experience of, 117
  medical model of, 27
  memoirs and physical decline, 218
  pro-aging and feminist views of, missing in dominant culture, 32–34, 105, 107–11, 113–15, 118, 148, 152, 175, 202
  See also body-mind; decline *entries*; face(s)

body-mind, the, 35, 36, 41, 134, 142, 205, 218, 222
  bodily integrity: as basis for rejecting cosmetic surgery, 107, 118; from infancy, 116, 122–23, 142
  as integrated whole, 34

brain, as declining organ, 193, 195, 198
  failures of brain scientists, 177–78
  mind reduced to, 177
  "steroids" for, 178, 193
  versus theory of neurogenesis, 177, 189
  See also medicalization of aging-past-youth; memory loss *entries*; mind

breast cancer after 2002
  legal suits, 86
  rates of, 85–86
  See also under estrogen carcinogenesis

"burden" (old/er people as), 5, 13, 26, 50, 55, 60, 194
  hard on families, 50
  mainly women seen as, 30

right-wing ageism, in public policies, 29, 81

term overheard by young/er people, 43

See also ageism in language and images; decline *entries*; stereotypes of later life

capitalism, American (multinational, postindustrial), 2, 11, 30, 122

assures young people inequality, 154

exploits midlife age class, 193

helps produce decline: 4, 9, 14, 49, 178

productivity crisis of, 193

weakens seniority, 4, 9, 14, 82, 153

See also commerce in aging; middle-ageism, as a historical phenomenon: economic construction

caregiving to elders, 173–74, 176, 181, 195, 201

elder abuse, 26, 37

improvements in, 26, 190, 199–200, 202

need for socialized long-term care, 27, 60, 193–94

unburdened by Alzheimer's label, 173, 179–80

unpaid, 174

cartoons, 2, 15–16, 21, 39, 105, 199

childhood, 25, 75, 151, 166, 184

children, 64, 76

and bodily integrity, 116, 122–23, 142

hearing progress and decline narratives, 40, 147–49, 151, 155, 162, 165

learning ageism early, 6, 25

need of, to learn anti-ageism, 39

chronic illness, 59, 75, 76, 77, 219, 221

and sexuality, 140

treatment of, in United States, 27, 52, 54

and young/er people, 75–76, 221, 230n42

classism, 64, 185

and ageism, 31, 56, 223

decreased longevity and poor health, 75–76

medical care rationed by class before age sixty-five, 27

relation to sexual longevity, 140

relation to telling progress narrative, 152, 156–57, 159, 165

See also middle-ageism, as a historical phenomenon: economic construction

cognitive competition and hierarchies, 184–86

cognitive impairments, 71, 170, 178–89, 181

alternative attitudes toward, 179–81, 198–202

before Age of Alzheimer's, 169–74

confused with Alzheimer's, 188, 190–91

danger of rationing treatment of, 194–96

in hypercognitive society, 179, 184–86

memoir about man with, 199, 209–12

neuroatypicality widespread, non-aged-graded, 198

personal fears of costs of, 193–95

problems diagnosing, 188, 189, 190, 195

selfhood remains despite, 174–75, 186–90, 212

shunning of people with, 183–86

social support for people with, 187–91, 199–200, 209–12

as term preferred to "dementia," 198

without dementia, 195

See also Alzheimer's; "dementia"; "dementias"; memory loss *entries*; mind

commerce in aging, the, 33, 34

"anti-aging" researchers, 14, 34, 99, 97, 177–78

Baby Boomers and, 9

defined, 96

depends on ideology of decline through aging, 14, 89, 101, 105

"dysfunction industries," 126

menopause of 10 percent of women as a centerpiece of, 92

requires ageism, 100

resistance to, 101–2, 122, 223

commerce in aging (*continued*)
  "uglification industries," 34, 96, 34,
    96, 100–101, 105–6, 111, 119–20,
    122
  See also anti-ageism; "anti-aging"
    products, services, ideology; cos-
    metic surgery; cult of youth; medi-
    calization of aging-past-youth;
    menopause discourse; pharmaceu-
    tical companies; rejuvenation
cosmetic surgery (CS, age-related),
    103–23
  critiques of surgeons, 106, 111, 113, 114,
    117, 121, 122
  death and other harms from, 104, 105,
    106, 112–14
  desire for, fought by bodily integrity,
    107, 116–18
  economic reasons for, 119–20
  history of normalization of looking
    younger through, 103, 105, 106,
    111–12, 122
  media hype about, 103, 106, 113, 115,
    119
  odd coalition against, 121
  pop scorn of, 104–5
  resisters' pro-aging attitudes, 107–9,
    115, 117–18, 121, 123
  statistics about, 103–4, 106, 112, 113
  users, 106, 107, 111–14, 120–21
  waning of era of normalization, 104,
    107, 112, 114–21
  See also cult of youth; rejuvenation;
    uglification industries
creativity in later life, 21, 23; threatened
    by cult of youth, 46–47
cult of youth, 13, 14, 32, 40, 46–47, 115,
    154, 176, 205
  delusory, 35
  and sex trafficking, 132
  sources of, 1, 7, 9, 95, 96, 101, 106
  See also cosmetic surgery; dysfunc-
    tion industries; estrogen, as
    twentieth-century treatment;
    middle-ageism *entries*; rejuvena-
    tion; uglification industries

death, 24, 25, 38, 53, 44, 74, 131; social
    death, 183
death, of midlife and old/er people
  of author's father, 44, 148, 207–8
  from cosmetic surgery, 104, 112, 113
  and "death shortage," 49
  "excess deaths" by age, concept of, 63,
    78, 234n5
  excessive, among men, 140
  the good, 24, 57
  of uninsured people between ages
    fifty-five and sixty-four, 75–76
  See also ageism in behavior: lethal;
    dying; "end of life"; Katrina
decline (through aging), narratives about.
    See age narratives: decline through
    aging; age narratives: decline
    versus progress
decline (through aging), as system, 5, 17,
    35–37, 74, 221
  includes ageism, middle-ageism, and
    aging-past-youth, 7, 15, 24–25, 33,
    38, 95, 103, 126, 128, 165
  language of, 5, 7, 38, 81, 122, 126, 128,
    142–43, 173, 188, 191, 204–5, 207
  opposition to, 5, 16, 34–35, 41, 43, 61,
    89, 115, 141, 143, 207, 223
  socioeconomic and cultural changes
    worsen aging-past-youth, 7–9,
    43, 165–66: aging-past-youth
    portrayed as personal physical
    deterioration, 27, 33, 35, 57, 99, 126,
    138–39; dangers of, 4, 15, 38, 39, 61,
    57, 140, 222; harms to women, 82,
    88, 95–96, 105, 117–18; ideology of,
    6, 13–14, 17, 23, 26, 36–37, 39, 43, 61,
    101; sources of "the new regime
    of," 8, 14–15, 33, 39, 87, 96, 120
  See also ageism *entries*; com-
    merce in aging; dysfunction
    industries; medicalization of
    aging-past-youth; middle-ageism
    entries; midlife job loss; uglification
    industries
"dementia," 95, 188, 210
  as ageist hate speech, 195, 198

anticipated as inevitable, 36, 173, 178, 216

confused with Alzheimer's, 179

in cultural/political contexts, 10, 51, 181–82, 192–94

and the duty to die, 51–2, 54, 194

epidemic of fear of, 36, 191–93, 198, 200

as obsolete term, 195, 198

"dementias," the, 85, 198. *See also* cognitive impairments; "dementia"; memory loss in midlife and beyond

demography by age, 223. *See also* longevity

depression, in later life

ageism and, 43, 45–47

cultural contexts of, 10, 59, 49–51, 59

"geriatric," 14, 53

not more common than earlier, 53

often goes untreated, 53

and suicide, 53–54

and women, 51, 92, 96

disability, people with a, 34, 56, 69, 80, 186, 208–15

and ageism, 60, 63, 67, 79–80, 185

and disability rights movement, 50, 135

in *Doonesbury*, 199

in Katrina, 63, 64

among non-old, 76, 248n2

sexual romance of, in later life, 124, 211, 213–14, 216

women, 77

See also ableism; cognitive impairments

disease mongering, 97

disparate impacts by age, in later life, 82

through death, 62, 65–66 passim

through employment discrimination, 1, 2, 3 passim, 237n75

through neglect, 63–67

See also ageism *entries*; invisibility

doctors, 12, 34, 52, 56, 58, 66, 75, 77, 115, 165

and ageism awareness, 29, 59, 80–81, 141

ageist attitudes of, toward old/er people, 29–30, 35, 49, 51, 53

and cosmetic surgery, 106, 111–14

drug companies' compensation of, 97, 99

medical homicide, 29–30, 194

professional responsibilities of, 66, 80, 90, 122

rarely read medical articles, 98–99

treating menopause as a disease, 90–91, 94, 96, 97–99, 126

untrained in geriatrics, 66, 140, 189, 222

"duty to aid," 57, 65

duty to care, 6, 60

"duty to die"

for the cognitively impaired, 36, 194

discourses of "burden" produced by, 5, 13, 26, 43, 50, 55, 60, 194

and health policy, 27

lethal consequences of, 51, 55, 57

need of old/sick people to justify continued living, 55

opposition to, 56–58, 195

proponents of, 14, 27, 50, 57–58

for sick elders, 27, 51, 56, 195

See also aging *entries*; "Eskimo . . ."; suicide in late life

dying, 25, 45, 50, 59

doctors' difficulty confronting, 58

"high-tech," 52, 54

at home, 44, 52

through lack of health insurance, 1–2, 75–76

living with, 58, 164, 208, 216, 248n3

need for choice concerning, 58

terminally ill people, 51, 53, 58

true cost of, under Medicare, 13, 52

See also death *entries*; "duty to die"; "end of life"

dysfunction industries, 60, 94, 125–26, 139. *See also* uglification industries

emergency preparations for at-risk populations, 63–64, 67, 74–75, 79–82

"end of life," the, 52, 181

feelings at, 53, 55, 164, 208, 209
home care at, 27, 44, 56, 60 166, 193
hospice, 50, 60, 123, 194
language of "sustainability" about
    costs of, 12–13, 51–52
reforms needed, 58, 195
treatment at, debated: "high-tech,"
    52, 54; "overtreatment," 12–13,
    51–52, 55, 194; undertreatment
    (rationing), 13, 51–53
various meanings of term, 159, 164–65
women's wishes at, neglected, 51
See also dying; death *entries*; "duty to
    die"; "Eskimo . . ."; Medicare;
    right to die; suicide *entries*
"Eskimo on the ice floe," 21–31, 36,
    221–22
    as critique of American culture, 28–30
    as fantasy of having old people disap-
        pear, 22–23, 25–29, 38
    as fantasy of suicide to avoid aging,
        23–25, 39
    See also ageism *entries*; "burden";
        decline *entries*; generations
estrogen, as twentieth-century treatment
    and breast cancer rates, 86
    and deficiency theory of menopause,
        14, 89–90, 94–95, 97, 98
    Food and Drug Administration (FDA)
        and, 89, 90, 97, 98
    and hormone debacle of 2002, 85–89,
        91, 93, 97–98, 101
    no paradigm shift, 89–90
    nostalgia for era of estrogen promise,
        14, 90–91, 94, 95
    opposition to, 85–86, 88, 97
    promotion of, 91, 93, 94, 95, 96, 98, 101
    rejuvenation myth, 94, 98, 120
    risks of, 85–87, 93, 95
    See also menopause discourse
estrogen carcinogenesis, 14, 86–87,
    89–90, 101
ethical philosophy, 25, 80, 122
ethicist(s), 13, 52, 57, 200; bioethicist(s),
    49, 50
European Americans, 33, 73

face (s), 69
    beauty of, lost with cosmetic surgery,
        108, 121
    facelifts, 105, 107, 108
    hardest body part to reclaim from
        uglification industries, 33–34
    See body
father(s), 8, 40, 171, 176
fears of aging/old age, 36, 61
    of "dementia," 36, 191–93, 198, 200
    fantasies of committing suicide to
        avoid, 23–25, 54–56, 60, 222
    people told to fear aging, 31
    rational and irrational, 32, 41, 56
    young/er people's, 25, 30, 18
    See also memory loss in midlife and
        beyond: terror of
feminism, 8, 16, 48, 108
    affirming the female body, 32, 105, 107,
        109–11, 113–15
    and anti-ageism, 43, 44, 46, 49, 56, 115,
        118, 122
    battle against estrogen "replacement"
        and deficiency theory, 85–86, 88,
        90, 101
    focus on younger women, 76
    and later life, 31, 107–8, 111, 138, 168,
        176, 200, 211–12
    and sexuality, 124–26, 127, 132, 135–36,
        141
    and women's movement, 45, 48,
        135
feminists, 37, 38, 42, 44, 103, 109
fiction. *See* novels
filial relations. *See* adult offspring
Food and Drug Administration (FDA),
    89, 90, 97, 98, 99, 115
forgetfulness in midlife and beyond.
    See memory loss in midlife and
    beyond

"Generation X," 28
gender in later life, 45, 46, 48
generational solidarity, 11, 15–16, 41, 157,
    175–6, 181; a weapon against de-
    cline, 222. *See also* adult offspring

generations, construction of hostility between the, 7, 11, 26, 40, 49, 152

"geriatric" depression, 14, 53

geriatric education, 66, 70, 79; geriatricians and 58, 66, 70, 72, 81, 140, 190

geronticide. *See* ageicide

gerontocracy, 175–76. *See also* patriarchy

gerontologists (feminist/critical/ humanist), 16, 38, 43, 57, 77, 81, 194, 200; specific critiques of ageism, "anti-aging," 4, 12, 14, 57, 77, 99–100. *See also* age critic(s)

gerontology, 178, 191, 198, 215
   biogerontologists, 34, 37, 99, 205
   biogerontology, 178, 223
   gerontophobia, 14, 26

globalization, and progress narrative, 156–58

"golden" years/age, 3, 5, 8, 10, 97

hate speech, ageist. *See under* ageism in language and images

health care
   inequality in, 27, 57, 75–76, 158
   national, 12, 60
   See also Medicare

health care at midlife and later life, 27
   ageist debate around cost of Medicare, 11–14, 51, 193–94
   denial of treatment, 52–53
   lack of insurance, 1, 10, 75, 76
   social causes of premature ill health, 74–76

health insurance, lack of
   for adolescents and emerging adult women, 127
   for long-term care, 181, 193
   10.7 percent of uninsured Boomers over age fifty-five die, 1–2, 75–76, 140

Heilbrun, Carolyn, 43, 59, 60
   and possible ageism, 45–47
   suicide of, 42–48

home care, 27, 44, 56, 60 166, 193

homeless old/er people, 69

hormone debacle of 2002, 85–89, 91, 93, 97–98, 101. *See also under* estrogen, as twentieth-century treatment

hormone "replacement therapy." *See* estrogen, as twentieth-century treatment

hospice, 50, 60, 123, 194

identity. *See* age identity(ies) across time

identity-stripping. *See under* age identity(ies) across time

individualism, 9, 48, 57, 154

illness in later life, chronic. *See* chronic illness

inequality, in income and health outcomes, 74–77

insurance for cosmetic surgery, 107, 113

internalization, 148
   deadliest is coerced suicide, 60
   of decline attitudes, 6, 45, 47, 57, 96, 118, 185
   internalization of pro-aging attitudes, 33, 107, 143, 148

invisibility, 42, 47, 48, 65, 67

Katrina (hurricane/flood/diaspora), 39, 50, 62–74
   and African Americans, 62, 64–65, 67–69, 71–72, 76
   aftermath of, 67–74
   age-related deaths, 38, 62–66, 234n2, 235n12
   "brain," 67, 71
   deaths of men, 62
   emergency preparations for at-risk populations, 63–64, 67, 75, 79–80
   lethal ageism, 64, 65, 66
   neglect of old/er people, 65–68
   old/er people as exiles, 71–72
   pro-elderly behavior, 66, 80–81
   resilience of old/er people, 65, 72–73
   triage, 66–67
   women, old/er, 62, 69, 71–72, 76

labor conditions. *See* working conditions

Latina women, 87

lesbian women, 77, 92, 137
life course, 156, 161, 190, 217
  anti-ageism as a process in, 111
  anticipated prospectively, 23 passim,
    148, 191, 218, 223
  as interplay between person and
    culture over time, 6
  attacked by decline forces, 4, 8–9,
    38, 56, 88–89, 91, 95, 101, 157, 165,
    222–23
  full selfhood accrues over, 61
  need for progress over entire, 15, 39,
    118, 143, 152, 159, 166, 223–24
  visions of a better, 6, 17, 35, 41, 58, 79,
    101–2, 141, 157, 166, 216, 224
  See also age auto/biography; age narra-
    tives; American dream of progress;
    longevity; progress
life-course storytelling/life writing. *See*
    age auto/biography; age narratives;
    memoirs
literary exits from decline narrative, 154,
    164, 206, 207–18, 221
living with dying, 58, 164, 208–9, 214–16,
    248n3
longevity (the new), in the United States,
    9–10, 17, 25, 38, 99, 140, 223
  alarmist demography, 10, 11, 49
  correlated with pro-aging attitude, 39
  democratized to a point, 22
  linked to economic class and
    health-care access, 9–10, 22, 27, 75,
    152, 221
  old/er people, wanting to live longer,
    38, 39, 49, 211
  positive aspects of, 9, 23
  "risk of," 32
  treated as a costly negative, 13, 40, 49,
    50, 51, 55, 193–94
  See also "anti-aging" products,
    services, ideology; "duty to die";
    "Eskimo . . ."
long-term care insurance, 181, 193
looks in later life
  and ads for youth, 33
  enticements to look younger, 96, 122

increasing popularity of "natural" ag-
    ing, 107–9, 115, 117–18, 123
  looksism, 118, 206
  visual progress narratives, 109–11, 115
  See also commerce in aging; pro-aging;
    uglification industries

media, independent, 101; feminist, 101,
    128
media, mainstream
  and ageism/middle-ageism, 48, 55, 58,
    76, 81, 111, 143: cause dissatisfac-
    tion with one's body, 128; cover
    untested "anti-aging" drugs, 91,
    93; create fear of people over age
    sixty-five needing costly health
    care, 49, 51; omitted in Katrina
    coverage, 64; promote cosmetic
    surgery, 103, 106, 113, 115, 119; raise
    fear of memory loss, Alzheimer's,
    178, 185, 192; role in advocacy of
    estrogen as treatment, 86, 89, 91,
    93–96, 99, 100–102; use language
    of right wing and medical model
    uncritically, 49, 100–101 (*see also*
    "anti-aging" products, services,
    ideology; "burden")
  and economy, 150: critique of the
    media, 107–8, 122
Medicaid, some states stingy with, 75
medical homicide, 29–30, 51, 194
medicalization of aging-past-youth, 95, 96
  critiqued, 216, 223
  of mind, 177–178
  of women, 87, 88, 91, 95
  See also estrogen, as twentieth-century
    treatment; menopause discourse;
    mind
Medicare, 75
  ageist debate around cost of, 11–14,
    51, 193–94
  cuts to, 70
  cutting may jeopardize health, 52
  only 3 percent incur very high costs
    under, 13, 52
  "overtreatment," 52, 55

people on, improve health, 76

undertreatment (rationing), 12–13,
29–30, 51–53, 60, 194

See also "burden"; "duty to die"; "end
of life"

medicine (research, training, practice), reforms needed in, 89–90,
100–101. *See also* pharmaceutical
companies

memoirs, 114, 150

of later life, 124, 137, 209–18

pressure to write positively, 217

See also novels

memory loss in midlife and beyond

age-related cognitive decline decreasing, 192

central to American decline narrative
of aging, 14, 39, 177, 191

connected to stereotypes and job loss,
192–93

heightened by anxiety, 16, 66, 67, 68,
191

heightened importance of good
memory, 36, 177–78

linked to a duty to die, 36, 194

normal, 5, 56, 163, 173, 177, 191, 192

overcoming terror of, 166, 189–91,
198–203

pathologized as "dementia," 100,
191–93

terror of, in hypercognitive society,
24, 54, 175, 181, 188–89, 191–93

treatment of, in Austen's *Emma*,
169–74

used by commerce in aging, 88, 96,
100, 193

See also Alzheimer's *entries*; brain;
cognitive impairments; "dementia"; mind

memory loss of young/er people, 191

men in middle life, 62, 90

"andropause" of, 91, 99

candidates for cosmetic surgery,
119–20

gay men, growing older, 29, 77

median income, 3

targeted by commerce in aging, 119

testosterone use of, 95, 99

vulnerable to middle-ageism, 31

wages for at median stagnant, 75

See also midlife job loss; sexuality of
men, at midlife and later life

menopause, 85–102, 139

as biocultural experience, 87–88, 91,
101

benefits of being postmenstrual, 86, 92

central to narrative of female midlife
decline, 88, 92, 95

deficiency theory of, 89–90, 93, 95, 97

hormone debacle of 2002, 85–88,
97–98, 101

important to commerce in aging, 96

most women never seek help, 87

See also estrogen, as twentieth-century
treatment; menopause discourse

menopause discourse, 86–103

hormone "replacement therapy," 85,
90, 91

media role in advocacy of estrogen as
treatment, 86, 89, 93–94, 96, 99,
100–102

"menoboom" of the 1990s, 96

"menopausal," 60

power of pharmaceutical companies,
91, 95

pro-estrogen bias, 93, 101

See also estrogen, as twentieth-century
treatment

mental illness, 45

and ageism, 58

and Katrina victims, 67–68, 72–74

See also depression, in later life

middle-ageism, 126, 205–6

damaging effects of, on people in
middle years, 1–3, 9, 75, 96, 100,
154

death and other harms from cosmetic
surgery, 104, 105, 106, 112–14

defined, 5

economic losses from, 1, 2, 3, 4, 9,
119, 153

hormone debacle of 2002, and con-

middle-ageism (*continued*)
    struction of nostalgic aftermath,
        89–96, 98
    looksism, 118, 206
    menopause central to narrative of
        female midlife decline, 88, 92, 95
    usefulness of term, 7
    and youth, 33
middle-ageism, as a historical phenom-
        enon
    bad luck of Baby Boomers, 2, 3, 5,
        8–10, 17, 152–53
    economic construction of midlife:
        age discrimination eliminates
        midlife workers, 1–2, 4, 81, 119, 153;
        capitalism weakens seniority, 4, 9,
        14, 82, 90, 153, 154; debt doubled in
        1990s, 75; Equal Employment Op-
        portunity Commission (EEOC)
        finds too little discrimination,
        4, 9; forgetfulness connected to
        stereotypes and job loss, 192–93;
        low age-wage peaks, 3, 74, 153;
        mass layoffs, 3, 152; men's median
        wage stagnant, 75; middle class be-
        coming vulnerable to, 2, 3, 10, 74,
        192–93; outsourcing, 153; Supreme
        Court weakening midlife job
        discrimination protections, 3–4,
        9, 82, 106, 153; unemployment,
        1–2, 9, 60, 75, 119, 153 192; unions
        weakened, 3, 9, 152, 153
    in language: "Oldtimers' disease," 5,
        193; "senior moments," 191–92;
        unproductive, 28
    sources of "anti-aging": cult of youth
        worsens, 1, 9, 47, 95, 96, 106,
        154; deficiency theory of meno-
        pause , 14, 89–90, 94–95, 97, 98:
        "dysfunction" industries develop
        for middle and later life, 60, 94,
        125–26, 139; medical model of
        aging-past-youth, 27; "menoboom"
        of 1990s, 96; normalization of
        looking younger through cosmetic
        surgeries, 103, 105–6, 106, 111–12,

    122; uglification industries grow,
        34, 96, 101, 120
    See also "anti-aging" products, ser-
        vices, ideology; "Baby Boomers";
        capitalism; commerce in aging;
        memory loss *entries*; menopause
        discourse; midlife job loss
middle-ageism, resistance to, 108–11, 120
    reforms needed, 140–41
    transformative goals, 122–23
    visual progress narratives, 109–10, 115
    See also feminism; positive aging; pro-
        aging; progress; unions
middle-class people at midlife and be-
        yond, 39, 64, 73
    apt to be viewed as "successful" at
        aging, 23, 75, 76
    vulnerable to middle-ageism, 2, 10, 74,
        192–93
    See also "Baby Boomers"; middle-
        ageism, as a historical phenom-
        enon: economic construction;
        midlife job loss
midlife job loss, 1–3, 21
    age discrimination and, 1–2, 4, 119,
        153, 184
    capitalism's race to the bottom, 9
    changes definition of life course, 4
    desire for cosmetic surgery, 120–21
    misery of, 2–3
    other negative consequences of, 9–10,
        75, 154
    resistance to, 17, 223
    Supreme Court's role in, 4, 9, 82, 106,
        153
    tacit business practice, 2
    trends in, 152–54
    unemployment, 1–2, 9, 60, 75, 119,
        153, 192
    for women versus men, 4, 119
    See also middle-ageism, as a historical
        phenomenon: economic construc-
        tion
midlife workers, 1–3
    household income of, lower than in
        1983, 153, 229n16

term more exact than "older worker," 230n20

mind: theories of, 176–78, 189–91, 198, 200. *See also* brain

narrative turn in the humanities, and memory, 177–78
narratives. *See* age narratives
neurogenesis, 177, 189
nostalgia, 46
    anti-nostalgia, 163, 217
    for era of estrogen promises, 90–91, 94, 95
    for pre-Alzheimer's era, 175, 181
novels
    decline-oriented, 74, 204–5
    caregiving represented in, 168–74
    about middle life, 168, 216
    about old/er characters, 167–74, 179–81, 205, 209, 216
    people with cognitive impairments in, 175–76
    plots a sign of wanting, 207
    See also writers and artists
nursing homes, 62, 77, 215

"old," 23, 76
old age, 3, 10, 23, 29, 42, 63, 180, 205
    Baby Boomers expected to transform, 5
    definitions of, dependent on class, 74, 76, 162
    entry into, defined by others, 29, 34, 184
    equated with dementia, 178–79, 216
    focus of commerce in "anti-aging," 99
    "good" old age harder to imagine, 24
    less feared formerly, 175–76
    plateau of health lasting into, 27
    poverty in, 9–11, 65, 76
    synonymous with illness, 24, 53, 99, 160
    telling progress narrative in, 49, 159
    See also "burden"; longevity; old/er people; suicide: fantasies of
old/er men
    die younger than women, 140

lack of social support, 65
old/er people, 29, 30, 71, 77
    as cornerstones of social life, 69–70
    equal rights needed by, 57–58, 60
    erosion of support for, 10–11, 53
    high expectations of behavior from, 165
    images of (*see* "Eskimo . . .")
    increasing number of, 11
    marriage rates of men and women, 140–41
    and pity, 190, 196, 202
    portrayed as rich, 11–12, 23, 49, 74
    resilience of, 72–73, 209, 219
    special needs of, in emergencies, 63–68, 78–80
    stigmatized as (costly and/or dependent) "burdens," 5, 11, 13, 26, 29, 50, 55, 60, 194
    sympathy for, 25, 40–41, 50, 54
    See also people over age sixty-five
older workers, 2. *See also* midlife workers
"old-old" people, 8
old/er women, 25, 29, 30, 51, 54, 181
    images of, 25, 33, 109–11
    in Katrina, 62, 69, 71–72, 76
    poverty of, 31, 64, 69, 72, 76, 77
    sexuality of, 137–38
    See also women *entries*
osteoporosis, 90, 98, 10
    distinguished from menopause, 91
    "osteopenia" as disease mongering, 97

parents of adult offspring, 2, 23, 25, 26, 92, 206
parents of young children, as tellers of life-course narratives, 25, 37, 40, 116, 148–51. *See also* adult offspring
patriarchy, 32, 45, 122, 128, 135, 171, 174, 176; as gerontocracy, 175–76
people over age eighty, 203
people over age eighty-five, "fastest growing segment," 81
people over age fifty, 38, 63, 74–75, 134
people over age forty, 5, 122, 192
people over age sixty, 124

people over age sixty-five, 11, 13, 35
    hostility to government assistance
        for, 21, 50, 51, 70, 77 (*see* right-wing
        ageism)
    majority are without cognitive im-
        pairment, 178, 192
    long-term care insurance needed for,
        181, 193
    in New Orleans, 64, 69, 72, 73, 76
    need to work, 3
    poorer than American children are, 31
    poverty of, 9, 65, 76: connected to ill
        health, 77; federal line set lower
        for, 76; higher rate of, than for
        people under age sixty-five, 31
    See also old/er people; retirement;
        women over age sixty-five
"perimenopause," 88, 91, 97
pharmaceutical companies (Big
    PhRMA), and "anti-aging," 86, 89,
    101, 102
    define "disease," 97
    downplayed hormone debacle, 93
    expand sexual dysfunction, 94–95,
        99, 126
    inventing "steroids for the brain,"
        178, 193
    permitted to advertise directly to
        consumers, 96
    promote deficiency theory of andro-
        pause, menopause, 91, 95
    Wyeth paid doctors for pro-estrogen
        articles, 94–95, 97–99
phenomenological psychologists, 200
plastic surgery. *See* cosmetic surgery
popular culture, 131
    ageism in, 14, 96
    salience of age in, 143
    scorn for bungled cosmetic surgery
        in, 104–5
positive aging, 107, 206
    boosterish side of, 124–25, 141, 154,
        161, 217
    class basis of "successful" aging, 23, 75
    relation of, to feminist pro-aging,
        111, 115

positive-aging stories, different from
        progress narratives, 141, 165, 217,
        219. *See also* age narratives: prog-
        ress; pro-aging
postmaternal women, 92
postmenstrual, 86, 92, 94, 96, 137
poverty before age sixty-five, 140
    connected to ill health, 25, 75
    high death rate for uninsured people
        between age fifty-five and Medi-
        care, 75–76
    high rate of poverty, for Baby Boom-
        ers aged forty to fifty, 9
    high spending on health care, 76
poverty, global, 156, 158
poverty over age sixty-five. *See* people
        over age sixty-five: poverty of
pro-aging
    default position in regard to body, 115
    derived from feminism, 107, 111
    favors seniority, 118
    fights decline view of body, 32–34
    has positive effect on longevity, 32
    possesses saving vision, 39–40, 121, 141
    views natural aging of body favorably,
        33, 118, 148, 152, 175, 202
    See also age gaze; anti-ageism; positive
        aging
progress
    importance of belief in, 5, 147–51, 160
    life-course, in relation to socioeco-
        nomic, 147, 151–52
    Sartre's theory of, 160–64, 219
    social changes necessary for democ-
        ratizing progress, 140–41, 152, 155,
        165–66, 223
    taught to children, 147–51, 155
    See also age narratives: progress
psyche embodied in culture, over time,
        108, 127, 136. *See also* selfhood over
        time
public health, 80–81, 127
    ageism and ableism a danger to, 58,
        100
    compression of morbidity, 22–23
    excess deaths, 39, 63

inequality and, 76
neglected issues of: cosmetic surgery,
    114, 122; entire decline system, 15;
    exogenous hormones, 87; sexual
    longevity, 140; unpaid informal
    care, 26

racism, 75, 184–85 (*see also*
    ageism-consciousness: intersec-
    tionality); antiracism, 74, 150, 223
readers of discourses about age, aging: 11,
    35, 94, 161–62, 168, 181, 204–5, 218
rejuvenation
    Baby Boomers' alleged desire for, 9
    enticements a form of bigotry, 122
    fantasies of, 37, 91, 94, 96, 98, 99, 106
    promises of, 7, 120–21
    See also "anti-aging" products, ser-
        vices, ideology; cosmetic surgery;
        estrogen, as twentieth-century
        treatment
remarriage, 131
rereading, over the life course, 167
resilience, 211–12; of old/er people, 72–73,
    209, 219–20
retirees, 67, 69, 76
    and better sex, 139
    income loss, 60
    as "unproductive," 49, 50, 74
retirement: 10, 11, 23, 46, 55, 75
    and age discrimination, 45
    disability the major cause of, 76
    losses resulting from, 31, 45, 48, 60,
        185
    premature and involuntary, 9, 14
    psychosocial dangers of, 45–46, 48
    women's new stress at, 48
right to die, 43, 44, 56, 58
right-wing ageism, in public policies,
    26, 81
    reducing social safety nets, 12, 31, 50, 70
    small-government advocacy, 14, 29

science, biomedical, 85–86
    Bush administration and, 98
    cognitive, 169, 177, 200

conflict over value of memory drugs,
    178
faulty about value of exogenous estro-
    gen, 97–98
and longevity, 9, 99, 205
See also mind
self-esteem in later life, 49; and social
    support, 189, 191, 162–64
selfhood, as embodied psyche, in culture,
    over time, 108, 127, 136
selfhood over time, 133
    continuity a fiction, 190
    and multiple sequential selves, 56, 136,
        151–52, 162–64, 190, 194
    nourished by progress narratives,
        151
"senility," 27, 36
seniority
    defined, 176
    erosion of, at midlife and beyond, 4,
        9, 14, 82, 153
    fights ageism, 14, 45
    importance of, for progress narrative,
        118, 140, 153, 166, 223
    learning it in the family, 40, 176
    relation to age hierarchy, 175–76
    strengthening, 122
    weakening of tenure in unions, aca-
        deme, 153
    See also Supreme Court's age-related
        decisions
sexism, 15, 30, 37, 54, 71, 75
    against young/er women, overlaps
        with other biases, 56, 63, 75, 80
    sexist ageism, 26, 31, 56, 84, 86, 98
    See also ageism-consciousness:
        intersectionality;
        ageism-consciousness: raising
sexual longevity, a class-based public
    health issue, 140–41
sexuality
    age-uninhibited, 143
    allegedly naturally "great," 127
    improves for many women as they get
        older, 132–39, 141–42, 143
    more than orgasm, 142

sexuality (*continued*)
  needs reforms based on later-life sex, 143
  as prospective decline story of age-related dysfunction, 126, 202
  sex ed poorly taught, 128
  socially constructed, 127, 132, 135, 222
  youth-centered, 142
sexuality, female
  celibacy, 131, 134, 136
  improvements in, since 1950s, 127
  masturbation, 127, 138
sexuality of girls, emerging-adult women, and young/er women, 94, 126–32, 139
  age-graded risks and sexual culture, 127, 129–33, 136–37
  encouraged by culture, 132
  See also women, young/er
sexuality of men, at midlife and in later life, 126, 127, 134, 135, 140, 214
  begrudging the time, 139
  becoming better partners, 136
  dying younger than women, 140
  and dysfunction, 139, 141, 176
  testosterone use, 95, 99
  Viagra, 139
sexuality of young/er men, 127, 140
sexuality of women at midlife and in later life, 7, 133–44, 211, 214
  contrasted with that of younger women, 133, 141
  dependent on extrinsic circumstances, 139
  discovering one's own normal, 138
  and the "dysfunction industries," 94, 125–26
  effects of ill health on, 140
  of lesbians, 129, 132, 136, 137
  menopause allegedly worsens, 125, 126, 135, 138, 142
  progress narratives about, 132–39, 141–42
  and sexual age autobiographies, 127, 136–37, 142–43, 152

social reforms needed to improve, 139–41
  "still doing it" rhetoric, 124–26, 134, 141
  undoing younger/older dichotomy, 126–27, 132
  See also estrogen, as twentieth-century treatment; menopause discourse
social death, 183
social responsibility for elders as age class, 41, 64
  becoming reduced, 57, 58
  family as model for, 40
Social Security, 6, 16, 21, 58, 71, 72, 76, 77
  attempts to reduce benefits of, 12, 31
  average woman's monthly check, 31
  poor women on, 77
  possibly bountiful, 81
social support for elders as individuals, 64–65, 160, 162–64, 171–72
social support for people with cognitive impairments, 187–91, 199–200, 209–12
stereotypes of later life, ageist, 6, 10, 55, 192
  shortening life, 16
  stereotype threat, 16
  See also ageism in language and images; "burden"; "Eskimo . . ."; middle-ageism, as a historical phenomenon: in language
suicide, 8, 44, 45, 46, 53, 105, 112
  fantasies of, to avoid aging/old age, 23–25, 54–56, 60, 222
  ideation versus act, 45–47, 57
  no duty to die for young/er people, 55–56, 60
  sexism, racism, ableism in, 56
suicide in late life, 3, 14, 49, 53
  ageist pressures to commit to avoid Alzheimer's/old age: 27–28, 43, 45–47, 51, 54–56, 195
  coerced, 22, 27, 51, 56, 60,
  physician-assisted, 51, 56, 58
  preemptive (surcease), 44, 53, 56, 195
  "rational," 42, 44, 45, 55, 56, 57

relation to depression, 45–46

resistance to: antiageist counseling, 58–60; attacks on decline, 222–23; will to live, 56, 222

right to die, 58, 59

"social autopsy" of, 43, 53

and women, 48–49, 51, 56

See also "burden"; "Eskimo . . ."; Heilbrun, Carolyn

Supreme Court's age-related decisions, 9, 106

Age Discrimination in Employment Act weakened, 82, 153

legalized age discrimination, 3–4

testosterone, 95, 99

therapy, 135–36

anti-ageist counseling for people with suicidal intent, 58–60

art, and writing, for people with Alzheimer's, 199–200

sex therapy, 134

"triage" in emergencies, 66–67

uglification industries, 34, 100–101, 119–20, 122

defined, 96

making rejuvenation normal, 106

See also beauty in later life; bodymind: bodily integrity; commerce in aging; cosmetic surgery

unemployment at midlife, 1–2, 9, 60, 75, 119, 192; lasting unemployment , 153, 244 n13, n14

unions

need for, 122, 141

weakened, 3, 9, 152, 153

United States of America, 41, 76; and national health care, 60, 76

wellness, 31–32

white people, 51, 62, 77, 130

women, 8, 23–24, 35, 54, 86, 88, 95

average size of, 33

as girls exposed to culture, 119, 128, 132

as main caregivers, 26

learning ageism from the culture, 88, 95

women, emerging-adult, 127, 132. *See also* women, young/er

women in middle life, 48–49, 64

discrimination against, 1–3, 4, 8

economic conditions of, 3, 75, 77

and feminism, 32, 51

health of, 140

peak income of at median, 153

prime candidates for surgery, age thirty-five to fifty, 103

and sexual desire, 136

stereotypes, 7, 138

suffer age discrimination ten years younger than men, 119

See also cosmetic surgery; menopause; middle-ageism; sexuality *entries*

women over age sixty-five, 43

later-life strength of, 49, 69, 72

a majority, subject to ageism, 30–31, 51

poverty of, 31, 64, 69, 72, 76, 77

and retirement, 30–31, 43, 45, 48–49, 51

sexuality of, 142

See also people over age sixty-five, women *entries*

women, single, 69, 77

women, young/er, 32, 41, 47, 48, 87, 90; average size of, 33

Women's Heath Initiative (WHI), 85, 91. *See* estrogen, as twentieth-century treatment: hormone debacle of 2002

women's health movement, 85–86, 97, 99, 101

workers, older, 3. *See also* midlife workers

working conditions

capitalism weakens seniority, 4, 9, 14, 82, 153

degradation of, 9, 154, 192

mass layoffs, 3, 152–53

reforms needed, 141

weakening of unions, 3, 9, 152, 153

See also capitalism; seniority; unemployment at midlife

writers and artists, 48, 109
  on age, aging, end-of-life, midlife, 38,
    46, 109–11, 160, 168, 199, 205–6,
    216–9
  future roles as anti-ageists, 206, 223
  late style, 164–65
  vulnerable to ageism, 46–47
  See also memoirs; novels: about
    midlife; novels: about old/er
    characters

young/er (non-old) people, 6, 11, 38, 47,
    65, 69
  and anti-ageist activism, 80–81
  as audience for age knowledge, 14,
    38, 224
  duty to live, 56, 60
  economic life getting harsher for, 154
  employers' bias toward, 1, 9, 153

fantasies of suicide to avoid old age,
    23–25, 54–56, 60, 222
  and fears of aging-past-youth/old age/
    old people, 23–25, 42–44, 53, 80,
    154, 188, 216, 222
  ignorant about old age/aging/old/er
    people, 38–39, 184, 216–17
  portrayed as enemies of old/er people,
    21–22, 49, 50
  warned about expenses of old age, 49
  See also under sexuality
youth, as superiority complex, 6, 68, 81,
    185
  considered as cultural capital, 32–33,
    46, 47, 48, 206
  for women, identified with feminin-
    ity, 94
  See also aging-past-youth: cult of
    youth